Frommer's®
Vancouver &
Victoria 17th Edition

by Chris McBeath & Chloë Ernst

D0094134

WILEY

John Wiley & Sons, Inc.

Published by:
John Wiley & Sons, Inc.
111 River St.
Hoboken, NJ 07030-5774

ISBN 978-1-118-09313-9 (paper); ISBN 978-1-118-10160-5 (ebk); ISBN 978-1-118-10162-9 (ebk); ISBN 978-1-118-10161-2 (ebk)

Editors: Gene Shannon & William Travis
Production Editor: Heather Wilcox
Cartographer: Lohnes+Wright
Photo Editors: Richard Fox, Cherie Cincilla
Design and Layout by Vertigo Design
Graphics and Prepress by Wiley Indianapolis Composition Services

Front cover photo: Kayaking in False Creek, downtown skyline in background, Vancouver, British Columbia ©Kerrick James / Alamy Images
Back cover photos: *Left:* Canada, Vancouver, Stanley Park, Totem pole, close-up ©Jerry Driendl / Getty Images. *Middle:* Man downhill skiing ©Scott Markewitz / Getty Images. *Right:* Legislative buildings and Inner Harbour at dusk, Victoria, British Columbia, Canada ©Shaun Cunningham / Alamy Images

For information on our other products and services or to obtain technical support, please contact our Customer Care Department within the U.S. at 877/762-2974, outside the U.S. at 317/572-3993 or fax 317/572-4002.

Wiley also publishes its books in a variety of electronic formats. Some content that appears in print may not be available in electronic formats.

Manufactured in China

5 4 3 2 1

CONTENTS

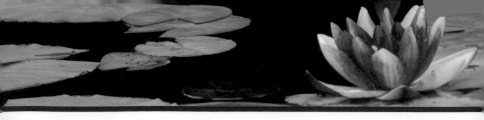

LIST OF MAPS

HOW TO CONTACT US

In researching this book, we discovered many wonderful places—hotels, restaurants, shops, and more. We're sure you'll find others. Please tell us about them, so we can share the information with your fellow travelers in upcoming editions. If you were disappointed with a recommendation, we'd love to know that, too. Please write to:

Frommer's Vancouver & Victoria, 17th Edition
John Wiley & Sons, Inc. • 111 River St. • Hoboken, NJ 07030-5774
frommersfeedback@wiley.com

AN ADDITIONAL NOTE

Please be advised that travel information is subject to change at any time—and this is especially true of prices. We therefore suggest that you write or call ahead for confirmation when making your travel plans. The authors, editors, and publisher cannot be held responsible for the experiences of readers while traveling. Your safety is important to us, however, so we encourage you to stay alert and be aware of your surroundings. Keep a close eye on cameras, purses, and wallets, all favorite targets of thieves and pickpockets.

ABOUT THE AUTHORS

As a west-coast travel writer, **Chloë Ernst** has skied on the slopes overlooking her Vancouver home, rafted rivers in Whistler, and caught waves on Pacific beaches. She also contributes to *Frommer's British Columbia*, as well as various print and online publications. Read more about the travel writer's journeys at www.chloeernst.com.

   With a lifetime of travel under her belt, **Chris McBeath** says she has yet to find a destination that beats the natural beauty and cosmopolitan nature of her home British Columbia. A seasoned travel writer with experience in many facets of the tourism industry, from chambermaid to management, aboard cruise ships and in top-ranked hotels, Chris brings to this book an insider's eye for what makes a great travel experience. In addition to bylines that include print, online, and i-app publications worldwide, Chris maintains her own travel website (www.greatestgetaways.com), is the contributing editor of "The Art of a Getaway" for the Arts & Cultural Guide to British Columbia (www.art-bc.com), and is the author for *Frommer's: Vancouver Island, the Gulf Islands & the San Juan Islands.*

FROMMER'S STAR RATINGS, ICONS & ABBREVIATIONS

Every hotel, restaurant, and attraction listing in this guide has been ranked for quality, value, service, amenities, and special features using a **star-rating system.** In country, state, and regional guides, we also rate towns and regions to help you narrow down your choices and budget your time accordingly. Hotels and restaurants are rated on a scale of zero (recommended) to three stars (exceptional). Attractions, shopping, nightlife, towns, and regions are rated according to the following scale: zero stars (recommended), one star (highly recommended), two stars (very highly recommended), and three stars (must-see).

In addition to the star-rating system, we also use seven feature icons that point you to the great deals, in-the-know advice, and unique experiences that separate travelers from tourists. Throughout the book, look for:

special finds—those places only insiders know about

fun facts—details that make travelers more informed and their trips more fun

kids—best bets for kids and advice for the whole family

special moments—those experiences that memories are made of

overrated—places or experiences not worth your time or money

insider tips—great ways to save time and money

great values—where to get the best deals

The following abbreviations are used for credit cards:

AE	American Express	**DISC**	Discover	**V**	Visa
DC	Diners Club	**MC**	MasterCard		

TRAVEL RESOURCES AT FROMMERS.COM

Frommer's travel resources don't end with this guide. Frommer's website, **www. frommers.com**, has travel information on more than 4,000 destinations. We update features regularly, giving you access to the most current trip-planning information and the best airfare, lodging, and car-rental bargains. You can also listen to podcasts, connect with other Frommers.com members through our active-reader forums, share your travel photos, read blogs from guidebook editors and fellow travelers, and much more.

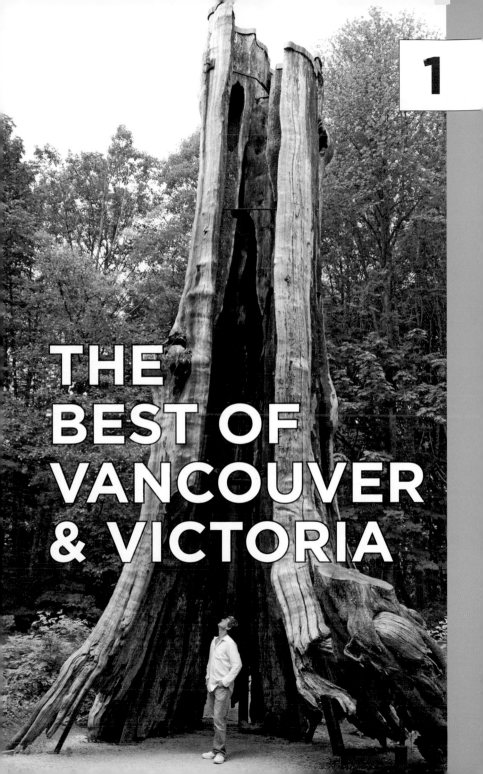

THE BEST OF VANCOUVER & VICTORIA

Ringed by snow-capped, forested mountains dropping down to miles of sandy beaches, **Vancouver** is a city where you can snowboard and sail on the same day. Against the stunning scenic backdrop, you'll find a medley of sophisticated restaurants, leafy parks, and lively, earthy brew pubs. As Vancouver pulsates with a smug and sassy youthfulness, **Victoria,** British Columbia's capital city, is more seasoned—like that of an elder sister whose English beauty is more than skin deep.

Things to Do   Giant, colorfully carved totem poles tower above an impressive collection of First Nations masks and sculptures at the **Museum of Anthropology.** Visit the belugas, otters, and dolphins at the **Vancouver Aquarium** in Stanley Park, before seeing historic and modern art at the downtown **Vancouver Art Gallery.** To reach Granville Island's plentiful **Public Market,** hop on a tiny ferry to cross False Creek. In Victoria, stroll the cobblestone streets of **Old Town** before taking traditional afternoon tea at the **Fairmont Empress.**

Active Pursuits   When the sun is shining, you'll join a stampede of Vancouverites heading to the city's beaches, hiking trails, and mountain slopes. Biking, running, or walking the **Stanley Park Seawall** rates highly for its at-your-own-pace vibe and panoramic views. In Victoria, you can take a **jeep-safari** through farms and vineyards, or spot harbor seals, whales, and dolphins on a **whale-watching tour.**

Eating & Drinking   Amid a rich culinary region, seafood is king in Vancouver and Victoria. Try a six-course seafood medley, paired with a glass of wine from an Okanagan winery, at five-star **Yaletown** dining rooms. Dining options are plentiful and often cheap, be it delectable Thai in **Kitsilano,** a raw food menu near **Main Street,** or inventive Chinese tapas in **Chinatown.** In Victoria, you'll find a variety of culinary styles **downtown.**

Nightlife & Entertainment   In Vancouver, you can rub shoulders with the nightclub crowd on funky **Granville Street** downtown. Hip **Yaletown** offers up swanky cocktail bars and clubs. For more laid-back surrounds, join the relaxed beach crowd at a variety of watering holes in **Kitsilano.** In summer, picnic in **Stanley Park** and watch **Theatre Under the Stars.** In Victoria, stop for a pint at a convivial **waterside brewpub,** or visit the cool bar in the **Fairmont Express** for blue martinis with hot jazz.

THE most UNFORGETTABLE VANCOUVER EXPERIENCES

o **Taking a Carriage Ride Through Stanley Park:** One of the largest urban parks in the world, Stanley Park is nothing short of magnificent. Sample the highlights on a delightful 1-hour carriage ride that winds through the forest,

PREVIOUS PAGE: **A man admires one of the many giant trees in Stanley Park.**

along Burrard Inlet, past cricket fields, rose gardens, and the park's superlative collection of First Nations totem poles. See p. 119.

o **Wandering the West End:** Encompassing the über-shopping strip known as Robson Street, as well as cafe-lined Denman and a forest of high-rise apartments, the West End is the urban heart of Vancouver. Enjoy the lush trees lining the streets, the range of architecture, the diversity of cultures, the latest fashions and fashionistas, and neat little surprises on every side street. See "Walking Tour 1," p. 158.

o **Dining Out on Local Seafood:** Visitors are rightly amazed at the abundance of fresh-that-day seafood available in Vancouver's restaurants. This is a city where an appetizer of raw oysters often precedes a main course of wild salmon or halibut. See chapter 6.

o **Visiting the Vancouver Aquarium:** It's a Jacques Cousteau special, live and right there in front of you. Fittingly enough, the aquarium has an excellent display on the Pacific Northwest, plus sea otters (cuter than they have any right to be), beluga whales, sea lions, and a Pacific white-sided dolphin. See p. 122.

o **Exploring Chinatown:** Fishmongers call out their wares before a shop filled with crabs, eels, geoducks, and bullfrogs, while farther down the street elderly Chinese women haggle over produce as their husbands hunt for deer antler or dried sea horse at a traditional Chinese herbalist. When you're tired of looking and listening, head inside to any one of a dozen restaurants to sample succulent Cantonese cooking. See "Walking Tour 2: Gastown & Chinatown," p. 164.

o **Marveling at First Nations Artwork in the Museum of Anthropology:** The building—by native son Arthur Erickson—is worth a visit in itself, but this is also one of the best places in the world to see and learn about west coast First Nations art and culture. See p. 128.

The Vancouver Aquarium brings you up close to the aquatic life of the Pacific Northwest.

o **Browsing the Public Market on Granville Island:** Down on False Creek, this former industrial site was long ago converted into a truly eye-popping and sense-staggering indoor public market. Hop on the mini-ferry at the foot of Davie Street in Yaletown, and in 10 minutes, you'll be there. At the market, you'll find incredible food and goodies; put together a picnic and sit outside by the wharf to people- or boat-watch as you nosh. See p. 125.

Pick up fresh food at the Granville Island public market for a nearby picnic.

o **Kayaking on Indian Arm:** Vancouver is one of the few cities on the edge of a great wilderness, and one of the best ways to appreciate its splendor is by kayaking on the gorgeous Indian Arm. Rent a kayak or go with an outfitter—they may even serve you a gourmet meal of barbecued salmon. See "Outdoor Activities" on p. 143.

o **Discovering the Paintings of Emily Carr at the Vancouver Art Gallery:** It's always a thrill to discover a great artist, and Emily Carr's work hauntingly captures the primal appeal of BC's rugged, rain- and wave-washed forests and shores. See p. 123.

THE BEST websites FOR VANCOUVER & VICTORIA

o **Tickets Tonight** (www.tickets tonight.ca): This site offers half-price night-of tickets and general entertainment information in the Vancouver area.

o **Pacific Rim Visitor Centre** (www. pacificrimvisitor.ca): This area-specific site is a great place to learn more about Vancouver Island's west coast.

o **Tourism BC** (www.hellobc.com): The official site of the provincial government tourism agency, this site provides good information on

attractions, as well as higher-end accommodations.

o **Tourism Vancouver** (www.tourism vancouver.com): The official city tourism agency site provides a great overview of attractions, including an excellent calendar of events, plus a few last-minute deals on accommodations.

o **Vancouver BC** (www.vancouverbc. com): This site offers a nice mix of Vancouver-related stories with Top 10 picks in various categories.

Walk above a forested canyon on the Capilano Suspension Bridge.

o **Crossing the Capilano Suspension Bridge:** Stretched across a deep forested canyon, high above trees and a rushing river, this pedestrian-only suspension bridge has been daring visitors to look down for more than 100 years. Now, you can explore the giant trees, too, on a series of artfully constructed tree walks. See p. 131.

o **Watching the Sunset from a Waterside Patio:** Why else live in a city with such stunning views? Many places on False Creek, English Bay, and Coal Harbour have great waterside patios. See chapter 7.

o **Vancouver Magazine** (www.vanmag.com): An online Vancouver news magazine with news and features, restaurant reviews, entertainment, and shopping.

o **Victoria's Food Secrets** (www.victoriasfoodsecrets.com): Victoria (a person, not the city) munches her way through Vancouver and provides restaurant reviews and foodie gossip between bites.

o **Tourism Victoria** (www.tourismvictoria.com): Victoria's official tourism site functions much the same as Vancouver's, with up-to-date, comprehensive information about what to do and see around the city.

o **Victoria BC Magazine** (www.victoriabcmagazine.com): Check out this site for general information and event news about Victoria.

o **Whistler Blackcomb Ski Resort** (www.whistlerblackcomb.com): This site offers a particularly helpful overview of activities and accommodations options available at North America's premier ski resort.

THE most UNFORGETTABLE TRAVEL EXPERIENCES: VICTORIA

o **Strolling Victoria's Inner Harbour:** Walk along a paved pathway that winds past manicured flower gardens, waterfront residences, and all manner of seafaring activity and aquatic wildlife. The best stretch runs south from the Inner Harbour near the century-old Provincial Legislature Buildings and the Fairmont Empress hotel. See "Walking Tour 1," p. 295.

o **Touring the Royal BC Museum:** One of the best small museums in the world, the Royal BC does exactly what a good regional museum should do—explain the region and its people. See p. 277.

o **Marveling at Butchart Gardens:** This world-class garden, 20 minutes north of downtown Victoria, is a must-see attraction. Gorgeous during the day and subtly illuminated on summer evenings, it takes on a whole new personality when the famous fireworks begin. Saturday nights in the summertime, you get both. See p. 273.

o **Whale-Watching:** Of all the species of orcas (killer whales), those on the Washington and BC coasts are the only ones that live in large, extended families which are relatively easy to find. There's something magical about being out on the water and seeing a pod of 15 animals surface just a few hundred feet away. Adventurous souls might want to trying kayaking excursions. See "Whale-Watching," in chapter 15.

o **Discovering the Paintings of Emily Carr at the Art Gallery of Greater Victoria:** If you didn't get to see the works by this great local artist at the Vancouver Art Gallery, you can view several canvases at the Art Gallery here, in

FROM LEFT: The world-class Butchart Gardens is only 20 minutes from downtown Victoria; traditional afternoon tea at the Fairmont Empress is one of Victoria's highlights.

Pods of Orca whales can be found just off the coast of Vancouver Island.

Emily Carr's hometown, as well as visit her family residence: Emily Carr House. See p. 272.

o **Scooting about on a Mini-Ferry:** Catch a Victoria Harbour Ferry and take a 45-minute tour around the harbor, past the floating neighborhood of West Bay, or up the gorge, where tidal waterfalls reverse direction with the changing tide. Moonlight tours depart every evening at sunset. See "Getting Around," in chapter 12, and "Organized Tours," in chapter 15.

o **Biking the Dallas Road:** This is the "Cycling Capital of Canada," so there are plenty of pedal power opportunities for the entire family. This bike path runs alongside the ocean with a backdrop of high mountain peaks, past heritage homes, cruise ships, windsurfers, and kite-flyers. Cut back to downtown through Beacon Hill Park and add rhododendrons, lily-filled ponds, and meadows to your scenic itinerary. See p. 306.

THE most UNFORGETTABLE EXPERIENCES BEYOND VANCOUVER & VICTORIA

o **Skiing and Mountain Biking at Whistler Blackcomb Resort:** The two best resorts in North America merged in 1997 for a total of more than 200 runs on two adjoining mountains. In the summer, the same slopes become a world-class mountain biking network. See chapter 11.

o **Ziptrekking at Whistler:** Once you're strapped into your safety harness and hooked onto cables suspended hundreds of feet above a wild river, leap off, and away you go. Safe for everyone from 8 to 80, Ziptrek is an exhilarating adventure you'll never forget. See p. 224.

o **Looking for Bald Eagles in Squamish:** The bald eagle is the national symbol of the United States, but in winter, when the salmon are running, you can see more of these huge birds in Squamish than just about anywhere else in the world. See "Wildlife-Watching," in chapter 7.

o **Discovering Pacific Rim National Park:** The drive to this rugged maritime park on Vancouver Island's west coast is stunning, and once there, you're in a world of old-growth temperate rainforests and surf-pounded beaches. It's a place where you can experience the primal glories of nature amid the pampering luxuries of a first-class resort. See chapter 19.

Whistler-Blackcomb is considered one of the best ski and snowboard resorts in North America.

o **Meandering Through the Wineries:** Located within an hour's drive north of Victoria, the Cowichan Valley is home to numerous vineyards, cideries, cottage farms, and art studios. Touring is as easy as following the burgundy-and-white Wine Route signs. The Saanich Peninsular is smaller, and just as pretty. See chapter 15.

Pacific Rim National Park has miles of beautiful, rugged beaches.

Nearly half a million spectators take in the summer fireworks over English Bay.

THE best THINGS TO DO FOR FREE (OR ALMOST) IN VANCOUVER

o **Walk the Stanley Park Seawall:** Or jog, blade, bike, skate, ride—whatever your favorite mode of transport is, use it, but by all means, get out to enjoy this superlative and super-exhilarating path at the water's edge. See p. 119.

o **Watch the Fireworks Explode over English Bay:** Every August during the July/August Celebration of Light, three countries compete by launching their best fireworks displays over English Bay. As many as 500,000 spectators cram the beaches around English Bay, while those with boats sail out to watch from the water. See p. 31.

o **Stroll the Beach:** It doesn't matter which beach, there's one for every taste. Wreck Beach below the University of British Columbia is for nudists, Spanish Banks Beach is for dog walkers, Jericho Beach is for volleyballers, Kitsilano Beach is for serious suntanning, and English Bay Beach is for serious people-watching. See p. 143.

o **Picnic at the Lighthouse:** One of the prettiest picnic spots is Lighthouse Park on the North Shore. Not only do you get to look back over at Vancouver, but also the walk down to the rocky waterline runs through a pristine, old-growth rainforest. See p. 136.

o **Hike the North Shore:** The forests of the North Shore are at the edge of a great wilderness and only 20 minutes from the city. Step into a world of muted light and soaring cathedral-like spaces beneath the tree canopy. See "Hiking," in chapter 7.

Lighthouse Park is one of the prettiest picnic spots in Vancouver.

THE best THINGS TO DO FOR FREE (OR ALMOST) IN VICTORIA

o **Climb Mount Douglas:** Actually, you don't even have to climb. Just drive up and walk around. The whole of the Saanich Peninsula lies at your feet. See p. 278.

o **Beachcomb:** Just find a beach, preferably a rocky one, and turn stuff over or poke through the tide pools. The best beaches are along Highway 14A, starting with East Sooke Regional Park, and moving out to French Beach, China Beach, Mystic Beach, and (the very best of all) Botanical Beach Provincial Park, some 60km (37 miles) away by Port Renfrew. Remember to put the rocks back once you've had a peek. See "Beaches," "Especially for Kids," and "Watersports," in chapter 15.

o **Travel the Galloping Goose Trail:** Whether you cycle, rollerblade, jog, or walk, this rail-to-trail conversion starts in Victoria at the south end of the Selkirk Trestle, and weaves the back roads through urban, rural, and semi-wilderness landscapes. Different access points, many with parking areas, mean you can explore for an hour, a morning or the entire day. See p. 287.

Botanical Beach Provincial Park is an unbeatable site for beachcombing.

VANCOUVER & VICTORIA IN DEPTH

Vancouver is imposing and intimate, sophisticated and laid-back, glossy and gritty. **Victoria,** on the southeastern tip of Vancouver Island, leans more toward the quaint and the quiet (though you may not think so if you visit in the mobbed summer months).

A bustling, prosperous city, Vancouver almost miraculously combines a contemporary, urban-centered consciousness with the free-spirited magnificence of nature on a grand scale. In other words, the city offers residents and visitors the best of both worlds: an exciting cityscape set within a landscape of rugged, eye-catching beauty.

Victoria, British Columbia's capital, is only a short ferry ride from Vancouver, but the two cities are miles apart in their ambience and aesthetics. Where Vancouver trades its image as a brash, glamorous destination, Victoria offers a destination where refinement and a well-mannered style hold sway.

This chapter delves into the past and dishes about the present. Just what is it that makes these two cities so unique and so popular? How did they get to be the way they are? Who are the people who left their mark in years gone by, and who are the people who live in Vancouver and Victoria today? What makes the landscapes they inhabit so unique and so memorable? If you're curious, read on. The answers may surprise you.

VANCOUVER & VICTORIA TODAY
Boomtown Vancouver

With a population of about 612,000 (about 2,250,000 in the metro area), Vancouver is the largest metropolitan area in Western Canada and the third-largest city in the country. It's an ethnically diverse place where, according to the 2006 census, 52% of the residents have a first language other than English. And it's a popular place, with a population expected to grow to over 3 million by 2021. Though you'd never think so, given the amount of greenery and water, Vancouver is one of the most densely populated cities in North America, coming in fourth after New York City, San Francisco, and Mexico City. If forecasts are correct, by 2021, Vancouver will be in second place for urban density.

Most people think of Vancouver as something of a glamor-puss, thanks to its booming film industry, and the overall impression is one of glossy affluence. But, in fact, the city's basic economic underpinnings are built on trade and industry. Its location on the Pacific Rim at the western terminus of Canada's transcontinental highway and rail routes has helped to make Vancouver one of the largest industrial centers in Canada. Port Metro Vancouver, Canada's largest and most diversified, does more than C$75 billion in trade with over 160 countries

PREVIOUS PAGE: **The work of Haida artist Bill Reid is on display at Vancouver International Airport.**

annually. And it's no surprise, given that British Columbia's economy is based on what's euphemistically called "resource extraction," that Vancouver is also the headquarters of forest product and mining companies.

In recent years, however, the economy, like the population, has become more diverse and appears to be quite strong. Vancouver has become an increasingly important center for software development, biotechnology, and (of course) film development. Tourism is the third most important economic driver (behind forestry and fishing), and although Vancouver took a hit during the worldwide recession, the 2010 Winter Games (and the strong Canadian dollar) helped offset some of the loss. Roughly speaking, over a million people annually pass through Vancouver, many of them en route to a cruise-ship vacation, usually to Alaska. (The C$1-billion-a-year cruise-ship business has taken a hit, too, as some cruise lines such as Disney have decided to use Seattle or Victoria as their departure points.)

Vancouver is one of the "newest" cities you'll ever visit, and certainly it's one of the most cosmopolitan. A showy, energetic youthfulness pervades, along with a certain Pacific Northwest chic (and cheek). I can guarantee you that part of your trip will be spent trying to figure out what makes Canada's largest west coast metropolis so appealing. Nature figures big in that equation, but so does enlightened city planning and the diversity of cultures. Vancouver is a city where people *want* to live.

As Diverse as It Gets

Vancouver is the second-most popular destination for immigrants in Canada, after Toronto. People of English and Scottish origin formed the largest ethnic groups when the city was founded (the same was true in Victoria), and elements of British society and culture are still visible in the South Granville and Kerrisdale neighborhoods. But the largest visible ethnic group in the city today is the Chinese. In the 1990s, an influx of immigrants from Hong Kong, mainland China, and Taiwan arrived to create one of the largest concentrations of ethnic Chinese residents in North America. Vancouver is home to the largest population of Chinese outside of Asia.

Not to suggest that Vancouver's population is either British or Chinese. Other significant Asian ethnic groups in Vancouver are South Asian (mostly Punjabi, usually referred to as Indo-Canadian), Vietnamese, Filipino, Indonesian, Korean, Cambodian, and Japanese. The city has a growing Latin-American population from Peru, Ecuador, and more recently, Mexico. Vancouver and its surrounding metropolitan region are also home to the largest native (aboriginal) community in British Columbia and support a substantial gay community. British Columbia was the second Canadian jurisdiction to legalize same-sex marriage as a constitutional right, shortly after Ontario.

Victoria Today

For years, Victoria marketed itself quite successfully as a little bit of England on the North American continent. While the Empire Englishness still remains, the place that once only seemed to attract "the newly wed and the nearly dead" has

Pulling Rank

Vancouver is consistently ranked one of the "most livable cities" in the world, and Victoria earns some kudos, too. This ranking business always seems a bit silly but it does provide a snapshot insight in terms of expectations. Here are some recent rankings for Vancouver and Victoria, based on a variety of factors, surveys, and statistics used by various magazines and organizations:

Vancouver

○ "Best City in the Americas" (Conde Nast Readers' Choice Awards, 2010, 2009, 2006, 2005, 2004)

○ "World's most liveable city" (The *Economist* Intelligence Unit's Global Liveability Rankings, 2010, 2009, 2007, 2005)

○ "Most Walkable City in Canada" (*Up!* Magazine, 2010, 2009)

○ "Highest quality of life in the world" (Mercer Human Resource Consulting, 2010, 2009)

○ "Number One gay travel destination in Canada" and "Number Two international gay travel destination" (Community Marketing, Inc., 2008)

○ "6th most overpriced real estate market in the world," second in North America after *really* overpriced Los Angeles *(Forbes)*

○ "10th cleanest city in the world" *(Forbes)*

Victoria

○ "Number One Destination to Visit in Canada (TripAdvisor's Travellers' Choice, 2010)

○ "Best City for Young Professionals to Live and Work (Canada's "Next Cities," 2009)

○ "Best Place to Live (*MoneySense,* 2009)

○ "Top 10 Romantic Destinations (Gayot. com, 2009)

○ "Top North American Island (Conde Nast Readers' Choice Awards, 2008)

ramped up its appeal. The city has become cool. Restaurants have a collective focus on sublimely fresh, local, seafood, ethnic, and fusion cuisines, most of which have innovative spins that make food intriguingly delicious. Among the top draws to Victoria are all its eco-activities—whale-watching, kayaking, wind surfing, cycling, hiking, and mountain-biking have added a "natural" cache to its traditional London-style double-decker bus tours. The result? Victoria is the only city in the world where you can zoom out on a boat in the morning to see a pod of killer whales and make it back in time for an expansive afternoon tea. Still, life in Victoria remains much quieter and more laid-back than life in glam-seeking Vancouver. And that's part of Victoria's charm.

LOOKING BACK AT VANCOUVER & VICTORIA

Though **Vancouver** today has all the trappings of a sexy, showy, metrosexual metropolis, it began life as a hardscrabble pioneer town.

Victoria, on the other hand, has never shaken its colonial air and, in fact, embraces and celebrates it. The Victoria you see today retains much of its historic character and charm.

European Claims

In 1791, José María Narváez of Spain became the first European to explore the coastline of present-day Vancouver (Point Grey). The following year, 1792, an English sea captain named George Vancouver explored the inner harbor of Burrard Inlet, giving various places British names. The explorer and fur trader Simon Fraser and his crew, working for the North West Company, were the first Europeans known to have set foot on the site of present-day Vancouver. In 1808, they descended the Fraser River perhaps as far as Point Grey, near where the University of British Columbia stands today. The entire region, including present-day Victoria, came under British rule in the mid–19th century, when the Strait of Juan de Fuca became one of the new dividing lines between the U.S. and Canada.

Gold Rush & Boomtown

Though trappers and traders with the Hudson Bay Company had been active in the area since the 1820s (building forts in Victoria and Fort Langley near Vancouver), Vancouver really began its life as a boomtown during the Fraser Canyon Gold Rush of 1861, when 25,000 men, mostly from California, traveled to the mouth of the Fraser River and began prospecting for gold. The first European settlement was established in 1862, just east of the ancient village of Musqueam in what is now Marpole. Vancouver (and Victoria) boomed again during the 1898 Klondike Gold Rush, except this time, the cities served as profitable trading posts where merchants sold equipment and provisions to gold-hungry prospectors on their way north.

Vancouver's first sawmill was established on the north shore of Burrard Inlet in 1863 and was quickly followed by mills on the south shore. Hastings Mill, near the foot of Gore Street, formed the nucleus of nascent Vancouver, though the mill's central role in the city waned after the arrival of the Canadian Pacific Railway. The settlement of Gastown—the oldest section of Vancouver still standing today—grew up around a makeshift tavern established by "Gassy Jack" Deighton in 1867 on the edge of Hastings Mill. The British colonial government surveyed the settlement in 1870 and laid out a town site, renaming it "Granville," in honor of Granville Leveson-Gower, 2nd Earl Granville, the British Secretary of State for the Colonies.

East Meets West: The Canadian Pacific Railway

Big changes were in store for the newly named settlement of Granville, for it was soon selected to be the terminus for the Canadian Pacific Railway (CPR), dashing the hopes of Victoria, which had also vied to be the railhead. The building of

A SHORT history OF FIRST NATIONS

When Captain Vancouver arrived in English Bay in 1792, he entered the traditional territories of the Skwxwú7mesh, Xwméthkwyiem, and Tsleil-Waututh peoples of the Coast Salish language group. Their villages dotted the land that we now recognize as Vancouver's Stanley Park, False Creek, the Burrard Inlet, West Vancouver, and Point Grey. Exactly where each tribe lived, when Captain Vancouver arrived, and how many members each had are matters of some controversy, but evidence suggests that the coastal areas around Vancouver and Victoria had about 10,000 native residents and had been settled for some 10,000 years.

Pre-contact, First Nations society was divided into a nobility of chief families, commoners, and slaves (mostly war captives taken during raids). Living in the rainforest, all of these coastal peoples developed an extremely rich and complex culture, using cedar as their primary building material and, for food, harvesting marine resources such as herring, shellfish, and especially salmon. The richness of the local environment allowed these peoples ample surplus; their spare time was devoted to the creation of stories and art. Now undergoing a revival, coastal art, whether in wood, glass, or precious metals, usually depicts stylized figures from native mythology, including such universal figures as the Raven or tribal totems such as the Bear, Frog, or Killer Whale.

The central ceremony of the coastal First Nations was and is the potlatch, a gathering of tribes held to mark a significant event such as the raising of a totem pole or the coming-of-age of a son or daughter. Invited tribes sing and dance traditional songs, while the host, both to thank his guests and to demonstrate his wealth, gives away presents.

In the years after contact, the coastal First Nations were decimated by disease.

It's estimated that of some 10,000 people living along the coastal waterways, all but 600 of them were killed by smallpox carried by white settlers. The loss of traditional fishing rights, the repression of traditional rituals such as the potlatch, and the forced assimilation into English-Canadian culture all had a major impact on First Nations life and culture. In the decades after World War II, an entire generation of native children was forced into residential schools, where speaking native languages and learning native stories were forbidden. (In 2008, the Canadian government issued a formal apology to all Canadian First Nations tribes and established a fund to pay for past abuses in the residential schools.) The 1970s saw the first steps toward a long and slow recovery. The term "First Nations" came into common usage in the '70s, replacing the word "Indian," which some regarded as derogatory. There is no legal definition of "First Nations," but the term "First Nations peoples" generally refers to all the indigenous peoples in Canada. Though still beset by problems, the First Nations communities are on their way back to becoming a powerful and important force on the BC coast.

the railway was among the preconditions for British Columbia joining the Confederation in 1871. It was an enormous task, but finally, in 1886, the railway moved in and set up shop. A new era and a new name arrived with the railroad: The name Granville was scrapped, and the city was rechristened Vancouver. Just 4 years after the railway arrived, Vancouver's population grew from 400 to 13,000.

From 1886 to 1986: One Helluva Century

The year 1886 looms large in Vancouver's history. In that 1 year, the city incorporated, the first transcontinental Canadian Pacific train arrived, and a massive fire broke out and razed the entire city. Not surprisingly, 1886 was also the year the Vancouver Fire Department was established. The city quickly rebuilt and, thanks to the railroad and burgeoning port, grew even faster. Vancouver was now poised to become the key land and sea port for the natural bounty of British Columbia and the rest of Canada. Industry became the driving force behind Vancouver's phenomenal growth over the next century.

By 1901, the Steveston canneries were shipping out a record 7.3 million kg (16 million lb.) of salmon. The opening of the Panama Canal in 1914 proved enormously beneficial to Vancouver by shortening ocean journeys between British Columbia and Europe, and spurring the port's continued growth in grain exports.

By 1923, Vancouver had become the third-largest city in Canada. Though the city struggled through the 1930s, World War II pulled Vancouver out of the Great Depression as shipyards began to build warships and minesweepers. But the war also fueled anti-Japanese sentiment, and in 1942, following the Japanese bombing of Pearl Harbor, Japanese-Canadians were herded into holding areas at Hastings Park and removed to government camps in the Interior.

The turbulent 1960s was marked by anti-war protests, peace rallies, marches, and the appearance of hippies, who made Vancouver's West 4th Avenue (Kitsilano) their neighborhood. About the same time, the environmental activist group Greenpeace was formed in a Dunbar-neighborhood living room.

The city's infrastructure was expanded in the 1970s with a new shipping-container facility and coal port that dramatically increased Canada's economic links to the Pacific Rim. At the same time, Granville Island was converted from an industrial island into the big public market and retail/restaurant sector that continues to be popular today. Its transformation is widely considered one of the most successful inner city developments in North America.

The whirlwind century ended with two milestones demonstrating just how far Vancouver had come from its humble frontier-town beginnings. Expo '86 (the last world's fair to be held in North America) coincided with Vancouver's 100th anniversary and drew more than 21 million visitors. By the end of the 1980s, the Port of Vancouver was handling more imports/exports than any other port in North America.

The last big world-draw event to take place in Vancouver (and nearby Whistler and Cypress Mountain) was the 2010 Winter Games and Paralympic Games, held in February of that year.

Impressions

To realize Victoria, you must take all that the eye admires most in Bournemouth, Torquay, the Isle of Wight, the Happy Valley at Hong Kong, the Doon, Sorrento and Camps Bay; add reminisces of the Thousand Islands, and arrange the whole round the Bay of Naples, with some Himalayas in the background.
— Rudyard Kipling on Victoria
(after visiting in 1908)

VICTORIA'S secret

Founded in 1843, during Queen Victoria's reign, Victoria became the capital of British Columbia in 1866 when Vancouver Island united with the mainland—which is why a statue of the unamused monarch stands in front of the Provincial Legislature Buildings (still called "Parliament" by some). With colony-hood (and a big gold rush) came colonists, lots of them English and Scots, who imported British customs and brought a kind of domesticating old-world sensibility to their wild, new-world home. (They assumed they were bringing civilization, but that certainly wasn't how the First Nations tribes that had been in the area for at least 10,000 years saw it.) British patriotism and customs might have faded away altogether except that, in the 1920s, Victoria's population began to drop as business shifted over to Vancouver. Local merchants panicked. And it was then that San Francisco–born George Warren of the Victoria Publicity Bureau put

forward his proposal: Sell the Olde England angle. Warren had never been to England and had no idea what it looked like, but to him, Victoria looked "English." Warren's scheme clicked big-time with the city's merchants and boosters, and for three-plus generations, it served the city well. While Vancouver was leveling its "old" downtown in the name of urban renewal, Victoria nurtured and preserved its heritage buildings, adding gardens and city parks. Eventually, it possessed that rarest of commodities for a North American city—a lively, walkable, historic city center. True, the "let's pretend we're in England" mindset meant ignoring certain details. Whales sometimes swam into the Inner Harbour; snowcapped mountain peaks loomed just across the water from Ross Bay; and trees in the surrounding forests towered far higher than Big Ben. So be it. It worked, and Victoria didn't turn into Disneyland in the process.

VANCOUVER & VICTORIA ARCHITECTURE & ART
Wood, Brick & Glass: The Fabric of Vancouver

Old Vancouver was a city built of wood and brick, the complete antithesis of today's slender glass towers. The earliest wooden structures of pioneer Vancouver were destroyed in the Great Fire of 1886, after which brick became more common for commercial buildings. Walk through **Gastown** ("Walking Tour 2," p. 164), and you'll get a glimpse of what "downtown" Vancouver looked like in the late 19th century. If you stroll through the residential **West End** on the first walking tour in chapter 8, you'll encounter remnants of Old Vancouver in the form of big sturdy wooden houses with high front porches and sober, not-too-extravagant trim.

Though some "heritage buildings" still remain in Vancouver's Old Town and Chinatown, the face of the city you see today is undeniably new. Starting in the 1960s, misguided city planners and developers seemed intent on demolishing every last vestige of the city's pioneer past, replacing old brick and wood buildings with an array of undistinguished concrete high-rises and blocky eyesores. It was called "urban renewal." Citizen outcry finally got the bulldozers to stop their rampage. A few tiny pockets of original buildings are scattered among the downtown high-rises, most notably **Mole Hill** (See "Walking Tour 1: Downtown & the West End," in chapter 8).

What was lost? Vancouver as it used to be—a place where you could stand at any downtown street corner and have an unobstructed view of the sea in every direction. With a couple of notable exceptions, such as the **Sun Tower** (p. 167), the tallest building in the British Empire when it was built at Beatty and Pender streets in 1911, the 25-story **Marine Tower** (which took over the title as tallest building in the British Empire when it was built in 1929 at Burrard and Hastings sts.), and the **Fairmont Hotel Vancouver** (p. 64), the big Canadian Pacific Railroad hotel built downtown in 1939, the city was more low-rise than high-rise. Luckily, all three of those landmarks remain, as does the **Vancouver Art Gallery** (p. 123), a neoclassical gem built in 1907 to serve as the city's courthouse.

The same city planners responsible for bulldozing so much of the old city in the late 1950s and 1960s encouraged the development of high-rise residential towers in Vancouver's West End, a scheme that was intended to create a compact urban core amenable to public transit, cycling, and pedestrian traffic. According to the 2006 census (the last available), Vancouver's population density on the downtown peninsula is 5,335 people per sq. kilometer (13,817 people per sq. mile). Vancouver is rare among North American cities for having this kind of dense (and desirable) downtown core where people live, work, and play.

A building boom for Expo '86 was spurred on by enormous amounts of cash pouring in (along with thousands of immigrants) from Hong Kong and Asia. The new quarter-block residential towers, made of glass and steel, are much lighter looking than those from times past, and have helped to generate Vancouver's hip, international image. It's this new construction, with the "view corridors" and sustainable urban planning that go with it, that have made Vancouver a model for livability.

The Vancouver Art Gallery originally served as the city's courthouse.

FRANCIS RATTENBURY: FAMOUS ARCHITECT
& murder victim

Born in Leeds, England, Francis Mawson Rattenbury moved to the new Canadian province of British Columbia in 1891, where he won (despite having no formal architectural training) a competition to build a new legislative building in Victoria. Built on a grand scale in the Romanesque style, the **Legislature (Parliament) Buildings** opened in 1898 and led to more commissions. In Victoria, as Western Division Architect for the Canadian Pacific Railway, Rattenbury designed the château-style **Empress Hotel,** which opened in 1908, and the original CPR Steamship Terminal (1924). In Vancouver, he designed the Victorian **Roedde House** (1893) and the neoclassical Courthouse (1907) that serves today as the **Vancouver Art Gallery.** Then, as quickly as he'd become famous, Rattenbury and his architecture fell out of favor. Financial speculations led to conflicts with his business partners, and in 1923, he left his wife and two children for 27-year-old Alma Pakenham, an affair that led to public ostracism and contributed to his decision to leave Victoria and move to Bournemouth, England, in 1929. There, his relationship with Alma disintegrated as his financial problems worsened, and she began an affair with George Percy Stoner, her 18-year-old chauffeur. In 1935, aged 68, Rattenbury was murdered in his sitting room, suffering blows to the head with a carpenter's mallet from his killer. His wife and Stoner were charged, and Stoner was convicted and sentenced to death, although the sentence was later commuted to a life imprisonment (he served 7 years). Alma committed suicide a few days after the charges against her were dropped. The event was made into the 1977 play *Cause Célèbre* by Terence Rattigan.

A strong economy and the 7-year frenzy leading up to the 2010 Winter Games fueled what many believe was Vancouver's last major building boom; there simply isn't any more land to transform. Hence, the city continues to pursue progressive policies intended to increase density as an alternative to sprawl and to encourage environmental sustainability. For example, proposals to build high-rises in historic Chinatown are on a developer's agenda, a seeming extension for conversions of some of Gastown's heritage warehouses into funky condos and offices. The new buildings are characterized as mixed-use development, allowing street-level commerce and life to flourish. Though this booming city may now have its head in the clouds, it retains a street-level friendliness and accessibility. In fact, developing urban centers with mixed-use development has been referred to as "Vancouverism" because of the apparent success of such development.

Victoria's Architectural Charm

If you miss the old in Vancouver, you'll find plenty of it in Victoria. Victoria took the opposite approach from Vancouver and preserved nearly all its heritage buildings. As a result, British Columbia's capital, beautifully sited on its own Inner Harbour, is one of the most charming small cities you'll ever find (it has about 325,000 residents in the Greater Victoria area, compared to over two and a quarter million in Vancouver). The city's most famous architectural landmarks are the

Empress Hotel, dating from 1908, and the **Legislature Building,** completed in 1898, both located on the Inner Harbour, the most visible spot in the city.

Most of the buildings in the downtown core are built of stone or brick, and most of them are low-risers (newer hotels being the exception). But wood was the primary building material for houses, and a drive through any of Victoria's quiet residential neighborhoods will provide an architectural panorama of residential building styles from about the 1880s onward, including many English-style "cottages" that were popular in the 1920s. Victoria's neighborhoods are enhanced by lovely gardens, mature trees, and landscaping based on English gardening styles.

Emily Carr: Visionary from Victoria

Victoria was the birthplace of one of British Columbia's most distinguished early residents, the painter and writer Emily Carr. Though trained in the classical European tradition, Carr developed her own style in response to the powerful landscapes of the Canadian west coast. Eschewing both marriage and stability, she spent her life traveling the coast, drawing inspiration from the land, seascapes, and native peoples for her vivid and striking works. In addition to visiting the great collection of Carr's paintings at the **Art Gallery of Greater Victoria** (p. 272), you can visit the **Emily Carr House** (p. 274), where she was born. The **Vancouver Art Gallery** (p. 123) also has a major collection of Carr's hauntingly evocative paintings.

Emily Carr is one of British Columbia's most distinguished artists.

Bill Reid: First Among First Nations Artists

William (Bill) Ronald Reid is the best-known of Canada's aboriginal or First Nations artists, and the man who helped to save and revitalize the traditions of Haida art and culture. Born in Victoria to a father of European descent and a mother from the Haida people, Reid first learned about his aboriginal heritage from his maternal grandfather, a Haida artist of great renown. While working as a radio announcer in Toronto, Reid developed his interest in Haida art and studied jewelry making. In 1951, he returned to Vancouver to help salvage many intricately carved totem poles decaying in abandoned Haida village sites and to aid in the reconstruction of a Haida village in the University of British Columbia's Museum of Anthropology. Working in traditional Haida forms, Reid made jewelry of gold, silver, and argillite before branching out into larger sculptures. Visitors to Vancouver can see two of Bill Reid's most magnificent works—the **Jade Canoe,** at **Vancouver International Airport,** is a large bronze sculpture

NATIVE ART OF THE NORTHWEST: A CULTURE OF carving

The art of the first peoples of the Pacific Northwest is colorful, distinctive, and absolutely unique. It is, in its essence, sacred art meant to provide a bridge between the spirit and animal world (through a shaman) and the world of humans. Pacific Northwest First Nations art was almost always carved from rot-resistant cedar wood (or alder wood) and brightly painted with natural pigments; hairlike strands of cedar bark were sometimes attached. Totem poles, the most familiar pieces of native art, were originally erected in front of village longhouses to identify clans, memorialize ancestors, and denote status. But the great carving tradition of the First Nations artists also includes dramatic and sometimes frightening ceremonial and transformation masks; drums and rattles; boxes, feast dishes, and spoons; and canoes and paddles. The distinctive carvings and painted surfaces memorialize myths and mythological creatures; spirits both good and bad; and familiar animals of the sea, sky, and land.

By the 1950s, after a century of physical and cultural decimation, the great carving traditions were on the verge of being lost forever. Efforts by Bill Reid, working with the University of British Columbia Museum of Anthropology (p. 128) in Vancouver and the Royal BC Museum (p. 277) in Victoria, helped to save major First Nations artworks and revive the carving tradition.

Figures that recur over and over in Pacific Northwest First Nations art include the mythological Thunderbird and the more familiar animals that native tribes encountered, observed, and hunted: Raven, Bear, Salmon, Eagle, Killer Whale (Orca), Beaver, Hawk, Owl, Kingfisher, Wren, Grouse, Frog, and Bee. Stylized masks represent humans and elements of the natural world (Sun, Wind, Moon). These spirits' images are often carved into masks (note that many variant spellings exist for these names):

o **Bakwas**   Wild man of the woods, chief of the ghosts

o **Dzunukwa**   Giant wild woman of the woods, bringer of gifts at the potlatch

o **Huxwhukw**   Cannibal bird

o **Kolus**   One of the great thunderbirds, ancestor

o **Kumugwe**   Lord of the Undersea

o **Noomis**   Ancestor, born an old man at the beginning of time

o **Nulamal**   Fool dancer

o **Pugmis**   Sea equivalent of Bakwas, collector of souls

o **Pugwis**   Messenger of the Lord of the Undersea

o **Pook-ubs**   Figure who is a victim of the sea with white body and skeletal face

o **Sisiutl**   Double-sided serpent with face in the middle of a canoe filled with human and animal figures; the **Legend of the Raven and the First Humans,** a Haida creation myth carved from Nootka cypress (yellow cedar), occupies pride of place at the **UBC Museum of Anthropology** (p. 128)—and also visit the **Bill Reid Gallery of Northwest Coast Art** (p. 118), which showcases a selection of his work. Reid's work is also featured on the **C\$20 note** in the Bank of Canada's *Canadian Journey* (2004) issue.

VANCOUVER & VICTORIA IN POP CULTURE: BOOKS, FILM & MUSIC

Books

The following is a list of some titles that will give you a deeper insight into the multicultural richness of Vancouver and Victoria:

o *The Black Canoe: Bill Reid and the Spirit of the Haida Gwaii,* by Robert Bringhurst (Douglas & McIntyre): A poet and storyteller pays tribute to the great Haida artist Bill Reid.

o *City of Glass: Douglas Coupland's Vancouver,* by Douglas Coupland (Douglas & McIntyre): Generation X author Coupland's homage to his hometown is both a personal memoir and an alternative history of Vancouver's cultural icons.

o *The Concubine's Children: Portrait of a Family Divided,* by Denise Chong (Penguin Canada): A moving narrative of a Chinese immigrant family at the dawn of the 20th century.

o *The Complete Writings of Emily Carr* (University of Washington Press): Born in Victoria in the late 19th century, Emily Carr went on to become one of Canada's greatest and most original artists. In addition to painting, Carr also wrote, and this collection contains her remarkable autobiography, journals, and fiction. *Emily Carr,* part of the *Extraordinary Canadians* series (Penguin Canada), is a new biography of the artist by Lewis DeSoto. (For more on Emily Carr, see "Emily Carr: Visionary from Victoria," p. 21.)

o *Empress Letters,* by Linda Rogers who, until November 2011, was Victoria's poet laureate (Cormorant Books): Stories of a sea voyage in the 1920s mixed with opium secrets and a few cameos by island notables like Emily Carr and frequent visitor Tallulah Bankhead.

o *Making Vancouver,* by Robert A. J. McDonald (UBC Press): A scholarly history of Vancouver's development to 1913.

o *Obasan,* by Joy Kogawa (Anchor): The author was 7 years old in 1942 when the outbreak of war with the Japanese prompted Canada to send its Japanese citizens to internment camps in the BC Interior. The book draws on her experiences during that period.

o *Shoeless Joe,* by W.P. Kinsella (Mariner Books): This novel by Vancouver storyteller and raconteur Kinsella was adapted into the popular movie *Field of Dreams.*

THE CITY AS stand-in: FILMS FILMED IN VANCOUVER

It's really a bit ironic: Though hundreds of films and television shows have been shot in and around Vancouver, the city and the surrounding region usually serve as stand-ins for some other metropolis, country, or region. TV series have included *Chaos* and *Smallville;* here is a very brief list of some of the better-known movies filmed in Vancouver.

○ *2012* (2009)   We're in that year when we're to find out if the world is really going to end, as predicted in this made-up Mayan prophecy; in the meantime, you might recognize bits of Vancouver before disaster strikes.

○ *The 6th Day* (2000)   Arnold Schwarzenegger stars in this tale of a future when clones conspire to take over the world. The Vancouver Public Library (pictured here) serves as a stand-in for an evil corporation's headquarters.

○ *Best in Show* (2000)   In Christopher Guest's hilarious "mockumentary" about celebrity canines and their owners, Vancouver's venerable old Coliseum building doubles as the venue for a dog show.

○ *Christmas with the Kranks* (2004)   The Pacific Centre Mall in downtown Vancouver is easy to spot in this comedy about a suburban

family trying to skip the crass commercialism of Christmas.

○ *Dreamcatcher* (2003)   The town of Steveston is meant to be a quaint Maine village in this Stephen King balderdash about aliens terrorizing a group of buddies vacationing in a cabin.

○ *Elf* (2003)   Vancouver does a stellar job of standing in for Manhattan in

○ *There Is a Season,* by Patrick Lane (McClelland & Stewart): Although an award-winning memoir about the author's relationship between his garden and his own recovery from alcoholism, the words are so beautifully crafted, they come together as the definitive book about Victoria, aka the Garden City.

○ *Vancouver Cooks* and *Vancouver Cooks 2,* edited by Jamie Maw (Douglas & McIntyre): Fifty of the area's best-known chefs contributed to this celebration of the amazing food culture and restaurants of Vancouver, the Lower Fraser Valley, and southern Vancouver Island.

○ *The Vancouver Stories: West Coast Fiction from Canada's Best Writers* (Rain-coast Books): With stories by the likes of Pauline Johnson, Emily Carr, Alice Munro, Malcolm Lowry, and many others, this wide array of short fiction reveals just how varied Vancouver really is.

this Christmas flick starring Will Ferrell.

○ **The Exorcism of Emily Rose** (2005)   The University of British Columbia campus gets screen time in this tale of a young girl killed by a priest during an exorcism.

○ **The Five People You Meet in Heaven** (2004)   A TV mini-series based on the book by Mitch Albom about a man who meets up with some important people in the afterlife.

○ **Gods and Monsters** (1998)   This fascinating film, starring Ian McKellen as James Whale, the director of the original Frankenstein, would be worth watching even if it weren't filmed in Vancouver.

○ **Herbie Fully Loaded** (2005)   Lindsay Lohan starred in this family-friendly remake of a Disney movie about a cute little Volkswagen.

○ **Night at the Museum** (2006)   The Vancouver Art Gallery stars as the Museum of Natural History in New York.

○ **Scary Movie** (2000) and **Scary Movie 4** (2006)   These idiotic horror-film spoofs, filmed all over the Lower Mainland, have raked in gazillions.

○ **Strange Magic** (2011)   Gastown's cobblestone streets are a stand-in for London's Leicester Square and the film premiere of Harry Potter.

○ **Timecop** (1994)   Granville Island is featured in this time-warp thriller starring Jean-Claude Van Damme.

○ **The Twilight Saga: New Moon** (2010) and **Eclipse** (2008)   The film adaptations of Stephanie Meyer's teen vampire romances suck in blood and big bucks at the box office; New Moon was the first Twilight flick shot in IMAX.

○ **The X-Files** (1998), **X-Men 2** (2003), and **X-Men: The Last Stand** (2006)   These three movies (as well as the X-Files TV series) give nods to Robson Square in downtown Vancouver and that black-glass high-rise known as the Sheraton Wall Centre.

○ *Victoria: The Unknown City,* by Ross Crockford (Arsenal Pulp Press): Tales of hidden intrigue and historic curiosities in Canada's westernmost provincial capital, whose polite, "just-like-England" exterior conceals a surprisingly quirky and rough-edged heart.

Music

A number of notable punk-rock bands originated in Vancouver. D.O.A., the most famous, has been performing for 30 years and is often referred to as the founders of hardcore punk. Other early punk bands from Vancouver include the Subhumans; the Young Canadians; the Pointed Sticks; Active Dog; the Modernettes; UJ3RK5; I, Braineater; and Nomeansno (originally from Victoria). In the 1990s, when alternative rock hit the mainstream, several Vancouver groups rose to

Sarah McLachlan is one of Vancouver's more famous local musicians.

prominence, including 54-40, Odds, Moist, the Matthew Good Band (2011 Juno Rock Album of the Year), and Econoline Crush. More recent successes include Gob and Stabilo.

Today, Vancouver is home to a lively independent music scene, including bands such as the New Pornographers, Destroyer, Frog Eyes, the Organ, Veda Hille, and Black Mountain. Vancouver also produced the influential metal band Strapping Young Lad and pioneering electro-industrial bands Skinny Puppy and Front Line Assembly. Popular musical artists from Vancouver include Bryan Adams, Sarah McLachlan, Michael Bublé, Nickelback, and from Vancouver Island, Diana Krall. Notable hip hop artists from Vancouver include the Rascalz, Swollen Members, and Sweatshop Union.

EATING & DRINKING IN VANCOUVER & VICTORIA

In the past 2 decades, Vancouver has become one of the top dining destinations in the world, bursting with an incredible variety of cuisines and making an international name for itself with its audacious and adventuresome Pacific Northwest cooking. The food mantra here is "buy locally, eat seasonally," a philosophy that lets chefs support local farmers and fishermen, and take full advantage of bountiful local organic produce, game, and seafood. Victoria has an even stronger farm-to-fork ethos and, as an island, the collaboration between chef and supplier adds a creative dimension to the eating experience.

Regional Richness

This part of the world has always been known for the bounty of its land, rivers, and sea. The First Nations tribes of the Pacific Northwest were among the richest in the world, thanks to the abundance and seasonal variety of their food, which included year-round fish, game, berries, and wild edible plants. During the tribal feast and gift-giving celebration known as potlatch, the natural wealth of the coastal rainforest, and its rivers and coastlines, was fully evident. You'll still find one of the most popular potlatch dishes—alderwood-smoked salmon—on menus in Vancouver and Victoria.

As you might expect, salmon and shellfish became dietary staples for the new immigrants arriving from England, Scotland, and Europe. An enormous salmon cannery (it's now a national historic landmark) in Steveston, on the Fraser River, packaged and exported millions of tons of sockeye—until the stocks dwindled and the industry collapsed in the 1970s.

The first European settlers were not known for inventive cooking. Victoria, in particular, took its culinary cues from England, and a large German population in Vancouver spawned so many delicatessens that Robson Street was formerly nicknamed *Robsonstrasse*. Up until the 1980s, restaurants in Vancouver and Victoria relied on the fried and true, serving fish, seafood, and area produce, but without the flair and imagination that rules the dining scene today.

What changed it all? A generation of young, creative, ambitious BC and Canadian chefs who trained in Europe and came back to experiment with the riches at home. That and a rising number of ethnic restaurants—at first mostly Chinese and Japanese, but today encompassing just about every cuisine you can think of. It wasn't long before chefs started crossing culinary lines and borrowing influences (and spices) from Asian and Indian cooking. Fusion is big. It's Italian (Vancouver has several excellent Italian restaurants), French, sushi, and dim sum. Add to this, the region's craft beer culture (Victoria's brewpubs are numerous and classy), and you have a plethora of tasting opportunities and pairings—usually you just have to ask and presto, you'll be in for a treat whether with hand-made chocolates, charcuterie, or multiple tapas!

Uncorking BC Wines

Be sure to try a British Columbian wine with your meal. BC wines are now winning international acclaim and rival vintages from California, Australia, France, and Germany. The big wine-producing areas are in the Okanagan Valley (in southern BC's dry interior) and on southern Vancouver Island (the Cowichan Valley). Some of these wines are truly wonderful, but you won't find them outside of Canada (and sometimes not outside of Vancouver). They're not produced in large enough quantities to export, and the restaurants usually snap up what's available.

WHEN TO GO
Weather

A rainforest species like the western red cedar needs at least 76cm (30 in.) of precipitation a year. Vancouver gets about 116cm (46 in.) a year, a cause for celebration among the local cedar population. *Homo sapiens* simply learn to adjust.

Most of that precipitation (usually in the form of showers and drizzle, not downpours) arrives in the winter, when (with a 30-min. drive to the mountains) you can trade the rain for snow. Skiing and snowboarding are popular from mid-December until the mountain snowpack melts away in June. Except in Whistler, hotels in the winter are quieter and the restaurants less busy.

Both Vancouver and Victoria enjoy moderately warm, sunny summers and mild, rainy winters; their weather is the mildest in Canada. Victoria gets half as much rain as Vancouver (58cm/23 in.), thanks to the sheltering Olympic Peninsula to the south and its own southeasterly position on huge Vancouver Island. You can find **current weather conditions** for Vancouver at http://vancouver.weatherpage.ca.

Around mid-February, the winds begin to slacken, the sun shines a bit more, the buds on the cherry trees appear, and early daffodils blossom. By late-March, azaleas, rhododendrons, and most other flowers are in bloom, and the sun is more frequent though this doesn't always hold through April, which can serve up a bit of everything from glorious warmth to sudden arctic chills.

June sees more sun per summer day than farther south (mid-June sees 16 hr. of daylight). Only 10% of the annual rainfall occurs during the summer months, and the sun stays out through summer until the rains close in again in mid-October. These spring/summer/early autumn months are prime visiting time and when most visitors arrive. The first cruise ships start appearing in late April/early May.

Daily Average High Temperatures & Total Precipitation for Vancouver, BC

	JAN	FEB	MAR	APR	MAY	JUNE	JULY	AUG	SEPT	OCT	NOV	DEC
TEMP (°F)	41	45	50	57	64	70	73	73	64	57	48	43
TEMP (°C)	5	7	10	14	18	21	23	23	18	14	9	6
PRECIPITATION (IN.)	5.9	4.9	4.3	3	2.4	1.8	1.4	1.5	2.5	4.5	6.7	7

Holidays

The official British Columbia public holidays are as follows: New Year's Day (Jan 1); Good Friday, Easter, Easter Monday (Apr 9, 2012); Victoria Day (May 21, 2012); Canada Day (July 1); British Columbia Day (first Monday in Aug); Labour Day (Sept 3, 2012); Thanksgiving (Oct 8, 2012); Remembrance Day (Nov 11); Christmas (Dec 25); and Boxing Day (Dec 26).

Vancouver & Victoria Calendar of Events

The various festivals and special events held in Vancouver and Victoria every year draw tens of thousands of visitors and reflect an extraordinary diversity of cultures. Things may seem a little quiet in the winter and early spring, but that's because most residents simply head for the ski slopes. Resorts in **Whistler Blackcomb** (© **800/944-7853;** www.whistler.com) have events happening nearly every weekend. If no contact number or location is given for any of the events listed below, **Tourism Vancouver** (© **604/683-2000;** www.tourismvancouver.com) can provide further details.

For an exhaustive list of events beyond those listed here, check **http://events.frommers.com,** where you'll find a searchable, up-to-the-minute roster of what's happening in cities all over the world.

VANCOUVER EVENTS

JANUARY

Polar Bear Swim, English Bay Beach. Thousands of hardy citizens show up in elaborate costumes to take a dip in the icy waters of English Bay. Call ℂ **604/665-3418** or visit http://vancouver.ca for more information. January 1.

Dine Out Vancouver. For a limited time every January into early February, Vancouver's hottest restaurants offer three-course dinners for C$18, C$28, and C$38 per person. Contact www.tourism vancouver.com for more information.

PuSh International Performing Arts Festival, venues throughout Vancouver. An international performing arts festival featuring over 100 performances, involving 18 works in the main program and seven satellite shows by 23 companies at 16 venues. For more information, visit www.pushfestival.ca. Late January to early February.

FEBRUARY

Chinese New Year, Chinatowns in Vancouver and Richmond. This is when the Chinese traditionally pay their debts and forgive old grievances to start the new lunar year with a clean slate. These Chinese communities launch a 2-week celebration, ringing in the new year with firecrackers, dancing dragon parades, and other festivities. Call ℂ **604/662-3207** or visit www.vancouverchinesegarden. com for information. Dates vary yearly.

International Bhangra Celebration, downtown. Vancouver's East Indian population of 60,000-plus celebrates with Bhangra, a lively form of folk music and dance that originates in the Punjab. Events include live music and dance demonstrations, workshops, and competitions. Details are at www.vibc.org. Mid-February.

Dine Out Victoria. For 10 days, from late February to early March, Victoria's hottest restaurants offer three-course dinners for C$18, C$28, and C$38 per person. Contact Tourism Victoria (www. tourismvictoria.com) for details.

MARCH

CelticFest, downtown. For 5 days each year, the sounds of fiddles, bagpipes, bodhrans, dancing feet, and voices resound throughout downtown Vancouver in celebration of Celtic culture. Hundreds of local and international artists at more than 60 events are scheduled at dozens of popular venues and two outdoor stages along Granville Street. For information, visit www.celticfest vancouver.com. Mid-March.

Vancouver Playhouse International Wine Festival. This is a major wine-tasting event featuring the latest international vintages. For more ticket information, call ℂ **604/873-3311** or visit www.playhousewinefest.com. Early March.

APRIL

Baisakhi Day Parade. The Sikh Indian New Year is celebrated with a colorful parade around Ross Street near Marine Drive. It sets the stage for daylong festivities on Fraser Street, and at 49th Avenue/Main Street, aka "Little India" where streets are packed with vendors giving away traditional food—free, as well as Indian music and dancing. Contact Tourism Vancouver (ℂ **604/683-2000;** www.tourismvancouver.com) for more information. Mid-April.

Vancouver Sun Run. This is Canada's biggest 10K race, featuring more than 60,000 runners, joggers, and walkers who race through 10 scenic kilometers (6¼ miles). The run finishes at BC Place Stadium. Call ℂ **604/689-9441** for information or register online at www. sunrun.com.

MAY

Vancouver International Marathon. Runners from around the world compete here. For information, call ℂ **604/872-2928** or visit www.van marathon.com. First Sunday in May.

International Children's Festival.
Activities, plays, music, and crafts for children are featured at this annual event held in Vanier Park on False Creek. For information, call ☎ **604/708-5655** or visit www.childrensfestival.ca. Mid-May.

JUNE

Festival d'Eté Francophone de Vancouver/ Francophone Summer Festival. This 4-day festival celebrating French music uses various venues and includes a street festival. Call ☎ **604/736-9806** or check www.lecentreculturel.com for information. Mid-June.

Alcan Dragon Boat Festival. Traditional dragon-boat racing is a part of the city's cultural scene. Watch the races from False Creek's north shore, where more than 150 local and international teams compete. Four stages of music, dance, and Chinese acrobatics are presented at the **Plaza of Nations** (750 Pacific Blvd.), and along the shores of False Creek. For more info, call ☎ **604/688-2382** or visit http://dragonboatbc.ca. Third weekend in June.

National Aboriginal Day Community Celebration. This event gives the public an opportunity to learn about Canada's First Nations cultures. Many events take place at the **Vancouver Aboriginal Friendship Centre** (1607 E. Hastings St., at Commercial St.). Call ☎ **604/251-4844** or visit www.vafcs.org for information. June 21.

Vancouver International Jazz Festival. More than 800 international jazz and blues players perform at 25 venues, ranging from the Orpheum Theatre to the Roundhouse. Many are free performances. Call the **Jazz Hot Line** (☎ **604/872-5200**) or visit www.coastaljazz.ca for more information. Late June/early July.

Bard on the Beach Shakespeare Festival, Vanier Park. Four of Shakespeare's plays are performed in a tent overlooking English Bay. Call the box office

(☎ **604/739-0559**) or check www.bardonthebeach.org. Late May through late September, Tuesday through Sunday.

JULY

Canada Day. Canada Place Pier hosts an all-day celebration that begins with the induction of new Canadian citizens. Music and dance are performed outdoors throughout the day. A 21-gun salute at noon, precision acrobatics teams in the afternoon, and a nighttime fireworks display on the harbor lead the festivities. Granville Island, Grouse Mountain, and other locations also host Canada Day events. For more information, call ☎ **604/683-2000** or check www.tourismvancouver.com. July 1.

BCMTA Kayak Marathon. Competitors race sea kayaks in Georgia Strait. The **Ecomarine Kayak Centre** (☎ **604/689-7575;** www.ecomarine.com), at Jericho Beach, hosts the race and can provide details. Mid-July.

Harrison Festival of the Arts, Harrison Hot Springs, lower mainland. This arts festival in the Fraser River valley, just east of Vancouver, attracts performing artists from around the world. Call ☎ **604/796-3664** or visit www.harrisonfestival.com for more information. Early to mid-July.

Dancing on the Edge. Canadian and international dance groups perform modern and classic works at the **Firehall Arts Centre** and other venues. For information, call ☎ **604/689-0926** or visit www.dancingontheedge.org. Early to mid-July.

Vancouver Folk Music Festival. International folk music is performed outdoors at Jericho Beach Park. Contact the **Vancouver Folk Music Society** at ☎ **604/602-9798** or visit www.thefestival.bc.ca for more information. Second or third weekend in July.

Illuminares Lantern Festival, Trout Lake, John Hendry Park (Victoria Dr. and 15th

Ave.). This evening lantern procession circling Trout Lake is a phantasmagoric experience, complete with drums, costumes, fire-breathing apparitions, and lots of elaborate handcrafted lanterns. Various performances start at dusk. For info, call ☎ **604/879-8611** or visit www.publicdreams.org. Third or fourth Saturday in July.

Caribbean Days Festival, North Vancouver. The Trinidad and Tobago Cultural Society of BC hosts the city's premier Caribbean event at Waterfront Park in North Vancouver, featuring live music, authentic Caribbean food, arts, crafts, and a parade. For info, call ☎ **604/515-2400** or visit www.ttcsbc.com. Third or fourth weekend in July.

Harmony Arts Festival, West Vancouver. This event highlights the talent of North Shore artists, offering free exhibitions, demonstrations, studio tours, theater, concerts, markets, and workshops. Call ☎ **604/925-7268** or visit www.harmonyarts.net for more information. Late July and early August.

Celebration of Light. Three international fireworks companies compete for a coveted title by launching their best displays accompanied by music over English Bay Beach. Don't miss the big finale on the fourth evening. It's mainly a free event with some paid-seating available. *Note:* Because of the crowds, some streets are closed to vehicles at night. Other prime viewing locations include Kitsilano Beach and Jericho Beach. Call **Tourism Vancouver** (☎ **604/683-2000)** or check www.vancouverfireworks.ca for information. End of July to first week of August.

AUGUST

Summer Dancing in Robson Square. Every Friday night in August, Robson Square in downtown Vancouver hosts a free night of dancing under the stars. The evening starts with a free dance lesson given by a local instructor,

followed by showcase dancers and then a "general dance" where everyone (all ages and dance levels) is encouraged to join in. For more information, visit www.dancesportbc.com.

Powell Street Festival. An annual fete of Japanese culture includes music, dance, food, and more. Contact the Powell Street Festival Society (☎ **604/739-9388;** www.powellstreetfestival.com) for info. First weekend of August.

Gay Pride Parade. This huge and hugely popular gay- and lesbian-pride parade begins at noon in the West End and serves as the culmination of Pride Week. Celebrations at many local gay and lesbian nightclubs take place around town on the same long holiday weekend (BC Day weekend). For more info, contact the Pride Society (☎ **604/687-0955;** www.vancouverpride.ca). First Sunday in August.

MusicFest Vancouver. National and international artists perform orchestral, choral, opera, world music, chamber music, and jazz concerts in venues throughout Vancouver. For information, call ☎ **604/688-1152** or visit www.musicfestvancouver.ca. First 2 weeks in August.

Abbottsford International Air Show, Abbottsford. Barnstorming stuntmen and precision military pilots fly everything from Sopwith Camels to Stealth Bombers. This is one of the biggest air shows in the world. Call ☎ **604/852-8511** or visit www.abbotsfordairshow.com for more info. Second weekend in August.

Pacific National Exhibition. The city's favorite fair includes one of North America's best all-wooden roller coasters. Special events include livestock demonstrations, logger competitions, fashion shows, and a midway. Call ☎ **604/253-2311** or visit www.pne.bc.ca for more details. Mid-August to Labour Day.

Vancouver Wooden Boat Festival, Granville Island. Call ☎ **604/519-7400** or visit www.vancouverwoodenboat.com for more info. Third weekend of August.

Vancouver Fringe Festival. The Fringe Festival is centered on Granville Island, Commercial Drive, and Yaletown's Roundhouse, and features more than 500 innovative and original shows performed by more than 100 groups from Canada and around the world. Call ☎ **604/257-0350** or check out www.vancouverfringe.com for more info. First and second week of September.

Mid-Autumn Moon Festival, Dr. Sun Yat-Sen Chinese Garden. This outdoor Chinese celebration includes a lantern festival, storytelling, music, and (of course) moon cakes. For info, call ☎ **604/662-3207** or visit www.vancouverchinesegarden.com. Early to mid-September, according to the lunar cycle (15th day of the eighth month of the Chinese calendar).

Vancouver International Film Festival. This highly respected festival features 250 new works, revivals, and retrospectives, representing filmmakers from 40 countries (particularly Asia). Call ☎ **604/685-0260** or visit www.viff.org for details. Late September and first 2 weeks of October.

Vancouver International Writers and Readers Festival. Public readings by Canadian and international authors, as well as writers' workshops, take place on Granville Island and at other locations in the lower mainland. Call ☎ **604/681-6330** or check www.writersfest.bc.ca for details. Mid-October.

Parade of the Lost Souls, Grandview Park. This bizarre and intriguing procession takes place around Commercial Drive to honor the dead and chase away bad luck. For more information, call

☎ **604/879-8611** or visit www.public dreams.org. Last Saturday of October.

Remembrance Day. Celebrated throughout Canada, this day commemorates Canadian soldiers who gave their lives in war. Vintage military aircraft fly over Stanley Park and Canada Place. At noon, a 21-gun salute is fired from Deadman's Island. November 11.

Carol Ship Parade of Lights Festival. Harbor cruise ships decorated with colorful Christmas lights sail around English Bay, while onboard guests sip cider and sing their way through the canon of Christmas carols. For more info, call ☎ **604/878-8999** or check out www.carolships.org. First 3 weeks in December.

Festival of Lights. Throughout December, the VanDusen Botanical Garden is transformed into a magical holiday land with seasonal displays and more than 20,000 lights. Call ☎ **604/878-9274** or visit www.vandusengarden.org for info.

Stanley Park Festival of Lights. Throughout December, the plaza in the middle of Stanley Park becomes a festive gathering point with more than a million twinkling lights transforming the surrounding forest and children's farmyard. The Stanley Park holiday train winds its way through the illuminated forest. For more information, call ☎ **604/257-8400** or visit http://vancouver.ca/parks.

VICTORIA & SOUTHERN VANCOUVER ISLAND EVENTS

Annual Bald Eagle Count, Goldstream Provincial Park, Vancouver Island. Hundreds of bald eagles take up residence to feed on the salmon, which begin to run in October. The eagle count usually takes place in mid- to late January, when the numbers peak. Throughout December and January, the park offers educational programs, displays, and guest speakers. Call ✆ **250/478-9414** or visit www.goldstreampark.com for dates.

FEBRUARY

Chinese New Year, Chinatown. See "Vancouver Events," earlier in this chapter. Late January or early February.

Trumpeter Swan Festival, Comox Valley. A weeklong festival celebrates these magnificent white birds as they gather in the Comox Valley. Check dates with the Vancouver Island tourist office (✆ **250/754-3500**).

MARCH

Pacific Rim Whale Festival, Tofino, Ucluelet, and Pacific Rim National Park. Every spring, more than 20,000 gray whales migrate past this coastline, attracting visitors to Vancouver Island's west coast beaches. The event features live crab races, storytelling, parades, art shows, guided whale-spotting hikes, and whale-watching boat excursions. Call ✆ **250/726-4641** or visit www. pacificrimwhalefestival.com for more information. Mid-March to early April.

MAY

Swiftsure International Yacht Race. International sailing races make for spectacular scenery on the waters around Victoria. For information, call ✆ **250/953-2033** or visit www.tourism victoria.com. Third or fourth weekend in May.

JUNE

JazzFest International. Jazz, swing, bebop, fusion, and improv artists from across the globe perform at various venues around Victoria during this 10-day festival (✆ **250/388-4423;** www.jazz victoria.ca). Late June/early July.

JULY

Canada Day. Victoria, the provincial capital, celebrates this national holiday with events centered on the Inner Harbour, including music, food, and fireworks. July 1.

Organic Island Festival & Sustainability Expo. Little wonder that this young, annual event is gaining traction in the mainstream. More than 150 exhibits and displays share all sorts of "green" and intriguing ideas for energy savings, food cultivations, and more at Victoria's Glendale Gardens. Call ✆ **250/658-8148** for information or visit www. organicislands.ca.

Victoria Pride Celebration. Victoria's gay and lesbian community celebrates with a week of activities that culminates in a downtown parade and festival at Fisherman's Wharf Park. For more info, visit www.victoriapridesociety.org. First week in July.

AUGUST

First Peoples Festival. This free event highlights the heritage of the Pacific Northwest First Nations with performances, carving demonstrations, and cultural displays at the Royal BC Museum (✆ **250/384-3211**). Second week in August.

Fringe Festival. Anything goes at this annual alternative-theater festival. The festival is a 12-day celebration of some of the most innovative theater offered anywhere in the country. For more information, call ✆ **250/383-2663** or visit www.intrepidtheatre.com. Late August/ early September.

Victoria Dragon Boat Fest. Although a smaller version to Vancouver's races, the races are just as exciting. More than 90 teams help to transform the entire Inner Harbour into action central with food vendors, street performers, and pageantry. Check out www.victoriadragon boat.com for details.

SEPTEMBER

Classic Boat Festival. Boaters from around the world converge in Victoria's Inner Harbour for this annual Labour Day–weekend celebration, which includes races, a parade of steam vessels, a cruise up the Gorge Waterway, and vessels open for tours. For more information, call ☎ **250/383-8306** or visit www.classicboatfestival.ca. First weekend in September.

The Great Canadian Beer Festival. Featuring samples from the province's best microbreweries, this event is held at the Victoria Conference Centre, 720 Douglas St. For more information, call ☎ **250/ 383-2332.** Early September.

OCTOBER

Royal Victoria Marathon. This annual race attracts runners from around the world (there's a half-marathon course available, too). Call ☎ **250/658-4520** or go to www.royalvictoriamarathon. com for more info. Early October (Canadian Thanksgiving weekend).

NOVEMBER

Remembrance Day. See "Vancouver Events," earlier in this chapter. November 11.

DECEMBER

First Night. The Inner Harbour becomes the venue for street performers, music, food vendors, and a fireworks show. Very family friendly. Drinking is prohibited. Call **Tourism Victoria** at ☎ **250/953-2033** for more details. December 31.

THE LAY OF THE LAND
Way Back When

Thousands of years ago, a giant glacier sliced along the foot of today's North Shore mountains, carving out a deep trench and piling up a gigantic moraine of rock and sand. When the ice retreated, water from the Pacific flowed in and the moraine became a peninsula, flanked on one side by a deep natural harbor (today's Port of Vancouver on Burrard Inlet) and on the other by a river of glacial meltwater (the Fraser River). Vast forests of fir and cedar covered the land, and wildlife flourished. The First Nations tribes that settled in the area developed rich cultures based on cedar and salmon.

Urban Recreation

Although Vancouver is one of the most densely populated cities in North America, it also has over 1,298 hectares (3,207 acres) of parks and green space. At 404 hectares (998 acres), **Stanley Park** is the largest and most famous. Eighteen kilometers (11 miles) of **beaches** surround Vancouver, including one at English Bay (First Beach) and two in Stanley Park (Second Beach and Third Beach), all three easily reachable from anywhere in central Vancouver. Kitsilano Beach is the pride and joy of the west-side Kitsilano neighborhood. The other city beaches—Jericho, Locarno, Spanish Bank East, Spanish Bank Extension, Spanish Bank West, and Sunset—are farther south, near the University of British Columbia.

Across **Burrard Inlet** and visible from just about anywhere in Vancouver, the nearby **North Shore Mountains** are home to three ski areas (Cypress Mountain, Grouse Mountain, and Mount Seymour), each within 20 to 30 minutes by car from downtown Vancouver. The **Capilano River, Lynn Creek,** and **Seymour River,** all less than half an hour from downtown, provide opportunities for salmon fishing (late summer), and some whitewater kayaking during periods of rain and spring melt.

Kitsilano Beach is a haven for urban recreation.

Victoria, Where Are You?

Many visitors arrive thinking Victoria is on the British Columbia mainland. It's not. Victoria is on the southeastern tip of **Vancouver Island,** which lies southwest of Vancouver across the **Strait of Georgia** and **Haro Strait.** Victoria is 72km (45 miles) south of the 49th parallel, the border between most of Canada and the contiguous United States. British Columbia's island capital looks south across the **Strait of Juan de Fuca** to Port Angeles, Washington, and Washington state's snowcapped Olympic peninsula. Anacortes, Washington, is almost due east.

Ferry Tales
Instead of road rage, Victoria residents have "ferry stress." In order to get on or off their island, they have to take a ferry (or a float-plane), which takes time and involves some planning, especially on summer and holiday weekends. But gliding through the waters of the Pacific Northwest, with mountains gleaming and orcas (maybe) splashing, is really not the same as driving at breakneck speed along a freeway or sitting in bumper-to-bumper traffic. So the stress isn't really all that stressful.

Tiiiiiimber!

The original vegetation of most of Vancouver and Victoria was dense temperate rainforest, consisting of conifers—a mix of Douglas fir, Western red cedar, and Western hemlock—with scattered pockets of maple, alder, and around Victoria, Garry oaks (indigenous to Vancouver Island). The forest you see today in Vancouver's Stanley Park is mostly second and third growth, and evidence of old-fashioned logging techniques such as springboard notches can still be seen there. British Columbia has been heavily logged, as you'll see if you venture out of Vancouver or Victoria, but it has also preserved the largest area of temperate rainforest left in the Northern Hemisphere (the **Great Bear Rainforest,** p. 341). Clear-cutting of old-growth forest has spurred major environmental action, especially in the area around Clayoquot Sound on the west coast of Vancouver Island (see chapter 19).

As the Eagle Flies

Keep your eyes open, and you may spot a bald eagle or two in Vancouver and Victoria, though most of these magnificent raptors hang out in less populated and fishier areas. In fact, the largest concentration of American bald eagles in North America annually congregates at **Brackendale,** about an hour north of Vancouver. Brackendale Art Gallery (✆ **604/898-3333;** www.brackendaleartgallery.com) has hosted counts every year for more than 25 years, and has witnessed a decline of numbers which, in 1994, numbered more than 3,700 birds in one day along a 15km (9¼-mile) stretch of the Squamish Valley; in 2008, the number dropped to 895, and in 2011, it fell to 627. The eagles congregate at the junction of Howe Sound at the mouths and tributaries of the Cheakamus, the Mamquam, and the Squamish rivers, to feed on spawning salmon. The mature trees—mixtures of fir, cedar, hemlock, and skeletal deciduous trees—provide perfect roosting spots for these huge birds. The birds are also commonly sighted in and around Tofino and **Pacific Rim National Park** (p. 323). For more information on the annual Brackendale Eagle Count, see the Vancouver Calendar of Events for January, p. 32.

Gray Whales & Orcas

From mid- to late March, thousands of gray whales pass along the coast of British Columbia on their annual migration from Alaska down to their breeding grounds in Baja. The best places to view these giant mammals are **Tofino** and **Ucluelet** on the western coast of Vancouver Island, which celebrate the annual event with the Pacific Rim Whale Festival (see "Special Events," in chapter 19). But when companies in Victoria or Vancouver advertise "whale-watching" excursions, it is the orca, or killer whale, they are referring to. These animals are closer at hand and easier to spot—in fact, a pod of them lives year-round in the waters near Victoria on the southern tip of Vancouver Island.

RESPONSIBLE TRAVEL

In 2006, after years of protests and negotiations by First Nations tribes and environmentalists, Canada declared British Columbia's Great Bear Rainforest off-limits to loggers. This landmark decision preserves the largest remaining temperate coastal rainforest in the world, some 6 million hectares (15 million acres) that are home to rare white bears and support the highest concentration of grizzly bears in North America (p. 341). It must also be noted that much of British Columbia's economy is based on "resource extraction" of one kind or another, logging being the most prevalent.

Vancouver and Victoria are meccas of ecotourism in all its many guises. From patronizing restaurants that use only locally harvested foods (the 110-mile diet was conceived in Vancouver) and non-endangered fish to enjoying natural, non-polluting fun by paddling kayaks and hiking through beautiful rainforests, you can enjoy green holidays in both of these cities without sacrificing any fun or flavor. Many hotels in both cities take green practices so seriously that they've almost turned sustainability into a one-upmanship competition. Incidentally, if you're ordering fish, look for the "Ocean Wise" logo on the menu—it indicates what fresh, non-endangered fish has been sustainably harvested for the restaurant.

See **www.frommers.com/planning** for more tips on responsible travel.

TOURS
Special Interest Trips

Both Vancouver and Victoria are fit, outdoors-oriented cities with plenty of opportunities to explore urban activities alongside soft adventures. You'll find special low-impact walking tours and ecotours in and around **Vancouver** in "Organized Tours" (p. 141) and "Outdoor Activities" (p. 143). For **Victoria,** turn to "Organized Tours" (p. 284) and "Outdoor Activities" (p. 286). Ecotours of various sorts are also available in **Whistler** (see "What to See & Do Outdoors," in chapter 11), and they're especially popular in and around **Tofino** and the **Pacific Rim National Park** on the west coast of Vancouver Island.

Escorted General-Interest Tours

Escorted tours are structured group tours, with a group leader. The price usually includes everything from airfare to hotels, meals, tours, admission costs, and local transportation.

Uniglobe Specialty Travel (© **800/455-0007** or 604/688-8816; www.uniglobespecialtytravel.com) in Vancouver offers multiday escorted tours of Vancouver and Victoria, highlighting the major attractions in both cities. **Globus Tours** (© **866/755-8581;** www.globusjourneys.com), one of the largest tour companies in the U.S., provides escorted tours throughout Western Canada, including Vancouver and Victoria, as part of a larger west coast itinerary.

Package Tours

Package tours are simply a way to buy the airfare, accommodations, and other elements of your trip (such as car rentals, airport transfers, and sometimes even activities) at the same time and often at discounted prices.

One good source of package deals is the airlines themselves. **Air Canada Vacations** (© **888/247-2262;** www.aircanadavacations.com) offers an array of package deals covering a whole series of travel bargains ranging from city packages to fly/drive tours, escorted tours, motor-home travel, and ski holidays. Other airlines with Canadian package holidays include **American Airlines** (© **800/321-2121;** www.aavacations.com), **Delta** (© **800/800-1504;** www.deltavacations.com), **Continental Airlines** (© **800/301-3800;** www.co vacations.com), and **United** (© **888/854-3899;** www.unitedvacations.com).

Several big **online travel agencies**—Expedia, Travelocity, Orbitz, and Lastminute.com—also do a brisk business in packages.

VANCOUVER & VICTORIA IN DEPTH

Tours

3

SUGGESTED VANCOUVER & VICTORIA ITINERARIES

Vancouver and Victoria are preeminently maritime cities, and the visitor is always aware of water and the closeness of the immense Pacific. Vibrant Vancouver is (mostly) on the British Columbia mainland, but charming Victoria occupies the southern tip of Vancouver Island, about 45km (28 miles) to the west.

To get the most out of this glorious part of Canada, you'll need a car, and you'll likely have to take a ferry to reach Victoria. In both Vancouver and Victoria, you can ditch your car and use public transportation or walk, but to enjoy the almost limitless sightseeing opportunities outside the cities, a car is essential.

In addition to the itineraries below, we provide walking tours of Vancouver in chapter 8 and Victoria in chapter 16.

THE BEST OF VANCOUVER IN 1 DAY

This tour is meant to show off the city as a whole, giving you an overview of what makes it so appealing. Some places you'll explore on foot, and for others, you'll drive to reach the destination. Nature, art, culture, and coffee are all part of today's itinerary.

1 Canada Place ★★

Start your day outside, on the upper (deck) level of the city's giant convention center and cruise-ship terminal, which juts out into Burrard Inlet across from the Tourism Vancouver visitor center. From here, you'll get a good sense of Vancouver's natural and urban topography, with the North Shore Mountains rising up before you; low-rise, historic Gastown to the east; Stanley Park to the west; and a forest of glass residential towers in

Get your bearings and take in the views from Canada Place; PREVIOUS PAGE: At the top of the challenging Grouse Grind trail you'll get excellent views of the entire region.

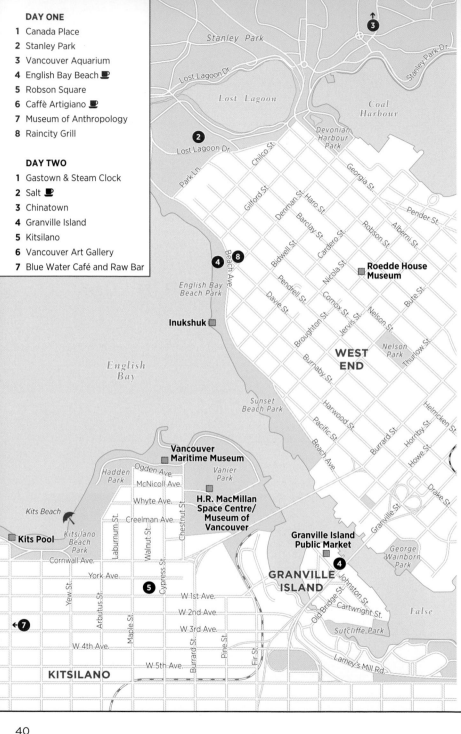

Stanley Park

Lost Lagoon Dr.

Lost Lagoon

Coal Harbour

Devonian Harbour Park

Lost Lagoon Dr.

Park Ln.

Chilco St.

Gilford St.

Georgia St.

Denman St.

Haro St.

Barclay St.

Cardero St.

Robson St.

Pender St.

Alberni St.

Bidwell St.

Nicola St.

Roedde House Museum

Beach Ave.

English Bay Beach Park

Pendrell St.

Comox St.

Jervis St.

Nelson St.

Bute St.

Thurlow St.

Inukshuk

Davie St.

Broughton St.

WEST END

Nelson Park

English Bay

Sunset Beach Park

Burnaby St.

Harwood St.

Pacific St.

Beach Ave.

Burrard St.

Hornby St.

Howe St.

Helmcken St.

Vancouver Maritime Museum

Hadden Park

Ogden Ave.

McNicoll Ave.

Vanier Park

Drake St.

Whyte Ave.

H.R. MacMillan Space Centre/ Museum of Vancouver

Kits Beach

Creelman Ave.

Chestnut St.

Walnut St.

Laburnum St.

Kits Pool

Kitsilano Beach Park

Cornwall Ave.

York Ave.

Granville Island Public Market

Granville St.

George Wainborn Park

GRANVILLE ISLAND

Johnston St.

Old Bridge St.

Cartwright St.

False

W 1st Ave.

Yew St.

Arbutus St.

Maple St.

Cypress St.

W 2nd Ave.

W 3rd Ave.

Burrard St.

Pine St.

Fir St.

Sutcliffe Park

W 4th Ave.

W 5th Ave.

Lamey's Mill Rd.

KITSILANO

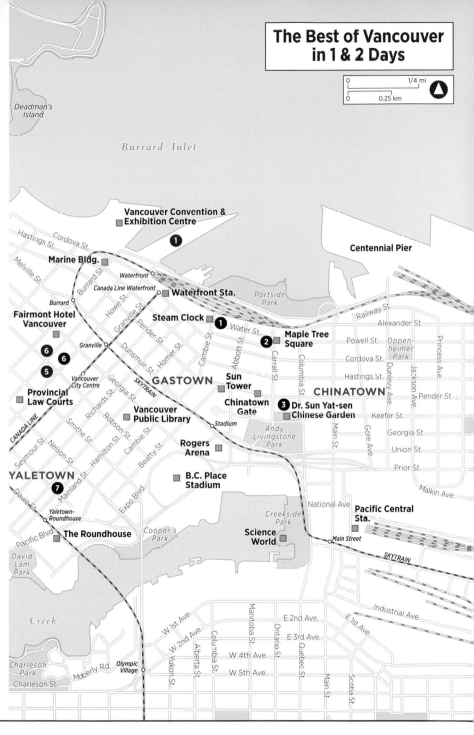

0   1/4 mi

0   0.25 km

Deadman's
Island

Burrard Inlet

Vancouver Convention &
Exhibition Centre

1

Centennial Pier

Hastings St.

Cordova St.

Melville St.

Marine Bldg.

Burrard St.

Waterfront

Canada Line Waterfront

Waterfront Sta.

Portside
Park

Railway St.

Alexander St.

Burrard

**Fairmont Hotel
Vancouver**

Howe St.

Granville St.

Pender St.

Homer St.

Steam Clock

1

Water St.

**Maple Tree
Square**

2

Powell St.

Oppen-
heimer
Park

Princess Ave.

Granville

Dunsmuir St.

Cambie St.

Abbott St.

Carrall St.

Columbia St.

Cordova St.

Hastings St.

Dunlevy Ave.

Jackson Ave.

Pender St.

6

6

5

Vancouver
City Centre

Georgia St.

GASTOWN

**Sun
Tower**

CHINATOWN

Gore Ave.

**Provincial
Law Courts**

Richards St.

Robson St.

**Vancouver
Public Library**

**Chinatown
Gate**

Stadium

3 **Dr. Sun Yat-sen
Chinese Garden**

Keefer St.

Georgia St.

CANADA LINE

Smithe St.

Seymour St.

Nelson St.

Hamilton St.

Cambie St.

Beatty St.

**Rogers
Arena**

Andy
Livingstone
Park

Main St.

Union St.

Prior St.

Malkin Ave.

YALETOWN

7

Mainland St.

Expo Blvd.

**B.C. Place
Stadium**

National Ave.

Creekside
Park

**Pacific Central
Sta.**

Davie St.

Yaletown-
Roundhouse

Pacific Blvd.

The Roundhouse

Cooper's
Park

**Science
World**

Main Street

SKYTRAIN

David
Lam
Park

Creek

W 1st Ave.

W 2nd Ave.

Yukon St.

Columbia St.

Alberta St.

Manitoba St.

Ontario St.

Quebec St.

E 2nd Ave.

E 3rd Ave.

E 1st Ave.

Industrial Ave.

Charleson
Park

Charleson St.

Moberly Rd.

Olympic
Village

W 4th Ave.

W 5th Ave.

Main St.

Scotia St.

SKYTRAIN

between. Canada Place is busiest in summer, when up to three giant cruise ships may dock in 1 day. For more on Canada Place, see "Walking Tour 2: Gastown & Chinatown," in chapter 8.

2 Stanley Park ★★★

You can't really appreciate Stanley Park by driving through it in a car, so park your vehicle and head in on foot via Lagoon Drive. Surrounded by a famed pedestrian seawall, this giant park invites hours of exploration. A 1-hour carriage ride (p. 121) is the perfect way to see the highlights. See p. 119.

3 Vancouver Aquarium Marine Science Centre ★★

One of the best aquariums in North America is located right in Stanley Park. Don't miss the Arctic Canada exhibit with its beluga whales and the Wild Coast Gallery, where you can see Pacific white-sided dolphins, sea otters, and other denizens of Pacific Northwest waters. See p. 122.

4 English Bay Beach ★★ ☕

If the weather is warm, head to **English Bay Beach,** an all-seasons gathering spot on the south side of Stanley Park. You can pick up picnic eats or find takeout food on nearby Denman Street.

5 Robson Street & the West End

How you explore the West End is up to you. You can walk from English Bay Beach down Denman Street, and then turn southeast on Robson, taking in as much of the throbbing shopping and cafe scene as you want. It's also fun to explore the West End as a living neighborhood—one of the most densely populated in North America. For extra suggestions on exploring the West End, see "Walking Tour 1: Downtown & the West End," in chapter 8.

6 Caffè Artigiano ★★ ☕

For the best latte in town, as well as grilled Italian sandwiches and snacks, stop in at this busy cafe right across from the Vancouver Art Gallery. The patio in front is perfect for people-watching. 763 Hornby St. ☏ **604/694-7737.** See p. 106.

7 Museum of Anthropology ★★★

Hop in your car or on the bus for the 20-minute drive to the outstanding Museum of Anthropology at the University of British Columbia. Here, in one of North America's preeminent collections of First Nations art, you'll encounter powerful totem poles, spirit masks, and totemic objects. See p. 128.

8 Dinner

For a romantic dinner that will introduce you to the best of Vancouver's "eat local" food philosophy (there's a 100-mile tasting menu), reserve a table at

The Museum of Anthropology houses one of North America's preeminent collections of First Nations art.

Raincity Grill, 1193 Denman St. (℡ **604/685-7337**), where the windows overlook English Bay and the regional cuisine provides the perfect excuse to linger. See p. 97.

THE BEST OF VANCOUVER IN 2 DAYS

If you've already made your way through "The Best of Vancouver in 1 Day," above, you'll find that your second full-day tour takes in a roster of new sights and adventures. Today's itinerary will give you an entertaining handle on Vancouver's past and introduce you to some of Vancouver's most appealing neighborhoods.

1 Gastown & the Steam Clock

Gastown is the oldest part of Vancouver, a low-rise brick district from the late 19th century, that has made a comeback after years of neglect. Stroll down Water Street, timing your visit so you'll be in front of the famous steam clock when it steams and chimes at noon. You might also want to shop for a piece of First Nations art at one of Gastown's specialty galleries (see "First Nations Art & Crafts," in chapter 9). For a complete tour of Gastown, see "Walking Tour 2: Gastown & Chinatown," in chapter 8.

2 Salt ★ ☕

If it's lunchtime, head over to one of Gastown's smart new eateries. **Salt** is one of Vancouver's favorite charcuteries, serving cured meats, soups, and artisan cheeses. 45 Blood Alley. ℡ **604/633-1912.** See p. 95.

There is great shopping throughout upscale Kitsilano.

3 Chinatown

Vancouver's Chinatown lies just east of Gastown, and you can walk there or drive. Though parts of Chinatown are touristy, the street markets are lively and authentic. Don't miss the **Dr. Sun Yat-Sen Classical Chinese Garden ★★**. For a complete tour of Chinatown, see "Walking Tour 2: Gastown & Chinatown," in chapter 8.

4 Granville Island ★★★

You can easily drive to Granville Island via the Granville Bridge, but it's more fun to hop on a mini-ferry from Yaletown Landing and take the 10-minute trip across False Creek. The **public market ★★★** is pure sensory overload, crammed with every kind of produce, seafood, and food product imaginable, while the area around it is a browser's heaven of shops, galleries, and outdoor-adventure outfitters. (See p. 125.) For a complete tour of Granville Island, see "Walking Tour 3: Yaletown, Granville Island & Kitsilano," p. 170.

5 Kitsilano

You can drive, walk, or catch a bus to Kitsilano, the funky, hippie-turned-upscale neighborhood west of Granville Island. Check out the buffed beach scene at Kitsilano Beach. One of the world's longest saltwater pools is here if you want a summertime swim. For a complete walking tour of Kitsilano, see "Walking Tour 3: Yaletown, Granville Island & Kitsilano," p. 170.

6 Vancouver Art Gallery ★★

You can drive or take a no. 4 or 7 bus on West 4th Avenue for the 15-minute ride back to downtown Vancouver. Head for the Vancouver Art Gallery, and make your way specifically to the museum's collection of hauntingly atmospheric paintings by BC native Emily Carr. Her moodily expressive works sum up all that is grand and glorious in the Pacific Northwest landscape. See p. 123.

7 Dinner

Cap off your day with a memorable meal at **Blue Water Cafe and Raw Bar** (1095 Hamilton St.; ℭ **604/688-8078**), a culinary high point of the city and winner of *Vancouver* magazine's Best Restaurant Award in 2010 and Best Formal Dining Restaurant in 2011. See p. 87.

THE BEST OF VICTORIA IN 1 DAY

Victoria is less than a quarter of the size of Vancouver, and you can easily hit the highlights in 1 day if you arrive on an early ferry. The scenic ferry ride—from Vancouver, Seattle, Anacortes, or Port Angeles—is part of the fun. Although it's easy to experience Victoria by foot, bike, and public transportation, having a car will help to maximize your sightseeing.

1 Inner Harbour

A stroll along the Inner Harbour takes you past the **Provincial Legislature Buildings ★★**, a massive stone edifice completed in 1898, and the famous Fairmont Empress hotel, which dates from 1908. Along the busy waterfront, you'll also find information on whale-watching excursions, a popular Victoria pastime. For a complete walking tour of the Inner Harbour, see "Walking Tour 1: The Inner Harbour," p. 295.

Victoria's Inner Harbour is home to several of the city's top attractions.

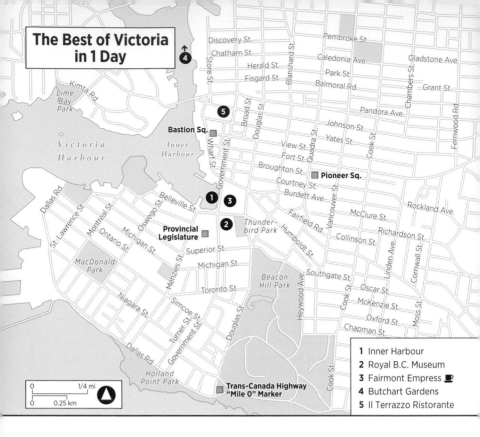

Discovery St. | Pembroke St. | Gladstone Ave.
Chatham St. | Caledonia Ave.
Herald St. | Park St.
Fisgard St. | Balmoral Rd. | Grant St.

Kimta Rd.
Lime Bay Park

Pandora Ave.

Johnson St.

Bastion Sq.

Yates St.

Victoria Harbour

Inner Harbour

View St.
Fort St.
Broughton St.
Courtney St.
Burdett Ave.

■ **Pioneer Sq.**

Rockland Ave.

Belleville St.

1 **3**

McClure St.
Richardson St.
Collinson St.

Provincial Legislature ■

2

Thunder-bird Park

MacDonald Park

Michigan St.
Superior St.
Michigan St.

Beacon Hill Park

Southgate St.
Oscar St.
McKenzie St.
Oxford St.
Chapman St.

Niagara St.
Simcoe St.
Toronto St.

Holland Point Park

Trans-Canada Highway "Mile 0" Marker ■

0 ___ 1/4 mi
0 ___ 0.25 km

1 Inner Harbour
2 Royal B.C. Museum
3 Fairmont Empress 🍵
4 Butchart Gardens
5 Il Terrazzo Ristorante

2 Royal BC Museum ★★★

The highlight of this excellent museum is the First Peoples Gallery, an absorbing and thought-provoking showplace of First Nations art and culture. The other exhibits pale by comparison, but do have a look at the life-size woolly mastodon. See p. 277.

3 Fairmont Empress ★★ 🍵

Tea at the **Empress** is a traditional affair that has remained a real treat, despite its fame. Make it your main meal of the day (seatings at 12:30, 2, 2:30, and 5pm) and be sure to reserve in advance. 721 Government St. ℭ **250/384-8111.** See "Taking Afternoon Tea," in chapter 14.

4 Butchart Gardens ★★★

This century-old garden is one of the gardening wonders of the world, meticulously planned and impeccably maintained. Though hordes of tourists can jam the paths in the summer months, time your visit for late afternoon, and you'll have more room, plus you can stay for the fabulous summer fireworks display. See p. 273.

5 Dinner

If there's time, have dinner at Victoria's best Italian restaurant, **Il Terrazzo Ristorante** (555 Johnson St.; ℭ **250/361-0028**). See p. 260.

Taking tea at the Empress hotel is one of Victoria's grand traditions.

THE BEST OF VANCOUVER, VICTORIA & WHISTLER IN 1 WEEK

Lucky the traveler who gets to spend a whole week or more exploring this ruggedly beautiful part of the Pacific Northwest. If you don't arrive with a car, you can rent one in either Vancouver or Victoria. Most visitors travel to Victoria by car ferry. The assumption here is that your week begins and ends in Vancouver, the major travel hub. For reference, see the map on the inside front cover of this book.

1 & 2 Vancouver ★★★

Start your week in Vancouver, following "The Best of Vancouver in 1 Day" and "The Best of Vancouver in 2 Days," above.

3 North Vancouver

Use your third day to get out of the city. At **Capilano Suspension Bridge & Park ★** (p. 131), you can test your love-hate relationship with heights on the narrow, bouncy suspension footbridge that spans a scenic ravine, or step out onto the new **Cliffhanger** walkways for views of granite cliffs and the Capilano Canyon through glass. Afterward, drive to the nearby **SkyRide gondola** and be transported to the summit of **Grouse Mountain ★★★**, where you'll enjoy panoramic views of the entire region (p. 131). Capilano and Grouse Mountain have casual dining and picnic areas, or you can enjoy fine Pacific Northwest cuisine and a panoramic waterfront view at the **Beach House at Dundarave Pier ★★** (p. 106), a restored 1912 teahouse located on the water's edge.

Test your tolerance for heights at the Capilano Suspension Bridge and Park.

4 Vancouver to Whistler ★★★

Take Georgia Street from downtown Vancouver and head west through Stanley Park, across the scenic Lions Gate Bridge, and hook up with the **Sea-to-Sky Highway,** which winds along the edge of Howe Sound and climbs into the mountains. It should take you about 2 hours to reach **Whistler Village.** Once you get to Whistler, ski (it is one of North America's greatest ski resorts,

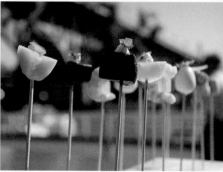

FROM TOP: **There are endless hiking options around Whistler; Fresh fare from the restaurant Coast.**

after all) . . . or mountain bike, or hike, or Ziptrek, or shop, or pamper yourself with a spa treatment. A casual and delicious lunch or dinner at **Ciao-Thyme Bistro ★** (p. 217; *€* **604/932-7051**) will set you up for whatever activities are on your agenda. You'll find a complete rundown of Whistler possibilities in chapter 11.

5 Whistler to Vancouver

Spend the night in Whistler. Before leaving the area, drive to **Nairn Falls Provincial Park ★★**, where the Green River shoots through basaltic rock formations and forms a series of thundering waterfalls (p. 222). Once back in Vancouver, enjoy seafood at **Coast ★★★** (p. 91; *€* **604/685-5010**) or local farm-sourced fare at **West ★★★** (p. 100; *€* **604/738-8938**).

6 Vancouver to Victoria ★★★

Spend day six of your weeklong adventure in Victoria, preferably taking an early-morning ferry through the Gulf Islands. For your day in Victoria, see "The Best of Victoria in 1 Day," above.

7 Victoria to Vancouver

If time allows, make a trip from Victoria to **Pacific Rim National Park ★★★**, a temperate rainforest with old-growth trees and a wildly magnificent coastline on the west coast of Vancouver Island (a 4½-hr.

The temperate rainforest of Pacific Rim National Park has many good trails to help you explore the park.

drive or 45-min. flight). For a complete summary of what's there, including famous lodges and dining choices, see chapter 19. Otherwise, this is the day you return to Vancouver by ferry. Back on the mainland, the Tsawassen ferry terminal is the closest to the Vancouver airport and hooks up with I-5 south to Seattle or north to Vancouver. Or you can travel back via Port Angeles, a gateway to Washington's Olympic National Park, or Anacortes.

GETTING TO KNOW VANCOUVER

4

T

he setting is majestic and the city is exciting, so it's no wonder that Vancouver lures visitors from around the globe. The rest of the world has taken notice of the blessed life people in these parts lead, and surveys generally list Vancouver as one of the 10 best cities in the world to live in. Not bad for a city that some 20 years ago was routinely derided as the world's biggest mill town.

ORIENTATION

Getting lost as you wander around a fascinating new neighborhood is part of the fun of traveling. And getting lost in Vancouver, or at least losing your directional bearings, is possible, mostly because the main grid of streets doesn't run strictly north-south, but rather northwest to southeast like a parallelogram.

If you do become directionally challenged, just look for the mountains. They are to the north, across a body of water called Burrard Inlet. If you're facing the mountains, east is to your right, west is to your left, and the back of your head is pointing south. That one tip will generally keep you pointed in the right direction, no matter where you are. You'll also find that Vancouverites are incredibly friendly: If you're scratching your head over a map, almost inevitably someone will ask if he or she can help.

Vancouver Airport

Vancouver International Airport (YVR; ✆ 604/207-7077; www.yvr.ca) is a 14km (8⅔-mile) journey south of downtown. The International Terminal features an extensive collection of First Nations sculptures and paintings set amid grand expanses of glass under soaring ceilings. Before you leave the International Terminal, catch a glimpse of Bill Reid's huge bronze sculpture, the *Jade Canoe*.

Two **Tourist Information Centres** are located in the airport's arrivals areas: The information center on Level 2 of the Domestic terminal is open daily from 8:30am to 9:30pm, while the desk on Level 2 of the International terminal is open 24 hours.

GETTING TO & FROM THE AIRPORT The easiest, fastest, and cheapest way to get into Vancouver from the airport is by the **Canada Line SkyTrain,** opened in late 2009 and operated by **Translink** (✆ **604/953-3333;** www.translink.ca). The train zips into Vancouver in 26 minutes, stopping at stations in Yaletown, City Centre (downtown), and Waterfront (the SeaBus Terminal, near the Canada Place cruise-ship terminal). For airport passengers, there is a C$5 surcharge on top of Translink two-zone fares, bringing the total Canada Line ticket price to C$8.75 for adults on weekdays, C$7.50 after 6:30pm weekdays and all day on weekends. Purchase tickets at the machines clustered around the Canada Line entrance; machines give change.

PREVIOUS PAGE: **The Gastown steam clock is a well-known local landmark.**

Aeroshuttle (✆ **877/921-9021** or 604/299-4444; www.aeroshuttle yvr.ca) provides **airport shuttle bus service** from both the Domestic and International terminals to downtown hotels on two loops: one through Yaletown and downtown, the other through downtown and the West End. Hotels serviced by the shuttle include the Georgian Court, the Metropolitan, Sutton Place, Westin Bayshore, and the Fairmont Waterfront. Shuttles for each route leave the airport hourly from 8am to 8pm from May to September, 8am to 7pm October to April. Buses pick up passengers at downtown hotels from about 5am to 5pm from May to September, 6am to 5pm October to April. Check with your hotel or the shuttle website for an exact schedule. The trip takes 60–75 minutes, depending on the pickup location, and costs C$14 for adults and C$8.40 children 12 and over. Round-trip discounts available. Major credit cards and cash accepted, and you can purchase tickets from the driver.

The average **taxi** fare from the airport to a downtown Vancouver hotel is approximately C$35, plus tip, but the fare can run up to C$40 if the cab gets stuck in traffic. **Aerocar Service** (✆ **888/821-0021** or 604/298-1000; www.aerocar.ca) provides flat-rate sedan or stretch-limousine service from the airport, and fares are quoted based on destination. Sedan service runs C$43 per trip to downtown and C$52 to Canada Place, plus taxes and tip. Limousine service for up to six passengers costs C$50 to downtown and C$63 to Canada Place. Rates also available for groups of up to eight passengers. Look for Aerocars in front of the terminal; drivers accept cash or major credit cards.

Although no longer the official limousine provider at the airport, **LimoJet** (✆ **604/273-1331;** www.limojetgold.com) also offers transport to downtown and other points. Meet-and-greet service at the arrivals area plus transportation to downtown costs C$75, plus tax and tip, for up to three people (C$80 for up to six passengers). The drivers accept all major credit cards.

Most major **car-rental firms** have airport counters and shuttles. Drivers heading into Vancouver from the airport should take the Arthur Laing Bridge, which leads directly to Granville Street, the most direct route to downtown.

The Train & Bus Station

VIA Rail and Amtrak trains, and Greyhound buses arrive at **Pacific Central Station** (1150 Station St., at Main St. and Terminal Ave.; Amtrak ✆ **800/872-7245**; VIA Rail ✆ **888/842-7245**; Greyhound ✆ **604/661-0328**), the main Vancouver railway station, located just south of Chinatown. You can reach downtown Vancouver from there by cab for about C$10. Plenty of taxis wait at the station entrance. One block from the station is the SkyTrain's Main Street–Science World Station; within minutes, you'll be downtown. The Granville and Waterfront SkyTrain stations are two and four stops away, respectively.

Visitor Information

The **Tourism Vancouver Visitor Centre** (200 Burrard St., Plaza Level; ✆ **604/683-2000;** www.tourismvancouver.com), is your single best travel information source about Vancouver and the North Shore. An incredibly helpful and

Orientation

GETTING TO KNOW VANCOUVER

well-trained staff provides information, maps, and brochures, and can help you with all your travel needs, including hotel, cruise-ship, ferry, bus, and train reservations. The center also has a **half-price ticket office** (Tickets Tonight; ℃ **604/684-2787;** www.ticketstonight.ca) for same-day shows and events. The Touristinfo Centre is open daily from 8:30am to 6pm (closed Sun in winter). If you're driving, a **Touristinfo Centre** is located just north of the **U.S. Canada Peace Arch border crossing,** at 298 Hwy. 99, Surrey (no phone).

The free weekly tabloid the ***Georgia Straight*** (℃ **604/730-7000;** www. straight.com), found in cafes, bookshops, newspaper boxes, and restaurants, provides up-to-date schedules of concerts, lectures, art exhibits, plays, recitals, and other happenings. Also free and published weekly with event listings is the ***West Ender*** (℃ **604/742-8686;** www.westender.com). Not free but equally good—and with more attitude—is the glossy city magazine ***Vancouver*** (℃ **604/877-7732;** www.vanmag.com), available at newsstands. The free guide called ***Where Vancouver*** (℃ **604/736-5586;** www.where.ca/vancouver) is available in many hotels and lists attractions, entertainment, upscale shopping, and fine dining. It also has good maps.

Two free monthly tabloids, ***BC Parent*** (℃ **604/221-0366;** www.bc parent.ca) and ***West Coast Families*** (℃ **604/249-2866**), available at grocery stores and cafes around the city, are geared toward families with young children, listing many kid-friendly current events. Gay and lesbian travelers will want to pick up a copy of ***Xtra! West*** (℃ **604/684-9696;** www.xtra.ca), a free biweekly tabloid available in cafes, bars, shops, and restaurants throughout the West End.

City Layout

With four different bodies of water lapping at its edges and miles of shoreline, Vancouver's geography can seem a bit complicated. **Downtown Vancouver** is on a peninsula: Think of it as an upraised thumb on the mitten-shaped Vancouver mainland. **Stanley Park,** the **West End, Yaletown,** and Vancouver's business and financial center (downtown) are located on this thumb of land bordered to the north by Burrard Inlet, the city's main deepwater harbor and port, to the west by English Bay, and to the south by False Creek. Farther west beyond English Bay is the Strait of Georgia, part of the Pacific Ocean. Just south across False Creek is **Granville Island,** famous for its public market, and the beach community of **Kitsilano.** This part of the city, called the **West Side,** covers the mainland, or the hand of the mitten. Its western shoreline looks out on the Strait of Georgia with the Pacific beyond, and the north arm of the Fraser River demarcates it to the south. Pacific Spirit Park and the University of British Columbia (UBC), a locus for visitors because of its outstanding Museum of Anthropology, take up most of the western tip of the West Side; the rest is mostly residential, with a sprinkling of businesses along main arterial streets. Both the mainland and peninsula are covered by a simple rectilinear street pattern. **North Vancouver** is the mountain-backed area across Burrard Inlet from downtown.

MAIN ARTERIES & STREETS   On the downtown peninsula are four key east-west streets (to be more directionally exact, the streets run southeast to northwest). Robson Street starts at BC Place Stadium on Beatty Street, flows through the West End's more touristed shopping district, and ends at Stanley Park's Lost Lagoon on Lagoon Drive. Georgia Street—far more efficient for drivers than the pedestrian-oriented Robson—runs from the Georgia

Viaduct on the eastern edge of downtown through Vancouver's commercial core, through Stanley Park, and over the Lions Gate Bridge to the North Shore. Three blocks north of Georgia is Hastings Street, which begins in the West End, runs east through downtown, and then skirts Gastown's southern border as it runs eastward to the Trans-Canada Highway. Davie Street starts at Pacific Boulevard near the Cambie Street Bridge, travels through Yaletown into the West End's more residential shopping district, and ends at English Bay Beach.

Three **north-south downtown streets** will get you everywhere you want to go in and out of downtown. Three blocks east of Stanley Park is **Denman Street,** which runs from West Georgia Street at Coal Harbour to Beach Avenue at English Bay Beach. This main West End thoroughfare is where locals dine out. It's also the shortest north-south route between the two ends of the Stanley Park Seawall.

Eight blocks east of Denman Street is **Burrard Street,** which starts near the Canada Place Pier and runs south through downtown, crosses the Burrard Bridge, and then forks. One branch, still **Burrard Street,** continues south and intersects West 4th Avenue and Broadway before ending at West 16th Avenue on the borders of the ritzy Shaughnessy neighborhood. The other branch becomes **Cornwall Avenue,** which heads west through Kitsilano, changing its name to **Point Grey Road** and connecting via West 4th Avenue and **Northwest Marine Drive** to the University of British Columbia campus.

Granville Street starts near Waterfront Station on Burrard Inlet and runs the entire length of downtown, crosses the Granville Street Bridge to Vancouver's West Side, and carries on south across the breadth of the city before crossing the Arthur Laing Bridge to Vancouver International Airport.

On mainland Vancouver, the city's east-west roads are successively numbered from 1st Avenue at the downtown bridges to 77th Avenue by the banks of the Fraser River. The most important east-west route is **Broadway** (formerly 9th Ave.), which starts a few blocks from the University of British Columbia as West 10th Avenue before extending across the city to the border of neighboring Burnaby, where it becomes the **Lougheed Highway.** In Kitsilano, **West 4th Avenue** is an important east-west shopping and commercial corridor. Intersecting with Broadway at various points are a number of important north-south commercial streets, each defining a particular neighborhood. The most significant of these streets are (from west to east) **MacDonald Street** in Kitsilano; **Granville, Cambie,** and **Main streets;** and **Commercial Drive.**

FINDING AN ADDRESS   In many Vancouver addresses, the suite or room number precedes the building number. For instance, 100-1250 Robson St. is Suite 100 at 1250 Robson St.

In downtown Vancouver, Chinatown's **Carrall Street** is the east-west axis from which streets are numbered and designated. Westward, numbers increase progressively to Stanley Park; eastward, numbers increase approaching Commercial Drive. For example, 400 W. Pender would be 4 blocks from Carrall Street heading toward downtown; 400 E. Pender would be 4 blocks on the opposite side of Carrall Street. Similarly, the low numbers on north-south streets start on the Canada Place Pier side and

What's West?

The thing to keep in mind when figuring out what's where in Vancouver is that this is a city where property is king, and the word *west* has such positive connotations that folks have always gone to great lengths to associate it with their particular patch of real estate. Thus we have the **West End,** the **West Side,** and **West Vancouver,** which improbably enough is located immediately beside **North Vancouver.** It can be a bit confusing for newcomers, but fortunately, each west has its own distinct character. The West End is a high-rise residential neighborhood on the downtown peninsula. The West Side is one-half of Vancouver, from Ontario Street west to the University of British Columbia. (The more working-class **East Side** covers the mainland portion of the city, from Ontario St. east to Boundary Rd.) Very tony West Vancouver is a city unto itself on the far side of Burrard Inlet. Together with its more middle-class neighbor, North Vancouver, it forms the **North Shore.**

increase southward in increments of 100 per block (the 600 block of Thurlow St. is 2 blocks from the 800 block) toward False Creek and Granville Island.

Off the peninsula, the system works the same, but **Ontario Street** is the east-west axis. Also, all east-west roads are avenues (for example, 4th Ave.), while streets (for example, Main St.) run exclusively north-south.

STREET MAPS   To get you off on the right foot, check out the detailed Vancouver map tucked inside the back cover of this guide. Tourist information centers (see "Visitor Information," above) and most hotels can also provide you with a detailed downtown map. *Where Vancouver* (✆ 604/736-5586; www.where.ca/vancouver), a free guide available at most hotels, has good maps. A good all-around metropolitan area map is the Rand McNally Vancouver city map. If you're an auto-club member, the Canadian Automobile Association (CAA) map is also good. It's not for sale, but it's free to both AAA and CAA members, and is available at AAA offices across North America.

GETTING AROUND
By Public Transportation

Vancouver's public transportation system is the most extensive in Canada and includes service to all major tourist attractions, so it's not really necessary to have a car (especially if you're staying in the downtown area).

The **Translink** (✆ **604/953-3333;** www.translink.ca) system includes electric trolley and diesel buses, the SeaBus catamaran ferry, and the light-rail SkyTrain. It's an ecologically friendly, highly reliable, inexpensive system that allows you to get everywhere, including the beaches and ski slopes. Regular service runs from about 5am to 2am.

Schedules and routes are available online, at tourist information centers, at many major hotels, and on buses. The back cover of this book has a downtown Vancouver transit map.

FARES   Fares are based on the number of zones traveled and are the same for buses, the SeaBus, and the SkyTrain. One ticket allows you to transfer from one mode of transport to another, in any direction, within 90 minutes. A one-way, one-zone fare (everything in central Vancouver) costs C$2.50. A two-zone fare—C$3.75—is required to travel to nearby suburbs such as Richmond or North Vancouver, and a three-zone fare—C$5—is required for travel to the far-off city of Surrey. To reach the airport costs an additional C$5 over the two-zone fare, unless you purchase a booklet of FareSaver tickets (available at many convenience and drugstores). After 6:30pm on weekdays and all day on weekends and holidays, you can travel anywhere in all three zones for C$2.50. **DayPasses,** good on all public transit, cost C$9 for adults and C$7 for seniors, students, and children. They can be used for unlimited travel.

Tip: Keep in mind that drivers do not make change, so you need the exact fare or a valid transit pass. Pay with cash or buy tickets and passes from ticket machines at stations, tourist information centers, both SeaBus terminals, and convenience stores, drugstores, and outlets displaying the FAREDEALER sign; most of these outlets also sell a transit map showing all routes.

BY BUS   Both diesel and electric-trolley buses service the city. Regular service on the busiest routes is about every 5–15 minutes from 5am to 2am. Wheelchair-accessible buses and bus stops are identified by the international wheelchair symbol. Some key routes to keep in mind if you're touring the city by bus: **no. 5** (Robson St.), **no. 6** (Davie St.), **no. 10** (Granville St.), **no. 4** (UBC**), no. 2** (Kitsilano Beach to downtown), **no. 50** (Granville Island), **no. 19** (Stanley Park), **no. 240** (North Vancouver), and bus **no. 250** (West Vancouver–Horseshoe Bay). Call © **604/953-3333** for general public transportation information.

BY SKYTRAIN   The SkyTrain is a fast, light-rail service between downtown Vancouver and the suburbs. The **Expo Line** trains operate from Waterfront to King George station, running along a scenic 27km (17-mile) route from downtown Vancouver east to Surrey through Burnaby and New Westminster in 39 minutes. There are 20 stations along this route; three downtown stations are underground and marked at street level. The **Millennium Line** makes the same stops from Waterfront to Columbia, then branches to Sapperton, Braid, Lougheed town center, and beyond before looping back to Commercial Drive. All stations are wheelchair accessible; trains arrive every 2 to 8 minutes. **Canada Line,** the newest SkyTrain, began operating in October 2009 and links the Vancouver Airport to Yaletown, City Centre, and Waterfront Station (SeaBus terminal). Trains run every 4–20 minutes.

BY SEABUS Double-ended catamaran ferries take passengers, cyclists, and wheelchair riders on a scenic 12-minute commute across Burrard Inlet between downtown's Waterfront Station and North Vancouver's Lonsdale Quay. On weekdays, a SeaBus leaves Waterfront Station every 15 minutes from 6:16am to 6:46pm, then every 30 minutes until 12:46am. SeaBuses depart Waterfront Station on Saturdays every half-hour from 6:16am to 10:16am, then every 15 minutes until 6:46pm, and then every half-hour until 12:46am. On Sundays and holidays, runs depart downtown every half-hour from 8:16am to 11:16am, every 15 minutes until 6:46pm, and finally every 30 minutes until 11:16pm. If catching the SeaBus from Lonsdale, all times are 14 minutes earlier than departure times from Waterfront Station. A lot to keep straight? Thankfully there's a countdown clock in each terminal that lets you know how long you'll wait until the next crossing. The crossing is a two-zone fare on weekdays until 6:30pm.

By Taxi

Cab fares start at C$3.20 and increase at a rate of C$1.85 per kilometer. In the downtown area, you can expect to travel for less than C$12, plus tip. The typical fare for the 13km (8-mile) drive from downtown to the airport is C$35–C$40.

Taxis are easy to find in front of major hotels, but flagging one down can be tricky—especially late at night or on rainy days. Most drivers are usually on radio calls. But thanks to built-in satellite positioning systems, if you call for a taxi, it usually arrives faster than if you go out and hail one. Call for a pickup from **Black Top** (© 604/731-1111), **Yellow Cab** (© 604/681-1111), **Vancouver Taxi** (© 604/871-1111), or **MacLure's** (© 604/731-9211).

By Car

Vancouver's road system and traffic are easier to handle than those in many other cities, in large part because the city has no freeways. Traffic thus tends to move more slowly. If you're just sightseeing around town, public transit and cabs will easily see you through. However, if you're planning to visit the North Shore mountains or pursue other out-of-town activities, then a car is necessary. Gas is sold by the liter, averaging at press time around C$1.35 per liter; so a gallon of gas costs approximately C$5.11. Car insurance is compulsory in British Columbia. *Note:* In Canada, speeds and distances are posted in kilometers. The speed limit in Vancouver is 50kmph (31 mph); highway speed limits vary from 90 to 110kmph (56–68 mph).

RENTAL CARS Rates vary widely depending on demand, style of car, and special offers. If you're over 25 and have a major credit card, you can rent a vehicle from **Avis** (757 Hornby St.; © **800/879-2847** or 604/606-2868); **Budget** (416 W. Georgia St.; © **800/472-3325** or 604/668-7000); **Enterprise** (550 Bute St.; © **800/736-8222** or 604/689-7377); **Hertz Canada** (1270 Granville St.; © **800/263-0600** or 604/606-4711); **National** (999a Canada Place; © **800/387-4747** or 604/609-7160); or **Thrifty** (413 Seymour St.; © **800/847-4389** or 604/606-1666). These firms all have counters and shuttle service at the airport, as well. To rent a recreational vehicle,

4

GETTING TO KNOW VANCOUVER

Getting Around

contact **Go West Campers** (32 Fawcett Rd., Coquitlam; ℂ **800/661-8813** or 604/528-3900; www.go-west.com).

PARKING   All major downtown hotels have guest parking, either in-house or at nearby lots. Secure valet parking at most hotels costs upwards of C$30 per day, plus 21% parking sales tax and 12% harmonized sales tax. Public parking is found at **Robson Square** (enter at Smithe and Howe sts.), the **Pacific Centre** (Howe and Dunsmuir sts.), and **The Bay** department store (Seymour St. near Dunsmuir St.). You'll also find larger **parking lots** at the intersections of Thurlow and Georgia, Thurlow and Alberni, and Robson and Seymour streets.

Street meters accept C$2 and C$1 coins as well as quarters (25 cents), dimes (10 cents), nickels (5 cents), and pennies (1 cent). Rules are posted and strictly enforced; generally, downtown and in the West End, metered parking is in effect 7 days a week until 10pm. (**Note:** Drivers are given about a 2-min. grace period before their cars are towed away when the 3pm no-parking rule goes into effect on many major thoroughfares.) Unmetered parking on side streets is often subject to neighborhood residency requirements: Check the signs. If you park in such an area without the appropriate sticker on your windshield, you'll get ticketed and towed. If your car is towed away or you need a towing service and aren't a CAA or an AAA member, call **Unitow** (ℂ **604/251-1255**) or **Busters** (ℂ **604/685-8181**). If you are parking on the street, remove all valuables from your car; break-ins are not uncommon.

SPECIAL DRIVING RULES   Though photo radar is no longer in use in BC, photo-monitored intersections are alive and well. If you're caught racing through a red light, fines start at C$167.

AUTO CLUB   Members of the American Automobile Association (AAA) can get assistance from the **Canadian Automobile Association** (**CAA;** ℂ **604/268-5600** or for road service 604/293-2222; www.caa.ca).

By Bike

Vancouver is a biker's paradise. Along Robson and Denman streets near Stanley Park are plenty of places to rent bikes. (For specifics, see p. 147.) Paved paths crisscross through parks and along beaches. Helmets are mandatory, and riding on sidewalks is illegal except on designated bike paths.

You can take your bike on the SeaBus anytime at no extra charge. Bikes are not allowed in the George Massey Tunnel, but a tunnel shuttle operates 10 times daily from May to mid-October and about 6 times daily the rest of the year to transport you across the Fraser River. All of the West Vancouver blue buses (including the bus to the Horseshoe Bay ferry terminal) can carry two bikes—first-come, first-served—free of charge.

By Mini-Ferry

Crossing False Creek to Granville Island or beautiful Vanier Park on one of the zippy little mini-ferries is cheap and fun. These small, covered boats connect various points of interest; they are privately operated, so your public transit pass or ticket is not valid. It's well worth the extra money, though.

The **Aquabus** (☎ 604/689-5858; www.theaquabus.com) docks at the south foot of Hornby Street, the Public Market on Granville Island, David Lam Park, Stamp's Landing, Yaletown at Davie Street, Plaza of Nations, and Science World. Ferries operate daily from about 7am to 10:30pm (9:30pm in winter) and run every 3–15 minutes or so, but schedules change monthly and depend on the route. One-way fares are C$3.25 to C$6.50 for adults and C$1.75 to C$3.50 for seniors and children. A day pass is C$14 for adults and C$8 for seniors and children. You can take a 25-minute scenic boat ride (one complete circuit) for C$7 adults, C$4 seniors and children.

False Creek Ferries (☎ 604/684-7781; www.granvilleislandferries. bc.ca) runs a similar route, stopping at the Maritime Museum, Aquatic Centre, Granville Island, David Lam Park, Yaletown, Stamp's Landing, Science World, and Plaza of Nations. Most routes run from about 9am to 8pm, depending on the leg and season. One-way fares are C$3 to C$6 for adults and C$1.50 to C$2 for seniors and children.

[FastFACTS] VANCOUVER

Business Hours Vancouver **banks** are open Monday through Thursday from 10am to 5pm and Friday from 10am to 6pm. Some banks, like TD Canada Trust and Vancity, are also open on Saturday. **Stores** are generally open daily from 10am to 6pm. Last call at **restaurant, bars,** and **cocktail lounges** is usually at 1 or 2am and about midnight on Sundays, although legislation allows last call as late as 3am.

Child Care If you need to rent cribs, car seats, playpens, or other baby accessories, **Wee Travel** (☎ 604/222-4722; www. weetravel.ca) delivers them right to your hotel or the airport.

Dentists Most major hotels have a dentist on call. **Vancouver Centre**

Dental Clinic (Vancouver Centre Mall, 11-650 W. Georgia St.; ☎ **604/682-1601**) is another option. You must make an appointment. The clinic is open Monday to Thursday 8:30am to 5pm (Wed until 6pm) and Friday 8:30am to 2pm.

Doctors Hotels usually have a doctor on call. **Ultima Medicentre** (Bentall Centre, 1055 Dunsmuir St.; ☎ **604/683-8138**) is a drop-in clinic open Monday through Friday 8am to 5pm. Another drop-in medical center, **Care Point Medical Centre Walk-in Clinic** (1175 Denman St.; ☎ **604/681-5338**), is open Monday through Wednesday 8:30am to 9pm, Thursday to Saturday from 9am to 9pm, and Sunday 9am to 8pm. See also "Hotlines," below.

Hospitals **St. Paul's Hospital** (1081 Burrard St.; ☎ **604/682-2344**) is the closest facility to downtown and the West End. West Side Vancouver hospitals include **Vancouver General Hospital Health and Sciences Centre** (855 W. 12th Ave.; ☎ **604/875-4111**) and **BC Children's Hospital** (4480 Oak St.; ☎ **604/875-2345**). In North Vancouver, there's **Lions Gate Hospital** (231 E. 15th St.; ☎ **604/988-3131**).

Hotlines Emergency numbers include the **Crisis Centre** (☎ 604/872-3311), **Rape Crisis Centre** (☎ 604/255-6228), **Rape Relief** (☎ 604/872-8212), **BC Drug and Poison Information Centre** (☎ 604/682-5050), **Crime Stoppers** (☎ 800/222-8477), and **SPCA** animal emergency (✆ 604/879-3571). Or dial ✆ **911** for any emergency police, fire, or ambulance service.

Internet Access   Free Internet access is available at the Vancouver **Public Library** Central Branch (350 W. Georgia St.; ✆ **604/331-3600**). **Internet Cafe** (616 Seymour St.; ✆ **604/681-1088**) charges C$2.50 for 30 minutes and is open until 10pm.

Laundry & Dry Cleaning   **Westend Laundry** (1061 Davie St.; ✆ **604/682-2717**) offers self-service, drop-off service, and dry cleaning. **Swan Laundry** (1352 Burrard St.; ✆ **604/684-0323;** www.swanlaundry. com) is unmissable with its bubblegum pink window and is open daily. Also,

almost all hotels have laundry service.

Luggage Storage & Lockers   Lockers are available at the main Vancouver railway station (which is also the main bus depot), **Pacific Central Station,** 1150 Station St., near Main Street and Terminal Avenue (✆ **604/661-0328**).

Newspapers & Magazines   The two local papers are the *Vancouver Sun* (www.vancouversun. com), published Monday through Saturday, and the *Province* (www.the province.com), published Sunday through Friday. The free alt-weekly paper, the *Georgia Straight* (www.straight.com), comes out on Thursday, as does the *West Ender* (www.westender.com).

Pharmacies   **Shopper's Drug Mart** (1125 Davie St.; ✆ **604/669-2424**) is open 24 hours. Several Safeway supermarket pharmacies are open late; the one on Robson and Denman streets is open until midnight.

Police   For emergencies, dial ✆ **911**. This is a free call. Otherwise, the **Vancouver City Police** can be reached at ✆ **604/717-3535.**

Post Office   The **main post office** (349 W. Georgia St., at Homer St.; ✆ **866/607-6301**) is open Monday through Friday from 9am to 5:30pm. You'll also find post office outlets in some Shopper's Drug Mart and 7-Eleven stores with longer open hours than the main post office.

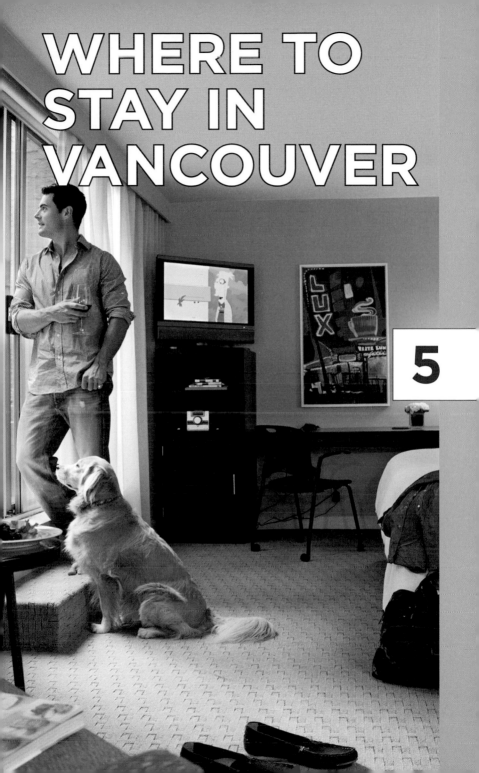

WHERE TO STAY IN VANCOUVER

5

ancouver hotels come dressed in sleek, modern towers, grand dames, and boutique B&Bs. Most of Vancouver's hotels are in the downtown area or the West End. Covering a peninsula, downtown Vancouver is small and easily walkable, so you'll often be no more than a 20-minute walk from most major sights, services, and nightlife.

BEST VANCOUVER HOTEL BETS

- **Best New Hotel:** Because it offers something so different that anything else you'll find in Vancouver, **The Waldorf Hotel** stands out for its clean-lined rooms and on-site historic Tiki Bar with Polynesian artifacts and bamboo screening. See p. 82.
- **Best Historic Hotel:** The **Fairmont Hotel Vancouver** harks back to a more gracious and traditional era. Even with all the modern amenities and services you could wish for, it wraps you up in old-fashioned charm and comfort. See p. 64.
- **Best for Business Travelers:** The **St. Regis Hotel** really goes beyond with Wi-Fi and international calling—at no extra charge. The hotel, located conveniently near the main business core, offers room rates a little lower that most downtown hotels; plus there's a full breakfast included. See p. 72.
- **Best Splurge:** There are two. In trendy Yaletown, the stylish **Opus Hotel** houses an array of room types appointed in luscious colors and contemporary decor that sets it apart, plus an ultra-hip bar and a fine restaurant. See p. 68. The newer **Loden Vancouver,** a 14-story tower on the edge of Coal Harbour, envelops you in a sophisticated West Coast aesthetic that features spa-type bathrooms and a marvelous restaurant. See p. 68.
- **Best for a Romantic Getaway:** The **Wedgewood Hotel,** one of the few boutique hotels downtown, has a comfy, rich, European elegance that brings out the romance in everyone. See p. 70.
- **Best for Families:** The **Coast Plaza Hotel & Suites** offers large one- and two-bedrooms suites near the beaches of English Bay and the attractions of Stanley Park. There's also a sizeable basement pool. See p. 77.

price CATEGORIES

Very Expensive	C$275 and up
Expensive	C$175–C$274
Moderate	C$100–C$174
Inexpensive	Under C$100

PREVIOUS PAGE: The stylish decor at the Opus Hotel makes it one of the city's best splurge options.

Best Vancouver Hotel Bets

WHERE TO STAY IN VANCOUVER

WHAT YOU'LL really PAY

Hotels listings below provide the rack rates, or the rates you would receive if you walked in off the street and requested a room. The highest prices tend to be during high season—June to September—but many Vancouver properties also scale their pricing based on occupancy, so when the hotel is busy you'll pay more for the last few rooms. With that in mind, it is advised to make reservations well ahead for summer travel, but note that even stretches of April and May can be busy.

By checking the hotel's website, you'll almost always find lower rates, including special "romance packages" and weekend-getaway specials.

Online discounts on third-party sites can often slash away an attractive percentage off the room rates listed here. Searching through websites such as Hotels.com and Expedia is a good place to start. But hotels are becoming increasingly aware of luring guests back from booking through independent sites, often offering incentives for guests to book through their own reservations lines.

Call and let them know if you've found a lower rate than on their website, and ask if they will match or beat it. (See "Getting the Best Deal;" on p. 84 for more tips).

In Vancouver, 12% harmonized sales tax (HST) is added to all rooms—an exception is the **YWCA Hotel/Residence** (p. 76), which as a nonprofit organization charges a reduced tax rate of 3.5%.

Note: Discount rates rarely include breakfast, parking, or other fees that may be included in a package deal.

- **Best Value:** With all the facilities of a convention center, plus cheap, comfortable rooms, the **University of British Columbia Conference Centre** is the best inexpensive choice in the city. See p. 81.

- **Best Service:** Built in 1905 by two Vancouver photographers, the **West End Guest House** is not only filled with the artists' work and a collection of Victorian antiques, but you also get fresh-baked brownies or cookies with your evening turndown service. See p. 79.

- **Best Location:** Everyone's definition of a great location is different, but the **Westin Bayshore Resort & Marina** is right on the Seawall, just steps from Stanley Park and Denman Street, and only 10 blocks from downtown. See p. 76.

- **Best Views:** So many Vancouver hotels have outstanding views that it's difficult to choose just one—so how about three? The luxe and lively **Fairmont Pacific Rim** has fabulous rooms where you can take in water views from deep soaker tubs. See p. 64. With a tad more spectacular views but slightly less divine amenities, the **Westin Bayshore Resort & Marina** offers magnificent water/mountain/park views. See p. 76. With a recent update of the decor to simple lines and fresh colors, the **Empire Landmark** offers stunning, panoramic views from most of the rooms in this 40-year-old tower; plus there's a top-floor revolving restaurant for the full 360-degree effect. See p. 78.

DOWNTOWN & YALETOWN

Downtown—the financial district, the area around Canada Place convention center and cruise-ship terminal, the central shopping-business area around Robson Square, and the warehouse district of Yaletown—is buzzing during the day but pretty quiet at night. All downtown hotels are within 5 to 10 minutes' walking distance of shops, restaurants, and attractions.

BEST FOR: First-time visitors to Vancouver who are unfamiliar with the city layout and love the proximity to lively clubs, top restaurants, and entertainment venues.

DRAWBACKS: You pay for location—so the area has the highest prices you'll see in Vancouver.

Very Expensive

The Fairmont Hotel Vancouver ★★ ☺ A landmark in the city since Queen Elizabeth first opened the property in 1939, the Fairmont Hotel Vancouver has been brought up to 21st-century standards but retains its traditional, old-fashioned elegance—such as the glass-fronted mail chute that runs through every floor and trunk-sized closets. The rooms are spacious, quiet, and comfortable. The bathrooms (with tub/shower combinations) look a bit dated when compared with other newer downtown hotels in this price range, but that's part of the rich heritage charm. One-bedroom suites feature a luxuriously furnished living room, separated from the bedroom by French doors. Guests can use the state-of-the-art gym with heated indoor pool in an airy, glassed atrium. Off the grandiose lobby, find high-end boutique shopping at the likes of Louis Vuitton. The hotel is family friendly and even has two resident dogs (former Seeing Eye dogs) that can be taken out for walks.

900 W. Georgia St., Vancouver, BC V6C 2W6. www.fairmont.com/hotelvancouver. ℂ **866/540-4452** or 604/684-3131. Fax 604/662-1929. 556 units. C$180–C$410 double. Children 18 and under stay free in parent's room. AE, DC, DISC, MC, V. Parking C$43 (includes taxes). **Amenities:** 2 restaurants; bar; babysitting; concierge; executive-level rooms; health club; Jacuzzi; indoor pool; room service; sauna; spa. *In room:* A/C, TV w/pay movies, hair dryer, Internet (C$15/day), minibar.

Fairmont Pacific Rim ★★★ Fairmont's newest Vancouver property is a real show-stopper. Located across from the new addition to the Canada Place Convention Centre, the Pacific Rim is far more luxurious than the nearby Fairmont Waterfront (see below) and is as up-to-date, with all the amenities you could possibly want. The rooms—many of which have water views—are beautifully designed, especially the 18 suites with freestanding Japanese-style soaking tubs that look out over Burrard Inlet and the North Shore mountains. For families or sun lovers, book a Pool View room where the balcony opens up onto the rooftop pool deck. Finishes throughout are sumptuous and superbly crafted. Dining options include Giovane, the hotel's Italian-inspired, local-focused cafe/bakery/deli, and Oru, a pan-Asian bistro. The signature Willow Stream Spa offers a complete menu of pampering treatments. It's hard not to feel a bit posh at this hotel, and the staff works hard to make you feel special.

1038 Canada Place Way, Vancouver, BC V6C 0B9. www.fairmont.com/pacificrim. © **877/900-5350** or 604/695-5300. Fax 604/695-5301. 377 units. C$300–C$450 double; C$400–C$7,500 suite. Children 18 and under stay free in parent's room. AE, DC, DISC, MC, V. Valet or self-parking C$43 (incl. taxes). SkyTrain: Waterfront Station. **Amenities:** Restaurant; cafe/deli; bar; babysitting; concierge; executive-level rooms; health club; Jacuzzi; outdoor pool; room service; sauna; spa. *In room:* A/C, TV w/pay movies, DVD player, hair dryer, Internet (C$14/day), minibar.

The Fairmont Waterfront ★ ☺ This large Fairmont hotel occupies a triangular high-rise tower right across the street from Canada Place, offering front-row views of the cruise-ship terminal and its hulking vessels. The Pan Pacific (p. 68) is the only other hotel in Vancouver as conveniently located for cruisers. The Fairmont features large, traditionally styled rooms with big windows and some great views; if you want to see the giant cruise ships right below you, ask for a harbor-view room on the ninth floor or above; for something really special and kid friendly, book one of the terrace rooms that have doors leading out to the hotel's rooftop garden and swimming pool. The hotel has its own beehives that produce pounds of honey each fall. The more expensive Fairmont Gold rooms come with a dedicated concierge, breakfast, and evening hors d'oeuvres.

900 Canada Place Way, Vancouver, BC V6C 3L5. www.fairmont.com/waterfront. © **866/540-4509** or 604/691-1991. Fax 604/691-1999. 457 units. C$270–C$440 double. Children 18 and under stay free in parent's room. AE, DC, DISC, MC, V. Parking C$43 (incl. tax). SkyTrain: Waterfront Station. **Amenities:** Restaurant; bar; babysitting; concierge; executive-level rooms; health club; Jacuzzi; outdoor pool; room service; sauna. *In room:* A/C, TV w/pay movies, hair dryer, Internet (C$14/day), minibar.

Four Seasons Hotel ★★★ ☺ For over 30 years now, the Four Seasons has reigned as one of Vancouver's top hotels with its lively restaurant, bright rooms, and serene decor. From the outside, this huge high-rise hotel across from the Vancouver Art Gallery is rather unappealing. But the large, light-filled rooms are wonderfully comfortable with superb beds and interesting views of downtown with glimpses of the mountains. The marble bathrooms are on the small side but well designed. For a slightly larger room, reserve a deluxe corner room with wrap-around floor-to-ceiling windows. One of the glories of this hotel is its health club with an enormous heated pool—half indoor, half outdoor—on a terrace. The Four Seasons completed a top-to-bottom renovation in 2007 and opened its noteworthy bar/lounge/restaurant **Yew** (p. 92).

791 W. Georgia St., Vancouver, BC V6C 2T4. www.fourseasons.com/vancouver. © **800/819-5053** or 604/689-9333. Fax 604/684-4555. 373 units. Nov–Apr C$255–C$1,750; May–Oct C$375–C$2,750. AE, DC, DISC, MC, V. Parking C$41. **Amenities:** Restaurant; bar; babysitting; concierge; exercise room; indoor and heated outdoor pool; room service; sauna. *In room:* A/C, TV, hair dryer, minibar, Wi-Fi (C$12–C$17/day).

Le Soleil Hotel & Suites ★ A boutique hotel midway between Robson Square and the financial district, Le Soleil is a 1980s-era building decorated to look like a French manor, with crystal chandeliers, plush carpeting, and gilded ceilings. Most units are suites with pullout sofa beds; for maximum space, corner

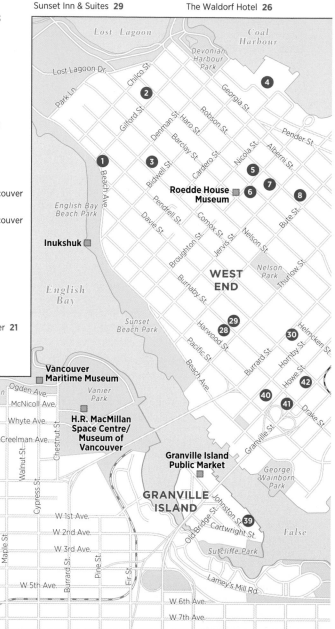

Vancouver Hotels

Wedgewood Hotel **18**
West End Guest House **6**
Westin Bayshore Resort
   & Marina **4**
The Westin Grand **33**
YWCA Hotel/Residence **36**

0   1/4 mi
0   0.25 km

Deadman's Island

Burrard   Inlet

Vancouver Convention &
Exhibition Centre

Canada Place

Centennial Pier

Cordova St.
Hastings St.
9
10
11
12
Marine Bldg.
13
14
Melville St.
Burrard St.
16
Waterfront
Canada Line
Waterfront
Howe St.
15
Burrard
Waterfront Sta.
Portside Park
Railway St.
Alexander St.
Steam Clock
Granville St.
Pender St.
25
Water St.
Maple Tree Square
Powell St.
Oppenheimer Park
Princess Ave.
19
21
20
22
Granville
23
24
Cambie St.
Abbott St.
Carrall St.
Columbia St.
Cordova St.
Jackson Ave.
17
18
Robson Square
Vancouver City Centre
Homer St.
Dunsmuir St.
Hastings St.
CHINATOWN
Dunlevy Ave.
26 →
27 →
GASTOWN
Sun Tower
Pender St.
Provincial
Law Courts
Georgia St.
32
Smithe St.
Richards St.
33
Vancouver Public Library
Chinatown Gate
Dr. Sun Yat-sen Chinese Garden
Keefer St.
Gore Ave.
Georgia St.
CANADA LINE
Stadium
Andy Livingstone Park
Main St.
Union St.
31
Seymour St.
Nelson St.
Robson St.
34
36
35
Rogers Arena
Prior St.
YALETOWN
Mainland St.
Hamilton St.
Cambie St.
Beatty St.
B.C. Place Stadium
Malkin Ave.
Davie St.
Yaletown-Roundhouse
Expo Blvd.
National Ave.
Pacific Central Sta.
43
Pacific Blvd.
The Roundhouse
Cooper's Park
Creekside Park
Science World
Main Street
SKYTRAIN
David Lam Park
Creek
W 1st Ave.
E 2nd Ave.
E 1st Ave.
Industrial Ave.
Charleson Park
Moberly Rd.
Olympic Village
Charleson St.
W 2nd Ave.
Yukon St.
Alberta St.
Columbia St.
Manitoba St.
Ontario St.
W 4th Ave.
W 5th Ave.
E 3rd Ave.
Quebec St.
Main St.
Scotia St.

suites with soaker tubs are best. In some units the sitting areas have no windows and consequently feel somewhat confined, despite the Biedermeier-style furniture and richly colored wallpapers and fabrics. Where Le Soleil shines is in its personal service, but if you're looking for a luxury boutique hotel, also check out the Wedgewood, the Loden, and the Opus (see below).

567 Hornby St., Vancouver, BC V6C 2E8. www.lesoleilhotel.com. © **877/632-3030** or 604/632-3000. Fax 604/632-3001. 119 units. C$370–C$700 double. AE, DC, MC, V. Valet parking C$26. **Amenities:** Restaurant; concierge; access to YWCA fitness facilities next door; room service. *In room:* A/C, TV w/pay movies, hair dryer, minibar, Wi-Fi (C$9/day).

Loden Vancouver ★★ 🎒 This luxury boutique hotel opened in spring 2008 at the edge of Coal Harbour. The building is a narrow urban tower tucked in among other high-rise buildings just a couple of blocks from Burrard Inlet and the Seawall, and within easy walking distance of Robson Street and the West End. Standard rooms and one-bedroom suites are chic and comfortable at the same time, with a rich palette of fabrics, colors, and materials—including thoughtfully placed precious stones, and floor-to-ceiling windows that offer "view-corridor" views of the water and North Shore mountains. Garden Terrace rooms have a Zen quality with private patios, and are close to the light-filled, well-equipped fitness area. The bathrooms in every room have been designed to open up (if you want them to) into the bedroom area; it's like having your own private spa, with a soaker tub and a big glass-walled shower. **Tableau** (p. 98), the Loden's new restaurant that opened in 2011, is a friendly spot to dine.

1177 Melville St. (at Bute St.), Vancouver, BC V6E 0A3. www.theloden.com. © **877/225-6336** or 604/669-5060. Fax 604/662-8904. 77 units. C$220–C$280 double; C$460 suite. AE, DC, MC, V. Parking C$35. **Amenities:** Restaurant; bar; babysitting; concierge; exercise room; Jacuzzi; room service; sauna. *In room:* A/C, TV/DVD, hair dryer, minibar, Wi-Fi ($15/day).

Opus Hotel ★★★ If you want to stay in a hip, happening, luxury hotel, try the Opus—various reader polls have consistently voted it one of the world's top hotels. It's the only hotel truly in Yaletown, a vibrant area for shopping, nightlife, and dining. Each room is furnished according to one of five "personalities," with its own layout, color, and flavor. The luscious room colors—from tangerine and cotton candy pink to serene blue—are eye candy if you're tired of blah hotel interiors. The heated-floor bathrooms are fitted with high-design sinks, soaker tubs, or roomy rain showers (or both). The cool Opus Bar serves an international tapas menu, and on weekends becomes one of Yaletown's see-and-be-seen scenes. (Be forewarned: This area of Yaletown is "club central" and can be noisy until the wee hours; book a courtyard room if you don't want to be disturbed.) There's also a restaurant—in 2011 it was a popular "pop-up" dining spot called **One Hundred Nights**—that at the time of writing was on the cusp of being revamped.

322 Davie St., Vancouver, BC V6B 5Z6. www.opushotel.com. © **866/642-6787** or 604/642-6787. Fax 604/642-6780. 96 units. May–Oct C$360–C$550 double; from C$815 suite; Nov–Apr C$230–C$430 double, from C$740 suite. Children 17 and under stay free in parent's room. AE, MC, V. Valet parking C$29. **Amenities:** Restaurant; bar; bikes; concierge; small exercise room; room service. *In room:* A/C, TV w/pay movies, hair dryer, minibar, Wi-Fi (C$15/day).

Pan Pacific Vancouver ★★★ This 23-story luxury hotel atop Canada Place is a key landmark on the Vancouver waterfront. Despite its size, the hotel excels in comfort and service, and it provides spectacular views of the North Shore mountains, Burrard Inlet, and cruise ships arriving and departing from the terminal below. The rooms are spacious and comfortable, with contemporary furnishings and a soothing color palette. Bathrooms are large and luxurious. Guests have use of a heated outdoor pool and Jacuzzi that feels private and overlooks the harbor. Spa Utopia offers a full array of pampering treatments.

300-999 Canada Place, Vancouver, BC V6C 3B5. www.panpacificvancouver.com. ☎ **800/937-1515** in the U.S., 800/663-1515 in Canada, or 604/662-8111. Fax 604/685-8690. 503 units. C$240–C$540 double; C$450–C$7,500 suite. AE, DC, DISC, MC, V. Valet parking C$39. **Amenities:** 2 restaurants; bar; babysitting; concierge; health club; Jacuzzi; outdoor heated pool; room service; sauna; spa. *In room:* A/C, TV w/pay movies, hair dryer, Internet (C$5–C$15/day), minibar.

Rosewood Hotel Georgia ★★★   From its original layout to the renovated hotel that opened in mid 2011, the 1927 Hotel Georgia has halved its number of rooms and created roomier suites, multiple restaurants, and a saltwater pool. The design elements—tones of ivory, taupe, and chocolate brown—are unimposing, allowing the comforts of the space and the vast collection of Canadian art to stand out. Bathrooms are exceptional, each with a separate tub and shower, heated floors, and double vanities. For the best views, request a southeast exposure to overlook the Vancouver Art Gallery. On-site you'll find a basement bar called **Prohibition,** buzzing lobby lounge **1927,** and inventive dining at street-level **Hawksworth Restaurant** (p. 91). Indeed, with so many options for guests and locals, the Hotel Georgia is poised to once again become a social hub in the city.

801 W. Georgia St., Vancouver, BC, V6C 1P7. www.rosewoodhotelgeorgia.com. ☎ **888/767-3966** or 604/682-5566. 155 units. July–Oct from $375 double; Nov–June from $295 double. AE, MC, V. Valet parking. **Amenities:** 3 restaurants; lounge; bar; babysitting; concierge; room service; fitness center; indoor pool; sauna; spa. *In room:* A/C, TV, DVD, hair dryer, minibar, MP3 docking station, Wi-Fi (free).

Shangri-La Hotel ★★★   For all-around luxury and excellent, unobtrusive service, the new Shangri-La, opened in 2009, can't be beat; its only rival is the Four Seasons (reviewed above). This is the first North American property for Shangri-La, and it's an impressive one, with the hotel occupying the lower 15 floors of Vancouver's tallest residential tower. The rooms are large and furnished with a quiet good taste that combines contemporary furnishings with Asian accents; over half of them have balconies (the smaller balconies are more like a glass enclosure with an open window). Bathrooms, finished in white marble, are sumptuous. Chi, the hotel's spa, offers a unique menu of treatments utilizing Asian and Tibetan techniques. And to cap it all off, the hotel's restaurant, **MARKET by Jean-Georges** (as in Vongerichten; p. 92), is one of Vancouver's hottest haute spots.

1128 W. Georgia St., Vancouver, BC V6E 0A8. www.shangri-la.com/vancouver. ☎ **604/689-1120.** Fax 604/689-1195. 119 units. C$355–C$405 double. AE, DC, DISC, MC, V. Valet parking C$35. **Amenities:** Restaurant; lounge; babysitting; concierge; health club; Jacuzzi; outdoor heated pool; room service; sauna; spa. *In room:* A/C, TV w/pay movies, hair dryer, minibar, Wi-Fi (free).

The Sutton Place Hotel ★★   Don't let the bland, corporate-looking exterior fool you: This hotel has won many awards, and is known to hotel cognoscenti as one of the best in Vancouver in terms of overall comfort and service. Once you enter the lobby, elegantly decorated with marble, fresh flowers, chandeliers, and

French-leaning European furnishings, it's pure luxury, comparable to the Four Seasons (reviewed above). The rooms, decorated in a traditional European style, don't skimp on size or comfort. The European-style health club and spa has a big heated pool and sun deck. In the end, it's the outstanding service that really stands out. A tower of 164 spacious one- and two-bedroom apartments is connected to the hotel and designed for long-stay guests.

845 Burrard St., Vancouver, BC V6Z 2K6. www.vancouver.suttonplace.com. ℂ **866/378-8866** or 604/682-5511. Fax 604/682-5513. 397 units. C$209–C$409 double. AE, DC, DISC, MC, V. Underground, self-, or valet parking C$40. **Amenities:** Restaurant; lounge (w/bistro fare); bakery/cafe; bikes; concierge; health club; Jacuzzi; indoor pool; room service; sauna; spa. *In room:* A/C, TV w/ pay movies, hair dryer, minibar, Wi-Fi (C$15/day).

Wedgewood Hotel ★★★ If you're searching for a romantic, sophisticated hotel with superb service, spacious rooms, fine detailing, a good restaurant, and a full-service spa, and a central downtown location, you can't do any better than the Wedgewood. One feature that makes the award-winning Wedgewood so distinctive is that it's independently owned (by Greek-born Eleni Skalbania), and the owner's elegant personal touch is evident throughout. All 83 units are spacious and have balconies (the best views are those facing the Vancouver Art Gallery and Law Court). Furnishings, original art, and antiques are of the highest quality, and the limestone- and marble-clad bathrooms with deep soaker tubs and separate walk-in Roman showers are simply the best. Bacchus, the cozy hotel restaurant, serves a modern French menu of fish, pasta, and meat. It is a member of the Relais & Châteaux group.

845 Hornby St., Vancouver, BC V6Z 1V1. www.wedgewoodhotel.com. ℂ **800/663-0666** or 604/689-7777. Fax 604/608-5349. 83 units. C$250–C$500 double; C$300–C$1,500 suite. AE, DC, MC, V. Valet parking C$20. **Amenities:** Restaurant; concierge; executive-level rooms; exercise room; room service; spa; Wi-Fi (free) in common areas. *In room:* A/C, TV/DVD, CD player, hair dryer, minibar.

The Westin Grand ★★ ☺ It's such a pleasure to find a luxury-level hotel that's elegant instead of garish, and understated rather than pompous. Located across from Library Square, the Westin Grand provides high-end all-suite accommodations within easy walking distance of Yaletown, Rogers Arena, and Robson Street shopping. The spacious suites are brightened by natural light pouring in through the floor-to-ceiling windows and the varied layouts eschew any boxy feel; if you can, spring for one of the deluxe 09 or 03 units, which have balconies. Sitting rooms come with a concealed kitchenette and loads of business-friendly amenities. The furnishings throughout are clean-lined and contemporary; bathrooms are roomy, most with separate tub and shower. Kids get a special welcome kit. Check the website for special deals. The hotel's restaurant **Hidden** opened in 2010, serving a tapas menu.

433 Robson St., Vancouver, BC V6B 6L9. www.westingrandvancouver.com. ℂ **888/680-9393** or 604/602-1999. Fax 604/647-2535. 207 suites. Mid-Oct to Apr C$240–C$440 suite; May to mid-Oct C$280–C$480 suite. Up to 2 children 18 and under stay free in parent's room. AE, DC, DISC, MC, V. Valet parking C$31. **Amenities:** Restaurant; babysitting; concierge; executive-level rooms; health club; Jacuzzi; outdoor pool; room service; sauna. *In room:* A/C, TV w/pay movies, hair dryer, kitchenette, minibar, Wi-Fi (C$15/day).

Expensive

Coast Coal Harbour Hotel ★ 👜 Newly opened in 2010 just in time for the Olympic Winter Games, this comfortable, contemporary hotel is one of the best deals in Vancouver. The hotel has implemented an admirable zero-waste initiative: All rooms have small bins for recyclables and organics. Bulk amenities in the bathrooms minimize plastic and waste. The property doesn't draw attention to itself like so many of Vancouver's showier hotels, and that is part of what makes it a pleasant place to stay. Rooms aren't skimpy in size, and the bathtubs are big enough for a relaxing soak. Try to get a corner room (big windows on two sides) on one of the higher floors, which have views of Burrard Inlet. Standard rooms on the fifth floor lead out onto a rooftop terrace. The Coast Hotel group has another hotel in the West End (Coast Plaza Hotel & Suites; p. 77). The hotel restaurant **Prestons** has booths that are fun for groups as well as a communal plank table.

1180 W. Hastings St., Vancouver, BC V6B 1L6. www.coasthotels.com. ☎ **800/716-6199** or 604/697-0202. Fax 604/697-0123. 220 units. Oct–Apr C$230–C$310; May–Sept C$270-C$360. AE, DC, DISC, MC, V. Valet parking C$28. **Amenities:** Restaurant; concierge; fitness center; outdoor pool; room service. *In room:* A/C, TV w/pay movies, hair dryer, MP3 docking station, Wi-Fi (free).

Delta Vancouver Suites ★ ☺ The Delta Vancouver Suites is a full-service, all-suites hotel with a special appeal to business and convention travelers. It sits across the street from the Lookout observation tower (p. 122), just minutes from the cruise ships at Canada Place, great nightlife in Gastown, cultural sites in Chinatown, and shopping along Robson Street. Waterfront Station, the downtown Canada Line stop, lies just one block away. The look throughout is high-end, with an attractive lobby connecting to a state-of-the-art conference facility. Each suite has a desk and mini-office/living area, and elements are often moveable to personalize the space. Corner 09 rooms are long and narrow with a full wall of floor-to-ceiling glass. A C$40 upgrade to the Signature Club gets you a room on the top three floors and access to the Signature Lounge, which puts out a good continental breakfast and afternoon hors d'oeuvres (both included in the upgrade). Kids are given a welcome pack on arrival.

550 W. Hastings St., Vancouver, BC V6B 1L6. www.deltahotels.com. ☎ **888/890-3222** or 604/689-8188. Fax 604/605-8881. 225 units. C$130–C$260 double. Children 17 and under stay free in parent's room. AE, DC, DISC, MC, V. Valet parking C$26. **Amenities:** Restaurant; bar; babysitting; concierge; executive-level rooms; exercise room; indoor pool; room service. *In room:* A/C, TV w/pay movies and games, hair dryer, Internet (C$15/day), minibar.

Georgian Court Hotel ★ 🍴 This modern, 14-story brick hotel is convenient to BC Place Stadium, Rogers Arena, the Queen Elizabeth Theatre, the Vancouver Playhouse, and the Vancouver Public Library. You can walk to Robson Square in about 10 minutes. The guest rooms are relatively large, nicely decorated, and have good-size bathrooms. And while the big-time celebs are usually whisked off to the glamorous top hotels, their entourages often stay at the Georgian Court, as it provides all the amenities and business-friendly extras such as two phones in every room, brightly lit desks, and complimentary high-speed Internet access. Booking on the Orchid Floor adds extra comfort for female travelers—including flat irons, curling irons, yoga mats, and an emergency kit with items like nylons and a sewing kit.

773 Beatty St., Vancouver, BC V6B 2M4. www.georgiancourt.com. ☎ **800/663-1155** or 604/682-5555. Fax 604/682-8830. 180 units. C$200–C$250 double. AE, DC, MC, V. Parking C$16. **Amenities:** Restaurant; bar; exercise room; Jacuzzi; room service; sauna; downtown shuttle (drop-off only). *In room:* A/C, TV, fridge, hair dryer, Internet (free).

Metropolitan Hotel Vancouver ★★

Centrally located between the financial district and downtown shopping areas, the Metropolitan is geared toward business and leisure travelers who want traditional luxury and full service. Guest rooms feature large, marble-tiled bathrooms with separate tub and shower, and wonderfully comfortable beds with Frette Italian linens. Most guest rooms are newly refurbished, with the wood cabinetry and muted tones updated to a fresh white with bright accents. Many units in the 18-story hotel have small balconies, but the views are not the hotel's selling point as the building is dwarfed by the Four Seasons across the street. Guests have use of a sauna and steam rooms. There are pay-per-use Zip Cars (☎ **604/697-0550;** www.zipcar.com) stationed in the hotel parkade and the hotel's restaurant, **Diva at the Met** (p. 87), is regarded as one of Vancouver's top eateries.

645 Howe St., Vancouver, BC V6C 2Y9. www.metropolitan.com/vanc. ☎ **800/667-2300** or 604/687-1122. Fax 604/602-7846. 197 units. C$200–C$400 double; C$250–C$700 suite. Children 17 and under stay free in parent's room. AE, DC, DISC, MC, V. Underground parking C$40. **Amenities:** Restaurant; bar; concierge; exercise room; Jacuzzi; indoor pool; room service; squash court. *In room:* A/C, TV w/pay movies, hair dryer, minibar, MP3 docking station, Wi-Fi (included in C$9 daily facility fee).

Rosedale on Robson Suite Hotel ★ ☺ ✦

Across the street from Library Square, the Rosedale provides good value, particularly when it comes to amenities. All rooms are one- or two-bedroom suites and feature separate living rooms with a pullout couch and full kitchenettes (with microwaves, stoves, and ovens); the decor is a tad dated but cozy. The designated two-bedroom family suites include two single beds in the kids' bedrooms. The small gym has an indoor lap pool with toys for the kids to enjoy. The hotel does a lot of business with tour groups. Check the website for seasonal deals, which can be lower than the rack rates listed below.

838 Hamilton St. (at Robson St.), Vancouver, BC V6B 6A2. www.rosedaleonrobson.com. ☎ **800/661-8870** or 604/689-8033. Fax 604/689-4426. 217 units. C$170–C$650 suite. Additional adult C$25. Rates include continental breakfast. AE, DC, MC, V. Parking C$11. **Amenities:** Restaurant; babysitting; concierge; executive-level rooms; small exercise room; Jacuzzi; indoor lap pool; room service; sauna. *In room:* A/C, TV w/pay movies, fax, hair dryer, Internet (C$5/day), kitchenette, MP3 docking station.

St. Regis Hotel ★ ⛺

Many hotels in downtown Vancouver occupy newer buildings, so it's a pleasure to find one—and especially one as nice as the St. Regis—in a so-called "heritage building," dating from 1913. The owners have transformed it into a unique boutique hotel that's handsome inside and out, filled with contemporary art, and wired for up-to-the-minute Wi-Fi. The redesigned rooms and suites have a savvy, comfy, contemporary look to them. Plus, an impressive full breakfast is included in the room rate—it's the only downtown hotel to do so—and there's a great after-work crowd at the on-premises brewpub. The hotel is just 3 short blocks from the financial district, and close proximity to the shops at Pacific Centre. The new Canada Line SkyTrain from the airport stops a half block away at Granville and Dunsmuir. The only other heritage hotel in Vancouver to have this kind of updated flair is the Moda (p. 74).

602 Dunsmuir St., Vancouver, BC V6B 1Y6. www.stregishotel.com. © **800/770-7929** or 604/681-1135. Fax 604/683-1126. 65 units. C$170 double; C$275–C$509 suite. Rates include breakfast. AE, MC, V. **Amenities:** Restaurant; bar/pub; Starbucks; concierge; executive-level rooms; access to nearby health club. *In room:* A/C, TV w/pay movies, hair dryer, minibar (in suites), MP3 docking station, Wi-Fi (free).

Moderate

Best Western Downtown Vancouver   The 12-story Best Western is just a 5-block walk from the theater area on Granville Street at the south end of downtown. All rooms are comfortable, and some have harbor views. The corner rooms are a bit smaller than the rest, but they receive more light. This hotel is not overflowing with amenities, but the rooms are cleanly furnished and the location is convenient. Rooms with a full kitchen are available for an additional C$20. Keep in mind, however, that while quite safe and usually quiet, the hotel is located in a nightlife-oriented downtown neighborhood. You shouldn't book here unless you have a reasonable tolerance for the realities of street life.

718 Drake St. (at Granville St.), Vancouver, BC V6Z 2W6. www.bestwesterndowntown.com. © **888/669-9888** or 604/669-9888. Fax 604/669-3440. 143 units (30 with full kitchen). C$100–C$190 double. AE, DC, DISC, MC, V. Parking C$14. **Amenities:** Restaurant; babysitting; bikes; downtown shuttle (drop-off only); rooftop exercise room; hot tub; sauna. *In room:* A/C, TV, hair dryer, Internet (free).

The Burrard ★   Echoing the successful transformation of East Vancouver's **The Waldorf Hotel** (p. 82), the Burrard follows suit by hinging its vibe of a 1956 motor inn into a hip hotel. The difference is the Burrard is right downtown, making it wonderfully convenient to clubs on Granville Street and dining in the West End. Besides replanting the spectacular inner courtyard that all the motel-like units face, a gutting renovation has brought a fun freshness to the inn. Gone are the pink tubs, instead replaced with white enamel and tiling, Moroccan ottomans, and triple-sheeting. Double-glazed windows have minimized traffic noise from busy Burrard Street, but it may still be best to request a room on the alley side.

1100 Burrard St., Vancouver, BC, V6Z 1Y9. www.burrardinn.com. © **800/663-0366** or 604/681-2331. 72 units. C$186–C$206 double. AE, MC, V. Parking C$20. **Amenities:** Bicycles; courtyard garden; access to nearby fitness club. *In room:* A/C (portable units), TV w/movie channels, fridge, hair dryer, Internet (free), MP3 docking station.

Days Inn Downtown   Located in a heritage building that's been a hotel since 1918, the well-maintained Days Inn Downtown is conveniently located in the heart of Vancouver's financial district and within easy walking distance of just about everything. For travelers who don't need all the amenities of a large hotel, these small, newly refurbished rooms are comfortable and convenient, but if you check out other hotel websites, you might find a much nicer place for not much more money. The heritage aspect allows for some neat touches, such as the hotel's original safe (although the combination has been lost). Ten of the rooms have showers only. Ask for a water view or consider a harbor-facing suite; rooms facing east stare directly at the concrete walls of the building next door.

5

921 W. Pender St., Vancouver, BC V6C 1M2. www.daysinnvancouver.com. ✆ **877/681-4335** or 604/681-4335. Fax 604/681-7808. 85 units. C$105–C$219 double. AE, DC, DISC, MC, V. Valet parking C$25. **Amenities:** Restaurant; bar; concierge; downtown shuttle (drop-off only). *In room:* A/C, TV w/pay movies, fridges (in all but standard rooms), hair dryer, Internet (free).

The Inn at False Creek ☺ 🍴 The Inn at False Creek is on the cusp of Yaletown, Downtown, Granville Island, and the West Side—which makes the location convenient to reach most Vancouver attractions. The decor is fresh and contemporary, and on-site amenities make this a good choice for this price range, but street traffic is ever-present as the hotel sits next to the Granville Bridge on-ramp. Although rooms at the back are preferable, the traffic noise is largely minimized in the front by double-pane windows and blackout curtains. Suites are great for families—some have full kitchens and narrow, glassed-in balconies. The Inn has a nice outdoor pool and private patio (open summer only).

1335 Howe St. (at Drake St.), Vancouver, BC V6Z 1R7. www.innatfalsecreek.com. ✆ **800/663-8474** or 604/682-0229. Fax 604/662-7566. 157 units. Oct–Apr C$90–C$150 double; May–Sept C$149–C$249 double. AE, DC, DISC, MC, V. Parking C$15. **Amenities:** Restaurant; bar; concierge; access to nearby health club; outdoor pool (summer only); room service. *In room:* A/C, TV w/pay movies, hair dryer, Wi-Fi (free).

Moda Hotel ★ 🛎 Situated downtown, across from the Orpheum Theatre and close to the clubs on Granville Street, the Moda offers lots of modern style and heritage flair for a superb value. Rooms and suites in this 1908 heritage building feature a sleek, tailored, European look with punchy colors, luxury beds and linens, flatscreen TVs, custom-tiled bathrooms with a tub/shower, and double-glazed windows to dampen the traffic noise. The only thing the refurbishers couldn't change was the slant in some of the old wooden floors. Anyone with a bit of adventure and a taste for something out of the ordinary will enjoy a stay here. Suites are located in a newer building across the street, and offer soaring ceilings, a wall of windows with lots of light, and upgraded amenities. Other pluses include the on-site wine bar **Uva** and a buzzing Italian restaurant called **Cibo.**

900 Seymour St., Vancouver, BC V6B 3L9. www.modahotel.ca. ✆ **877/683-5522** or 604/683-4251. Fax 604/683-0611. 67 units. C$100–C$230 deluxe double; C$220–C$290 suite. AE, DC, MC, V. **Amenities:** 2 restaurants; bar. *In room:* A/C, TV, Internet (free), minibar.

Inexpensive

Hostelling International Vancouver Downtown Hostel Located in a converted nunnery, this modern, curfew-free hostel offers a convenient base of operations for exploring downtown. The beach is a few blocks south; downtown is a 10-minute walk north. Most beds are in quad dorms, with a limited number of doubles and triples available. Except for two rooms with private bathrooms, all bathroom facilities are shared. Rooms and facilities are accessible for travelers with disabilities. There are common cooking facilities, as well as an enviable rooftop patio and game room with pool table. The hostel is extremely busy in the summertime, so book ahead. Many organized activities such as ski packages and tours can be booked at the hostel. The hostel also provides a free shuttle service to the bus/train station and Jericho Beach.

1114 Burnaby St. (at Thurlow St.), Vancouver, BC V6E 1P1. www.hihostels.ca. ✆ **888/203-4302** or 604/684-4565. Fax 604/684-4540. 67 units (44 4-person shared dorm rooms, 23 double or private rooms). C$30–C$35 dorm (IYHA members), C$33–C$39 dorm (nonmembers);

C$75–C$92 private (members), C$83 C$100 private (nonmembers). Rates include full breakfast. Annual adult membership C$35. MC, V. Limited free parking. **Amenities:** Bikes. *In room:* No phone, Wi-Fi (free).

The Kingston Hotel ⚓ An affordable downtown hotel is a rarity for Vancouver, but if you can do without the frills, the Kingston offers a clean, safe, inexpensive place to sleep and a complimentary continental breakfast to start your day. You won't find a better deal anywhere, and the premises have far more character than you'll find in a cookie-cutter motel, with a cozy lounge and a quiet clientele. The Kingston is a Vancouver version of the kind of small budget B&B hotels found all over Europe, and the manager is the fourth generation to head up this family-run hotel. Just 13 of the 52 rooms have private bathrooms; the rest have hand basins and shared showers and toilets on each floor. The premises are well kept, and the location is central, so you can walk everywhere. The staff is friendly and helpful, and if you're just looking for a place to sleep and stow your bags, you'll be glad you found this place.

757 Richards St., Vancouver, BC V6B 3A6. www.kingstonhotelvancouver.com. ℂ **888/713-3304** or 604/684-9024. Fax 604/684-9917. 52 units (13 with private bathroom). C$85–C$95 double with shared bathroom; C$105–C$175 double with private bathroom. Additional adult C$20. Senior discount. Rates include continental breakfast. AE, MC, V. Parking C$25 across the street. **Amenities:** Restaurant; bar; sauna. *In room:* TV (in units w/private bathrooms), Wi-Fi (free).

Ramada Inn and Suites The Ramada was converted from a rooming house into a tourist hotel, and has a fun, modern style that matches the adjacent weekend-only lounge and lively pub. The location is convenient for exploring downtown and Yaletown, as well as Granville Island or Kitsilano—but the south end of Granville, though gentrifying, is not yet a scenic or shopping area. The motel-like rooms were completely remodeled in 2010. For any kind of view, ask for a room facing Granville; otherwise, you may be looking out at a wall. Suites feature a sofa bed, kitchenette, and small dining area, making them useful for families. Guests have full access to a nearby sports club. The Ginger62 Ultra Lounge is a smart new addition.

1221 Granville St., Vancouver, BC V6Z 1M6. www.ramadavancouver.com. ℂ **888/835-0078** or 604/685-1111. Fax 604/685-0707. 116 units. C$90–C$260 double. Children 16 and under stay free in parent's room. AE, DC, DISC, MC, V. Valet parking C$15. **Amenities:** Restaurant; bar/lounge; access to nearby health club. *In room:* A/C, TV w/pay movies, hair dryer, kitchenette (in suites), Wi-Fi (free).

Urban Hideaway Guesthouse 🏠 World travelers Janine and Ken have created a quiet, creative guesthouse inside one of Vancouver's oldest buildings and the only remaining house downtown. Spaces—be it the well-stocked kitchen, rooftop garden, or two bathrooms—are shared, so a stay here is best suited to independent-minded folks who are okay with a communal feel. All rooms have European-style sinks and the loft bedroom has a private bathroom. Guest rooms tend to fill up well in advance. Allergy sufferers beware—there are two indoor cats in-residence.

581 Richards St., Vancouver, BC, V6B 2Z5. www.urban-hideaway.com. ℂ **604/694-0600.** 7 units. Oct–Apr C$70–C$110 double; May–Sept C$110–C$160 double. Breakfast included. **Amenities:** Bikes, kayaks, TV/DVD, kitchen.

5

WHERE TO STAY IN VANCOUVER

Downtown & Yaletown

YWCA Hotel/Residence ★ ⚡ This attractive 12-story residence next door to the Georgian Court Hotel is an excellent choice for travelers on limited budgets and attracts a large percentage of international travelers. Bedrooms are simply furnished; the basic, shared-bathroom singles, though, do not have TVs. Quite a few reasonably priced restaurants and a number of grocery stores are nearby. Three large and two small communal kitchens are available for guests' use, and all rooms have mini-fridges. The Y has three TV lounges and free access to the best gym in town, the nearby coed YWCA Fitness Centre. Perhaps best of all, the sales tax at this nonprofit hotel is only 3.5% and all proceeds support the YWCA's projects.

733 Beatty St., Vancouver, BC V6B 2M4. www.ywcahotel.com. ℭ **800/663-1424** or 604/895-5830. Fax 604/681-2550. 155 units (about ⅓ with private bathroom). C$70–C$90 double with shared bathroom; C$85–C$130 double with private bathroom. Weeklong discounts available. AE, MC, V. Parking C$12. **Amenities:** Access to YWCA facility. *In room:* A/C, TV, fridge, hair dryer, Wi-Fi (C$10/day).

THE WEST END

A 10-minute walk from downtown, the West End is green, leafy, and residential, a neighborhood of high-rise apartment houses, beautifully landscaped streets, and close to Coal Harbour, Stanley Park, and the best beaches. While downtown gets quiet at night, the West End starts hopping; dozens of restaurants, cafes, and bars line Robson, Davie, and Denman streets.

The West End's hotels are nestled along Robson Street and amid the tree-lined, garden-filled residential streets bordering Stanley Park. Have no fear: You will not be out of the loop if you stay here, though the area's relaxed, beachy ambience is very different from downtown. While the area has fewer hotels than downtown, the choices are more diverse—and so are the people who live here.

BEST FOR: Families who want to be close to beaches, the Seawall, and Stanley Park will love the West End. The neighborhood is also a favored destination for gay and lesbian travelers.

DRAWBACKS: Parking can be a hassle on the resident- and pedestrian-friendly streets. To counter that, become familiar with a few bus routes: namely the no. 5 Robson and no. 6 Davie.

Very Expensive

Westin Bayshore Resort & Marina ★★★ ☺ This is Vancouver's only resort hotel with its own marina, and the mountain and water views from all but a handful of its rooms are stunning. The Bayshore overlooks Coal Harbour and Stanley Park on one side, and Burrard Inlet and the city on the other. The hotel is in two buildings: the original low-rise from 1961 and a newer tower, with a giant pool, restaurant, and conference center between them. All the rooms, which received a makeover in 2009, are appointed with comfortable, contemporary West Coast decor and have floor-to-ceiling windows that open wide. In the newer tower, the rooms are a bit larger and have narrow balconies. The bathrooms in both buildings are nicely finished but fairly small. Children receive their own welcome package and will enjoy the indoor and outdoor pools.

1601 Bayshore Dr., Vancouver, BC V6G 2V4. www.westinbayshore.com. ℭ **800/937-8461** or 604/682-3377. Fax 604/687-3102. 511 units. C$460 double; C$560 suite. Children 17 and under stay free in parent's room. AE, DC, MC, V. Self-parking C$36; valet parking C$41. **Amenities:** 2

restaurants; bar; Starbucks; babysitting; concierge; health club; Jacuzzi; 2 pools (1 indoor, 1 outdoor); room service; sauna; spa. *In room:* A/C, TV w/pay movies, hair dryer, minibar, Wi-Fi (C$15/day).

Expensive

The Listel Hotel ★★ 🎒 What makes the Listel unique is its artwork in the guest rooms, meeting spaces, and common areas—but it's the headline Artist Series Suites that delight the most with collections by artists such as Otto Rogers, Carmelo Sortino, Bernard Gantner, and Jean Pierre Cassigneul. Hallways and suites on the top two Gallery floors are decorated with original pieces from the Buschlen Mowatt Gallery or, on the Museum floor, with First Nations artifacts from the Museum of Anthropology (p. 128). Also unique is the fact that the Listel is the first Vancouver hotel to really go "green" with the use of solar power-generating panels. The hotel is luxurious without being flashy, and all the rooms and bathrooms feature top-quality bedding and handsome furnishings—though some bathrooms are larger than others, with separate soaker tub and shower. The roomy upper-floor suites facing Robson Street, with glimpses of the harbor and the mountains beyond, are the best bets. Rooms at the back are quieter but face the alley and nearby apartment buildings. In the evenings, you can hear live jazz at **O'Doul's** (p. 194), the hotel's restaurant and bar. Downtown or Stanley Park is a 10-minute walk away.

1300 Robson St., Vancouver, BC V6E 1C5. www.thelistelhotel.com. ☏ **800/663-5491** or 604/684-8461. Fax 604/684-7092. 129 units. C$200–C$290 double; C$400–C$600 suite. AE, DC, DISC, MC, V. Parking C$26. **Amenities:** Restaurant; bar; concierge; executive-level rooms; exercise room; room service. *In room:* A/C, TV w/pay movies, hair dryer, minibar, Wi-Fi (free).

Moderate

Blue Horizon ⚓ This 31-story high-rise built in the 1960s has a great location on Robson Street, and underwent a top-to-bottom room renovation in 2011 that included new windows, fresh decor, and comfortable, modern furniture. Its rates remain a bargain almost year-round and upper floors have sweeping views; rooms feel a bit little like a high-rise motel but they are spacious and quiet. Most rooms are on a corner with wraparound windows and a balcony; superior rooms on floors 15 to 30 offer the best views. Book 05 and 07 rooms for a great vantage of the water and Stanley Park. Overall, the Blue Horizon is a good deal for this location. The hotel uses energy-efficient lighting, low-flow shower heads, and recycling bins, and the entire hotel is nonsmoking.

1225 Robson St., Vancouver, BC V6E 1C3. www.bluehorizonhotel.com. ☏ **800/663-1333** or 604/688-1411. Fax 604/688-4461. 214 units. C$100–C$220 double; C$110–C$230 superior double; C$190–C$330 suite. Children 15 and under stay free in parent's room. AE, DC, MC, V. Parking C$15. **Amenities:** Restaurant; small exercise room; Jacuzzi; indoor pool; sauna. *In room:* A/C, TV w/pay movies, fridge, hair dryer, Internet (free).

Coast Plaza Hotel & Suites ★ 😊 🎒 Built originally as an apartment building, this 35-story hotel atop Denman Place Mall has spacious floor plans and a superb location that attracts a wide variety of guests, from business travelers and tour groups to film and TV actors. They come for the nearby amenities, the affordable one- and two-bedroom suites, and great views of English Bay. The two-bedroom corner suites are bigger than most West End apartments and afford spectacular panoramas. The spacious one-bedroom suites and standard rooms feature floor-to-ceiling windows and balconies; about half the units have full kitchens, and all are nonsmoking. The proximity to parks and beaches will stand out for most families. While the hotel has a good-size heated pool that's great for kids to splash around, it's in the not-particularly appealing basement.

1763 Comox St., Vancouver, BC V6G 1P6. www.coasthotels.com. ℂ **800/716-6199** or 604/688-7711. Fax 604/688-5934. 269 units. C$140–C$280 double; C$170–C$310 suite. Children 18 and under stay free in parent's room. AE, DC, DISC, MC, V. Self-parking C$25; valet parking C$34. **Amenities:** Restaurant; bar; babysitting; concierge; access to health club in mall below; Jacuzzi; indoor pool; room service; sauna. *In room:* A/C, TV, fridge, hair dryer, Internet (free).

Empire Landmark   At 42 stories high, this tower hotel is the tallest building in the West End. But it's the lack of surrounding buildings that guarantees the awesome views of the mountains, Stanley Park, and the water. Here's the thing about the Empire Landmark: It's a big hotel that handles a lot of tour groups and conferences, so it feels pretty anonymous. The standardized rooms have been freshened up with bright, clean-lined furnishings, giving the rooms an urban feel. Some rooms decorated in an older, blander style remain on the lower floors. For the best panoramas, ask for a room on floor 20 or higher. The top floor features a revolving restaurant-lounge, **Cloud 9,** where you can have a drink with all of Vancouver spread out before you. Also in this hotel's favor is the location, right on Robson Street (ask about the shopping program, which provides discounts at select merchants), close to English Bay and Stanley Park. For smokers, the hotels is one of a decreasing number that still designates smoking guest rooms.

1400 Robson St. (btw. Broughton and Nicola sts.), Vancouver, BC V6G 1B9. www.empire landmarkhotel.com. ℂ **800/830-6144** or 604/687-0511. Fax 604/687-7267. 357 units. C$170–C$230 double. AE, DC, DISC, MC, V. Parking C$15/day. **Amenities:** Restaurant; bar. *In room:* A/C, TV, fridge, Wi-Fi (C$8/day).

Sunset Inn & Suites ★ ☺ ✍   Just a couple of blocks from English Bay on the edge of the residential West End, the family-owned Sunset Inn offers roomy studios or one-bedroom apartments with balconies and fully equipped kitchens. Like many other hotels in this part of town, the Sunset Inn started life as an apartment building (although briefly), meaning the rooms are larger than at your average hotel. Request an upper floor for better views; the executive rooms have been upgraded with touches like double vanities and rain showers. For those traveling with children, the one-bedroom suites have a separate bedroom and a pullout couch in the living room. All the rooms were refurbished in 2008 with ongoing upgrades since. The beds are comfy, the staff is helpful and friendly, and the location is great for this price. Also, parking is free: a convenience that will run hefty charges at all downtown hotels.

1111 Burnaby St., Vancouver, BC V6E 1P4. www.sunsetinn.com. ℂ **800/786-1997** or 604/688-2474. Fax 604/669-3340. 50 units. Oct–May C$90–C$160 studio, C$110–C$210 1-bedroom; June–Sept C$160–C$230 studio, C$180–$475 1-bedroom. Additional adult C$10. Children 9 and under stay free in parent's room. Rates include continental breakfast. Weekly rates available. AE, DC, MC, V. Free parking. **Amenities:** Small exercise room. *In room:* A/C, TV, kitchen, MP3 docking station, Wi-Fi (free).

The West End

WHERE TO STAY IN VANCOUVER

Sylvia Hotel   Lots of folks love the Sylvia, mostly for its fabulous location, and many are eager to recommend it, but pretty as the old girl is from the outside, inside she's a modest, plain-Jane sort of place. This is a "heritage building" hotel (the original wing, anyway) that underplays style and doesn't believe in glamour. That's why you're not going to find waterfront accommodations anywhere else at Sylvia's prices. If you do stay, the best rooms are located on the higher floors facing English Bay. Quirky room layouts range from small budget rooms to suites that have fully equipped kitchens and are large enough for families. The newer low-rise annex rooms offer less atmosphere. The location is superb in summer— close to English Bay, the outdoor Second Beach pool, and Stanley Park.

1154 Gilford St., Vancouver, BC V6G 2P6. www.sylviahotel.com. ℭ **604/681-9321.** Fax 604/682-3551. 120 units. May–Sept C$160–C$255 double; Oct–Apr C$120–C$175 double. Children 17 and under stay free in parent's room. AE, DC, MC, V. Parking C$15. **Amenities:** Restaurant; bar; concierge; room service. *In room:* TV, hair dryer, Internet (free).

West End Guest House ★ 🎁   A heritage home built in 1906, the West End Guest House is a handsome example of what the neighborhood looked like before concrete towers and condos replaced the original Edwardian homes in the early 1950s. Decorated with early-20th-century antiques and a serious collection of vintage photographs of Vancouver taken by the original owners, this gay-friendly B&B is a calm, charming respite from the hustle and bustle of the West End. The seven guest rooms feature feather mattresses and down duvets and one is allergy free with a silk duvet and foam mattress; the Grand Queen Suite, an attic-level bedroom with a brass bed, fireplace, sitting area, claw-foot bathtub, and skylights, is the best and most spacious room. Owner Evan Penner and his partner, Ron Cadarette, pamper their guests with a scrumptious breakfast and serve iced tea and sherry in the afternoon.

1362 Haro St., Vancouver, BC V6E 1G2. www.westendguesthouse.com. ℭ **888/546-3327** or 604/681-2889. Fax 604/688-8812. 7 units. Oct–May C$90–C$195 double; June–Sept C$200–C$275 double. Rates include full breakfast. AE, DISC, MC, V. Free off-street parking. **Amenities:** Bikes. *In room:* TV/DVD player, hair dryer, MP3 docking station, Wi-Fi (free).

Inexpensive

Buchan Hotel 🏂   Built in 1926, this three-story building is tucked away on a quiet residential street in the West End, and it's a bargain for the location: just 2 blocks from Stanley Park and Denman Street. Like the Kingston (see above) downtown, this is a small European-style budget hotel that doesn't bother with frills or charming decor; unlike the Kingston, it isn't a B&B, so don't expect the second B. The standard rooms are quite plain; be prepared for close quarters and tiny bathrooms, half of which are shared. The best rooms are the executive rooms: four nicely furnished front-corner rooms with private bathrooms. Historic touches throughout the property include heritage photographs and inlaid hardwood floors. The hotel also has in-house bike and ski storage, a patio restaurant, and a reading lounge.

1906 Haro St., Vancouver, BC V6G 1H7. www.buchanhotel.com. ℭ **800/668-6654** or 604/685-5354. Fax 604/685-5367. 60 units (29 with private bathroom). C$60–C$85 double with shared bathroom; C$75–C$120 double with private bathroom; C$110–C$155 executive room. Children 12 and under stay free in parent's room. Weekly rates available. AE, DC, MC, V. Limited parking C$10. **Amenities:** Lounge. *In room:* TV, hair dryer, no phone, Wi-Fi ($2/day).

THE WEST SIDE

Right across False Creek from downtown and the West End is Vancouver's West Side, where you'll find cozy B&Bs and hotels. It's the perfect location if your agenda includes a stop at Granville Island, exploration of the laid-back Kitsilano neighborhood and Kits Beach, visits to the Museum of Anthropology and famed gardens on the University of British Columbia campus, seeing the sunken garden at Queen Elizabeth Park, or being close to the airport without staying in an "airport hotel."

BEST FOR: The West Side is a haven for repeat visitors to Vancouver who don't mind a quick bus ride to downtown as well as foodies who love to explore the culinary markets, fisheries docks, and unheralded ethnic eateries.

DRAWBACKS: This is not an ideal base for those in town for the nightlife in Gastown and along Granville Street.

Expensive

Granville Island Hotel ★ 🏨   One of Vancouver's best-kept secrets, this hotel is tucked away on the edge of Granville Island in a unique waterfront setting, a short stroll from theaters, galleries, and the fabulous Granville Island public market (p. 125). Rooms in the original wing are definitely fancier, so book these if you can, but the new wing is fine, too. Rooms are fairly spacious with decor hinting at the nautical location and large bathrooms with soaker tubs and rain showers; some units have balconies and great views over False Creek. If you don't have a car, the only potential drawback to a stay here is the location. During the daytime, when the False Creek ferries are running, it's a quick ferry ride to Yaletown or the West End. After 10pm, however, you're looking at a C$15 to C$20 cab ride or an hour walk. The Island after dark is reasonably happening, and the hotel's waterside restaurant and brewpub are good-weather hangout spots with outdoor seating.

1253 Johnston St., Vancouver, BC V6H 3R9. www.granvilleislandhotel.com. ✆ **800/663-1840** or 604/683-7373. Fax 604/683-3061. 82 units. Oct–Apr starting at C$160 double, C$400 penthouse; May–Sept starting at C$260 double, C$500 penthouse. AE, DC, DISC, MC, V. Parking C$12. **Amenities:** Restaurant; brewpub; babysitting; small fitness room; Jacuzzi; room service; sauna; access to nearby tennis courts. *In room:* A/C, TV w/pay movies, hair dryer, minibar, Wi-Fi (free).

Inexpensive

Hostelling International Vancouver Jericho Beach Hostel   Located in a former military barracks, this hostel (May–Sept only) is surrounded by an expansive park adjacent to Jericho Beach. Individuals, families with children, and groups are welcome, although children 4 and under must stay with parents in a private room. The nine private rooms can accommodate up to four people each. These particular accommodations go fast, so if you want one, call far in advance. The dormitory-style arrangements are well maintained and supervised. Linens are provided. Basic, inexpensive food is served in the cafe, or you can cook for yourself in the shared kitchen. The hostel's program director operates tours and activities.

1515 Discovery St., Vancouver, BC V6R 4K5. ✆ **888/203-4303** or 604/224-3208. Fax 604/224-4852. www.hihostels.ca. 252 beds in 15 dorms; 9 private family units (without private bathroom). C$27–C$36 dorm (IYHA members), C$31–C$40 dorm (nonmembers); C$65–C$95 private room (members), C$73–C$103 private room (nonmembers). MC, V. Parking C$6. Bus: 4. Children 4 and under must stay in a private room. **Amenities:** Cafe; bikes. *In room:* No phone, Wi-Fi (free).

The University of British Columbia Conference Centre ★ ✦ The University of British Columbia Conference Centre is in a pretty, forested setting on the tip of Point Grey, convenient to Kitsilano and the University itself. If you don't have a car, it's a half-hour bus ride from downtown. Although the on-campus accommodations are actually student dorms most of the year, rooms are usually available. The rooms are nice, and many are being updated with a sleek, west coast decor. The 17-story Walter Gage Residence offers comfortable accommodations, many on the upper floors with sweeping views of the city and ocean. One-bedroom suites come equipped with private bathrooms, kitchenettes, TVs, and phones. Each studio has a twin bed; each one-bedroom features a queen-size bed; a six-bed Towers room—a particularly good deal for families—features one double bed and five twin beds. The West Coast Suites, with a fresh Pacific style, are the most appealing and have a very reasonable price. A continental breakfast buffet at the Student Union Building cafeteria is included with all rooms.

5961 Student Union Blvd., Vancouver, BC V6T 2C9. www.ubcconferences.com. ℂ **888/822-1030** or 604/822-1000. Fax 604/822-1001. 1,500 units. Walter Gage Residence units available approx. May 11–Aug 25; Pacific Spirit Hostel units available May 15–Aug 15; West Coast Suites and Marine Drive Residence units available year-round. Walter Gage Residences and Marine Drive Residences C$46–C$57 single with shared bathroom, C$120–C$140 studio, C$150–C$180 suite; Pacific Spirit Hostel C$33–C$35 single, C$65–C$70 double; West Coast Suites C$160–C$200 suite. AE, MC, V. Parking C$7. Bus: 4, 14, 44, 84, or 99. **Amenities** (on campus): Restaurant; cafeteria; pub; fitness center; access to campus Olympic size swimming pool; sauna (C$5/person); tennis courts. *In room:* TV, hair dryer, Wi-Fi (free).

THE EAST SIDE

Vancouver's East Side is an up-and-coming art district, especially around the Main Street–Mount Pleasant area. The streets are lined with residential heritage homes, often renovated into apartments. Shopping along Commercial Drive makes for a fun exploration of cooperative businesses and unique boutiques.

BEST FOR: Truly independent travelers will thrill in discovering the East Van art scene.

DRAWBACKS: There isn't a concentration of attractions on the East Side; instead, expect artist studios, community cafes, and craft markets.

Moderate

Commercial Drive Accommodations Close to Commercial Drive with its lively shopping, dining, and bar scene, these short-stay apartments blend international touches with a flair of Art Deco design to create modern, livable spaces. The top-floor, one-bedroom Inukshuk loft has a large deck overlooking the quiet backyard. Art books and extra touches (like a sewing kit, playing cards, and sticky notes) make the apartments fabulously comfortable, as does the in-suite laundry, overstocked kitchen, and separate dining area. There's a luxe two-bedroom apartment on the main floor and a three-bedroom basement suite. Owner Joanne Renwick also operates the **House on Dunbar B&B** (3926 West 20 Ave.; www.houseondunbarbandb.com; ℂ **604/786-6355**) on Vancouver's West Side.

Staying on the North Shore (North Vancouver & West Vancouver)

The North Shore cities of North and West Vancouver are pleasant, lush, and much less hurried than Vancouver. Staying here also offers easy access to the North Shore mountains, including hiking trails (such as the Grouse Grind, or "Nature's Stairmaster"); the Capilano Suspension Bridge and Park; and the ski slopes on Mount Seymour, Grouse Mountain, and Cypress Bowl. The disadvantage is that if you want to take your car into Vancouver, there are only two bridges, and during rush hour, they're painfully slow. The passenger-only Sea-Bus, however, is quick, scenic, inexpensive (C$3.75), and runs until after midnight.

The **Lonsdale Quay Hotel** (123 Carrie Cates Court; www.lonsdalequayhotel.com; *©* **800/836-6111** or 604/986-6111), across Burrard Inlet from Canada Place, sits at the water's edge above the convenient and busy Lonsdale Quay Market, and adjacent to the SeaBus terminal. A few of the 70 rooms have 180-degree harbor and city views, while the majority look down on the docks and boats of the working waterfront. The hotel has the feeling of a cruise ship with its long halls. Doubles run C$140 to C$450.

With more amenities, however, is the largely undiscovered 106-room **Pinnacle Hotel at the Pier** (138 Victory Ship Way; www.pinnaclehotelatthepier.com; *©* **877/986-7437** or 604/986-7437). Opened in 2010, the property offers comfortable rooms with great skyline views of Vancouver, modern bathrooms with glass dividing walls so you can savor the view while you soak in the tub, an indoor pool and state-of-the-art fitness center (with a 25m pool), a good restaurant, and a convenient location next to the market at Lonsdale Quay and close to several North Shore restaurants. Rates for a double room begin at C$150 in low season (Oct–May), and C$199 in high season (June–Sept).

1734 E. 1st Ave., Vancouver, BC V5N 1B1. www.commercialdriveaccommodations.com. *©* **604/ 786-6355.** 3 units. C$140–C$325 suites. 2-night minimum. Weekly and monthly rates available. AE, MC, V. Free off-street parking. Bus: 20. *In room:* A/C, TV, phone, full kitchen, washer/dryer, Wi-Fi (free).

The Waldorf Hotel *☙* Originally transformed into a Tiki bar in 1955, the Waldorf Hotel reopened in 2010 with a modern take on its unique history. A neon palm tree still dons the streetside sign, but extensive renovations inside have reworked the space with sultry tones and Polynesian touches, including original velvet paintings by Edgar Leeteg. In the guest rooms, walls screened in bamboo, fresh linens, and original art create tranquil spaces away from the buzzing scene. Budget-friendly on-site restaurants (serving Mexican, Spanish, and Lebanese cuisines) are filled with an artsy, urban crowd that comes for the almost nightly events, be it film screenings, art shows, burlesque, or DJs. The downside of a stay here is that the hotel is smack in the middle of an otherwise markless stretch of East Hastings. But if you're game to explore outside downtown, the location won't faze you much.

1489 E. Hastings, Vancouver, BC V5L 1S4. www.waldorfhotel.com. *©* **604/253-7141.** 30 units. C$95–C$110 double. AE, MC, V. Free parking. Bus: 14. **Amenities:** Restaurant, bar. *In room:* TV, minibar, Wi-Fi (free).

PRACTICAL INFORMATION
The Big Picture

As an urban hub, Vancouver hotels tend to be well-equipped with technology. Most hotels have updated to flatscreen TVs and Wi-Fi, and many luxury properties have dataports to connect an array of devices. You'll find more hotels are smoke free, save a few like the Empire Landmark (p 78).

As a young city that completely burnt to the ground in 1886, Vancouver can be devoid of historic charm at times. Some of the larger hotels lack architectural character and blend in with the "Glass City" skyline, while it's the small boutique properties that deliver a delightful dose of heritage style.

One thing to keep in mind when booking a room downtown is that hotels on **Granville Street** (the Best Western Downtown Vancouver and the Ramada Inn and Suites) offer a central location without the high price tag, but the area they're in is not high-gloss (yet). Granville Street looks much better now, however, than it has for years. After a makeover in 2009, it is becoming trendy because of its large concentration of bars, lounges, and clubs, and has been dubbed the "Entertainment District." It's not dangerous, but be prepared for noisy revelry on warm summer Friday and Saturday nights.

Bus and/or public transportation information is given only for those hotels listed above that are outside of the Vancouver city center.

The opening of new hotels eased off following the 2010 Olympic Winter Games, and the months since have mostly seen re-openings of historic properties that have undergone multi-million-dollar renovations. The newly reopened **Rosewood Hotel Georgia** (p. 69) dates to 1927 and offers a fabulous location overlooking the Vancouver Art Gallery. **The Waldorf Hotel** (p. 82) is a fresh, welcomed concept of an artists' hub—renovations have revitalized the historic Tiki Bar and hotel. Although on traffic-heavy Burrard Street, **the Burrard** (p. 73) has been made over with a young urban polish that marks a fine balance of comfort, location, and price.

 Fido-Friendly Hotels

Vancouver is one of the dog-friendliest cities in the world. Nearly all downtown and West End hotels allow you to check in your canine companion, usually for an added daily charge of C$25 to C$75. The Fairmont Hotel Vancouver also has two canine ambassadors—Mavis and Beau—who greet dog and human guests.

Getting the Best Deal

Although Vancouver boasts a full complement of accommodations—from hostels and guest houses to luxury waterfront suites—rooms do fill up during the high-season (June–Sept) and when large conferences land in the city. Rates in the city fluctuate quite predictably with the seasons. Most properties offer package deals outside the busy season; these are usually advertised on hotel websites.

Also look online to find properties that offer a best-rate guarantee. With more travelers turning online to find the cheap deals, hotels are countering with promises to match or beat any online deal—often offering cash or points rewards for booking directly with them. Some in Vancouver that were advertising such guarantees in mid-2011 include the **Sutton Place** (p. 69), **Opus** (p. 68), **Georgian Court** (p. 71), **Moda Hotel** (p. 74), and the **Pinnacle Hotel at the Pier** (p. 82).

Reservation Services

Reservations are highly recommended May to September and during holidays. For additional information, call **Hello BC** at ℂ **800/435-5622** or 800/663-6000. You can also book a room by going to **Tourism Vancouver,** 200 Burrard St. (across from Canada Place), or by visiting **www.tourismvancouver.com**.

Alternative Accommodations

The majority of properties listed in this chapter are hotels, with a few hostels, bed-and-breakfasts and short-stay apartments included. Within these latter accommodation types, Vancouver boasts many more options that are listed earlier in the chapter. Bed-and-breakfasts especially can vary widely (from fussy frills to sleek and urban) and can be ideal for leisure travelers. For a list of quality local accommodations, check out **BC Bed & Breakfast Innkeepers Guild** (www.bcsbestbnbs.com).

Practical Information

WHERE TO STAY IN VANCOUVER

6

WHERE TO EAT IN VANCOUVER

ou may be surprised at the sophistication of Vancouver's food scene. It's a place with an established food culture, celebrity chefs, and soap (soup?) opera-ish twists and turns that are grist for the gourmet gossip mills. That's part of the fun, of course, but it also means that the food scene is constantly changing and evolving and reinventing itself.

BEST VANCOUVER DINING BETS

○ **Best Sustainable Dining:** There are two standouts in this category. **Raincity Grill** was one of the first Vancouver eateries to source all its products locally and responsibly, and it features a memorable "100 Mile" menu with food harvested, caught, or grown within 100 miles of Vancouver. See p. 97. Frank Pabst, the chef at **Blue Water Cafe and Raw Bar,** creates fabulously inventive dishes using only wild and sustainably harvested seafood. See p. 87.

○ **Best Pacific Northwest Cuisine: West** is the best—for an all-around, upscale, Pacific Northwest dining experience. But don't just take my word for it. This storied West Side eatery wins annual accolades, including an enduring top-three spot in *Vancouver* magazine's "Best Restaurant" category. See p. 100.

○ **Best View:** For a combination of top-notch food and a killer view of mountains, Burrard Inlet, and Stanley Park, try **Lift.** See p. 96.

○ **Best Chinese Cuisine:** The best Vancouver Chinese remains **Sun Sui Wah.** It's definitely worth the trip, although you need a group of at least four to sample a variety of dishes. See p. 104.

○ **Best Newcomer: Bao Bei** serves a series of inventive small Brasserie-style plates in its cheeky Gastown dining room. See p. 94.

○ **Best Sushi and Sashimi:** If you're looking for the best sushi and sashimi in Vancouver, **Tojo's Restaurant** is the place to go. It's expensive, but you'll be treated to the freshest fish and most exquisitely prepared seafood delicacies in BC. See p. 99.

○ **Best Outdoor Dining:** It's not fine dining, but for unsurpassed ocean views from Ferguson Point, reserve a table under the trees at the **Teahouse in Stanley Park.** This patio also doubles as the **best place to watch the sunset.** See p. 97.

PREVIOUS PAGE: The food is as sublime as the views at C.

price **CATEGORIES**

Very Expensive	Entrees C$30 and up
Expensive	C$20–C$29
Moderate	C$12–C$19
Inexpensive	Under C$12

DOWNTOWN & YALETOWN
Very Expensive

Blue Water Cafe + Raw Bar ★★★ SEAFOOD   If you had to describe this busy, buzzy place in one word, it would be *fresh*, as only the best from sustainable and wild fisheries make it onto the menu. In fact, Blue Water won the top prize for "Best Seafood" and "Best Formal Restaurant" in the 2011 *Vancouver* magazine restaurant awards. If you love sushi and sashimi, the raw bar under the direction of Yoshiya Maruyama offers up some of the city's finest. On the other side of the room, Frank Pabst, the restaurant's executive chef, creates his dishes in a large open kitchen. For starters, try a medley of local oysters with various toppings, a sushi platter, or smoked sockeye salmon velouté. Main courses depend on whatever is in season: It might be spring salmon, halibut, Arctic char, tuna, white sturgeon, or BC sablefish. The desserts are fabulous. A masterful wine list and an experienced sommelier assure fine wine pairings.

1095 Hamilton St. (at Helmcken St.). ℭ **604/688-8078.** www.bluewatercafe.net. Reservations recommended. Main courses C$25–C$46. AE, DC, MC, V. Daily 5–11pm. Valet parking C$10.

C ★★★ SEAFOOD/PACIFIC NORTHWEST   Since opening in 1997, the popularity of this award-winning trendsetter hasn't flagged. The dining room is a cool white space with painted steel and lots of glass; the waterside location on False Creek is sublime (book an outside table if the weather is fine). Ingredients make all the difference here: The chef and his highly knowledgeable staff can tell you not only where every product comes from, but also the name of the boat or farm. Expect exquisite surprises and imaginative preparations: For appetizers, sample the fresh BC oysters with tongue-tingling sauces, spot prawns, or the Pemberton beetroot salad. Mains are artfully created and might include slow-cooked sturgeon, sablefish with lobster gnocchi, or roasted duck with an apricot puree. Give executive chef Robert Clark a chance to show off, and order a six-course tasting menu or seafood platter as you watch the sun set over the marina. Excellent wine pairings, too.

1600 Howe St. ℭ **604/681-1164.** www.crestaurant.com. Reservations recommended. Main courses C$29–C$55; tasting menus C$84–C$175. AE, DC, MC, V. Daily 11:30am–2:30pm and 5–11pm. Valet parking C$7.

Diva at the Met ★ PACIFIC NORTHWEST   Diva's three-story lounge with a giant wall of glass makes for an elegant dining experience at breakfast, lunch, or dinner. **Yew** (p. 92), the scene-stealer at the Four Seasons, has lured away some of the business, but Diva still attracts diners who appreciate attentive service and good food. Chef Quang Dang's menu draws from the best of seasonal seafood and local meats served with an international flair. Appetizers might include warm

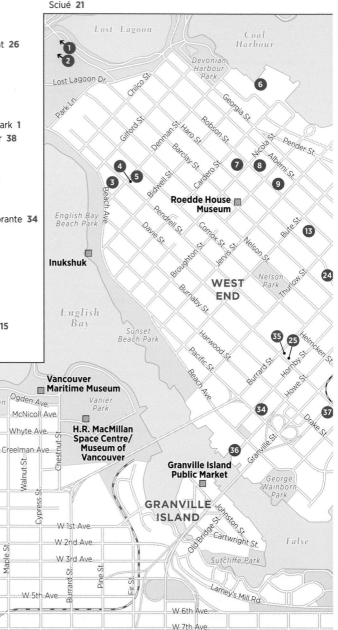

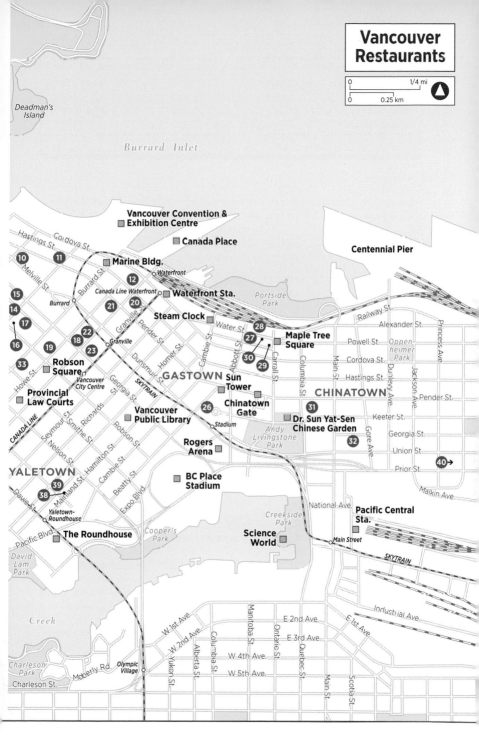

Vancouver Restaurants

0 ____ 1/4 mi
0 ____ 0.25 km

Deadman's Island

Burrard Inlet

Vancouver Convention & Exhibition Centre

Canada Place

Centennial Pier

Hastings St.

Cordova St.

Melville St.

⑩ ⑪

Marine Bldg.

Burrard St.

⑫

Waterfront

Canada Line Waterfront

Waterfront Sta.

Portside Park

⑮

Burrard

㉑ ⑳

Granville

Steam Clock

Water St.

㉘

Railway St.

Alexander St.

⑭

Pender St.

㉗

Maple Tree Square

Powell St.

Oppenheimer Park

Princess Ave.

⑰

㉒

Granville

⑱

Homer St.

㉚

Cordova St.

Jackson Ave.

⑯

⑲

㉓

Dunsmuir St.

Cambie St.

Abbott St.

㉙

Carrall St.

Columbia St.

Hastings St.

Main St.

Dunlevy Ave.

Pender St.

㉝

Robson Square

Vancouver City Centre

Georgia St.

SKYTRAIN

GASTOWN

Sun Tower

CHINATOWN

Keeter St.

Gore Ave.

Howe St.

Provincial Law Courts

Seymour St.

Richards St.

Robson St.

Vancouver Public Library

Chinatown Gate

㉛

Georgia St.

Nelson St.

Smithe St.

Hamilton St.

Cambie St.

㉖

Stadium

Dr. Sun Yat-Sen Chinese Garden

㉜

Union St.

CANADA LINE

Beatty St.

Rogers Arena

Andy Livingstone Park

Prior St.

㊵→

YALETOWN

Mainland St.

Expo Blvd.

BC Place Stadium

National Ave.

Malkin Ave.

㊴

Dawe St.

㊳

Yaletown-Roundhouse

Cooper's Park

Creekside Park

Pacific Central Sta.

David Lam Park

Pacific Blvd.

The Roundhouse

Science World

Main Street

SKYTRAIN

Creek

W 1st Ave.

W 2nd Ave.

Manitoba St.

E 2nd Ave.

E 3rd Ave.

E 1st Ave.

Industrial Ave.

Charleson Park

Moberly Rd.

Olympic Village

Yukon St.

Alberta St.

Columbia St.

Ontario St.

W 4th Ave.

W 5th Ave.

Quebec St.

Main St.

Scotia St.

Charleson St.

EATING ON A budget

If you're a foodie on a budget, then be sure to check out the 2-week event called Dine Out Vancouver, held in late January and early February. The event offers the opportunity to dine at over 200 of Vancouver's best restaurants for an amazing price of C$18, C$28, or C$38 for a 3-course meal. Visit **Tourism Vancouver** (www.tourismvancouver.com) for more details.

Dungeness crab salad, sherry-glazed squab, or short rib ravioli; mains include Fraser River salmon with a clam broth, lamb sirloin with orzo and fennel, or duck with mustard spaetzle. Diva's wine list is regularly rated one of the best in town. In the Metropolitan Hotel (p. 72), 645 Howe St. ℂ **604/602-7788.** www.metropolitan.com/diva. Reservations recommended. Main courses breakfast C$8–C$24, lunch C$16–C$28, dinner C$19–C$34; tasting menus C$69–C$95. AE, DC, DISC, MC, V. Daily 6:30am–11pm. Bus: 4 or 7.

Joe Fortes Seafood and Chop House ★ SEAFOOD   Named after the burly Caribbean seaman who became English Bay's first lifeguard, Joe Fortes is great if you're hankering for fresh seafood served the "old-fashioned" way, without a lot of modern culinary intrusions. The downstairs dining room evokes a kind of turn-of-the-20th-century saloon elegance, but if the weather's fine, try for a table on the rooftop patio. Stick with the seafood because it's what they do best, and most items are served simply and generally grilled with butter. The selection of seasonal oysters (Joe Fortes has the best oyster bar in Vancouver) is a Canadian sampling of renowned shellfish from both coasts. The famous seafood tower comes with an iced assortment of marinated mussels, poached prawns, scallop ceviche, Atlantic lobster, tuna sashimi, Manila clams, Dungeness crab, and local beach oysters. They also offer a good, fixed-price, three-course dinner for early diners. The wine list is well-rounded, with many BC wines available by the glass. 777 Thurlow St. (at Robson St.). ℂ **604/669-1940.** www.joefortes.ca. Reservations recommended. Main courses C$18–C$65; fixed-price dinner (from 4–6pm) C$29. AE, DC, DISC, MC, V. Daily 11am–11pm. Valet parking C$7. Bus: 5.

Expensive

Chambar Belgian Restaurant ★★ 🍴 BELGIAN   One of Vancouver's favorite restaurants, Chambar occupies an intriguing space in a kind of no man's land on lower Beatty Street between Yaletown and Gastown. Michelin-trained chef Nico Schuermans and his wife, Karri, have worked hard to make the place a success, and plenty of plaudits have come their way. The menu features small and large plates. Smaller choices typically include mussels cooked in white wine with bacon and cream (or with tomatoes and coconut cream), pistachio and chicken liver pâté, or coquilles St. Jacques. Main dishes feature *tagine* of braised lamb shank with honey, and sesame halibut with a squid tagliatelle salad. For dessert, try the espresso cheesecake with Belgian chocolate mousse or the lavender-milk chocolate pot de crème. Chambar specializes in Belgian beers, with some 40 varieties in bottles and on tap. 562 Beatty St. ℂ **604/879-7119.** www.chambar.com. Reservations recommended. Small plates C$13–C$22; main courses C$29–C$33; 3-course set menu C$60. AE, MC, V. Daily 5pm–midnight. Bus: 5 or 17.

Coast ★★★ SEAFOOD/INTERNATIONAL   This dashing restaurant moved to a new downtown location in 2009 and re-established itself as a culinary and people-watching spot of note. The concept at Coast is to offer an extensive variety of fresh and non-endangered seafood from coasts around the world. The dining room is a handsomely designed affair with a central oyster bar and seating at various levels, including a second floor that allows you to look out over the busy scene below. Coast excels at just about everything it does, and the price for top-quality seafood is actually quite reasonable. The signature seafood platter, for example, comes with halibut, wild sea tiger prawns, sockeye salmon, Qualicum scallops, vegetables, and potato gnocchi, and costs only C$34 per person. Try the super sushi (the innovative sushi chef has come up with a delectable fish-and-chips hand roll), or any of the fresh fish or shellfish offerings. Service here is deft, friendly, and always on the mark. Next door, O Lounge serves sushi and cocktails in a long narrow room of low-slung couches and high-top onyx tables.

1054 Alberni St. ⓒ **604/685-5010.** www.coastrestaurant.ca. Reservations recommended. Main courses C$18–C$46. AE, DC, MC, V. Mon–Thurs 11:30am–1am; Fri 11:30am–2am; Sat 4:30pm–2am; Sun 4:30pm–1am. Bus: 5 or 22.

Hawksworth Restaurant ★★★ PACIFIC NORTHWEST/SEAFOOD   On the street-level of the new Rosewood Hotel Georgia, Hawksworth Restaurant is the design of its namesake—Vancouver chef David Hawksworth. Three sections—a lounge, bright pearl room, and tranquil art room create a vibe that is at once intimate and buzzy. Dishes are Canadian twists on familiar plates: Start with the charred octopus salad or 72-hour beef short ribs served with a black pepper jam, before moving on to Sooke River trout with brown butter, or grilled sturgeon crowned with a bacon consommé. Hawksworth presents dishes with a fabulously creative flair that assures the restaurant will be a new Vancouver favorite.

In the Rosewood Hotel Georgia (p. 69), 801 W. Georgia St. ⓒ **604/673-7000.** www.hawksworth restaurant.com. Reservations recommended. Main courses C$20–C$30. AE, MC, V. Mon–Fri 6:30–10am and 11:30am–2pm; Sat–Sun 7am–2:30pm; daily for dinner 5–11pm.

Il Giardino di Umberto Ristorante ★★ ITALIAN   Restaurant magnate Umberto Menghi started a small restaurant, tucked away in a yellow heritage house at the bottom of Hornby Street, nearly 4 decades ago. It still serves some of the best Italian fare, and has one of the prettiest garden patios in town. This larger restaurant now adjoins Umberto's in the original house. The bright, spacious dining room re-creates the ambience of an Italian villa and the menu leans toward Tuscany, with dishes that emphasize pasta and game. Entrees usually include classics such as *osso buco* with saffron risotto, and that Roman favorite, spaghetti carbonara. A daily list of specials makes the most of seasonal fresh ingredients, often offering outstanding seafood dishes. The wine list is comprehensive and well chosen.

1382 Hornby St. (btw. Pacific and Drake sts.). ⓒ **604/669-2422.** www.umberto.com. Reservations recommended. Main courses C$20–C$44. AE, DC, MC, V. Mon–Fri 11:30am–3:30pm; Mon–Sat 5:30–11pm. Closed Sun and holidays. Bus: 22.

Le Crocodile ★ FRENCH   A secluded dining room gives way to delectable dishes presented by chef Michel Jacob. Le Crocodile is named for Michelin three-starred Au Crocodile in Strasbourg, France, but the seasonal ingredients such as white asparagus or spot prawns add a soupçon of West Coast. The

five-course tasting menu changes weekly to incorporate new offerings. Start with the subtle and comforting tomato and gin soup or escargot in pastry, followed by a main course Provençale-style lamb shank or duck with foie gras and an apple cider reduction. Service is attentive and the dining room private, busy, and casual.
100-909 Burrard St. ℭ **604/669-4298.** www.lecrocodilerestaurant.com. Reservations recommended. Main courses lunch C$14–C$38; dinner C$27–C$42. 5-course tasting menu C$75. AE, MC, V. Mon–Fri 11:30am–2:30pm; Mon–Thurs 5:30–10pm; Fri–Sat 5:30–10:30pm. Closed Sun.

MARKET by Jean-Georges ★★★ FUSION/INTERNATIONAL Jean-Georges Vongerichten is one of the world's most famous chefs, and his first restaurant in Vancouver is a paean to his long and highly successful career. You might call the menu here "The Greatest Hits of Jean-Georges" because what's on offer are the dishes he has perfected in his score of other restaurants. Try the sablefish in a nut-and-seed crust with sweet-and-sour broth, or soy-glazed short ribs with apple-jalapeño puree. The restaurant is calmly chic and not at all fussy. The place is usually packed, and it should be, because the fixed-price lunch and dinner menus list a selection of wonderful dishes at a remarkably reasonable price.
1115 Alberni St. (Level 3 in the Shangri-La Hotel). ℭ **604/695-1115.** Reservations recommended. Main courses C$16–C$44; fixed-price lunch C$35; tasting menu C$68. AE, DC, DISC, MC, V. Restaurant and cafe daily 7am–10:30pm; bar Sun–Wed 11:30am–midnight; Thurs–Sat 11:30am–1am.

Yew ★★ PACIFIC NORTHWEST/FUSION A multi-million-dollar makeover in 2008 transformed the old garden court dining room at the Four Seasons Hotel into a handsome new bar-lounge-restaurant that's drawing a whole new crowd of diners and lounge lizards. A sandstone fireplace divides the lounge area from the restaurant with its raw bar and open kitchen, but you can order from the same menu wherever you sit. For a delicious shared appetizer, try the lobster and mango roll with a sweet chili dipping sauce. Then choose fresh fish or oysters from the raw bar, or dine on one of the fish, meat, or pasta dishes from the kitchen. Comfort foods include a lobster macaroni and cheese and a lamb meatloaf panini, while noteworthy mains are the roasted venison with brown butter and sage jus or the miso-glazed sablefish. Wine lovers take note: With a two-glass minimum, you can order wine by the glass from any of the more than 300 available vintages.
In the Four Seasons Hotel (p. 65), 791 W. Georgia St. ℭ **604/692-4939.** www.yewrestaurant.com. Reservations recommended. Main courses C$18–C$36. AE, DC, DISC, MC, V. Daily 6:30am–midnight. Bus: 4, 7, 10, or 14.

Moderate

Bin 941 Tapas Parlour ★ TAPAS/CASUAL Still booming a decade after it opened its door, Bin 941 remains the place for trendy tapas dining. True, the music's too loud and the room's too small with carnival-esque mirrors, but the food that alights on the bar and eight tiny tables is delicious and fun, and the wine list is great. Look especially for local seafood such as scallops and tiger prawns. In this sliver of a bistro, sharing is unavoidable, so come prepared for socializing as you enjoy "tapatizers," or the renowned chocolate fondue. The tables start to fill up at 6:30pm, and by 8pm, the hip and hungry have already formed a long and eager line.
941 Davie St. ℭ **604/683-1246.** www.bin941.com. Reservations not accepted. Plates C$8–C$18. MC, V. Daily 5pm–1:30am. Bus: 4, 6, 7, or 10.

CHEAP, QUICK EATS DOWNTOWN: VANCOUVER food trucks

Making a major move beyond hotdogs and chestnuts, Vancouver's street food scene has expanded exponentially since 2010. A change to legislation allowed an initial 17 vendors to park their trucks on Vancouver streets, and in 2011 the city granted another 19 licenses and additional licenses for roaming vendors.

Food trucks can change location at the last minute, so follow them on Twitter or download an iPhone food truck app to confirm the locations.

Japadog The old-school stalwart of Vancouver street food, the innovative Japanese hot dog stand still grills its Kurabata and Bratwurst, serving them topped with miso, nori, and edamame. There's also a restaurant location at 530 Robson St. Twitter: @japadog

The Kaboom Box Easy to find at Robson and Granville streets, this red truck's smoked salmon "salmwich" is already being called world-famous. The salmon is smoked on-site and the fish is Ocean Wise certified sustainable. Fresh and local ingredients are the overarching theme, with a venison burger and oyster po'boy also on the menu. Twitter: @thekaboombox

La Brasserie The food truck extension of the West End restaurant of the same name, this mobile kitchen situated on West Georgia and Granville streets keeps things simple with a single sandwich: pulled chicken topped with French-fried onions on a buttermilk bun. A little gravy keeps the sandwich moist while mustard adds a distinct zip. Twitter: @La_Brasserie

The Re-Up BBQ Likewise here, there's just one sandwich on the menu, and thanks to the tangy-spicy secret sauce the sandwich is entirely memorable. Re-up serves its pulled pork outside the Vancouver Art Gallery, at Hornby and West Georgia streets. Twitter: @reupbbq

Roaming Dragon Vying for Vancouver's favorite street snack with its Chinese pork belly sliders and Korean short rib tacos, the Roaming Dragon truck regularly changes parking spots to serve Pan-Asian cuisine at farmers' markets and charity events, as well as its most-regular Burrard and Robson location. Twitter: @roamingdragon

glowbal grill steak & satay bar ★★ FUSION   glowbal has occupied a top spot in the trendy Yaletown dining scene since 2002 and started the craze for succulent satays of grilled meat or fish served with a dipping sauce. In 2009, it revamped, reinvented, and reinvigorated itself as a steakhouse (though the satays are still available); all prime cuts are on display in a meat case. Have one of their famous martinis as you peruse the menu and sample some of the delicious satays as an appetizer, then order a steak or the signature Kobe meatballs. As the evening rolls on, the in-crowd rolls into Afterglow, the small lounge behind the dining room. If you want to try the food but avoid the scene, go for the reasonably priced lunch Monday to Friday. glowbal also has one of the best Saturday and Sunday brunches in town.

1079 Mainland St. ℭ **604/602-0835.** www.glowbalgrill.com. Reservations recommended. Main courses lunch C$13–C$44, dinner C$18–C$44. AE, MC, V. Mon–Thurs 11:30am–1am; Fri 11:30am–2am; Sat 10:30am–2am; Sun 10:30am–1am. Canada Line: Yaletown-Roundhouse.

Sala Thai THAI   This family-run restaurant is a rarity for busy Burrard—an ethnic eatery that eschews the gleam of most downtown restaurants. Rich textiles and screens fill the dining room to give a touristy Thailand feel, while attentive staff serves up a vast array of classic meat and vegetarian dishes. Options tend to fall in a narrow price range, and are best shared family style with rice on the side. The spicy drunken noodle makes a well-priced lunch and daily drink specials blend tropical ingredients like passion fruit juice and cream of coconut. There's also a surprisingly long wine list.

102-888 Burrard St. ℂ **604/683-7999.** www.salathai.ca. Reservations recommended on weekends. Main courses C$10–C$16. AE, DC, DISC, MC, V. Sun–Thurs 11:30am–10pm; Fri–Sat 11:30am–10:30pm.

Inexpensive

Café Nuba ★ LEBANESE/VEGETARIAN   This sliver of a Seymour Street cafe is one of a growing number of Nuba Restaurants—a new favorite for quick, healthy, vegetarian and Lebanese eats. The secret-recipe falafel can make a cheap lunch in a pita (C$6) or as a platter with taboulleh, hummus, and rice or potatoes (C$10). A Gastown location (207 W. Hastings St.; ℂ **604/688-1655**) features a more formal dining room with longer hours.

1206 Seymour (at Davie St.). ℂ **778/371-3266.** www.nuba.ca. Main courses C$6–C$14. AE, MC, V. Mon–Sat 11:30am–9pm. Bus: 6.

Sciué ★ ITALIAN/DESSERTS/COFFEE   It's hard not to like a place that serves inexpensive Italian food and wonderful coffee in an airy, close-to-authentic Italian cafe setting. Sciué (pronounced *shoe*-eh) means "good and fast" in Italian regional slang, and that's how the food comes, but you can linger as long as you want and no one will bug you. Stop in for a double-shot espresso, a glass of Italian wine, or a dish of handmade gelato. For breakfast, you can get a fresh Italian pastry or a light, healthy meal. Lunch options include *pane Romano* (thin Roman bread topped with a selection of sauces, vegetables, cheeses, meats, or seafood, and sold by weight), fresh pastas, salads, and soups.

110-800 W. Pender St. (at Howe St.). ℂ **604/602-7263.** www.sciue.ca. Main courses C$5–C$10. AE, MC, V. Mon–Fri 6:30am–6:30pm; Sat 8am–6pm.

GASTOWN & CHINATOWN
Moderate

Bao Bei, A Chinese Brasserie ★★ CHINESE/TAPAS   Winning "Best New Restaurant" at the *Vancouver* Magazine 2011 Restaurant awards, Bao Bei often has an out-the-door line waiting to order from its innovate small-plates menu. The dining room is sleek, with a heritage Chinese charm that blends pale woods with floral textiles. Plates arrive as they are prepared, which promotes sharing but can mean a lag between dishes. The tofu duet serves up a marinated slice of soft soy bean curd alongside crisp agadashi-style blocks. Pot stickers are made fresh daily, and arrive crisp and not greasy. The restaurant only takes two reservations a night for large groups and none for smaller tables, so arrive early—even the tiny 12-seat bar and lounge is full by 6pm.

163 Keefer St. ℂ **604/688-0876.** www.bao-bei.ca. No reservations accepted (except large groups). Small plates C$8–C$18. AE, MC, V. Mon–Sat 5:30pm–midnight.

Jules FRENCH Jules is one of those places that is hard not to like, unless you catch the service on an off-day. Like Salt (see below), this casual French bistro is part of a mini-renaissance putting new life into Gastown. Jules can be really loud, but the staff is friendly and the food is honest, unpretentious, and reasonably priced. The menu's limited to just a few standard bistro items, all of them well prepared: steak frites (rib-eye or hanger steak with french fries), salmon Provençale, duck confit, steamed mussels, or a vegetarian offering. You can start with classics like French onion soup, escargots in garlic and herb butter, or country-style pâté. This is a good lunch spot, too.

216 Abbott St. ✆ **604/669-0033.** www.julesbistro.ca. Main courses C$16–C$24; 3-course fixed-price lunch C$24, fixed-price dinner C$26. AE, MC, V. Mon–Sat 11:30am–2:30pm and 5:30–10pm. Bus: 4, 7, 14, or 22.

Inexpensive

Judas Goat 🎒 TAPAS This tiny (28-seat) tapas parlor is a cool addition to the Gastown dining scene. It's located in the scarily named but now-gentrified Blood Alley, a couple of doors down from Salt (see below). At Judas Goat, you check off what you want from a small list of tapas-style offerings that might include beef brisket meatballs, maple sugar sablefish, marinated mussels, or fennel salad. There's a small wine and beer list.

27 Blood Alley. ✆ **604/681-5090.** www.judasgoat.ca. Tapas C$4–C$26. AE, MC, V. Tues–Sat 5–11pm or midnight. Bus: 4, 7, 14, or 22.

Old Spaghetti Factory 😊 🍴 FAMILY STYLE/ITALIAN The Old Spaghetti Factory, which celebrated its 40th anniversary in 2010, has a convenient location in the Gastown heritage district. This is a great place to take kids because it has a selection of half-size, half-price pasta dishes, including spaghetti with meatballs. For the older and more adventurous are more complicated pastas with clam or Alfredo sauce, as well as veal and steak. All entrees come with a green salad or minestrone soup, sourdough bread, coffee or tea, and spumoni ice cream. A small list of wines is offered, plus beer and chocolate milk.

53 Water St. ✆ **604/684-1288.** www.oldspaghettifactory.ca. Main courses C$9–C$18. AE, MC, V. Mon–Thurs 11am–10pm; Fri–Sat 11am–11pm; Sun 11am–9:30pm. Bus: 50.

Phnom Penh Restaurant ★ VIETNAMESE This family-run restaurant, serving Vietnamese and Cambodian cuisine, is a perennial contender for, and occasional recipient of, the *Vancouver* magazine award for the city's best Asian restaurant. Khmer dolls are suspended in glass cases, and the subdued lighting is a welcome departure from the harsh glare often found in inexpensive Chinatown restaurants. Try the hot-and-sour soup with prawns and lemon grass. The deep-fried garlic squid served with rice is a must-have, as is the tender, flame-kissed beef brochette. There's also the familiar (pho) and the foreign (frogs' legs). For dessert, the fruit-and-rice pudding is an exotic treat. The service can be brusque—don't be shy to catch a server's eye, and you may have to share a table.

244 E. Georgia St. (near Main St.). ✆ **604/682-5777.** Main courses C$7–C$18. AE, MC, V. Mon–Thurs 10am–9pm; Fri–Sun 10am–10pm. Bus: 3 or 8.

Salt ★ CHARCUTERIE The location of this dining spot in Gastown's Blood Alley might put some visitors off, and that's really a shame because Salt is unique and a wonderful place to get a good, fairly inexpensive meal. The minimalistically modern room is set with communal spruce dining tables. Salt has no kitchen, per se, as it serves only cured meats and artisan cheeses plus a daily soup, a couple of salads, and grilled meat and cheese sandwiches. For the tasting plate, you mix and match three of the meats and cheeses listed on the blackboard—be it local chèvre, red leicester, pancetta, or smoked beef. To drink, choose from a selection of beers, and several good wines and whiskeys, or opt for a wine flight. As Blood Alley has no apparent street numbers, look for the upside-down salt shaker flag over the doorway. Try it for lunch if you're in Gastown.

45 Blood Alley. ⓒ **604/633-1912.** www.salttastingroom.com. Tasting plates C$15; lunch specials C$12. AE, MC, V. Daily noon–midnight. Bus: 4, 7, 14, or 22.

THE WEST END

Expensive

Cin Cin ★★★ MODERN ITALIAN   Vancouverites looking for great food and a romantic atmosphere frequent this award-winning, second-floor restaurant on Robson Street. The spacious dining room, done in a rustic Italian-villa style, surrounds an open kitchen built around a huge wood-fired oven and grill; the heated terrace is an equally pleasant dining and people-watching spot. The dishes, inspired by Italy but using locally sourced ingredients, change monthly, but your meal might begin with house-made Dungeness crab sausage with herb salad and lemon vinaigrette, followed by bison-filled gnocchi or biodynamic rice with scallops. Mouthwatering main courses include local fish and meat cooked in the wood-fired oven or on the wood grill, and a delicious pizza with sautéed wild mushrooms, peppercorn pecorino, and caramelized onions. A number of sumptuous desserts cap the experience, including the zeppole ricotta doughnuts or dark chocolate and lemon semifreddo. The wine list is extensive, as is the selection of wines by the glass. The service is as exemplary as the food.

1154 Robson St. ⓒ **604/688-7338.** www.cincin.net. Reservations recommended. Main courses C$25–C$40; early (5–6pm) fixed-price menu C$45. AE, DC, MC, V. Daily 5–midnight. Bus: 5 or 22.

The Fish House in Stanley Park ★ SEAFOOD/PACIFIC NORTHWEST/ TEA   Reminiscent of a more genteel era, this green clapboard clubhouse from 1929 (which is in need of refurbishment) is surrounded by lawns and old cedar trees, and looks out over English Bay. In the summer, try for a table on the veranda and listen for the birds at the nearby heron rookery. Enjoy a traditional afternoon tea from 2 to 4pm, Sunday brunch, or a memorable lunch or dinner of fresh BC oysters and shellfish, fresh seasonal fish, and signature dishes such as maple-glazed salmon, flaming prawns (done at your table with ouzo), and a seafood cornucopia. Chef Karen Barnaby often creates special theme menus. The wine list is admirable; the desserts sumptuous.

8901 Stanley Park Dr. ⓒ **877/681-7275** or 604/681-7275. www.fishhousestanleypark.com. Reservations recommended. Main courses C$17–C$30; afternoon tea C$24. AE, DC, DISC, MC, V. Mon–Fri 11:30am–10pm; Sat–Sun 11am–10pm. Closed Dec 24–26.

Lift ★★ 🎁 PACIFIC NORTHWEST   Built on pilings right on Coal Harbour, Lift offers gorgeous mountain, water, and city views. The West Coast cuisine is equal to the sexy, waterside setting. The interior is luxe, with an illuminated onyx bar and different seating areas for drinking, eating, or both, as well as a rooftop patio. After 5pm, the restaurant serves "whet plates" (larger than an appetizer, but smaller than an entree), such as mussels with french fries, seared scallops, fried calamari with spicy salt, or watermelon salad. Main courses include ahi tuna, grilled venison, or swordfish with chorizo. The Sunday brunch is hopping, too, and reasonably priced. The wine list here is good with a variety of half-bottles available.

333 Menchions Mews (behind Westin Bayshore Resort). (C) **604/689-5438.** www.liftbarandgrill. com. Reservations recommended. Whet plates C$11–C$17; main courses C$21–C$42. AE, DC, MC, V. Mon–Fri 11:30am–midnight; Sat–Sun 11am–midnight. Bus: 240.

Raincity Grill ★★★ PACIFIC NORTHWEST This top-starred restaurant on a busy, buzzy corner across from English Bay is a gem—painstaking in preparation, arty in presentation, and yet completely unfussy in atmosphere. Raincity Grill was one of the very first restaurants in Vancouver to embrace the "buy locally, eat seasonally" concept and pioneered the Ocean Wise sustainable seafood organization. The menu focuses on seafood, game, poultry, and organic vegetables from British Columbia and the Pacific Northwest. The room is long, low, and intimate. To sample a bit of everything, I recommend the seasonal "100 mile" tasting menu, a bargain at C$69, or C$103 with wine pairings. One recent tasting menu included beetroot salad, steamed mussels, beef carpaccio, roasted duck with gnocchi, a cheese selection with hazelnuts, and crème brûlée—all of it made with ingredients found within 161km (100 miles) of the restaurant. The wine list is huge and, in keeping with the restaurant's philosophy, sticks pretty close to home. The restaurant also has a takeout window on Denman Street, where you can get delicious fish (lingcod) and chips to go for C$10.

1193 Denman St. (C) **604/685-7337.** www.raincitygrill.com. Reservations recommended. Main courses C$12–C$19; fixed-price lunch C$22. AE, MC, V. Mon–Fri 11:30am–2:30pm; Sat–Sun 10:30am–2:30pm; daily 5–10:30pm. Bus: 5 or 6.

The Teahouse in Stanley Park ★ PACIFIC NORTHWEST Perched on Ferguson Point overlooking English Bay, the Teahouse in Stanley Park is one of Vancouver's most venerable seaside landmarks. The menu sticks with safe but well prepared choices and a selection of what trendy Vancouverites are eating these days. Appetizers include salt and pepper squid, and mushrooms stuffed with crab, shrimp, and cream cheese. Main courses are divided between seafood and meat, with pasta thrown in for good measure. The view is perhaps most memorable: After the sun fades, the lights cast a magical glow on the trees and garden. Try for a seat on the outdoor patio or at a window-side table in the conservatory.

Ferguson Point, Stanley Park. (C) **604/669-3281.** www.vancouverdine.com. Reservations recommended. Small plates C$10–C$14; main courses C$16–C$34. AE, DC, MC, V. Mon–Fri 11:30am–10pm; Sat–Sun 10:30am–10pm.

Moderate

Hapa Izakaya ★ JAPANESE Dinner comes at almost disco decibels in Robson Street's hottest Japanese "eat-drink place" (the literal meaning of Izakaya), where chefs call out orders, servers shout acknowledgments, and the maitre d' and owner keep up a running volley to staff about the (often sizable) wait at the door. The menu features sushi-style dishes such as agedashi tofu and *negitori*—fresh tuna belly chopped with spring onions and served with bite-size bits of garlic bread. But look to the daily fresh sheets to select from inventive appetizers and meat dishes like a fish and chips roll or pork belly lettuce wrap. A scrumptious Korean hot pot and daily special vegetable goma-ae are also on the menu, for the non–raw fish eaters in your party. The service is fast and obliging, and the price per dish is reasonable. Other locations are in Kitsilano, at 1516 Yew St. (© **604/738-4272**), and Yaletown, at 1193 Hamilton St. (© **604/ 681-4272**).

1479 Robson St. © **604/689-4272.** www.hapa-izakaya.com. Reservations recommended on weekends. Small plates C$6–C$24. AE, MC, V. Sun–Thurs 5:30pm–midnight; Fri–Sat 5:30pm–1am. Bus: 5.

Tableau Bar Bistro ★ FRENCH   The dining room, now separate from the next-door Loden Vancouver hotel (p. 68), is a casual spot offering a varied menu of meat and seafood from executive chef Marc-André Choquette. Dark wood and heavy leather contrasts the Art Deco tiling in the dining room and long marble bar. Following the close of Voya, Tableau reopened in the same space with the intent to be more neighborly. And with intimate booths and an inventive, accessible menu, the restaurant is just that. Mains courses are substantial, be it the simple steak frites, half roasted-chicken, or cheese, broccoli, and brown rice casserole. The hominess continues with desserts, from chocolate éclairs to ice-cream sundaes, and (maybe if you're lucky) a rhubarb cake—the recipe courtesy of executive sous chef Tret Jordan's mother.

1181 Melville St., next to the Loden Vancouver. © **604/639-8692.** www.tableaubarbistro.com. Reservations accepted. Lunch C$12–C$21. Main courses dinner C$16–C$25. AE, MC, V. Mon–Fri 11:30am–2:30pm; Mon–Thurs 5–11pm; Fri–Sat 5pm–midnight; Sun 10:30am–3pm.

Tanpopo ✔ JAPANESE   Occupying the second floor of a corner building on Denman Street, Tanpopo has a partial view of English Bay, a large patio, and a huge menu of hot and cold Japanese dishes. But the line of people waiting 30 minutes or more every night for a table are here for the all-you-can-eat buffet. The unlimited fare includes the standards—*goma ae,* edamame, gyoza, tuna and salmon sashimi, California and BC rolls—as well as *tonkatsu,* tempura, chicken *karrage,* and oyster *motoyaki.* The quality is okay, a bit above average for an all-you-can-eat place. A couple of secrets to getting seated: You might try to call ahead, but they take only an arbitrary number of reservations for dinner each day. Otherwise, ask to sit at the sushi bar.

1122 Denman St. © **604/681-7777.** www.tanpoposushi.com. Reservations recommended for groups. Main courses C$8–C$15; all-you-can-eat buffet lunch C$14, dinner C$24. AE, MC, V. Daily 11:30am–11:30pm. Bus: 5.

Inexpensive

Banana Leaf ★ MALAYSIAN   One of the city's best spots for Malaysian food, Banana Leaf is just a hop and a skip from English Bay. The menu includes inventive specials such as a spicy papaya and seafood soup, delicious South Asian mainstays such as *gado gado* (a salad with hot peanut sauce), *mee goreng* (fried egg noodles with vegetables, beef, egg, shrimp, and tofu), and occasional variations such as an Assam curry (seafood in a tamarind-curry sauce). Must-tries are sambal green beans and a signature chili crab. For dessert, don't pass up *pisang gorong* fried banana with ice cream. The nine-course tasting menu (C$28 per person) lets you sample a bit of everything. The small room is tastefully decorated in dark tropical woods; service is very friendly. Other locations are at 820 W. Broadway (☎ **604/731-6333**) and in Kitsilano, at 3005 W. Broadway (☎ **604/734-3005**); same prices and hours apply.

1096 Denman St. ☎ **604/683-3333.** www.bananaleaf-vancouver.com. Reservations not accepted. Main courses C$11–C$20. AE, MC, V. Sun–Thurs 11:30am–10pm; Fri–Sat 11:30am–11pm. Bus: 5.

Gyoza King JAPANESE   Gyoza King features an entire menu of *gyoza*—succulent Japanese dumplings filled with prawns, pork, vegetables, and other combinations—as well as Japanese noodles and staples like *katsu-don* (pork cutlet over rice) and *udon* (a rich, hearty soup). This is the gathering spot for hordes of young Japanese students and visitors looking for reasonably priced eats that approximate home cooking. The staff is very courteous and happy to explain the dishes.

1508 Robson St. ☎ **604/669-8278.** Main courses C$4–C$14. AE, MC, V. Fri–Sun 11:30am–2:30pm; Mon–Thurs 5:30pm–1am; Fri 5:30pm–1:30am; Sat 6:30pm–1:30am; Sun 6–11:30pm. Bus: 5.

Hon's Wun-Tun House CHINESE   Hon Kwong Ip opened a Chinatown restaurant 40 years ago, and this big, bright dining room on Robson Street is now one of four Vancouver locations. The Hong Kong tastes of wun-tun noodles and pot stickers served here have been well received in Vancouver. The restaurant is also suited to family dining with a variety of barbequed meats and whole Peking ducks. The Chinatown location is at 268 Keefer St. (☎ **604/688-0871**).

1339 Robson St. ☎ **604/685-0871.** www.hons.ca. Main courses C$10–C$24. MC, V. Daily 11am–11pm. Bus: 5.

Ichiban-ya JAPANESE   In contrast to Hapa (see above), this small basement restaurant, with a rather dramatic red-and-black interior, has served old-fashioned, straight-up sushi for more than 2 decades. Options for non–sushi-philes include tempura, teriyaki, *udon,* and soba noodles. Service is fast although not always attentive, but the restaurant is standard amongst the cheap sushi options in Vancouver.

770 Thurlow St. ☎ **604/682-6262.** Reservations accepted. Main courses C$7–C$20. MC, V. Daily 11:30am–10pm (until midnight in summer). Bus: 5.

THE WEST SIDE
Very Expensive

Tojo's Restaurant ★★★ JAPANESE   Tojo's is considered Vancouver's top Japanese restaurant, the place where celebs and food cognoscenti come to dine on the best sushi in town. It's expensive, but the food is absolutely fresh, inventive, and boy is it good. The dining room's main area wraps around Chef Tojo (who invented the California and BC rolls) and his sushi chefs with a giant curved maple sake bar and an adjoining sushi bar. Tojo's ever-changing menu offers such specialties as sea urchin on the half shell, herring roe, lobster claws, tuna, crab, and barbecue eel. Go for the Chef's Arrangement—*omakase*—tell them how much you're willing to spend (per person), and let the good times roll. Many staff have been with the restaurant for upwards of a decade, and the polished, knowledgeable, and enthusiastic service is the best in Vancouver.

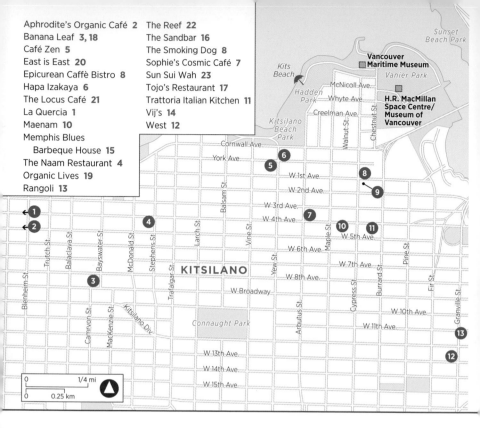

1133 W. Broadway. ✆ **604/872-8050.** www.tojos.com. Reservations required. Main courses C$34–C$45; sushi/sashimi C$12–C$55; Chef's Arrangement C$70–C$200. AE, DC, MC, V. Mon-Sat 5–10pm. Closed Christmas week. Bus: 9.

West ★★★ FRENCH/PACIFIC NORTHWEST The credo at West is deceptively simple: "True to our region, true to the seasons." That means fresh, organic, locally harvested seafood, game, and produce are transformed into extraordinary creations. The menu, and tasting menu in particular, changes regularly, but first courses might include BC spot prawns with chorizo and spring onions, smoked sablefish chowder, or spring lamb risotto. For a main course, you might find fillet of steelhead trout with pea ravioli, seared Qualicum Bay scallops, or duck breast served with duck confit cannelloni. For the ultimate dining experience, try one of the seasonal tasting menus—a multicourse progression through the best the restaurant has to offer. A carefully chosen wine list from one of the city's top sommeliers includes a selection of affordable wines by the glass and half-bottle. If you're really into cooking, reserve one of the two "chef tables" adjacent to the bustling kitchen.

2881 Granville St. ✆ **604/738-8938.** www.westrestaurant.com. Reservations recommended. Main courses lunch C$17–C$28, dinner C$29–C$37; tasting menus C$76–C$89. AE, MC, V. Mon-Fri 11:30am–2:30pm; Sat-Sun 11am–2:30pm; daily 5:30–11pm. Bus: 10.

Expensive

La Quercia ★★ ITALIAN   This intimate dining room has won plaudits for its Northern Italian fair served with flair by chefs Adam Pegg and Lucais Syme. A simple chalkboard lists what's fresh and flavorful for the day, and diners have the option of a five- or nine-course spread. Depending on the season, you might select from trout carpaccio or fresh anchovies followed by risotto, potato gnocchi with sausage, or grilled cuttlefish. The restaurant has been so welcomed by the neighborhood that the same team has opened a less-formal deli La Ghianda across the street (2083 Alma St.; *C* **604/566-9559;** www.laghianda.ca).

3689 W. 4th Ave. *C* **604/676-1007.** www.laquercia.ca. Reservations required. Main courses C$18–C$30. 5 courses C$43; 9 courses C$59. MC, V. Tues–Sun 5–10pm.

Vij's ★★★ INDIAN   Vij's doesn't take reservations, as is apparent by the line outside every night, but patrons huddled under the neon sign don't seem to mind since they're treated to tea and *papadums* (a thin bread made from lentils). Inside, the decor is as warm and subtle as the seasonings, which are all roasted, hand-ground, and used with studied delicacy. The menu changes monthly, though some of the more popular entrees remain constant. Recent offerings have included wine-marinated lamb popsicles and BC spot prawns and halibut with black chickpeas in coconut-lemon curry. Vegetarian selections abound, including vegetables and red beans in yellow mustard seed and coconut curry, and Indian lentils with naan and *raita* (yogurt-mint sauce). The wine and beer list is short but carefully selected. And for teetotalers, Vij has developed a souped-up version of the traditional Indian chai, the chaiuccino. In 2004 Vij opened Rangoli (see below), right next door, for lunch and takeout.

1480 W. 11th Ave. ℭ **604/736-6664.** www.vijsrestaurant.ca. Reservations not accepted. Main courses C$24–C$28. AE, MC, V. Daily 5:30–10pm. Bus: 10.

Moderate

Aphrodite's Organic Café ★ PACIFIC NORTHWEST/DESSERT It's only fair to talk about dessert first when describing Aphrodite's—organic greens aside, the business launched in 2003 with its home-baked pies. Customer favorites include double-crust classics like strawberry-rhubarb and blueberry, as well as the more decadent chocolate banana cream and chocolate pecan. If you opt for dinner first, the organic offerings include a wild salmon burger, a chicken shiitake quesadilla, or a simple bowl of leek and lentil soup.

3598 W. 4th Ave. ℭ **604/733-8308.** www.organiccafe.ca. Reservations recommended on weekends. Main courses C$12–C$17, pie slices C$7–C$9. MC, V. Daily 10am–9:30pm.

Maenam ★★ 🍴 THAI The feeling of freshness pervades in this white-walled, reed-screened eatery on West 4th Avenue, and the food delivers the same delight. From deceptively spicy green papaya salad to the wild prawn cakes with cucumber relish, dishes ring with simple and carefully selected ingredients. Service is attentive and the room quickly fills with a Kitsilano crowd of young professionals.

1938 W. 4th Ave. ℭ **604/730-5579.** www.maenam.ca. Reservations accepted. Main courses C$14–C$18. AE, MC, V. Tues–Sat 12–2:30pm; daily 5–11pm. Bus: 4 or 7.

Memphis Blues Barbeque House ★ 🍴 BARBECUE At the busy intersection of Granville and Broadway, this hole-in-the-wall barbecue pit has made a name for itself with corn-pone, Southern-boy barbecue smoked for hours over a low-heat, hardwood fire. Ribs come out tender enough to pull apart with your fingers (which is how food is eaten here; the cutlery is mostly for show), yet still sweet and firm. The beef brisket is cooked long enough that the fat is all rendered out, while the lean flesh remains juicy and tender. The pork butt is slow cooked until you can pull it apart with a fork. Those three meats (plus catfish and BBQ chicken) are essentially what's offered here. Put that meat on greens, and you've got a Southern salad. Put it on bread, and it becomes a sandwich. Serve it on a plate with beans and a potato, and it becomes a meal. Wines are sold by the glass and bottle, but what you want is the ice-cold, home-brewed beer. A second location lies farther east at 1342 Commercial Dr. (ℭ **604/215-2599**); the same hours apply.

1465 W. Broadway. ℭ **604/738-6806.** www.memphisbluesbbq.com. Main courses C$9–C$26. AE, MC, V. Mon–Thurs 11am–10pm; Fri 11am–11pm; Sat noon–11pm; Sun noon–10pm. Bus: 10, 14, or 16.

Rangoli ★ INDIAN Vij's (reviewed above) takes Indian cuisine to inventive new heights and tastes. But Vij's is open only for dinner, so right next door, you can get lunch, dinner, and takeout versions of Vij's curries and other specialties. Try lamb stewed with ginger and caramelized onions, spicy pulled pork, or beef short ribs in Kalonji curry. Rangoli has a hip, simple-looking interior with just a

few tables and a lot of stainless steel. On one side, a row of freezers stocks take-out-size envelopes of spiced curry sauces, cumin rice, and naan.
1488 W. 11th Ave. © **604/736-5711.** www.vijsrangoli.ca. Reservations not accepted. Main courses C$13–C$16. AE, MC, V. Daily 11am–10pm. Bus: 10.

The Sandbar CASUAL   The bar and patio here fill up with tables of 20- and 30-somethings and an assortment of baby boomers. Sunday to Thursday there's live piano music, while on Fridays and Saturdays a DJ spins at 10pm. Regardless of the scene, diners here on any night can sink their teeth into a number of fairly decent tapas and entrees. Shrimp and pork dumplings, lettuce wraps, pad Thai, and wok dishes provide the Asian component of a menu that spans the globe. Main courses range from cedar-planked grilled salmon to daily pasta and pizza specials. In summer, the third-floor patio is great for lazing about in the sunshine.
1535 Johnston St., Granville Island. © **604/669-9030.** www.vancouverdine.com. Reservations recommended on weekends. Main courses C$13–C$33; tapas C$7–C$17. AE, MC, V. Sun–Thurs 11:30am–midnight; Fri–Sat 11:30am–1am. Bus: 50 to Granville Island.

The Smoking Dog FRENCH   To date, the little Kitsilano neighborhood of Yorkville Mews has remained a local secret, perhaps because the few tourists who do venture into this delightful 1-block stretch are immediately confronted with a confusing variety of choices. This French bistro with international fusion overtones is generally a safe bet for a good meal. The menu features strip-loin steak with bordelaise sauce, pan-roasted halibut, steamed mussels and fries, risottos, and good pastas. If weather permits, take a seat on the heated patio and enjoy the bustling street life.
1889 W. 1st Ave. © **604/732-8811.** www.thesmokingdog.com. Main courses C$18–C$29. AE, MC, V. Mon–Fri 11:30am–11pm; Sat–Sun 11am–11pm. Bus: 2 or 22.

Trattoria Italian Kitchen ★ ITALIAN   The group behind glowbal, Coast, Sanafir, and Italian Kitchen have scored again, this time in Kitsilano. Trattoria is Kits-friendly, meaning it's more casual than their other restaurants, but the standards remain just as high and the prices just as reasonable. You can't make a reservation here, so plan accordingly. The line begins to form at 5:30pm, and by 7pm, you may have to wait an hour or more for a table (you can order a drink while you're waiting). The menu covers excellent pizzas with delicious toppings (house-made sausage with leeks and fingerling potatoes, or roasted squash and gorgonzola); pastas like linguine *vongole* with manila clams, spaghetti carbonara, or the sharable platter of spaghetti and meatballs (the meatballs are made of Kobe beef). Main courses are seasonal and might include seared wild spring salmon or grilled lamb chops. The wine list includes all the major Italian vintages.
1850 W. 4th Ave. © **604/732-1441.** www.trattoriakitchen.ca. Reservations not accepted. Main courses C$13–C$24. AE, MC, V. Mon–Thurs 11:30am–1am; Fri 11:30am–2am; Sat 10:30am–2am; Sun 10:30am–1am. Bus: 4 or 7.

Inexpensive

Café Zen CASUAL   A huge brunch menu, fast and efficient service, reasonable prices, and great eggs Benedict (plus the some of the best French toast in Vancouver) turn this little cafe into a packed dining room by 10am on weekends, when guests spill out the doorway and up the long, steep sidewalk. Sandal-clad traffic from Kits Beach (next door) heads here for breakfast and lunch during the week.

1631 Yew St. (at York Ave.). ☎ **604/731-4018.** Main courses C$6–C$12. MC, V. Daily 7am–4pm. Bus: 2, 4, 7, or 22.

The Naam Restaurant ★ ☺ VEGETARIAN   Back in the '60s, when Kitsilano was Canada's hippie haven, the Naam was tie-dye central. Things have changed since then, but Vancouver's oldest vegetarian and natural-food restaurant still retains a pleasant granola feel, and it's open 24/7. The decor is simple, earnest, and welcoming, and includes well-worn wooden tables and chairs, plants, an assortment of local art, a nice garden patio, and live music every night. The brazenly healthy fare ranges from all-vegetarian burgers, enchiladas, and burritos to tofu teriyaki, Thai noodles, and a variety of pita pizzas. The sesame spice fries topped with miso gravy are a Vancouver institution. And though the Naam is not quite vegan, they do offer specialties like the macrobiotic Dragon Bowl of brown rice, tofu, sprouts, and steamed vegetables.

2724 W. 4th Ave. ☎ **604/738-7151.** www.thenaam.com. Only group reservations accepted Mon–Thurs. Main courses C$8–C$15. AE, MC, V. Daily 24 hr. Bus: 2, 4, 7, or 22.

Sophie's Cosmic Café ☺ FAMILY STYLE/AMERICAN   For a fabulous home-cooked, diner-style breakfast in a laid-back but buzzy atmosphere, come to this Kitsilano landmark. On Saturday and Sunday mornings, get here early, or you may have to wait a half-hour or more to get in. You can also have a good, filling lunch or dinner here. Every available space in Sophie's is crammed with toys and knickknacks from the 1950s and 1960s so, understandably, children are inordinately fond of the place. Crayons and coloring paper are always on hand. The menu is simple and includes pastas, burgers and fries, great milkshakes, and a few classic Mexican and "international" dishes, but it's the breakfast menu that draws the crowds.

2095 W. 4th Ave. ☎ **604/732-6810.** www.sophiescosmiccafe.com. Main courses C$8–C$16. MC, V. Mon 8am–2:30pm; Tues–Sun 8am–8pm. Bus: 4 or 7.

THE EAST SIDE

These "east side" restaurants are on or near Main Street, which is on the borderlands between upscale west and working-class east. Main thus has some funky urban authenticity to go with its ever-increasing trendiness.

Expensive

Sun Sui Wah ★★ CHINESE/DIM SUM/SEAFOOD   One of the most visited and sophisticated Chinese restaurants in town, the award-winning Sun Sui Wah is well known for its seafood. Fresh and varied, the catch of the day can include fresh crab, geoduck, scallops, oyster, prawns, and more. Pick your meal from the tank or order from the menu if you'd rather not meet your food eye-to-eye before it's cooked. The restaurant's signatures dishes include Alaskan king crab and roasted squab, which is said to have healing properties in Chinese medicine. Dim sum is a treat, with the emphasis on seafood. Choices abound for meat lovers and vegetarians, though they will miss out on one of the best seafood feasts in town. The decor is in need of a shake-up, but don't let that stand in your way. It's best to dine with a group of four or more, so you can sample a variety of dishes family-style.

3888 Main St. ℂ **604/872-8822.** www.sunsuiwah.com. Main courses C$12–C$50. AE, DC, MC, V. Daily 10am–3pm and 5–10:30pm. Bus: 3.

Moderate

East is East ★ VEGETARIAN/INTERNATIONAL   Filled with rugs, pillows, and low wooden tables, East is East presents a harem of spices for food-lovers. The roti rolls come in a dozen combinations, from Spice Caravan (chickpeas and cauliflower) to the Silk Road (miso salmon in coconut milk).The Silk Road feast is a heartier all-you-can-eat option—diners start by selecting two dishes from a raft of vegetarian and meat dish choices. Even if you're just shopping along the Main Street boutiques, stop in for a veritably spicy chai tea (the best in Vancouver). There's a second location in Kitsilano at 3243 W. Broadway (ℂ **604/734-5881**) that serves the same menu.

4413 Main St. ℂ **604/879-2020.** www.eastiseast.ca. Reservations recommended on weekends. Main courses C$13–C$19. MC, V. Daily 11am–10pm.

The Locus Café CASUAL/SOUTHWESTERN   Even if you arrive by your lonesome, you'll soon have plenty of friends because the Locus is a cheek-by-jowl kind of place, filled with a friendly, funky crowd of artsy Mount Pleasant types. The big bar is overhung with "swamp-gothic" lacquer trees and surrounded by a tier of stools with booths and tiny tables. The cuisine originated in the American Southwest and picked up an edge along the way, as demonstrated in the pulled chicken sandwich with spicy black bean mayo served on a baguette. Keep an eye out for fish specials, such as grilled halibut with bacon and tomato vinaigrette. If you're in the mood for a burger, try the organic beef patty topped with caramelized onion and Edam cheese. Draft beers are pulled from local-favorite breweries, including Phillips in Victoria and North Vancouver's Red Truck.

4121 Main St. ℂ **604/708-4121.** www.locusonmain.com. Main courses C$12–C$24. MC, V. Mon–Wed 10am–midnight; Thurs–Fri 10am–1am; Sat 9am–1am; Sun 9am–midnight. Bus: 3.

The Reef ⚓ CARIBBEAN   The "JERK" in the phone number refers to a spicy marinade of Scotch bonnet peppers, allspice, garlic, soy, tomato, and ginger. The Reef serves a number of jerk dishes, including their signature quarter jerk chicken breast. Other dishes are equally tasty, including a tropical salad of fresh mango, red onions, tomatoes, and pumpkin seeds; shrimp with toasted coconut and avocado yoghurt; pan-seared marlin; and Trenton spiced ribs. With a glass of wine from the thoughtfully selected list, you have good dining at a bargain price. Afternoons, the tiny patio is drenched in sunlight. If you're lucky, a fresh batch of Jamaican fried dumplings—like savory doughnuts—will be ready on your arrival, although it's pure good luck to catch them.

4172 Main St. ℂ **604/874-JERK** [604/874-5375]. www.thereefrestaurant.com. Main courses C$10–C$18. AE, MC, V. Mon–Thurs 11am–11pm; Fri 11am–1am; Sat 10am–1am; Sun 10am–11pm. Bus: 3.

THE NORTH SHORE

Expensive

The Beach House at Dundarave Pier ★★ PACIFIC NORTHWEST   The Beach House offers a panoramic view of English Bay from its waterfront location. Diners on the heated patio get more sunshine, but they miss out on the rich interior of this restored 1912 teahouse. The food is consistently good—innovative, but not so experimental that it leaves the staid West Van burghers gasping for breath. Appetizers include fresh oysters with shaved horseradish; prawn dynamite rolls; and Dungeness crab cakes. Entrees might include linguine with wild prawns, scallops, tomatoes, and chilies; pan-roasted sablefish with baby bok choy; and a seasonal stuffed chicken breast. The Beach House is also a favorite West Van spot for Saturday and Sunday brunch.

150 25th St., West Vancouver. ✆ **604/922-1414.** www.thebeachhouserestaurant.ca. Reservations recommended. Main courses C$18–C$30. AE, DC, MC, V. Mon–Thurs 11:30am–10pm; Fri–Sat 11:30am–11pm; Sun 11am–10pm. Bus: 250 to Dundarave Village.

The Salmon House on the Hill ★ PACIFIC NORTHWEST/SEAFOOD High above West Vancouver, the Salmon House offers a spectacular view of the city and Burrard Inlet. An alder-wood-fired grill dominates the kitchen, lending a delicious flavor to many of the dishes. Try the "Taste of BC" menu, a three-course meal prepared with ingredients from British Columbia's different regions (C$30) and offered from 5 to 6pm. Alternately, you might start with bison carpaccio or clams and mussels in a cumin broth, go on to alder-grilled salmon with white asparagus, and finish with homemade Frangelico tiramisu.

2229 Folkestone Way, West Vancouver. ✆ **604/926-3212.** www.salmonhouse.com. Reservations recommended for dinner. Main courses C$27–C$40. AE, MC, V. Sat–Sun 10:30am–2:30pm; daily 5–10pm. Bus: 250 across the Lions Gate Bridge to Park Royal, and then transfer to 256.

Inexpensive

The Tomahawk Restaurant ☺ 🎁 FAMILY STYLE/AMERICAN   This is a typical American-style diner with one critical difference that makes it worth a visit: The Tomahawk is packed with native knickknacks and some truly first-class First Nations art. It all started back in 1926 when proprietor Chick Chamberlain began accepting carvings from Burrard Band First Nations in lieu of payment. Over the years, the collection just kept growing. So, how's the food? Great, in a burgers-and-fries kind of way. Portions are large, burgers are tasty (many made with organic beef), and milkshakes come so thick the spoon stands up straight as a totem pole. For an "only in BC" treat, try the oysters on toast. Tomahawk is also renowned for its hearty breakfasts with thick rashers of Yukon bacon.

1550 Philip Ave., North Vancouver. ✆ **604/988-2612.** www.tomahawkrestaurant.com. Reservations not accepted. Main courses C$5–C$17. AE, MC, V. Sun–Thurs 8am–9pm; Fri–Sat 8am–10pm. Bus: 240 to Philip Ave.

COFFEE, TEA, SWEETS & ICE CREAM

Caffè Artigiano ★★ 🎁   Absolutely the best lattes in town. The formula is to start with the perfect beans, brew the coffee to an exact temperature, give the steamed milk the respect it deserves, and pour it out ever so slowly, forming a leaf- or heart-shaped pattern in your cup. This is latte-making as an art form. Pop in for a light lunch or pastry, too. The original location at 1101 W. Pender St. (at Thurlow St.) in the financial district is less intimate than the digs on Hornby Street, right across from the Vancouver Art Gallery; the Hornby location has a little, often-packed outdoor patio perfect for people-watching. In the last 2 years many more locations have popped up, including on West Hastings Street, on West Broadway in Kitsilano, and on West 41st Avenue in Kerrisdale.

763 Hornby St. ✆ **604/694-7737.** www.caffeartigiano.com. Sweets and sandwiches C$4–C$10. AE, MC, V. Mon–Fri 5:30am–9pm; Sat 6:30am–9pm; Sun 6:30am–8pm (other locations closed evenings). Bus: 22.

Darryl's Coffee & Native Art Shop 🎁 Tucked just off busy Burrard Street, Darryl's blends art with baked goods and good coffee. The date oatmeal bars are utterly tasty. Open since 2003, Darryl's is a welcoming, neighborhood-focused joint.

945 Davie St. ✆ **604/689-5354.** Everything under C$10. V. Mon–Fri 8:30am–6:30pm; Sat noon–6pm; Sun closed. Bus: 2, 6, or 22.

Epicurean Caffè Bistro 🎁 The Epicurean brews a mean espresso, a real Italian *caffè* in Kitsilano. Locals and visitors flock to this tiny neighborhood deli, packing the sidewalk spots on nice days or the cozy small tables inside when the weather turns gray. Italian sweets, biscotti, and sorbet go well with any of the coffees, but for a savory treat, have a peek at the glass display case in the back. Freshly made antipasti, cold cuts, salads, panini sandwiches, and a daily pasta are just some of the delectables available for lunch or takeout. Eat in guests can sip a glass of wine with the fab food. The menu changes regularly, as the owners try out new recipes.

1898 W. 1st Ave. ✆ **604/731-5370.** www.epicureancaffe.com. Everything under C$14. MC, V. Sat–Wed 7:30am–6pm; Thurs–Fri 7:30am–9pm. Bus: 2 or 22 to Cornwall and Cypress sts.

La Casa Gelato ★ 🎁 No self-respecting ice-cream fiend could possibly pass up a visit to La Casa Gelato, where ice-cream lovers gather for a taste of one or more of the 218 flavors in store. Of course, you don't get that many flavors by simply serving up chocolate, vanilla, and strawberry. How about garlic, lavender, durian, basil, or hot chili ice cream, or pear with Gorgonzola sorbet? You're entitled to at least several samples before committing to one or two flavors, so go ahead and be adventurous. The downside: It's quite a trek out to this obscure industrial area near Commercial Drive, and sometimes the novelty tastes don't work as well as they should.

1033 Venables St. ✆ **604/251-3211.** www.lacasagelato.com. Everything under C$7. MC, V. Daily 11am–11pm. Bus: 22.

Mink, a Chocolate Cafe ★ 🎁 Baristas can make a fabulous cup of coffee, but chocolate—both hot and cold—is what Mink is all about. This unique chocolate cafe serves exceptionally fine chocolate beverages made with special spices and ingredients (like chipotle or blackberry). Their little handcrafted (made in Vancouver) chocolate bars are heavenly, and the bonbons . . . well, try one and you'll know what I mean. They also offer make-your-own s'mores and chocolate fondue.

863 W. Hastings St. (at Hornby St., on west side of Terminal City Club). ✆ **866/283-5181** or 604/633-2451. www.minkchocolates.com. Everything under C$10. MC, V. Mon–Fri 7:30am–6pm; Sat–Sun 10am–6pm. Bus: 10, 16, or 22.

PRACTICAL INFORMATION
The Big Picture

For travelers who love to dine out and dine well, Vancouver is a delightful discovery. It's so good, in fact, that you could come here just to eat. And here's the capper: A fabulous meal at one of Vancouver's top restaurants costs about a third less than a similar meal would cost in New York, London, or San Francisco. But one thing is certain: You will not encounter any snotty waiters or waitstaff in Vancouver. The friendly professionalism of everyone involved in the food industry in Vancouver adds to the pleasure of dining here.

Most of Vancouver's top restaurants offer tasting menus, and I recommend that you try them. In particular, the tasting menus at West, C, and Raincity Grill will give you a brilliant sampling of the best, freshest, and most creative cooking in Vancouver.

Sustainably harvested fish and seafood are available at most Vancouver restaurants; look for the Ocean Wise logo, which means the fish has been recommended by the Vancouver Aquarium as non-endangered and fished by sustainable methods.

But as once-plentiful fish becomes more expensive and harder to come by, more and more restaurants that formerly served seafood almost exclusively have added meat and game dishes to their menus. In addition to locally raised pork, beef, and fowl, don't be surprised if you encounter reindeer, buffalo, or ostrich on restaurant menus.

One thing to note about the Vancouver restaurants: Hotel dining rooms are very much a part of the fine-dining scene. Most hotel dining rooms in Vancouver are not updated coffee shops but serious restaurants.

Complement your dining experience with one of BC's award-winning wines. Vineyards in the Okanagan Valley in eastern BC and the Cowichan Valley on Vancouver Island produce some remarkable reds and a couple of delicious sparkling whites. The province's viniculture has helped to create a sophisticated wine culture in Vancouver, and every good restaurant has a sommelier or knowledgeable server who can steer you in the right direction.

Reservations

For dinner at Vancouver's top restaurants, reservations are essential for the best experience, although all also accommodate walk-ins diners. Many Vancouver restaurants now accept reservations through **Open Table** (www.opentable.com)—check individual websites for details.

Dining Hours

Restaurant hours vary. Lunch is typically served from noon to 2pm; Vancouverites begin dinner around 6:30pm—the busiest window is about 6 to 8pm—later in summer. Reservations are recommended at most restaurants and are essential on weekends at the city's top tables.

Tipping

The base-line tip in Vancouver calculates as 15%, with more offered for exceptional service. Groups of six or more can anticipate an automatic added service charge of 15% to 18%—this serves as the tip and diners are not expected to leave an additional amount unless service was outstanding. Keep in mind that restaurants in British Columbia add the 12% **harmonized sales tax (HST) to the bill.**

RESTAURANTS BY CUISINE

AMERICAN
Sophie's Cosmic Café ($, p. 104)
The Tomahawk Restaurant
($, p. 106)

BARBECUE
Memphis Blues Barbeque House ★
($$, p. 102)

BELGIAN
Chambar Belgian Restaurant ★★
($$$, p. 90)

CARIBBEAN
The Reef ($$, p. 105)

CASUAL
Bin 941 Tapas Parlour ★ ($$, p. 92)
Café Zen ($, p. 103)
The Locus Café ($$, p. 105)
The Sandbar ($$, p. 103)

CHARCUTERIE
Salt ★ ($, p. 95)

CHINESE/DIM SUM
Bao Bei ★★ ($$, p. 94)
Hon's Wun-Tun House ($, p. 99)
Sun Sui Wah ★★ ($$$, p. 104)

COFFEE/TEA
Caffè Artigiano ★★ ($, p. 106)
Darryl's Coffee & Native Art Shop
($, p. 107)
Epicurean Caffè Bistro ($, p. 107)
The Fish House in Stanley Park ★
($$$, p. 96)
Mink, A Chocolate Cafe ★ ($, p. 107)
Sciué ★ ($, p. 94)

DESSERTS
Aphrodite's Organic Café ★
($$, p. 102)
Caffè Artigiano ★★ ($, p. 106)
La Casa Gelato ★ ($, p. 107)
Sciué ★ ($, p. 94)

FAMILY STYLE
Old Spaghetti Factory ($, p. 95)
Sophie's Cosmic Café ($, p. 104)
The Tomahawk Restaurant ($, p. 106)

FOOD TRUCKS
Japadog ($, p. 93)
The Kaboom Box ($, p. 93)
La Brasserie ($, p. 93)
The Re-up BBQ ($, p. 93)
Roaming Dragon ($, p. 93)

FRENCH
Le Crocodile ★ ($$$, p. 91)
Jules ($$, p. 95)
Tableau Bar Bistro ★ ($$, p. 98)
The Smoking Dog ($$, p. 103)
West ★★★ ($$$$, p. 100)

FUSION
glowbal grill steak & satay bar ★★
($$, p. 93)
MARKET by Jean-Georges ★★★
($$$, p. 92)
Yew ★★ ($$$, p. 92)

INDIAN
Rangoli ★ ($$, p. 102)
Vij's ★★★ ($$$, p. 101)

INTERNATIONAL
Coast ★★★ ($$$, p. 91)
East is East ★ ($$, p. 105)
MARKET by Jean-Georges ★★★
($$$, p. 92)

KEY TO ABBREVIATIONS:
$$$$** = Very Expensive   **$$$** = Expensive   **$$** = Moderate   **$ = Inexpensive

ITALIAN

Cin Cin ★★★ ($$$, p. 96)
Il Giardino di Umberto Ristorante ★★ ($$$, p. 91)
La Quercia ★★ ($$$. p. 101)
Old Spaghetti Factory ($, p. 95)
Sciué ★ ($, p. 94)
Trattoria Italian Kitchen ★ ($$, p. 103)

JAPANESE

Gyoza King ($, p. 99)
Hapa Izakaya ★ ($$, p. 97)
Ichiban-ya ($, p. 99)
Tanpopo ($$, p. 98)
Tojo's Restaurant ★★★ ($$$$, p. 99)

LEBANESE

Café Nuba ★ ($, p. 94)

MALAYSIAN

Banana Leaf ★ ($, p. 98)

PACIFIC NORTHWEST

Aphrodite's Organic Café ★ ($$, p. 102)
The Beach House at Dundarave Pier ★★ ($$$, p. 106)
C ★★★ ($$$$, p. 87)
Diva at the Met ★ ($$$$, p. 87)
The Fish House in Stanley Park ★ ($$$, p. 96)
Hawksworth Restaurant ★★★ ($$$, p. 91)
Lift ★★ ($$$, p. 96)
Raincity Grill ★★★ ($$$, p. 97)
The Salmon House on the Hill ★ ($$$, p. 106)

The Teahouse in Stanley Park ★ ($$$, p. 97)
West ★★★ ($$$$, p. 100)
Yew ★★ ($$$, p. 92)

SEAFOOD

Blue Water Cafe + Raw Bar ★★★ ($$$$, p. 87)
C ★★★ ($$$$, p. 87)
Coast ★★★ ($$$, p. 91)
The Fish House in Stanley Park ★ ($$$, p. 96)
Hawksworth Restaurant ★★★ ($$$, p. 91)
Joe Fortes Seafood and Chop House ★ ($$$$, p. 90)
The Salmon House on the Hill ★ ($$$, p. 106)
Sun Sui Wah ★★ ($$$, p. 104)

SOUTHWESTERN

The Locus Café ($$, p. 105)

TAPAS

Bao Bei ★★ ($$, p. 94)
Bin 941 Tapas Parlour ★ ($$, p. 92)
Judas Goat ($, p. 95)

THAI

Maenam ★★ ($$, p. 102)
Sala Thai ($$, p. 94)

VEGETARIAN

Café Nuba ★ ($, p. 94)
East is East ★ ($$, p. 105)
The Naam Restaurant ★ ($, p. 104)

VIETNAMESE

Phnom Penh Restaurant ★ ($, p. 95)

EXPLORING VANCOUVER

Acity perched on the edge of a raw wilderness, Vancouver offers unrivaled opportunities for exploring the outdoors. But within the city limits, Vancouver is intensely urban, with buzzy sidewalk cafes and busy shopping streets.

A forest of glass-fronted high-rises rings the central part of the city, reminding some visitors of New York or Shanghai. Chinatown inevitably invites comparisons to San Francisco. But similarities with other places begin to pall as you come to realize that Vancouver is entirely its own creation: a young, self-confident, sparklingly beautiful city like no other on earth.

NEIGHBORHOODS TO EXPLORE

DOWNTOWN Most of Vancouver's commercial and office space is found in a square patch starting at Nelson Street and heading north to the harbor, with Homer and Burrard streets forming the east and west boundaries, respectively. Canada Place, on the waterfront facing Burrard Inlet, is part of the city's huge convention center and cruise-ship terminal. The most interesting avenues for visitors are West Georgia, Robson, and Granville streets. West Georgia Street—in addition to being the prime address for class-A commercial property—is where you'll find the Vancouver Art Gallery (p. 123), the Coliseum-shaped Vancouver Public Library (p. 172), and regional shopping mall Pacific Centre. Robson Street is "trend central," crammed with designer chains, restaurants, and cafes. Rapidly glitzifying Granville Street—where Vancouver's 1950s proliferation of neon is being re-introduced—is the home of bars, clubs, theaters, pubs, and restaurants.

THE WEST END This was Vancouver's first upscale neighborhood, settled in the 1890s by the city's budding class of merchant princes. By the 1930s, most of the grand Edwardian homes had become rooming houses, and in the late 1950s, some of the Edwardians came down and high-rise apartments went up. The resulting neighborhood owes more to the verticality of Manhattan than to the sprawling cities of the west, although the meld of brick buildings with lush landscaping, gardens, and gorgeous beaches along English Bay and Stanley Park is pure Northwest. It's Vancouver's most prominent gay neighborhood, where rainbow banners edge the streets, and the route for the colorful Gay Pride Parade traverses in late July or early August. All the necessities of life are contained within the West End's border, especially on **Denman, Davie,** and **Robson streets:** great cafes, good nightclubs, bookshops, and some of the city's best restaurants. That's part of what makes it such a sought-after address, but it's also the little things, like the street trees, the mix of high-rise condos and sturdy old Edwardians, and the way that, in the middle of such an urban setting, you now and again stumble on a view of the ocean or the mountains.

PREVIOUS PAGE: **A pond at the Dr. Sun Yat-Sen Classical Chinese Garden.**

Vancouver Attractions

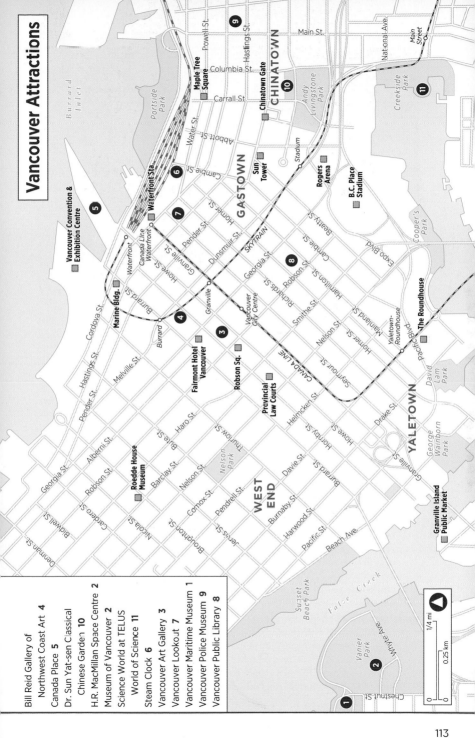

Bill Reid Gallery of
Northwest Coast Art **4**
Canada Place **5**
Dr. Sun Yat-sen Classical
Chinese Garden **10**
H.R. MacMillan Space Centre **2**
Museum of Vancouver **2**
Science World at TELUS
World of Science **11**
Steam Clock **6**
Vancouver Art Gallery **3**
Vancouver Lookout **7**
Vancouver Maritime Museum **1**
Vancouver Police Museum **9**
Vancouver Public Library **8**

Gastown is the only part of Vancouver to retain a Victorian style.

GASTOWN   The oldest section of Vancouver, Gastown has a charm that shines through the souvenir shops and panhandlers. It can be seedy—druggies and homeless people hang out around its fringes—but it's increasingly become home to some local-focused restaurants and unique-find stores. Its biggest charm, though, is as the only section of the city that has the feel of an old Victorian town—the buildings stand shoulder to shoulder, and cobblestones line the streets. The current Gastown was built from scratch just a few months after an 1886 fire wiped out the entire city. (Photographs of the time show proper-looking men in black coats selling real estate out of tents erected on the still-smoking ashes.) As you walk the streets, look for a new and experimental art gallery, a young fashion designer setting up shop, or a piece of beautiful, hand-carved First Nations art in one of the galleries along **Water** and **Hastings streets.** It's also the setting for the famous Steam Clock on Water Street (see "Walking Tour 2: Gastown & Chinatown," in chapter 8).

Alcohol has always been a big part of Gastown's history. The neighborhood is named for a saloonkeeper—Gassy Jack Deighton—who, according to local legend, talked the local mill hands into building a saloon as Vancouver's first structure in return for all the whiskey they could drink. Nowadays, Gastown is still liberally endowed with basement pubs and multi-level clubs—it's one of two or three main areas where Vancouverites congregate when the sun goes down.

CHINATOWN   Even though much of Vancouver's huge Asian population has moved out to Richmond, Chinatown remains a kick because it hasn't become overtly touristy. For the tens of thousands of Cantonese- and Mandarin-speaking Canadians who live in the surrounding neighborhoods, Chinatown is simply the place they go to shop. And for many others who have moved to more outlying neighborhoods, it's still one of the best places to come and eat. One of North America's more populous Chinatowns, the area was settled about the same time as the rest of Vancouver, by migrant laborers brought in to build the Canadian Pacific Railway and earn pittance in dangerous mines. Many white settlers resented the Chinese labor, and race riots periodically broke out. At one point, Vancouver's Chinatown was surrounded with Belfast-like security walls. By the 1940s and 1950s, however, the area was mostly threatened with neglect. The 1970s saw a serious plan to tear the whole neighborhood down and put in a freeway, but a huge protest stopped that, and now the area's future seems secure. For visitors, the fun is to simply wander, look, and taste.

YALETOWN & FALSE CREEK NORTH   Vancouver's former meatpacking and warehouse district, Yaletown has been converted to an area of apartment lofts, restaurants, and fledgling multimedia biz. It's a relatively tiny area, and the main streets of interest are **Mainland, Hamilton,** and **Davie.** For visitors, it features some interesting cafes, high-end shops, and a kind of refurbished-urban feel. The smidge of old-time authenticity—dating to when the CPR moved its repair shops here from Yale up the Fraser River—provides an essential anchor to the brand-new bevy of towers that have risen in the past 15 years on **Pacific Boulevard** along the north edge of False Creek. Officially (and unimaginatively) called False Creek North, the area is more often referred to as "the Concord lands" after the developer, or "the Expo lands" after the world's fair held in 1986 on the land where the towers now stand. Where the shiny newness of the Concord towers can prove a little disconcerting, gritty Yaletown provides the antidote. And vice versa. The two neighborhoods are slowly melding into one wonderful whole.

GRANVILLE ISLAND   Part crafts fair, part farmers market, part artist's workshop, part mall, and part industrial site, Granville Island seems to have it all. Some 35 years ago, the federal government decided to try its hand at a bit of urban renewal, so they took this piece of industrial waterfront and redeveloped it into . . . well, it's hard to describe. But everything you could name is here:

False Creek offers great access to the waterfront.

SOUTHEAST FALSE CREEK: VANCOUVER'S NEW post-olympics NEIGHBORHOOD

Where sawmills, foundries, and warehouses once stood, Vancouver's newest neighborhood has emerged. Southeast False Creek—which includes residential units, 4.5 hectares (11 acres) of park in the first phase, a community center, and a boating center—was first used as the Vancouver Olympic Village to house athletes during the 2010 Winter Games. Located on the waterfront, overlooking downtown Vancouver and BC Place Stadium, the neighborhood is considered among the greenest in the world and has earned platinum status from the LEED Green Building Rating System for its environmentally conscious architecture and building practices.

Southeast False Creek is easily accessed via the seawall that runs along the shores of False Creek, linking Granville Island, Science World, and Yaletown. The new seawall is great for biking or strolling, and it includes a timber boardwalk, granite seating blocks, and a kayak-shaped pedestrian bridge. Landscapers even put in a small island to increase the habitat available for local fish, plants, and birds. The historic station-red Salt Building, built in the 1930s and used as the athletes' lounge during the Games, is opening as a bakery, coffee shop, brewpub, and restaurant.

theaters, pubs, restaurants, artists' studios, bookstores, crafts shops, an art school, a hotel, parks, a community center, a cement plant, and lots and lots of people. One of the most enjoyable ways to experience the Granville Island atmosphere is to head down to the **Granville Island Public Market** (p. 125), grab a latte (and perhaps a piece of cake or pie, to boot), then wander outside to enjoy the view of the boats, the buskers, and the children endlessly chasing flocks of squawking seagulls.

KITSILANO Hard to believe, but in the 1960s, Kitsilano was a neighborhood that had fallen on hard times. Nobody respectable wanted to live there— the 1920s homes had all been converted to cheap rooming houses—so hippies moved in. The neighborhood became Canada's Haight-Ashbury, with coffeehouses, head shops, and lots of incense and long hair. Once the boomer generation stopped raging against the machine, they realized that Kitsilano—right next to the beach, but not quite downtown—was a very groovy place to live indeed, and a fine place to own property. Real estate began an upward trend that has never stopped, and "Kits" became thoroughly yuppified. Nowadays, it's a fun place to wander. You will discover trendy furniture and housewares shops, lots of consignment clothing stores, snowboard shops, coffee everywhere, and lots of places to eat (every third storefront is a restaurant). The best parts of Kitsilano are the stretch of **West 4th Avenue** between Burrard and Balsam streets, and **West Broadway** between Macdonald and Alma streets. Oh, and **Kits Beach** (p. 145), of course, with that fabulous heated saltwater swimming pool.

COMMERCIAL DRIVE Known as "The Drive," Commercial Drive is the 12-block section from Venables Street to East 6th Avenue. The Drive has a less glitzy, more down-to-earth, fading counterculture feel to it. It's an old immigrant neighborhood that, like everyplace else in Vancouver, has been rediscovered. The first wave of Italians left old-fashioned, delightfully tacky cafes such as **Calabria** (1745 Commercial Dr.; (C) **604/253-7017**). More recent waves of Portuguese, Hondurans, and Guatemalans have also left their mark. And more recently, lesbians, vegans, young families, and artists have moved in—the shops and restaurants reflect the mix. Think Italian cafe near a Marxist bookstore across from the vegan deli and a co-operative grocery store. After the relentless see-and-be-seen scene in the West End, it's nice to come out to the Drive for a bit of unpretentious fun.

SHAUGHNESSY Distances within the Shaughnessy neighborhood aren't conducive for a comfortable stroll (and you won't see many locals out walking), but Shaughnessy is a great place to drive or bike, especially in the spring, when trees and gardens are blossoming. Designed in the 1920s as an enclave for Vancouver's budding elite, this is Vancouver's Westmount or Nob Hill. Thanks to the stranglehold Shaughnessy exerts on local politics—every second mayor hails from this neighborhood—traffic flow is carefully diverted away from the area, and it takes a little bit of driving around to find your way in. It's an effort worth making, however, if only to see the stately homes and monstrous mansions, many of which are now featured in film shoots or rented by Hollywood movie stars while they're in town filming. This is also home to many old Vancouver families with a pioneer past. To find the neighborhood, look on the map for the area of curvy and convoluted streets between Cypress and Oak streets and 12th and 32nd avenues. The center of opulence is the Crescent, an elliptical street to the southeast of Granville and 16th Avenue.

RICHMOND Twenty years ago, Richmond was mostly farmland and blueberry fields with a bit of sleepy suburb. Now it's Asia West, an agglomeration of shopping malls geared to the new—read: rich, educated, and successful—Chinese immigrant. The residential areas of the city are not worth visiting (unless tract homes are your thing), but malls like the **Aberdeen Mall** or the **Yaohan Centre** are something else. It's like getting into your car in Vancouver and getting out in Hong Kong. For information on the famous Richmond Night Market, see "A Special Vancouver Experience: Asian Night Markets," p. 181.

PUNJABI MARKET India imported. Most of the businesses on this 4-block stretch of Main Street, from 48th Avenue up to 52nd Avenue, are run by and cater to Indo-Canadians, primarily Punjabis. The area is best seen during business hours, when the fragrant scent of spices wafts out from food stalls, and the sound of Hindi pop songs blares from hidden speakers. Young brides hunt through sari shops or seek out suitable material in discount textile outlets.

Sari shops are scattered throughout the Punjabi Market district.

SOUTH MAIN   South Main Street—awkwardly dubbed SoMa—enfolds artist studios in converted industrial buildings, hidden theater companies, and independent eco-fashion boutiques. Heritage Hall (3102 Main St.) is often the site of craft markets and swap meets. Vancouver's mixology scene draws crowds to slick lounges like Habit (2610 Main St.; ℂ **604/877-8582;** www.habitlounge.ca), which serves mix-your-own retro cocktails. Although hipster-tinged, the area truly thrives on community-minded businesses such as **The Rhizome Café** (317 E. Broadway; ℂ **604/872-3166;** www.rhizomecafe.ca) and **The Foundation** (2301 Main St.; ℂ **604/708-0881**). Nearby on Cambie Street lies City Hall, an Art Deco make-work project built in 1936.

THE TOP ATTRACTIONS
Downtown & the West End

Bill Reid Gallery of Northwest Coast Art ★★   Opened in 2008 a decade after the artist's death, this downtown museum-gallery showcases the work of the great Northwest coast aboriginal artist Bill Reid, who died in 1998 (see "Bill Reid: First Among First Nations Artists," in chapter 2). Permanent installations include the Raven's Trove: Gold and Silver Masterworks by Bill Reid; the monumental bronze sculpture *Mythic Messengers,* Reid's masterful composition of 11 intertwined figures recounting traditional Haida myths; a monumental cedar tribute pole carved by Haida Chief 7idansuu (James Hart) honoring Reid; and a tiny tea set that Reid carved in blackboard chalk when he was 12. Two exhibition spaces feature rotating exhibitions of Northwest Coast art, cultural performances, and lectures. The gift shop offers a good selection of Northwest Coast Native art, books, jewelry, and museum-quality collectibles.

639 Hornby St. ℂ **604/682-3455.** www.billreidgallery.ca. Admission C$10 adults, C$7 seniors and students, C$5 children 6–17; C$25 families. Wed–Sun 11am–5pm.

The Bill Reid Gallery of Northwest Coast Art displays some of the artist's most prominent works.

Canada Place ★★ If you've never been to Vancouver, this is a good place to orient yourself and see some of what makes BC's largest city so special. (Or you may arrive here on a cruise ship, in which case, this will be your first introduction to Vancouver.) With its five tall Teflon sails and bowsprit jutting out into Burrard Inlet, Canada Place is meant to resemble a giant sailing ship. Inside, it's a convention center on one level and a giant cruise-ship terminal below, with the Pan Pacific Hotel perched on top. Around the perimeter is a promenade, offering wonderful views across Burrard Inlet to the North Shore peaks and toward nearby Stanley Park, with plaques explaining the sights and providing historical tidbits. Continue around the promenade, and you'll get great city views and be able to see the older, low-rise buildings of Gastown, where Vancouver began. Bus sightseeing tours begin here, and there's a Tourism Vancouver Visitor Centre (see "Visitor Information," chapter 4) right across the street. In 2009, the new addition to the Canada Place Convention Centre opened. With its amazing "green" roof, marvelous light-filled interior spaces, and wonderful plazas and walkways, it has transformed the area adjacent to the "old" Canada Place.

Canada Place (at the north end of Burrard and Howe sts.). Promenade daily 24 hr.

Stanley Park ★★★ ☺ The green jewel of Vancouver, Stanley Park is a 400-hectare (988-acre) rainforest jutting out into the ocean from the edge of the busy West End. Exploring the second-largest urban forest in Canada is one of Vancouver's quintessential experiences.

The park, created in 1888, is filled with towering western red cedar and Douglas fir, manicured lawns, flower gardens, placid lagoons, and countless shaded walking trails that meander through it all. The famed **seawall ★★★** runs along the waterside edge of the park, allowing cyclists and pedestrians to experience the magical interface of forest, sea, and sky. One of the most popular free attractions in the park is the **collection of totem poles ★★★** at Brockton

STANLEY (fun) PARK

Stanley Park is the scene of several yearly events that have become part of the collective consciousness of Vancouverites. From the last weekend in November to early January, the Miniature Railway becomes the **Bright Nights Christmas Train** and runs through a forest illuminated with thousands of festive lights. For 3 weeks in October, the train is transformed into the **Stanley Park Halloween Ghost Train,** with actors portraying vampires and ghouls scaring delighted passengers as the train puffs through the forest. From July to mid-September, visitors can see a **Klahowya Village** in the train plaza.

From June to August, **Dance at Dusk** takes place Monday through Wednesday (on good-weather evenings) from 7 to 9 or 9:30pm, near Ceperley Playground's red fire engine. No partner is required, all ages are welcome, instruction is provided, and it's free. Summer is also the time to enjoy **Theatre Under the Stars,** a Stanley Park tradition at the Malkin Bowl since 1940. In mid-July, thousands of Vancouverites participate in the **Walk with the Dragon** festival, following a giant Chinese dragon along the entire length of the seawall. See the Stanley Park website (http://vancouver.ca/parks) for dates and details.

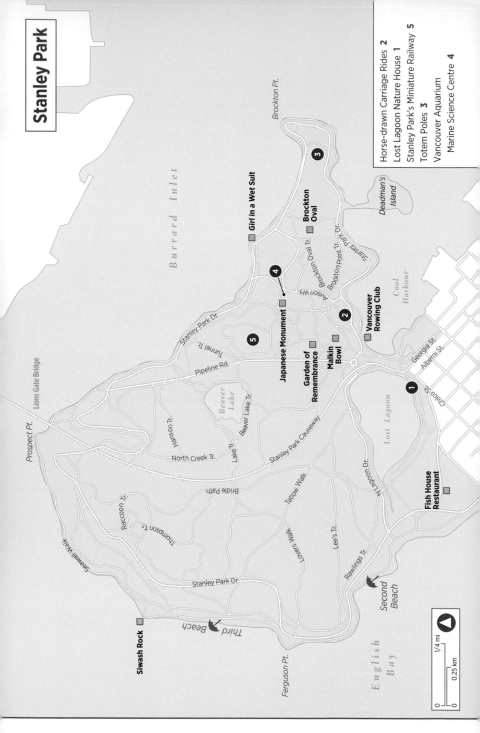

Stanley Park

Burrard Inlet

Brockton Pt.

Deadman's Island

Coal Harbour

English Bay

Prospect Pt.

Lions Gate Bridge

Seawall Walk

Siwash Rock

Third Beach

Ferguson Pt.

Second Beach

Stanley Park Dr.

Raccoon Tr.

Thompson Tr.

Hanson Tr.

North Creek Tr.

Beaver Lake Tr.

Lake Tr.

Beaver Lake

Bridle Path

Tatlow Walk

Lovers' Walk

Lee's Tr.

Rawlings Tr.

N. Lagoon Dr.

Lost Lagoon

Fish House Restaurant

Stanley Park Causeway

Pipeline Rd.

Tunnel Tr.

Stanley Park Dr.

Japanese Monument

Garden of Remembrance

Malkin Bowl

Girl in a Wet Suit

Brockton Oval

Brockton Oval Tr.

Avison Wy.

Brockton Point Tr.

Stanley Park Dr.

Vancouver Rowing Club

Georgia St.

Alberni St.

Chilco St.

1/4 mi
0   0.25 km
0

Horse-drawn Carriage Rides **2**
Lost Lagoon Nature House **1**
Stanley Park's Miniature Railway **5**
Totem Poles **3**
Vancouver Aquarium
Marine Science Centre **4**

120

Stanley Park's miniature railway takes riders through the forests of Stanley Park.

Point, most of them carved in the 1980s to replace the original ones that were placed in the park in the 1920s and 1930s. The area around the totem poles features open-air displays on the Coast Salish First Nations and a small gift shop/ visitor information center.

The park is home to lots of wildlife, including beavers, coyotes, bald eagles, blue herons, cormorants, trumpeter swans, brant geese, ducks, raccoons, skunks, and gray squirrels imported from New York's Central Park decades ago and now quite at home in the Pacific Northwest. (No, there are no bears.) For directions and maps, brochures, and exhibits on the nature and ecology of Stanley Park, visit the **Lost Lagoon Nature House** (© 604/257-8544; free admission; July 1 to Labour Day daily 10am–6pm, weekends only outside this period). Most Sundays at 9am or 1:30pm, rain or shine, they offer themed Discovery Walks of the park (pre-registration recommended). Equally nature-focused but with way more wow is the **Vancouver Aquarium ★★** (see below). The **Stanley Park's Miniature Railway ★** (© 604/257-8531) is a diminutive steam locomotive that pulls passenger cars on a circuit through the woods.

Swimmers head to **Third Beach** and **Second Beach** (p. 144), the latter with an outdoor pool beside English Bay. For kids, there's a free **Spray Park** near Lumberman's Arch, where they can run and splash through various water-spewing fountains. Perhaps the best way to explore the park is to rent a bike (p. 147) or in-line skates, and set off along the seawall. The wonderful **horse-drawn carriage ride ★★★** operated by **AAA Horse & Carriage Ltd.** (© 604/681-5115; www.stanleypark.com) is one of the most enjoyable ways to tour the park. Carriage tours depart every 20 to 45 minutes mid-March through October from the Coal Harbour parking lot, near the Georgia Street park entrance and the park information booth. The ride lasts an hour and covers portions of the park that many locals have never seen. Rates are C$30 for adults, C$28 for seniors and students, and C$16 for children 3 to 12.

Of the three restaurants located in the park, the best is the **Fish House in Stanley Park** (p. 96), where you can have lunch, afternoon tea, or dinner.

The **Vancouver Trolley Company** (© **604/801-5515**) operates an around-the-park shuttle bus mid-June to early September: C$10 for adults, C$5 for children 4 to 11, and C$25 for families.

Stanley Park. © **604/257-8400.** http://vancouver.ca/parks. Free admission. Park daily 24 hr. Bus: 19. Parking C$3/hr., C$10/day.

Vancouver Aquarium Marine Science Centre ★★ ☺ One of North America's largest and best, the Vancouver Aquarium houses more than 70,000 animals. From platforms above or through underwater viewing windows, you can watch the white beluga whales flashing through their pools. (One of the belugas gave birth in June 2008, and another in June 2009.) There are also sea otters, Steller sea lions, and Pacific white-sided dolphins. During regularly scheduled shows, the aquarium staff explains marine-mammal behavior while working with these impressive creatures. The Wild Coast area features a fascinating assortment of fish and sea creatures found in local waters, and there's always an interesting temporary exhibit or two.

For a substantial extra fee (C$130 adults, C$175 one adult and one child age 8–12), you can have a behind-the-scenes Beluga Encounter, helping to feed these giant white cetaceans, then head up to the Marine Mammal deck to take part in the belugas' regular training session. Beluga encounters are available daily at 3pm; book at least 1 day in advance. Other Animal Encounter tours take visitors behind the scenes to interact with dolphins (C$165 adults, C$225 adult and child), or help feed the Steller sea lions (C$39 adults, C$58 adult and child), sea turtles (C$39 adults, C$58 adult and child), and sea otters (C$24 adults, C$35 adult and child). Animal Encounter tours are available daily, but times vary. Call © **800/931-1186** to reserve all of these programs ahead of time. Children must be 8 or older to participate.

360 Degrees of Vancouver

The most popular (and most touristed) spot from which to view Vancouver's skyline and surrounding topography is high atop the space needle observation deck at the **Vancouver Lookout** ★ (555 W. Hastings St.; © **604/689-0421**; www.vancouverlookout.com). It's a great place for first-time visitors who want a panorama of the city. The 360-degree view is remarkable (yes, that is Mt. Baker looming above the southeastern horizon), but the signage identifying points of interest could be a lot better. Skylift admission is C$15 adults, C$12 seniors, C$10 students and children 13 to 18, C$7 children 6 to 12, and free for children 5 and under. It's open daily May to October from 8:30am to 10:30pm and from 9am to 9pm the rest of the year. Tickets are valid for the entire day.

The Vancouver Art Gallery hosts rotating exhibits of contemporary works alongside traditional West Coast art.

845 Avison Way, Stanley Park. ℂ **604/659-FISH** (604/659-3474). www.vanaqua.org. Admission C$27 adults; C$21 seniors, students and children 13–18; C$17 children 4–12; free for children 3 and under. June–Sept daily 9am–7pm; Oct–May daily 9:30am–5pm. Bus: 19. Around the Park shuttle bus mid-June to early Sept. Full-day parking June–Sept C$10 or C$3 per hour, Oct–May C$5 or C$2 for 2 hr.

Vancouver Art Gallery ★★ Designed as a courthouse by BC's leading early-20th-century architect Francis Rattenbury (the architect of Victoria's Empress Hotel and the Legislature buildings), and renovated into an art gallery by BC's leading late-20th-century architect Arthur Erickson, the Gallery is an excellent stop to see what sets Canadian and West Coast art apart from the rest of the world. Along with an impressive collection of paintings by BC native **Emily Carr ★★★** are examples of a unique Canadian art style created during the 1920s by members of the "Group of Seven," which included painter Lawren Harris who moved to Vancouver in 1940. The Gallery also hosts rotating exhibits of contemporary sculpture, graphics, photography, and video art from around the world. Watch for an occasional Friday event called FUSE—a melding of live performance, music, and art. DJs and gallery tours keep popular event going until 1am.

750 Hornby St. ℂ **604/662-4719.** www.vanartgallery.bc.ca. Admission C$20 adults, C$14 seniors, C$13 students, C$7 kids 5–12; C$50 families. Wed–Mon 10am–5pm; Tues 10am–9pm. SkyTrain: Granville. Buses: 4, 5, 6, 7, 10 all stop within 2 blocks.

Gastown & Chinatown

Dr. Sun Yat-Sen Classical Chinese Garden ★★ This small reproduction of a Classical Chinese scholar's garden truly is a remarkable place, but to get the full effect, it's best to take the guided tour (included in admission). Untrained eyes will only see a pretty pond surrounded by bamboo and oddly shaped rocks. The engaging guides, however, can explain this unique urban garden's Taoist yin-yang design principle, in which harmony is achieved through dynamic opposition. To foster opposition (and thus harmony) in the garden, Chinese designers place contrasting elements in juxtaposition: Soft-moving water flows across solid stone; smooth, swaying bamboo grows around gnarled immovable rocks; dark pebbles are placed next to light pebbles in the paving. Moving with the guide, you discover the symbolism of intricate carvings and marvel at the ever-changing views from covered serpentine corridors. This is one of two Classical Chinese gardens in North America (the other is in Portland, Oregon) created by master artisans from Suzhou, the garden city of China.

578 Carrall St. ✆ **604/662-3207.** www.vancouverchinesegarden.com. Admission C$12 adults, C$10 seniors, C$9 students, free for children 4 and under; C$25 families. Free guided tour included. May–June 14 and Sept daily 10am–6pm; June 15–Aug daily 9:30am–7pm; Oct–Apr Tues–Sun 10am–4:30pm. Bus: 19 or 22.

Steam Clock ☺   The Steam Clock in Gastown is a favorite photo op for tourists. Built by horologist Raymond Saunders in 1977 (based on an 1875 design), it was the world's first steam clock, powered by steam from an underground system of pipes that supply heat to many downtown buildings. The clock is supposed to sound its whistles (playing "The Westminster Chimes") every quarter-hour, with steam shooting out from vents at the top. Sometimes, however, it simply steams with no musical accompaniment. See "Gastown & Chinatown" walking tour in chapter 8.

Gastown (at the intersection of Water and Cambie sts.). Free.

Vancouver Police Museum   If you have a real fascination with crime, this museum will occupy an hour of your time; if not, I wouldn't recommend a visit. It's a well-meaning, old-fashioned place housed in the old Vancouver Coroner's Court (where actor Errol Flynn was autopsied in 1959 after dropping dead in the arms of a 17-year-old girl) and dedicated to memorializing some of the best cops and worst crimes in the city's short but colorful history. The confiscated illegal-weapons display is hair-raising; you can also see the old morgue, a simulated autopsy room (with pieces of damaged body parts in specimen bottles), and a forensics lab (sleuths of all ages can partake in the Forensic Science program, Sun noon–4pm). More fun and a lot more fascinating is the 2-hour **Sins of the City Walking Tour** ★, which departs from the museum Wednesdays, Fridays, and Saturdays at 4pm (early May to early Oct), and covers (or uncovers) the history of vice in a 10-block area around the museum. Tour cost (which includes museum entrance) is C$15 adults, C$12 seniors and students; it's essential to make reservations at least 1 day ahead.

240 E. Cordova St. ✆ **604/665-3346.** www.vancouverpolicemuseum.ca. Admission C$7 adults; C$5 seniors, students and children 7–13; C$20 families. Mon–Sat 9am–5pm. Bus: 4 or 7.

In a Summer Garden

Every Friday evening at 7:30pm from mid-July through the first weekend in September, the Dr. Sun Yat-Sen Classical Chinese Garden is the scene of musical performances and dances. The eclectic repertoire includes classical, Asian, world, Gypsy jazz, Slavic soul, and fusion music. Shows cost about C$20 and often sell out. The website provides a full listing of concerts; call ✆ **604/662-3207** to reserve tickets.

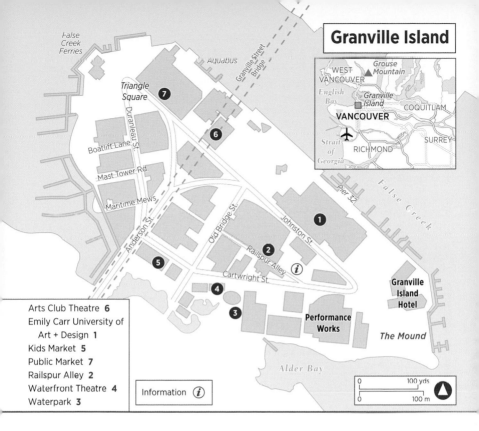

Granville Island

Arts Club Theatre	6
Emily Carr University of Art + Design	1
Kids Market	5
Public Market	7
Railspur Alley	2
Waterfront Theatre	4
Waterpark	3

Information (i)

The West Side

Beaty Biodiversity Museum   The suspended blue whale skeleton trumps the rows and rows of stored specimens at this underground museum. Unfortunately, a few interactive displays and backroom of microscopes don't provide enough to engage. But seeing a skeleton of world's largest mammal—a 25m (82 ft.) female blue whale, bigger than a brontosaurus—is worth the trip. A guide can explain how filter-feeding blue whales sift out krill from gallons of saltwater. Pinned butterflies, snakes jarred in alcohol, pressed flowers, and marine invertebrate show the diversity of the museum's collection.

2212 Main Mall, UBC. (C) **604/827-4955.** www.beatymuseum.ubc.ca. Admission C$12 adults; C$10 seniors and children 13–17; C$8 children 5–12. Daily 10am–5pm. Bus: 4 or 99.

Granville Island ★★★ ☺   Almost a city within a city, Granville Island is a good place to browse away a morning, an afternoon, or a whole day. You can wander through a busy public market jammed with food stalls, shop for crafts, pick up some fresh seafood, enjoy a great dinner, watch the latest theater performance, rent a yacht, stroll along the waterfront, or simply run through the sprinkler on a hot summer day; it's all there and more. If you have only a short period of time, make sure you spend at least part of it in the **Granville Island Public Market ★★★**, one of the best all-around markets in North America.

GRANVILLE'S greatest HITS

Even though the bustling **Public Market** ★★★ makes a fine destination in itself, Granville Island offers much more. To really get a feel for this neighborhood, stroll along the side streets and explore the alleys and lanes away from the main entrance. Check out the recommended attractions below:

○ Railspur Alley's artist studios are perfect for browsing; stop in at **Alarte Silk** in the Alley Gallery (1369 Railspur Alley; ✆ **778/370-4304**) to see some of the beautifully hand-painted wearable silk art; check out the wares at **Artisan Sake** (1339 Railspur Alley; ✆ **604/685-7253**), Canada's first boutique premium sake winery; or pause at the **Agro Café** (1363 Railspur Alley; ✆ **604/669-0724**) for a latte.

○ Art exhibits in the North Building at the **Emily Carr University of Art + Design** (1399 Johnston St.; ✆ **604/844-3800;** www.ecuad.ca) showcase the works of the institute's grads and students. You may be looking at the next Andy Warhol. Media and Concourse Galleries are free and open daily during university hours (usually early morning to midnight or later); the Charles H. Scott Gallery, showing exhibits of international work, is open Monday to Friday noon to 5pm, Saturday and Sunday 10am to 5pm.

○ In summer, check the **Carousel Theatre** (✆ **604/685-6217;** www.carouseltheatre.ca) schedule for free outdoor Shakespearean plays by a cast of teen actors or see what's playing at the **Arts Club Theatre** (✆ **604/687-1644;** www.artsclub.

com), **Performance Works** (✆ **604/687-3020;** www.performanceworks.ca), or the **Waterfront Theatre** (✆ **604/685-1731;** www.waterfronttheatre.ca).

○ Paddle off into the sunset by renting a kayak from one of the marinas on the west side of the island. Beginners can take lessons or head out on a guided tour. **Ecomarine Ocean Kayak Centre** (✆ **604/689-7575;** www.ecomarine.com) has everything to get you started. A 3-hour kayak lesson for C$76 teaches you the basic strokes. Or explore the waters of False Creek and English Bay on a 2½-hour tour with a guide for C$65. Experienced paddlers can rent single or double kayaks (C$89 single kayak, C$119 double kayak for full day) as well as standup paddleboards (C$19 for 1 hr., C$29 for 2 hr.).

○ Granville Island is one big playground. On a rainy day, duck into the **Kids Market** (daily 10am–6pm) to check out toys, kites, clothes, art supplies, and an indoor play area. On warm days, the free **water park** is the place to be. Open daily (weather permitting) from 10am to 6pm, late May until Labour Day.

Once a declining industrial site, Granville Island started transforming in the late 1970s when the government encouraged new, people-friendly developments. Maintaining its original industrial look, the former warehouses and factories now house galleries, artist studios, restaurants, and theaters; the cement plant on the waterfront is the only industrial tenant left. Access to Granville Island is by Aquabus from the West End, Yaletown, or Kitsilano (see "By Mini-Ferry," in chapter 4; the Aquabus drops you at the public market) or by foot, bike, or car across the

The Emily Carr University of Art + Design showcases the works of grads and students.

bridge/causeway at Anderson Street (access from W. 2nd Ave.). Avoid driving over on weekends and holidays—you'll spend more time trying to find a parking place than in the galleries. Check the website for upcoming events or stop by the information center, behind the Kids Market. Also see "Walking Tour 3: Yaletown, Granville Island & Kitsilano," p. 170.

If you can't bear to leave the island, consider staying at the **Granville Island Hotel** (p. 80). Even if you don't stay, it's worth stopping by the hotel's brewpub restaurant, the Dockside Brewery Company, for a brew with a view.

The south shore of False Creek (under the Granville St. Bridge). ℭ **604/666-5784** (information center). www.granvilleisland.com. Public market daily 9am–7pm. Bus: 50.

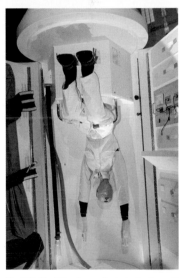

The H.R. MacMillan Space Centre's displays will delight space buffs.

H. R. MacMillan Space Centre ★ ☺   In the same building as the Museum of Vancouver (p. 129), the space center and observatory has hands-on displays and exhibits that will delight budding astronomy buffs and their parents (or older space buffs and their children). Displays are highly interactive: In the Cosmic Courtyard, you can try designing a spacecraft or maneuvering a lunar robot. Or punch a button and get a video explanation of the *Apollo 17* manned-satellite engine that stands before you. The exciting **Virtual Voyages Simulator** ★★ takes you on a voyage to Mars—it's a thrilling experience for kids and adults. In

The Museum of Anthropology has an outstanding collection of Northwest Coast Native art.

the GroundStation Canada Theatre, video presentations explore space, in general, and Canada's contributions to the space program. The StarTheatre shows movies—many of them for children—on an overhead dome. Evening laser and light shows feature cult-favorite albums (say by Pink Floyd or Radiohead) played loudly. 1100 Chestnut St. (in Vanier Park). ℭ **604/738-7827.** www.spacecentre.ca. Admission C$15 adults; C$11 seniors, students, and children 5–10; children 4 and under free; C$45 families (up to 5, maximum 2 adults). Evening laser shows C$11 adults. July to early Sept daily 10am–5pm; early Sept–June Mon–Fri 10am–3pm, Sat–Sun 10am–5pm; evening laser shows Fri–Sat 8:15, 9:20, and 10:25pm. Closed Dec 25. Bus: 22.

Museum of Anthropology ★★★ ☺ This isn't just any old museum. In 1976, BC architect Arthur Erickson created a classic native post-and-beam-style structure out of poured concrete and glass to house one of the world's finest collections of Northwest Coast Native art. A major renovation and rebranding completed in 2010 more than doubled the gallery space and added new luster to this remarkable showplace.

Enter through doors that resemble a huge, carved, bent-cedar box. Artifacts from different coastal communities flank the ramp leading to the Great Hall's **collection of totem poles.** Haida artist Bill Reid's masterpiece, *The Raven and the First Men,* is worth the price of admission all by itself. The huge carving in glowing yellow cedar depicts a Haida creation myth, in which Raven—the trickster—coaxes humanity out into the world from its birthplace in a clamshell. Some of Reid's fabulous jewelry creations in gold and silver are also on display.

The **Gallery 3**'s argillite sculptures, beaded and metalwork jewelry, and hand-carved ceremonial masks lead the way to the Multiversity Galleries, where more than 10,000 artifacts are arranged by culture. You can open the glass-topped drawers to view small treasures and stroll past larger pieces housed in tall glass cases.

Also at the museum is the somewhat incongruous Koerner Ceramics Gallery, a collection of European ceramics.

Behind the museum, overlooking Point Grey, are two **longhouses** built according to the Haida tribal style, resting on the traditional north-south axis. Ten hand-carved totem poles stand in attendance along with contemporary carvings on the longhouse facades. *Note:* You might want to pair this with a visit to the nearby UBC Botanical Garden & Nitobe Memorial Garden (see below). A number of trails also lead down to a few of Vancouver's most pristine beaches (p. 143). 6393 NW Marine Dr. (at Gate 4). ✆ **604/822-5087.** www.moa.ubc.ca. Admission C$14 adults; C$12 seniors, students and children 6–18; free for children 5 and under; C$7 for all Tues 5–9pm. Spring/summer daily 10am–5pm, Tues 10am–9pm; fall/winter Wed–Sun 10am–5pm, Tues 10am–9pm. Closed Dec 25 and 26. Bus: 4 or 99 (10-min. walk from UBC bus loop).

Museum of Vancouver Located in the same building as the H. R. MacMillan Space Centre (p. 127), the Museum of Vancouver is dedicated to the city's history, from its days as a native settlement and European outpost to its 20th-century maturation into a modern urban center. Of most importance here is the wonderful collection of First Nations art and artifacts. Hilarious, campy fun abounds in the 1950s Room, with its vinyl diner booth and neon signs. Next to this is another fun, and socially intriguing, room devoted to Vancouver's years as a hippie capital, with film clips, commentary, and a replica hippie apartment. 1100 Chestnut St. ✆ **604/736-4431.** www.museumofvancouver.ca. Admission C$12 adults, C$10 seniors, C$8 children 5–17. July–Aug Fri–Wed 10am–5pm, Thurs 10am–8pm; Sept–June Tues, Wed and Fri–Sun 10am–5pm; Thurs 10am–8pm. Bus: 2 or 22, then walk 3 blocks south on Cornwall Ave. Boat: False Creek Ferry to Heritage Harbour.

UBC Botanical Garden & Nitobe Memorial Garden ★   Serious plant lovers will love the University of British Columbia. The prime attraction on campus, besides the must-see Museum of Anthropology (see above), is the 44-hectare (110-acre) **UBC Botanical Garden,** home to more than 8,000 species of trees, shrubs, and flowers grouped into a BC native garden, a physic (or medicinal) garden, a food garden, and several others. You can also peruse the excellent plant and seed store. (*Note:* You can't bring plants in soil across the U.S. border or back into most countries, including the U.K.) Give yourself at least an hour if you want

The Nitobe Memorial Garden is considered one of the top five Japanese gardens in North America.

to explore this garden; it's best in spring when the flowering trees blossom. The **Greenheart Canopy Walkway** is ideal for energetic kids. Its platforms, suspended on wires at up to 18m (57 ft.) high, move in waves as you walk the metal planks. Take a guided tour to get a sense of the life within the forest canopy. Nearby is the **Nitobe Memorial Garden,** a beautiful traditional Japanese garden considered among the top five Japanese gardens in North America and one of the most authentic Tea and Stroll Gardens outside of Japan. Cherry blossoms peak in April and May, the irises bloom in June, and autumn brings colorful leaf displays.

Botanical Garden: 6804 SW Marine Dr., Gate 8. ℭ **604/822-4208.** www.ubcbotanicalgarden. org. Admission C$8 adults; C$6 seniors, students, and children 13–17; C$4 children 6–12; free for children 5 and under. With Greenheart Canopy Walkway: C$20 adults; C$15 seniors, students, and children 13–17; C$10 children 6–12. Family rates available. Nitobe Memorial Garden: 1895 Lower Mall. ℭ **604/822-6038.** www.nitobe.org. Admission C$6 adults, C$5 seniors and children 13–17, C$3 children 6–12, free for children 5 and under. Pass for all 3 attractions, C$24 adults; C$18 seniors, students, and children 13–17; C$12 children 6–12. UBC Botanical Garden open year-round; the Nitobe Memorial Garden closes during winter.

Vancouver Maritime Museum ☺   The museum's main attraction is the 1920s RCMP Arctic patrol vessel *St. Roch,* the first ship to travel the Northwest Passage both west-east and east-west, preserved with most of its original stores and equipment onboard. Tours of the *St. Roch* are popular with kids—they get to clamber around the boat, poking and prodding stuff. It also serves as a starting point to illuminate life in Canada's North, be it touching polar bear hair or measuring narwhal tusks.

Model ships, maps, and prints will appeal only to nautical nuts. If the weather is pleasant, walk across the front lawn at the edge of False Creek to Heritage Harbour, where the museum keeps a collection of vintage boats. You can also catch the mini-ferry there to Granville Island or the West End.

1905 Ogden Ave. (in Vanier Park). ℭ **604/ 257-8300.** www.vancouvermaritimemuseum.com. Admission C$11 adults, C$8.50 seniors and children 6–18, free for children 5 and under; C$30 families. Late May–Aug daily 10am–5pm; Sept–May Tues–Sat 10am–5pm, Sun noon–5pm. Bus: 2 or 22, then walk 4 blocks north on Cypress St. Boat: False Creek ferries dock at Heritage Harbour.

The East Side

Science World at TELUS World of Science ★ ☺   Science World is impossible to miss: It's the big blinking geodesic dome (built for Expo '86 and now partnered with TELUS, a communications company, hence the branded name) on the eastern end of False Creek. Inside, it's

Science World is loaded with first-rate adventures for kids from toddler age to early teens.

a hands on scientific discovery center where you and your kids can (depending on the current exhibits) light up a plasma ball, walk through a maze, wander through the interior of a camera, create a cyclone, watch a zucchini explode as it's charged with 80,000 volts, stand inside a beaver lodge, play in wrist-deep magnetic liquids, create music with a giant synthesizer, and watch mind-bending three-dimensional slide and laser shows, as well as other optical effects. Science World is loaded with first-rate adventures for kids from toddler age to early teens; you'll want to spend at least a couple of hours here. Throughout the day, special shows, many with nature themes, are presented in the OMNIMAX Theatre—a huge projecting screen equipped with surround sound.

1455 Quebec St. ✆ **604/443-7443.** www.scienceworld.ca. Admission C$21 adults, C$17 seniors and students, C$14 children 4–12, free for children 3 and under; C$57 families (2 adults with up to 4 children). OMNIMAX ticket C$5 adults. Sept–June Mon–Fri 10am–5pm, Sat–Sun 10am–6pm; July–Aug daily 10am–6pm; holidays 10am–6pm. SkyTrain: Main St.–Science World.

North Vancouver & West Vancouver

Capilano Suspension Bridge & Park ★   Vancouver's first and oldest tourist trap (built in 1889), this attraction still works—mostly because there's still something inherently thrilling about walking across a narrow, shaky walkway 70m (230 ft.) above a canyon floor, held up by nothing but a pair of tiny (although exceedingly strong) cables. Set in a beautiful 11-hectare (27-acre) park about 15 minutes from downtown, the suspension bridge itself is a 137m-long (450-ft.) cedar-plank and steel-cable footbridge, which sways and bounces gently above the Capilano River. Visitors nervously cross above kayakers and salmon shooting the rapids far below. Opened in 2011, **Cliffhanger** connects suspended walkways to get a better view of granite cliffs and the Capilano Canyon. Some stretches have nothing but glass below. The **Treetops Adventure** attraction features more bridges and walkways, only these are attached to giant tree trunks 30m (100 ft.) above the rainforest floor.

In addition to the bridge, the park has a **carving center** where native carvers demonstrate their skill, an exhibit describing the region's natural history, guides in period costume who recount Vancouver's frontier days, and a pair of overpriced and poorly serviced restaurants. Though overall it's quite well done, it's hard to justify the exorbitant entrance fee, and the summer crowds can be off-putting. If the admission price is a roadblock, you can have a similar experience at the nearby Lynn Canyon Suspension Bridge, which is almost as high, set in a far larger forest, almost untouristed, and absolutely free (see "The Other Suspension Bridge," p. 137).

3735 Capilano Rd., North Vancouver. ✆ **604/985-7474.** www.capbridge.com. Admission C$30 adults, C$28 seniors, C$24 students, C$19 children 13–16, C$10 children 6–12, free for children 5 and under. May–Sept daily 8:30am–dusk; Oct–Apr daily 9am–5pm or later. Hours change monthly. Closed Dec 25. Bus: 246 or 236 from Lonsdale Quay. There is also a free shuttle from some downtown hotels. Car: Hwy. 99 north across Lions Gate Bridge to exit 14 on Capilano Rd.

Grouse Mountain ★★ ☺   Once a local ski hill, Grouse Mountain has developed into a year-round mountain recreation park that claims to be the number-one attraction in Vancouver. It's fun if you're sports minded or like the outdoors; if not, you might find it disappointing. Located only a 15-minute drive from

The Skyride gondola takes you toward the summit of Grouse Mountain.

downtown, the **Skyride gondola** ★★ transports you on the first leg toward the mountain's 1,250m (4,101-ft.) summit. (Hikers can take a near vertical trail called the Grouse Grind. See "Doin' the Grouse Grind," below.) On a clear day, the **view** ★★★ from the top is the best around: You can see the city and the entire lower mainland, from far up the Fraser Valley east across the Strait of Georgia to Vancouver Island. In the lodge, **Theater in the Sky** ★ shows wildlife movies. Outside, in the winter, you can ski and snowboard (26 runs, 13 runs for night skiing/snowboarding; drop-in ski lessons available), go snowshoeing, skate on the highest outdoor rink in Canada, and take a brief "sleigh ride" (behind a huge snow-cat), and the kids can play in a special snow park. In warmer weather, you can wander forest trails, take a scenic chair ride, enjoy a lumberjack show or Birds in Motion demonstrations, or visit the Refuge for Endangered Wildlife. Visible from downtown, the new **Eye of the Wind** turbine takes you up a farther 57m (187 ft.) to a 360-degree viewing tower atop the windmill. The extra admission belays the small numbers (just 36 in the viewing tower) the windmill can accommodate. Most of these activities are included in the rather exorbitant price of your Skyride ticket; you have to pay extra for a lift ticket and equipment rentals as well as the Eye of the Wind. Casual and fine-dining options, and a Starbucks,

Doin' the Grouse Grind

The "Grouse Grind," a popular 2.9km (1.8-mile) trail, often called "Mother Nature's Stairmaster" by locals, generally opens late spring or early summer. Over 100,000 hikers per year take on the challenge of the rugged terrain and steep climb. By the time you reach the plateau, your ascent will have gained 853m (2,799 ft.). Average completion time is usually 1½ hours, with the fastest official completion time sitting at just over 25 minutes (the unofficial record dips under 24 min.). Once you reach the top, you can take the tram back down for just C$5 per person. For a look at the terrain, visit www.vancouvertrails.com/trails/grouse-grind.

are in the lodge. If you make dinner reservations at **The Observatory** restaurant (ⓒ **604/980-9311**), you get free admission to the Skyride as well as other mountaintop activities.

6400 Nancy Greene Way, North Vancouver. ⓒ **604/984-0661.** www.grousemountain.com. Skyride C$40 adults, C$36 seniors, C$24 children 13–18, C$14 children 5–12, free for children 4 and under. Full-day ski-lift tickets C$55 adults, C$45 seniors and children 13–18, C$25 children 5–12. Skyride free with advance Observatory Restaurant reservation. Daily 9am–10pm. Bus: 240 from W. Georgia St. and transfer to bus 236, or take bus 232 from Phibbs Exchange. SeaBus: Lonsdale Quay, then transfer to bus 236. Car: Hwy. 99 north across Lions Gate Bridge, take North Vancouver exit to Marine Dr., then up Capilano Rd. for 5km (3 miles). Parking C$3 for 2 hr. in lots below Skyride.

VANCOUVER'S PLAZAS & PARKS

Plazas

Unlike many cities, Vancouver's great urban gathering places stand not at the center but on the periphery, on two opposite sides of the **seawall** that runs around Stanley Park: **English Bay,** on the south side of Denman Street, and **Coal Harbour,** on the northern, Burrard Inlet side. They are where Vancouverites go to stroll and be seen and, on warm sunny days, the two areas are packed. Another waterside gathering spot is **Canada Place** (p. 119), built for Expo '86 and enlarged in 2009 to add more convention space. Built in the shape of a cruise ship and serving as the city's cruise-ship terminal, it has wide walkways all around it that are super for strolling, and it offers fabulous views of the mountains.

Designed by architect Arthur Erickson to be Vancouver's central plaza, **Robson Square**—downtown, between Hornby and Howe streets from Robson to Smithe streets—has never really worked. The square, which anchors the north end of the Provincial Law Courts complex designed by Erickson in 1973, suffers from a basic design flaw: It's sunk below street level, making it difficult to see and to access. The Law Courts complex, which sits on a higher level, raised above the street, is beautifully executed with shrubbery, cherry trees, sculptures, and a tri-ple-tiered waterfall, but Robson Square below is about as appealing as a drained swimming pool. Just opposite Robson Square, however, the steps of the **Vancou-ver Art Gallery** (p. 123) are a great people place, filled with loungers, political agitators, and old men playing chess.

Library Square—a few blocks east from Robson Square at the corner of Robson and Homer streets—is an example of a new urban space that does work. It's been popular with locals since it opened in 1995. People sit on the steps, bask in the sunshine, read, harangue passersby with half-baked political ideas, and generally seem to enjoy themselves.

Library Square is popular with locals.

Parks & Gardens

Park and garden lovers are in heaven in Vancouver. The wet, mild climate is ideal for gardening, and come spring, the city blazes with blossoming cherry trees, magnolia or "tulip" trees, rhododendrons, camellias, azaleas, and spring bulbs—and roses in summer. Gardens are everywhere. For general information about Vancouver's parks, call the parks board at © **604/873-7000** or try http://vancouver.ca/parks. For information on **Stanley Park ★★★**, the lord of them all, see p. 119.

In Chinatown, the **Dr. Sun Yat-Sen Classical Chinese Garden ★★** (p. 123) is a small, tranquil oasis in the heart of the city, built by artisans from Suzhou, China; right next to it, accessed via the Chinese Cultural Centre on Pender Street, is the pretty (and free) **Dr. Sun Yat-Sen Park,** with a koi-filled pond, walkways, and plantings.

On the West Side, you'll find the magnificent **UBC Botanical Garden,** one of the largest living botany collections on the west coast, and the sublime **Nitobe Memorial Garden ★**; for descriptions of both, see p. 129.

Also on the West Side, **Queen Elizabeth Park**—at Cambie Street and West 33rd Avenue—sits atop a 150m-high (492-ft.) hill (thought to be an extinct volcano) and is the highest urban vantage point south of downtown, offering panoramic views in all directions. Along with the rose garden in Stanley Park, it's Vancouver's most popular location for wedding-photo sessions, with well-manicured gardens and a profusion of colorful flora. There are areas for lawn bowling, tennis, disc golf, pitch-and-putt golf, and picnicking. The **Bloedel Conservatory** (© **604/257-8584**) stands next to the park's huge sunken garden, an amazing reclamation of an abandoned rock quarry. A

The Bloedel Conservatory houses a tropical rainforest with more than 100 free-flying tropical birds.

21m-high (70-ft) domed structure, the conservatory (May–Sept Mon–Fri 9am–8pm and 10am–9pm weekends; Oct–Apr daily 10am–5pm) houses a tropical rainforest with more than 100 free-flying tropical birds. Admission to the conservatory is C$5 for adults, with discounts for seniors, children, and families. Take bus no. 15 to reach the park.

Vancouver's 22-hectare (54-acre) **VanDusen Botanical Gardens** (5251 Oak St., at W. 37th Ave.; ✆ **604/878-9274;** www.vandusengarden.org), located just a few blocks from Queen Elizabeth Park and the Bloedel Conservatory, concentrates on whole ecosystems. From towering trees to little lichens on the smallest of damp stones, the gardeners at VanDusen attempt to re-create the plant life of a number of different environments. Depending on which trail you take, you may find yourself wandering through the Southern Hemisphere section, the Sino-Himalayan garden, or the glade of Giant Redwoods. Should all this tree-gazing finally pall, head for the farthest corner of the garden to the devilishly difficult Elizabethan garden maze. Admission April through September costs C$10 adults, C$7.50 seniors and children 13 to 18, C$5.50 children 3 to 12, and C$24 families; it's free for children 2 and under. Reduced admission prices October through March. Open daily 10am to dusk. Take bus no. 17. **Note:** The garden lost hundreds of trees in the December 2006 windstorm that also devastated Stanley Park.

Adjoining the University of British Columbia (UBC) on the city's west side at Point Grey, **Pacific Spirit Regional Park,** called the **Endowment Lands** by longtime Vancouver residents, is the largest green space in Vancouver. Comprising 754 hectares (1,885 acres) of temperate rainforest, marshes, and beaches, the park includes more than 50km (31 miles) of trails ideal for hiking, riding, mountain biking, and beachcombing.

Across the Lions Gate Bridge, provincial and regional parks on the North Shore Mountains delight outdoor enthusiasts year-round. Good in winter or for those averse to strenuous climbing is the publicly maintained **Capilano River Regional Park** (4500 Capilano Park Rd.; ✆ **604/224-5739**) surrounding the Capilano Suspension Bridge & Park (p. 131). Hikers can follow a gentle trail by the river for about 7km (4.4 miles) down the well-maintained **Capilano Pacific trail** to Ambleside Park and the Lions Gate Bridge, or a mile upstream to **Cleveland Dam,** a launching point for white-water kayakers and canoeists.

The **Capilano Salmon Hatchery,** on Capilano Park Road (✆ **604/666-1790**), is on the river's east bank about .5km (¼ mile) below the Cleveland Dam. Approximately 2 million coho and chinook salmon are hatched annually in glass-fronted tanks connected to the river by a series of channels. You can observe the hatching fry (baby fish) before they depart for open waters, as well as the mature salmon that return to the Capilano River to spawn (Oct–Dec is best viewing time for chinook; June–Nov for coho; Mar–Apr for steelhead). Admission is free, and the hatchery is open daily from 8am to 7pm (until 4pm Oct–Apr). Drive across Lions Gate Bridge and follow the signs to North Vancouver and the Capilano Suspension Bridge. Or take the SeaBus to Lonsdale Quay and transfer to bus no. 236; the trip takes less than 45 minutes.

Lighthouse Park has fabulous views of Vancouver across the Strait of Georgia.

Ten kilometers (6 miles) west of Lions Gate Bridge on Marine Drive West, West Vancouver, is **Lighthouse Park ★**. This 75-hectare (185-acre) rugged-terrain forest has 13km (8 miles) of groomed trails and—because it has never been clear-cut—some of the largest and oldest trees in the Vancouver area. One of the paths leads to the 18m (59-ft.) **Point Atkinson Lighthouse,** on a rocky bluff overlooking the Strait of Georgia and a fabulous view of Vancouver. It's an easy trip on bus no. 250. For information about other West Vancouver parks, call ℂ **604/925-7200** on weekdays.

Driving up-up-up will eventually get you to the top of **Cypress Provincial Park.** Stop halfway at the scenic viewpoint for a sweeping vista of the Vancouver skyline, the harbor, the Gulf Islands, and Washington State's Mount Baker, which peers above the eastern horizon. The park is 12km (7½ miles) north of Cypress Bowl Road and the Highway 99 (also mapped as the Upper Level Highway and the Trans-Canada) junction in West Vancouver. Cypress Provincial Park has trails for hiking during the summer and autumn, and **Cypress Mountain** (ℂ **604/926-5612;** www.cypressmountain.com) grooms slopes for downhill and cross-country skiing during the winter.

Rising 1,449m (4,754 ft.) above Indian Arm, the peaks of **Mount Seymour Provincial Park** and its ski hill **Mount Seymour** (1700 Mt. Seymour Rd., North Vancouver; ℂ **604/986-2261;** www.mountseymour.com) offer another view of the area's Coast Mountains range. Higher than Grouse Mountain, Mount Seymour provides a spectacular view of Washington State's Mount Baker on clear days. It has challenging hiking trails that go straight to the summit, where you can see Indian Arm, Vancouver's bustling commercial port, the city skyline, the Strait of Georgia, and Vancouver Island. The trails are open all summer for hiking; during the winter, the paths are maintained for daily skiing, snowboarding, and snowshoeing.

THE *OTHER* suspension BRIDGE

Lynn Canyon Park—in North Vancouver, between Grouse Mountain and Mount Seymour Provincial Park, on Lynn Valley Road—offers a free alternative to the Capilano Suspension Bridge. True, the **Lynn Canyon Suspension Bridge** ★ is both shorter and a little lower than Capilano (p. 131), but the waterfall and swirling whirlpools in the canyon below add both beauty and a certain fear-inducing fascination. Plus, it's free.

The park is located in a gorgeous 249.7-hectare (617-acre) rainforest of cedar and Douglas fir and is also home to an **Ecology Centre** (3663 Park Rd.; *②* **604/990-3755;** www.dnv.org/ecology), which presents natural-history films, tours, and displays that explain the local ecology. Staff members lead frequent walking tours. The center is open June to September daily from 10am to 5pm (Oct–May Mon–Fri 10am–5pm; Sat–Sun noon–4pm). The park itself is open from 7am to 7pm in spring and fall, 7am to 9pm in summer, and 7am to dusk in winter; it's closed December 25 and 26,

and January 1. To get there, take the SeaBus to Lonsdale Quay, then transfer to bus no. 229; by car, take the Trans-Canada Highway (Hwy. 1) to the Lynn Valley Road exit (about a 20-min. drive from downtown) and follow Lynn Valley Road to Peters Road, where you turn right. The park's cafe serves sit-down and takeout meals.

About four kilometers (2½ miles) up Lynn Valley Road from the highway is **Lynn Headwaters Regional Park** (*②* **604/985-1690** for trail conditions), one of the best places close to the city to experience the breathtaking nature of the Northwest. Until the mid-1980s, this was inaccessible wilderness and bear habitat. The park and the bears are now managed by the Greater Vancouver Regional Parks Department. Some of the 14 marked trails and scrambles of various levels of difficulty meander by the riverbank, while others climb steeply up to various North Shore peaks, and one trail leads to a series of cascading waterfalls.

Historic Landmarks & Attractions

The **Burnaby Village Museum** (6501 Deer Lake Ave., Burnaby; ℂ **604/293-6501;** www.burnabyvillagemuseum.ca), is a 4-hectare (10-acre) re-creation of the town as it might have appeared in the 1920s. You can walk along boardwalk streets among costumed townspeople, shop in a general store, ride a vintage carousel, peek into an authentic one-room schoolhouse, and visit a vintage ice-cream parlor that's been in the same location since the turn of the 20th century. At Christmastime, the whole village is aglow in lights and Victorian decorations. Admission fees—waived in 2011 to celebrate the museum's 40th anniversary— are C$12 for adults; C$9 for seniors, students, and children 13 to 18; C$6 for children 6 to 12; and free for children 5 and under. From May to early September, it's open Tuesday to Sunday from 11am to 4:30pm; October 28 through October 30 ("Haunted Village") from 6 to 9pm; last weekend in November through mid-December noon to 4:30pm; and mid-December through January 1 ("Holiday Village") from noon to 8pm. It's closed December 24 and 25. From the Metrotown SkyTrain Station, take bus no. 144 SFU to Deer Lake.

The **Fort Langley National Historic Site** (23433 Mavis Ave., Fort Langley; ℂ **604/513-4777;** www.pc.gc.ca/fortlangley) is the birthplace of British Columbia. In 1827, the Hudson's Bay Company established this settlement to supply its provincial posts. Costumed craftspeople demonstrate blacksmithing, coopering, and woodworking, bringing this landmark back to life. It's open year-round; daily from 9am to 6pm in July and August, 10am to 5pm the rest of the year. Admission is C$7.80 adults, C$6.55 seniors, C$3.90 children 6 to 16, and free for children 5 and under; a family pass is C$20. To get there, take the Sky-Train to Surrey Central Station and transfer to bus nos. 501, 502, or 320 to Langley Centre, and then pick up the C62 Walnut Grove to 6 Ave. and Glover Rd. **Note:** The main street of Fort Langley Village, Glover Road, is packed with antiques shops, a bookstore, and cafes, and it's only a 2-minute stroll away.

ESPECIALLY FOR KIDS

Pick up copies of the free monthly newspapers *BC Parent* (ℂ **604/221-0366;** www.bcparent.ca) and *West Coast Families* (ℂ **604/249-2866;** www.west coastfamilies.com). *West Coast Families'* community calendar lists many current events, including festivals and museum programs. Both publications, as well as Tourism Vancouver's **Kids' Guide,** are available at Granville Island's Kids Market and the visitor center at 200 Burrard St.

To give kids an overview of the city, take the trolley tour offered by **Vancouver Trolley Company** (ℂ **888/451-5581** or 604/801-5515; www.vancouver trolley.com). Gas-powered trolleys run through Downtown, Chinatown, the West End, and Stanley Park (for info, see "Organized Tours," below).

Stanley Park ★★★ (p. 119) offers a number of attractions for children, including a fabulous and free **Spray Park** near Lumberman's Arch. Stanley Park's **Miniature Railway ★** (ℂ **604/257-8531**) is a diminutive steam locomotive with passenger cars that runs on a circuit through the woods. The railway is open from 11am to 6pm daily mid-May through early September, weekends 11am to 4pm from February through mid-May as well as Spring Break and Easter. There are also special evening hours for the Halloween Ghost Train and the Bright Lights Christmas Train. All hours depend on weather. Admission for the miniature railroad is C$6.25 adults, C$4.45 seniors and children 13 to 18, and

C$3.15 for kids 2 to 12. **Second Beach** on Stanley Park's western rim has a playground, a snack bar, and an immense heated ocean-side **pool** ★ (© **604/257-8371**), open from May through September. Admission is C$5.30 adults, C$3.70 seniors and children 13 to 18, and C$2.65 for children 3 to 12. Kids will also be impressed with the collection of giant **totem poles** ★★★ at Brockton Point in Stanley Park, and the entire family will enjoy the **horse-drawn carriage rides** ★★★ that begin near Lost Lagoon (p. 121).

Also in Stanley Park, the **Vancouver Aquarium** ★★ (p. 122) has sea otters, sea lions, whales, and numerous other marine creatures, as well as many exhibits and special programs geared to children.

On the East Side of town and quickly accessible by SkyTrain, **Science World at TELUS World of Science** (p. 130) is a terrific interactive kids' museum where budding scientists can get their hands into everything.

A trip to **Granville Island** ★★★ will delight kids, and there are a couple of specific places they will really enjoy. Granville Island's **Kids Market** (1496 Cartwright St.; © **604/689-8447**) is open daily from 10am to 6pm. Playrooms and shops filled with toys, books, records, clothes, and food are all child-oriented. At **Granville Island Water Park** (near the Kids Market at 1496 Cartwright St.), kids can really let loose with movable water guns and sprinklers. They can also have fun on the water slides or in the wading pool. The facilities are open during the summer daily (weather permitting) from 10am to 6pm. Admission is free; changing facilities are nearby at the False Creek Community Centre (© **604/257-8195**).

Across Burrard Inlet, **Maplewood Farm** (405 Seymour River Place, North Vancouver; © **604/929-5610**; www.maplewoodfarm.bc.ca) has more than 200 barnyard animals (from cows to chickens) living on its 2-hectare (5-acre) farm. A few working farms once operated in the area but were put out of business by competition from the huge agricultural concerns in Fraser River valley. The parks

The Granville Island Water Park has movable water guns and sprinklers to cool off the kids.

Anyone can try panning for gold at the Britannia Mine Museum.

department rescued this one and converted it into an attraction. The ticket booth (a former breeding kennel) sells birdseed for feeding the ducks and other fowl. The farm also offers pony rides. Visit for the late-May Sheep Fair, which demonstrates sheep herding, fleece carding, and wool spinning. The farm is open 10am to 4pm daily from April through October (closed Mon the rest of the year). Admission is C$6.25 adults, C$3.57 seniors and children. Take bus nos. 211 or 290 from downtown.

Greater Vancouver Zoo (5048 264th St., Aldergrove; ☎ **604/856-6825;** www.gvzoo.com), located about 55km (34 miles) east of downtown Vancouver on the Trans-Canada Highway, is a lush 48-hectare (119-acre) reserve filled with lions, tigers, ostriches, buffalo, elk, antelope, zebras, giraffes, a rhino, and camels; 135 species and more than 600 animals in all. The zoo also has food service and a playground. It's open daily 9am to 4pm from October through April, 9am to 7pm from May through September. Admission is C$18 adults, C$14 seniors and children 4 to 15, free for children 3 and under, and C$58 for families. Take the Trans-Canada Highway to Aldergrove, exit 73; parking is C$4 per day.

Walk high above the rushing waters at the **Capilano Suspension Bridge & Park** (p. 131) and the **Lynn Canyon Suspension Bridge** (p. 137). In winter, **Mount Seymour** (p. 136), **Cypress Mountain** (p. 136) and **Grouse Mountain Resort** (p. 151) offer ski programs for kids and adults; in summer, trails surrounding the peaks are great for hikes.

A 45-minute drive north of Vancouver, the **Britannia Mine Museum** (Hwy. 99, Britannia Beach; ☎ **800/896-4044;** www.britanniaminemuseum.ca) is impossible to miss. Located at the head of Howe Sound, it's marked by a 235-ton truck parked in front. Re-opening in late 2010 following extensive renovations, the museum offers guided tours of the old copper mine, demonstrations of mining techniques, and even a gold-panning area where anyone can try straining gravel for the precious metal. It's open daily 9am to 4:30pm. Call ahead for the tour schedule; allow about 1½ to 2 hours. Admission is C$22 adults, C$16 seniors and students, C$14 children 6 to 12, C$72 for families, and free for children 5 and under.

For a different speed, head out for a whale-watching excursion—one of the most exciting adventures you can give a kid. See "Wildlife-Watching," later in this chapter, for information.

ORGANIZED TOURS

Please note that the 12% Harmonized Sales Tax (HST) may be applied to the tour prices listed below.

Air Tours

Harbour Air ★★★ (1075 W. Waterfront Rd. [Coal Harbour terminal]; ✆ 800/665-0212 or 604/274-1277; www.harbour-air.com) and **West Coast Air** ★★★ (www.westcoastair.com) operate under the same company, offering daily floatplane flights from the downtown Vancouver terminal next to the Canada Place cruise-ship terminal. Floatplanes are single-prop, usually six-seater planes that take off and land on water. The 20-minute "Vancouver Panorama" tour (C$99 per person) flies over Stanley Park, the North Shore Mountains, and all around the metro region, giving you an unparalleled bird's-eye view of the magnificent terrain; on the Mail Run, small planes zip between island villages to pick up or drop off parcels (C$185 per person). Other tours will take you to Victoria, glacial lakes, and whale-watching spots. The full-day "Victoria Day Trip" tour (C$315 per person) flies you across the Strait of Georgia to Vancouver Island, where you can spend the night, go orca watching, or tour the world-famous Butchart Gardens.

From April through September, **Helijet Charters** (✆ 800/665-4354; www.helijet.com) offers a variety of daily tours that depart from their terminal next to Canada Place and their helipad on top of Grouse Mountain. The "Coastal Scenic Tour" is a 20-minute tour of the city, Stanley Park, and North Shore mountains for C$179 per person.

Boat Tours

Harbour Cruises (501 Denman St.; ✆ 604/688-7246; www.boatcruises.com) will take you on a 2½-hour Sunset Dinner Cruise, including a buffet meal and onboard entertainment. Cost is C$75 adults, seniors, and students; C$65 children 2 to 11. The cruise leaves daily at 7pm May through mid-October. The 4-hour Indian Arm Luncheon Cruise (May–Sept) includes a salmon or chicken lunch, with departure at 11am. Cost is C$65 per person.

Harbour Cruises also conducts a 1-hour narrated Harbour Tour aboard the MPV *Constitution*, a 19th-century sternwheeler with a smokestack. Tours depart at 11am, 12:15, 1:30, and 2:45pm daily from late April to late September (dates vary yearly). Fares are C$30 adults, C$25 seniors and children 12 to 17, C$10 children 5 to 11, and free for children 4 and under. This tour allows you to see harbor facilities and gets you out onto Burrard Inlet, but the narration, read from a script, is rather dull and unengaging.

Accent Cruises (1676 Duranleau St.; ✆ 800/993-6257 or 604/688-6625; www.accentcruises.ca) runs a 3-hour Sunset Cruise departing Granville Island daily at 6pm. Cost for adults is C$60 with dinner, C$30 for the cruise only.

Paddlewheeler Riverboat Tours operates the 19th-century SS *Native*.

Paddlewheeler Riverboat Tours (New Westminster Quay, New West-minster; ℭ **604/525-4465;** www.vancouverpaddlewheeler.com) operates Fraser River tours from New Westminster aboard the 19th-century vessel SS *Native*. The company offers a 3-hour Sunset Dine and Dance cruise Saturday evenings at 7pm. Ticket prices are C$65 adults, C$60 seniors, C$50 children 6–12. More interesting but less frequent are day trips to historic Fort Langley, Steveston, and Harrison Hot Springs; call or visit the website for dates.

Bus Tours

Big Bus (317 Water St.; ℭ **877/299-0701** or 604/299-0700; www.bigbus.ca) runs a fleet of double-decker buses on a 90-minute "hop-on, hop-off" sightseeing loop around the city. Two-day passes cost: C$45 adults, C$40 students and seniors, and C$25 children 6 to 12, free for children 5 and under, and C$100 family pass. Buses depart from Canada Place daily between 9am and 6pm, running every 15 to 20 minutes during peak summer hours; a 1-day pass is also available for weekend warriors.

    Landsea Tours (ℭ **877/669-2277** or 604/255-7272; www.vancouver tours.com) offers a wide array of tour options, including a 4-hour excursion through Vancouver in a 24-person van. Offered year-round at 9am, and April to early November at 2pm as well. The tour costs C$69 adults, C$45 children. The van picks you up from downtown hotels. You can also take a tour up to Grouse Mountain and the Capilano Suspension Bridge. Departing at 11am year-round (and 8am from early May to late Sept), it costs C$139 adults, C$99 children 3 to 12. Other options are tours of wineries, Victoria, and Whistler.

    Vancouver Trolley Company (875 Terminal Ave.; ℭ **888/451-5581** or 604/801-5515; www.vancouvertrolley.com) operates propane-powered trolleys on a route through downtown, the West End, Stanley Park, Kitsilano, Yaletown, and Chinatown. Between 9am and 6pm in spring and summer (until 5pm in fall and winter), passengers can get on and off at any of the 30 stops, explore, and catch another scheduled trolley. Onboard, drivers provide detailed commentary. Purchase 1-day and 2-day tickets from the driver (or, in summer, at the Gastown ticket booth at 157 Water St.) for C$38 adults, C$35 seniors and children 13 to 18, and C$25 children 4 to 12.

First Nations Tours

The Tsleil-Waututh Nation of North Vancouver leads a number of cultural and ecotours that provide an introduction to both First Nations culture and the stunning Indian Arm fjord. Their company, **Takaya Tours** (700 Apex Ave.; ☎ **604/ 904-7410;** www.takayatours.com) operates from the Cates Park Paddling Centre, North Vancouver in summer (☎ **604/985-2925**), and conducts a roster of outdoor tours such as excursions in traditional northwest canoes and plant nature walks. Prices run from C$35 to C$60, with dinner options available for groups.

Specialty Tours

Playing off Vancouver's growing reputation as a culinary tourism destination, **Chef and Chauffeur** (603-36 Water St.; ☎ **604/267-1000;** www.chefand chauffeur.com) has launched several tours of the Fraser Valley, located an hour east of the city, and the more distant Okanagan Valley, famed for its fruit, produce, meats, cheeses, and wines. Participants start the day with coffee, fresh orange juice, and cinnamon buns or berry scones while their guide maps out the day's adventures. The tours, in a luxury SUV, visit a variety of wineries, farms, bakeries, and cheese makers. Optional dinner and overnight add-ons are available. Tours range from C$195 to C$2,995 per person.

Walking Tours

Walkabout Historic Vancouver (☎ **604/720-0006**) offers three 2-hour walking tours (downtown and Gastown, Gastown and Chinatown, and Granville Island), and for large groups the guides dress as 19th-century schoolmarms. Tours depart daily at 10am and 2pm April through October, and by request during other months. Tours are wheelchair accessible. The cost is C$25 per person; you must reserve in advance.

During the summer months (July–Aug), the **Architectural Institute of BC** (☎ **604/683-8588,** ext. 306; www.aibc.ca) offers a number of **architectural walking tours ★★★** of downtown Vancouver neighborhoods, including Chinatown and Granville Island, for only C$10 per person. The 2-hour tours run on a rotating basis from Tuesday through Saturday, departing at 1pm sharp from the AIBC Architecture Centre, 440 Cambie St. Call or visit the website for details and to book.

The **Vancouver Police Museum** offers an entertaining "Sins of the City" walking tour; see the museum description (p. 124) for details.

Or devise your own walking tour with brochures from the Tourism Vancouver **Visitor Centre** at 200 Burrard St. (p. 52). Otherwise, turn to chapter 8.

OUTDOOR ACTIVITIES

If you don't find your favorite sport listed here, take a look at chapter 11; also check out "Parks & Gardens," earlier in this chapter.

An excellent resource for outdoor enthusiasts is **Mountain Equipment Co-op** (130 W. Broadway; ☎ **604/872-7858;** www.mec.ca).

Beaches

Only about 12% of Vancouver's annual rainfall occurs during June, July, and August; 60 days of summer sunshine is not uncommon, although the Pacific never really warms up enough for a comfortable swim. Still, **English Bay**

VISIT olympic sports VENUES

Now that the athletes have gone, it's your turn to walk, skate, ski, or snowboard in many of the same places where the world's best athletes did at the 2010 Winter Games. Here's a rundown of what you can do at the world-class sport venues open to the public:

○ **Skate at the Richmond Olympic Oval.** Located south of downtown Vancouver, the **Richmond Oval** (6111 River Rd., Richmond; ℂ **778/296-1400;** www.richmondoval.ca), a venue for speed skating during the 2010 Winter Games, now offers multiple skating rinks, ball courts, and a first-class fitness center. The facility is open Monday through Friday from 6am to 11pm, and weekends 8am to 9pm. Call for the public skating schedule or to enquire about speed-skating lessons.

○ **Ski and snowboard on Cypress Mountain.** For many winters to come, you'll be able to ski and snowboard the Olympic runs on Cypress Mountain, home of Canada's first gold medal of the 2010 Winter Games. NBC's *Today* show broadcast for the duration of the Olympics from the Grouse Mountain Resort (p. 151). For more information on Cypress Mountain, see the "Skiing & Snowboarding" section (p. 151).

○ **Swim at the Vancouver Olympic Centre.** Home to the Olympic and Paralympic curling events, the **Vancouver Olympic Centre** (4575 Clancy Loranger Way; http://vancouver.ca/parks/info/2010olympics/hillcrest.htm) now houses an aquatic center; eight curling ice sheets remain, too.

○ **Watch a hockey game.** You'll feel just like you're at the 2010 Winter Games when you attend an NHL Vancouver Canucks hockey game at **Rogers Arena,** site of the gold medal men's and women's hockey games. For more information, see the Hockey section under "Spectator Sports," p. 155.

○ **Discover an Olympic neighborhood.** Southeast False Creek was the site of the Vancouver Olympic Village. Walk the False Creek seawall from Science World (p. 130) toward Granville Island (p. 125) and check out the new Creekside community center, inviting public spaces, and historical Salt Building at 85 W. 1st Ave., which has been converted into a public restaurant.

Beach ★★—at the end of Davie Street, off Denman Street and Beach Avenue—is a great place to see sunsets. The bathhouse dates to the turn of the 20th century, and a huge playground slide is mounted on a raft just off the beach every summer.

On **Stanley Park**'s western rim, **Second Beach ★** is a short stroll north from English Bay Beach. A playground, a snack bar, and an immense heated ocean-side **pool ★** (ℂ **604/257-8371**), open from Victoria Day weekend (late May) through Labour Day weekend, make this a convenient and fun spot for families. Admission to the pool is C$5.95 adults, C$4.15 seniors and children 13 to 18, and C$2.95 children 3 to 12. Farther along the seawall, due north of Stanley Park Drive, lies secluded **Third Beach ★★**. Locals tote along grills and coolers to this spot, a scenic place for summer barbecues and sunset-watching.

South of English Bay Beach, near the Burrard Street Bridge, is **Sunset Beach** ★. Running along False Creek, it's actually a picturesque strip of sandy beaches filled with enormous driftwood logs that serve as windbreaks and provide a little privacy for sunbathers and picnickers. A snack bar, basketball courts, and a long, gently sloping grassy hill are available for people who prefer lawn to sand.

On the West Side, **Kitsilano Beach** ★★★, along Arbutus Street near Cornwall Street, is affectionately called Kits Beach. It's an easy walk from the Maritime Museum and the False Creek ferry dock. If you want to do a saltwater swim but can't handle the cold, head to the huge (135m/443-ft.) heated (25°C/77°F) **Kitsilano Pool** ★★. Admission is the same as for Second Beach Pool, above.

Farther west on the other side of Hastings Mill Park is **Jericho Beach** (Alma St. off Point Grey Rd.), another local after-work and weekend social spot. **Locarno Beach,** at the north end of Trimble and Tolmie streets, and **Spanish Banks,** on Northwest Marine Drive, lead to the Point Grey Foreshore that wraps around the northern point of the UBC campus and University Hill. (Be forewarned that beachside restrooms and concessions on the promontory end abruptly at Spanish Banks East.) Below UBC's Museum of Anthropology is **Point Grey Beach,** a restored harbor-defense site. The next beach is **Wreck Beach** ★★★—Canada's largest nude beach. You get down to Wreck Beach by taking the steep Trails 4 or 6 on the UBC campus lead down to the water's edge. Extremely popular with locals and maintained by its own preservation society, Wreck Beach is also the city's most pristine and least-developed sandy stretch, bordered on three sides by towering trees.

For information on any of Vancouver's many beaches, call © **604/738-8535** (summer only).

At the northern foot of the Lions Gate Bridge, **Ambleside Park** is a popular North Shore spot. The beach faces the Burrard Inlet.

Kitsilano Beach is an easy walk from the Maritime Museum and the False Creek ferry dock.

Canoeing, Kayaking & Paddleboarding

Both placid, urban False Creek and the incredibly beautiful 30km (19-mile) North Vancouver fjord known as Indian Arm have launching points that can be reached by car or bus. Prices range from about C$40 per 2-hour minimum rental to C$70 per 5-hour day for single kayaks and about C$60 for canoe rentals. Customized tours range from C$75 to C$150 per person. Paddleboards generally run C$19 per hour, or C$29 for 2 hours.

Ecomarine Ocean Kayak Centre (1668 Duranleau St., Granville Island; ℂ 888/425-2925 or 604/689-7575; www.ecomarine.com) has 2-hour, daily, and weekly kayak rentals, as well as courses and organized tours. The company also has an office at the Jericho Sailing Centre (1300 Discovery St., at Jericho Beach; ℂ 604/224-4177; www.jsca.bc.ca). In North Vancouver, Deep Cove Canoe and Kayak Rentals (2156 Banbury Rd., at the foot of Gallant St.; ℂ 604/929-2268; www.deepcovekayak.com) is an easy starting point for anyone planning an Indian Arm run. It offers hourly and daily rentals of canoes and kayaks, as well as lessons and customized tours.

Lotus Land Tours (2005-1251 Cardero St.; ℂ 800/528-3531 or 604/684-4922; www.lotuslandtours.com) runs guided kayak tours on Indian Arm that come with hotel pickup, a barbecue salmon lunch, and incredible scenery. The wide, stable kayaks are perfect for first-time paddlers. One-day tours are C$165 adults, C$155 seniors, C$125 children 5 to 12.

See also Takaya Tours, an excellent First Nations eco-outfitter (p. 143).

Cycling & Mountain Biking

Cycling in Vancouver is fun, amazingly scenic, and very popular. Cycling maps are available at most bicycle retailers and rental outlets. Some West End hotels offer guests bike storage and rentals. Hourly rentals run around C$8 to C$16 an

Vancouver has several places to enjoy an afternoon of kayaking.

There are several world-class mountain bike trails within a short drive of downtown Vancouver.

hour for a mountain or city bike, C$30 to C$60 for a day; helmets and locks are included. Popular shops that rent city and mountain bikes, child trailers, child seats, and in-line skates (protective gear included) include **Spokes Bicycle Rentals & Espresso Bar** (1798 W. Georgia St.; ℭ **604/688-5141;** www.spokesbicyclerentals.com), at the corner of Denman Street at the entrance to Stanley Park; and **Bayshore Bicycle and Rollerblade Rentals** (745 Denman St.; ℭ **604/688-2453;** www.bayshorebikerentals. ca). **Note:** Be advised that wearing a helmet is mandatory, and one will be included in your bike rental.

The most popular cycling path in the city runs along the **seawall ★★★** around the perimeter of Stanley Park. Offering magnificent views of the city, the Burrard Inlet, the mountains, and English Bay, this flat, approximately 10km (6¼-mile) pathway attracts year-round bicyclists, in-line skaters, and pedestrians. (**Note:** Runners and cyclists have separate lanes on developed park and beach paths.) Another popular route is the **seaside bicycle route,** a 15km (9¼-mile) ride that begins at English Bay and continues around False Creek to the University of British Columbia. Some of this route follows city streets that are well marked with cycle-path signs; the sights include the Plaza of Nations, Science World, Granville Island, the Pacific Space Centre, the Kitsilano Pool, the Jericho Sailing Centre, lush Pacific Spirit Park (p. 135), and the University of British Columbia, home to the Museum of Anthropology, UBC Botanical Garden, and Nitobe Memorial Garden (p. 129).

Serious mountain bikers also have a wealth of world-class options within a short drive from downtown Vancouver. The trails on **Mount Fromme** near Grouse Mountain are some of the lower mainland's best. Local mountain bikers love the cross-country ski trails on around **Hollyburn Lodge** in **Cypress Provincial Park,** just northeast of Vancouver on the road to Whistler on Highway 99. Closer to downtown, both **Pacific Spirit Park** and **Burnaby Mountain** offer excellent beginner and intermediate off-road trails.

Ecotours

Lotus Land Tours runs guided kayak tours on Indian Arm (see "Canoeing & Kayaking," above). From late November to the end of January, this small local company also offers unique float trips on the Squamish River to see the large concentration of bald eagles up close. **Rockwood Adventures** (ℭ **888/236-6606** or 604/741-0802; www.rockwoodadventures.com) has 4-hour **guided walks of the North Shore rainforest ★,** complete with a trained naturalist, stops in Capilano Canyon and at the Lynn Canyon Suspension Bridge (p. 137), and lunch. Cost is C$95 adults, C$85 seniors and students 12 to 25, and C$60 children 4 to 11.

Golf

With five public 18-hole courses, half a dozen pitch-and-putt courses in the city, and dozens more courses nearby, golfers are never far from their love. For discounts and short-notice tee times at more than 30 Vancouver-area courses, contact the **A-1 Last Minute Golf Hot Line** (✆ **800/684-6344** or 604/878-1833; www.lastminutegolfbc.com).

A number of excellent public golf courses, maintained by the **Vancouver Board of Parks and Recreation** (✆ **604/280-1818** to book tee times; http://vancouver.ca/parks), can be found throughout the city. **Langara Golf Course** (6706 Alberta St., around 49th Ave. and Cambie St.; ✆ **604/713-1816;** http://vancouver.ca/parks/golf/langara), built in 1926 by the Canadian Pacific Railway and recently renovated and redesigned, is one of the most popular golf courses in the province. Depending on the course, summer greens fees range from C$14 to C$43 for an adult, with discounts for seniors, children, off-season tee times, and advance booking online.

The public **University Golf Club** (5185 University Blvd.; ✆ **604/224-1818;** www.universitygolf.com) is a great 6,300-yard, par-72 course with a clubhouse, pro shop, locker rooms, bar and grill, and sports lounge.

Leading private clubs are situated on the North Shore and in Vancouver. Check with your club at home to see if you have reciprocal visiting memberships with one of the following: **Capilano Golf and Country Club** (420 Southborough Dr., West Vancouver; ✆ **604/922-9331;** www.capilanogolf.com), **Marine Drive Golf Club** (7425 Yew St.; ✆ **604/261-8111;** www.marine-drive.com), **Seymour Golf and Country Club** (3723 Mt. Seymour Pkwy., North Vancouver; ✆ **604/929-2611;** www.seymourgolf.com), **Point Grey Golf and Country Club** (3350 SW Marine Dr.; ✆ **604/261-3108;** www.pointgreygolf.com), and **Shaughnessy Golf and Country Club** (4300 SW Marine Dr.; ✆ **604/266-4141;** www.shaughnessy.org). Greens fees range from C$42 to C$75.

The University Golf Club is a great public par-72 course.

Lynn Canyon Park has less strenuous trails through Douglas fir and cedar.

Hiking

Great trails for hikers of all levels run through Vancouver's dramatic environs. You can pick up a local trail guide at any bookstore. Good trail maps are also available from **International Travel Maps and Books** (12300 Bridgeport Rd., Richmond; © **604/273-1400;** www.itmb.com), which also stocks guidebooks and topographical maps. The retail store is open Monday to Saturday from 9:30am to 5pm, or you can order maps online.

If you're looking for a challenge without a longtime commitment, hike the aptly named **Grouse Grind ★★** from the bottom of **Grouse Mountain** (p. 132) to the top; then buy a one-way ticket (C$5) down on the Grouse Mountain Skyride gondola.

For a bit more scenery with a bit less effort, take the Grouse Mountain Skyride up to the **Grouse chalet** and start your hike at an altitude of 1,100m (3,609 ft.). The trail north of **Goat Mountain** is well marked and takes approximately 4 to 5 hours round-trip, though you may want to build in some extra time to linger on the top of Goat and take in the spectacular 360-degree views of Vancouver, Vancouver Island, and the snowcapped peaks of the Coast Mountains.

Lynn Canyon Park, Lynn Headwaters Regional Park, Capilano River Regional Park, Mount Seymour Provincial Park, Pacific Spirit Park, and **Cypress Provincial Park** (see "The Top Attractions" and "Parks & Gardens," earlier in this chapter) have good, easy-to-strenuous trails that wind up through stands of Douglas fir and cedar, and contain a few serious switchbacks. Pay attention to the trail warnings posted at the parks (some have bear habitats) and always remember to sign in with the park service at the start of your chosen trail.

A little farther outside the city, the 9- to 12-hour hike to **Black Tusk** is one of the finest hikes in North America and is often completed over 2 days, overnighting at the primitive campground on Garibaldi Lake. Located in **Garibaldi Provincial Park** (© **604/898-3678**), the trail head is 34km (21 miles) north of Squamish, which is 65km (40 miles) north of downtown Vancouver along Highway 99 on the road to Whistler. The park has five access points; Black Tusk/Garibaldi Lake is the second marked turnoff (it takes about an hour to get there).

The trail switchbacks up nearly 1,000m (3,281 ft.) in about 9km (5.5 miles), then levels onto a rolling alpine plateau with fabulous views before another 850m (2,789 ft.) climb over 7km (4.3 miles) to Black Tusk. The best time to make this climb is for the wildflowers in late July and August, although the trail is usually clear through October.

Ice-Skating

The highest ice-skating rink in Canada is located on **Grouse Mountain;** see the Grouse Mountain description under "The Top Attractions," earlier in this chapter.

In the city, **Robson Square Ice Rink** (✆ **604/646-3557**) re-opened for the 2010 Winter Games after years of closure. During the winter, daily public skating is free and skate rentals are available for C$3. The **West End Community Centre** (870 Denman St.; ✆ **604/257-8333;** www.westendcc.ca) rents skates at its enclosed rink; during summer the rink is converted to a dry floor for other sports. The **Kitsilano Ice Rink** (2690 Larch St.; ✆ **604/257-6983;** http://vancouver.ca/parks) has ice surface through mid-June. Before the Vancouver Canucks moved out to UBC, the enormous **Burnaby 8 Rinks Ice Sports Centre** (6501 Sprott St., Burnaby; ✆ **604/291-0626;** www.icesports.com/burnaby8rinks) was the team's official practice facility. It has eight rinks, is open year-round, and offers lessons and rentals. Call ahead to check hours for public skating at all these rinks.

In-Line Skating

All over Vancouver, you'll find lots of locals rolling along beach paths, streets, park paths, and promenades. If you didn't bring a pair of blades, try **Bayshore Bicycle and Rollerblade Rentals** (745 Denman St.; ✆ **604/688-2453;** www.bayshorebikerentals.com). Rentals run C$10 for 2 hours or C$20 for 8 hours. For info on in-line skating lessons and group events, visit www.inlineskatevancouver.com.

Jogging

Local runners traverse the **Stanley Park seawall** ★★★ and the park paths around **Lost Lagoon** and **Beaver Lake.** If you're a dawn or dusk runner, take note that this is one of the world's safer city parks. However, if you're alone, don't tempt fate—stick to open and lighted areas. Other prime jogging areas are **Kitsilano Beach, Jericho Beach,** and **Spanish Banks** (see "Beaches," earlier in this chapter); all of them offer flat running paths along the ocean. You can also take the seawall path from English Bay Beach south along **False Creek.** If you feel like doing a little racing, competitions take place throughout the year; ask for information at any runners' outfitters, such as **Forerunners** (3504 W. 4th Ave.; ✆ **604/732-4535**) or **Running Room** (679 Denman St., at the corner of Georgia St.; ✆ **604/684-9771**). Check www.runningroom.com for information on clinics and events around Vancouver and British Columbia.

Paragliding

In Surrey, **Deimos Paragliding Flight School** (✆ **877/359-7413** or 604/200-2029; www.deimospg.com) offers tandem flights from Burnaby Mountain and other locations starting at C$160 per person. No experience is necessary for this

Cypress Bowl was home to the 2010 Winter Games freestyle skiing and snowboarding events.

unforgettable adventure, the actual flights, controlled by an experienced instructor, take 10–30 minutes.

Skiing & Snowboarding

World-class skiing lies outside the city at the **Whistler Blackcomb Ski Resort,** 110km (68 miles) north of Vancouver; see chapter 11. However, you don't have to leave the city to get in a few runs. It seldom snows in the city's downtown and central areas, but Vancouverites can ski before work and after dinner at the three ski resorts in the North Shore mountains. These local mountains played host to the freestyle and snowboard events in the 2010 Winter Games.

Grouse Mountain Resort (6400 Nancy Greene Way, North Vancouver; ℂ **604/984-0661,** or 604/986-6262 for a snow report; www.grousemountain. com) is about 8km (5 miles) from the Lions Gate Bridge and overlooks the Burrard Inlet and Vancouver skyline. Four chairs take you to 26 alpine runs, and there is a Magic Carpet (like a moving walkway) for beginners. The resort has night skiing, special events, instruction, and a spectacular view, as well as a terrain park for snowboarders. All skill levels are covered, with 3 beginner trails, 15 blue trails, 6 black-diamond runs, and 2 double-black-diamond runs: Purgatory and Devil's Advocate, which both drop down from close to the 1,250m (4,100-ft.) peak. Rental packages and a full range of facilities are available. Lift tickets good for all-day skiing are C$55 adults, C$45 seniors and children 13 to 18, C$25 children 5 to 12, and free for children 4 and under. Lift prices do not include your gondola ride to the summit.

Mount Seymour Provincial Park (1700 Mt. Seymour Rd., North Vancouver; ℂ **604/986-2261;** www.mountseymour.com) has the area's highest base elevation; it's accessible via four chairs and a tow. All-day lift tickets are C$45 adults, C$37 seniors, C$39 children 13 to 19, and C$23 children 6 to 12. Nighttime skiing from 4 to 10pm costs less. In addition to 39 runs for day or night skiing, the facility offers snowboarding, cross-country, and tobogganing as well as 10km (6⅕ miles) of snowshoeing trails. The resort specializes in teaching first-timers. Camps for children and teenagers, and adult clinics, are available throughout the winter. Mount Seymour has one of Western Canada's largest equipment rental shops, which will keep your measurements on file for return visits. Shuttle service is available during ski season from various locations on the North Shore, including the Lonsdale Quay SeaBus. **Cypress Bowl** (Top of Cypress Bowl Rd.; ℂ **604/926-5612,** or 604/419-7669 for a snow report; www. cypressmountain.com) was home to the 2010 Winter Games freestyle skiing (moguls and aerials), snowboarding (half-pipe and parallel giant slalom), and new ski-cross events. In the 2007/2008 season, Cypress opened nine new runs for intermediate and expert skiers and snowboarders, accessed by a new quad chairlift, and a new day lodge opened for the winter 2008/2009 season—prepping for its 2010 spotlight. Cypress has the area's longest vertical drop (610m/2,010 ft.), challenging ski and snowboard runs, and 19km (11⅘ miles) of track-set cross-country ski trails (including 7.5km/4⅔ miles set aside for night skiing).

Swimming

The **Vancouver Aquatic Centre** (1050 Beach Ave., at the foot of Thurlow St.; © 604/665-3424) has a heated, 50m (164-ft.) Olympic pool, saunas, whirlpools, weight rooms, diving tanks, locker rooms, showers, child care, and a tot pool. Admission is C$6 adults, C$3 children 3 to 12. The new, coed **YWCA Fitness Centre** (535 Hornby St.; © 604/895-5800; www.ywcahealthandfitness.com), in the heart of downtown, has a 6-lane, 25m (82-ft.), ozonated (much milder than chlorinated) pool, steam room, whirlpool, conditioning gym, and aerobic studios. A day pass is C$16 adults. UBC's **Aquatic Centre** (6121 University Blvd.; © 604/822-4522; www.aquatics.ubc.ca), located next door to the Student Union Building and the bus loop, sets aside time for public use. Admission is C$6 adults, C$5 children 13 to 17, and C$4 seniors and children 3 to 12. See also "Beaches," p. 143.

Tennis

The city maintains more than 180 outdoor hard courts that operate on a first-come, first-served basis (with a 30-min. time limit when all courts are full) from 8am until dusk. Predictably, heavy usage times are evenings and weekends. With the exception of the Beach Avenue courts, which charge a nominal fee in summer, all city courts are free.

Stanley Park has four courts near Lost Lagoon and 17 courts near the Beach Avenue entrance, next to the Fish House Restaurant on Stanley Park Drive. During the summer season (May–Sept), six courts are taken over for pay tennis and can be pre-booked by calling © 604/605-8224. **Queen Elizabeth Park**'s 17 courts service the central Vancouver area, and **Kitsilano Beach Park**'s ★ 10 courts service the beach area between Vanier Park and the UBC campus.

The **UBC Tennis Centre** (6160 Thunderbird Blvd.; © 604/822-2505; www.tennis.ubc.ca) re-opened in 2011 with 12 indoor courts and 1 outdoor court. Indoor courts are C$20 to C$26 per hour, depending on the time.

Wildlife-Watching

Orcas, or killer whales, are the largest mammals to be seen in Vancouver's waters (except for the odd gray whale, such as the one that swam into False Creek in May 2010). Three pods (families) of orcas, numbering about 80 whales, return to this area every year to feed on the salmon that spawn in the Fraser River starting in May and continuing into October. The eldest female leads the group; the head of one pod is thought to have been born in 1911. From April through October, daily excursions offered by **Vancouver Whale Watch** (12240 2nd Ave., Richmond; © 604/274-9565; www.vancouverwhalewatch.com) focus on the majestic whales, plus Dall's porpoises, sea lions, seals, eagles, herons, and other wildlife. The cost is C$125 per person (slightly lower rates for a semi-covered boat). **Steveston Seabreeze Adventures** (12551 No. 1 Rd., Richmond; ☎ **604/272-7200;** www.seabreezeadventures.ca) also offers whale-watching tours for about the same price. Both companies offer a shuttle service from downtown Vancouver.

Thousands of migratory birds following the Pacific flyway rest and feed in the Fraser River delta south of Vancouver, especially at the 300-hectare (740-acre) **George C. Reifel Bird Sanctuary** (5191 Robertson Rd., Westham Island; ☎ **604/946-6980;** www.reifelbirdsanctuary.com), which was created by a former bootlegger and wetland-bird lover. Many other waterfowl species have made this a permanent habitat. More than 268 species have been spotted, including a Temminck's stint, a spotted redshank, bald eagles, Siberian (trumpeter) swans, peregrine falcons, blue herons, owls, and coots. The huge, snowy white flocks of snow geese arrive in October and stay in the area until mid-December. (High tide, when the birds are less concealed by the marsh grasses, is the best time to visit.) An observation tower, 7km (4⅓ miles) of paths, birdseed for sale, and picnic tables make this wetland reserve an ideal outing spot from October to April, when the birds are wintering in abundance. The sanctuary is wheelchair accessible and open daily from 9am to 4pm. Admission is C$5 adults, C$3 seniors and children.

The **Richmond Nature Park** (11851 Westminster Hwy.; ☎ **604/718-6188**) was established to preserve the Lulu Island wetlands bog. It features a Nature House with educational displays and a boardwalk-encircled duck pond. On Sunday afternoons at 2pm, knowledgeable guides give free tours. Admission is by donation.

To hook up with local Vancouver birders, try the **Vancouver Natural History Society** (☎ **604/737-3074;** www.naturevancouver.ca). This all-volunteer organization runs birding field trips most weekends; many are free.

During the winter, thousands of bald eagles—in fact, the largest number in North America—line the banks of the **Squamish, Cheakamus,** and **Mamquam** rivers to feed on spawning salmon. To get there by car, take the scenic **Sea-to-Sky Highway** (Hwy. 99) from downtown Vancouver to Squamish and Brackendale; the trip takes about an hour. The route winds along the craggy tree-lined coast of Howe Sound through the town of Britannia Beach and past two beautiful natural monuments: **Shannon Falls** and the continent's tallest monolithic rock face, the **Stawamus Chief.** Alternatively, you can take a **Greyhound** bus from Vancouver's Pacific Central Station (1150 Station St.; ☎ **800/661-8747;** www.greyhound.ca); trip time is 1¾ hours. Contact the **Squamish Adventure Centre** (☎ **604/815-4994;** www.squamishchamber. com) for more information.

The annual summer salmon runs attract more than bald eagles. Tourists flock to coastal streams and rivers to watch the waters turn red with leaping coho and sockeye. The salmon are plentiful at the **Capilano Salmon Hatchery** (p. 135), **Goldstream Provincial Park** on Vancouver Island, and numerous other fresh waters.

Stanley Park (p. 119) is home to a heron rookery (the birds nesting in Pacific Spirit Park have moved on). You can see these large birds nesting just outside the Vancouver Aquarium. Ravens, dozens of species of waterfowl, raccoons,

You can try windsurfing at Jericho or English Bay beach.

skunks, beavers, gray squirrels (imported from New York's Central Park a century ago), and even coyotes are also full-time residents. The **Stanley Park Ecology Society** (✆ 604/257-8544) runs regular nature walks in the park. Call or check their website (www.stanleyparkecology.ca) for more information or drop by the **Lost Lagoon Nature House** in Stanley Park (p. 121).

Windsurfing

Windsurfing is not allowed at the mouth of False Creek near Granville Island, but you can bring a board to **Jericho** (p. 145) and **English Bay beaches** ★★ (p. 143), or rent one there. Equipment sales, rentals (including wet suits), and instruction can be found at **Windsure Windsurfing School** (1300 Discovery St., at Jericho Beach; ✆ 604/224-0615; www.windsure.com). Rentals start at about C$19 per hour, wet suit and life jacket included. Windsure also rents skimboards, C$18 per day, which can be used on the sandy flats along the Point Grey Foreshore.

SPECTATOR SPORTS

You can get schedules for all major events at Tourism Vancouver's **Visitor Centre** (200 Burrard St.; ✆ 604/683-2000; www.tourismvancouver.com). Purchase tickets from **Ticketmaster** (✆ 855/985-5000; www.ticketmaster.ca) or from dozens of outlets in the Greater Vancouver area. Popular events such as Canucks games sell out weeks or months in advance, so be sure to book ahead.

Baseball

At Nat Bailey Stadium (4601 Ontario St.), the minor league Vancouver Canadians (✆ 604/872-5232; www.canadiansbaseball.com) play a good game of baseball complete with hot dogs and beer. Tickets run C$13 to C$22, with a senior discount available.

Football

In 2011, the Canadian Football League's **BC Lions** (✆ **604/589-7627;** www.bclions.com) moved their home and Grey Cup championship games (in good seasons) from Empire Field to the 55,000-seat **BC Place Stadium** (777 Pacific Blvd. S., at Beatty and Robson sts.). The stadium has a newly finished retractable roof, cheerfully dubbed the "Blue Sky" roof. Canadian football differs from its American cousin: It's a three-down offense game on a field that's 10 yards longer and wider. Some of the plays you see will have American fans leaping out of their seats in surprise. Tickets for individual games are available from Ticketmaster (✆ **855/985-5000;** www.ticketmaster.ca); prices run from C$35 to C$85.

Hockey

The National Hockey League's **Vancouver Canucks** play at **Rogers Arena** (recently renamed from GM Place; 800 Griffiths Way; ✆ **604/899-4600,** or 604/899-7444 for the event hotline; www.canucks.com). Tickets start at C$65 and, while difficult to obtain because the season tends to sell out in advance, some individual seats are made available for every home game. Purchase tickets from **Ticketmaster** (✆ **855/985-5000;** www.ticketmaster.ca).

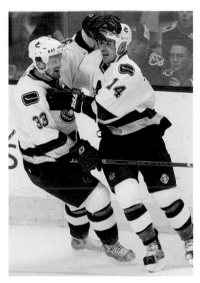

The **Vancouver Giants** (✆ **604/444-2687;** www.vancouvergiants.com) also offer an exciting hockey game. The minor league team plays at the Pacific Coliseum (100 N. Renfrew St.) for a bargain price: Tickets start at C$18, through Ticketmaster (✆ **855/985-5000;** www.ticketmaster.ca).

Tickets to see the Vancouver Canucks play can be difficult to obtain.

Horse Racing

Thoroughbreds run at **Hastings Park Racecourse** (Exhibition Park, 188 N. Renfrew St.; ✆ **604/254-1631;** www.hastingspark.com) from mid-April to October. Call ahead or check the website for the latest schedule. The racecourse has a decent restaurant, so you can make a full afternoon or evening of dining and racing.

Running

The **Vancouver Sun Run** in April and the **Vancouver International Marathon** (Canada's largest) in May attract thousands of runners from around the world and even more spectators. Contact the **Vancouver International**

Marathon Society (✆ 604/872-2928; www.bmovanmarathon.ca), or the Vancouver Sun Run (21-200 Granville St.; ✆ 604/689-9441; www.sunrun.com) for information.

Soccer

The **Vancouver Whitecaps** (✆ 604/899-9283; www.whitecapsfc.com) recently moved to **BC Place Stadium** (777 Pacific Blvd. S., at Beatty and Robson sts.) to play under the new retractable roof. The team joined the **MLS** professional league in 2011. Tickets are available through Ticketmaster (✆ 855/646-2277; www.ticketmaster.ca); admission is typically C$20 to C$55.

VANCOUVER STROLLS

8

n this rainy west coast city, an umbrella and perhaps rain boots are all that's needed to overcome any weather in the name of a walk. And you'll join a strong local contingent: "I'd rather walk than drive a car," said actress Kristin Kreuk—best-known for her role in the shot-in-Vancouver television series *Smallville*—to The WB in a 2003 interview. "In Vancouver, where I am from, you can get to just about anywhere you need to go on foot. Even if it's raining, I'll go out for a stroll."

Networks of waterside seawalls, urban park trails, and tree-lined streets make Vancouver a world-class city to take a stroll. In fact, WestJet's *Up* magazine named Vancouver as Canada's most walkable in 2009 and 2010.

If you have directional problems, remember that the grid of streets basically runs northwest to southeast, rather than straight north-south, and that the mountains (which you can almost always see) are north. The best way to get acquainted with this unique city is to explore its various neighborhoods on foot. The tours below provide a good overall introduction.

WALKING TOUR 1: DOWNTOWN & THE WEST END

START:	**The Fairmont Hotel Vancouver.**
FINISH:	**Cathedral Place.**
TIME:	**2 to 3 hours, not including museum, shopping, and eating stops.**
BEST TIME:	**Daytime, particularly during the week, when the Law Courts building is open.**
WORST TIME:	**Late in the evening when the shops and offices have closed.**

Once said to be the densest residential district west of Manhattan (now trumped by Toronto's St. James Town), it's surprising that Vancouver's West End doesn't overwhelm with tall buildings and concrete. Indeed, urban density has never been more beautifully planned or landscaped than in Vancouver. Every Edwardian house and every high-rise residential tower in the West End is surrounded by lush, beautiful plantings of trees, shrubs, and flowers. City council has given density bonuses to developers: trading more floors of condos for the preservation of heritage and trees. This appealingly green idea of the urban working *with* nature instead of against it carries over into Vancouver's commercial downtown, where the placement and orientation of buildings has been carefully controlled to preserve view corridors to the mountains and bodies of water. Remember to look up as you wander downtown—more often than not, you'll be rewarded with a peek-a-boo view of a North Shore peak.

PREVIOUS PAGE: **Canada Place was built to resemble a giant sailing ship.**

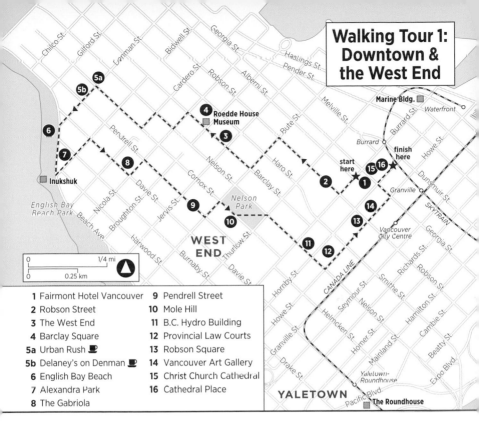

Marine Bldg. ■

Waterfront ○

Roedde House Museum

Burrard ○

finish here

start here ★

Inukshuk

English Bay Beach Park

Granville ○

WEST END

Nelson Park

Vancouver City Centre

SKYTRAIN

0 — 1/4 mi

0 — 0.25 km

▲

1 Fairmont Hotel Vancouver
2 Robson Street
3 The West End
4 Barclay Square
5a Urban Rush 🍴
5b Delaney's on Denman 🍴
6 English Bay Beach
7 Alexandra Park
8 The Gabriola

9 Pendrell Street
10 Mole Hill
11 B.C. Hydro Building
12 Provincial Law Courts
13 Robson Square
14 Vancouver Art Gallery
15 Christ Church Cathedral
16 Cathedral Place

YALETOWN

Yaletown-Roundhouse

■ The Roundhouse

1 The Fairmont Hotel Vancouver

At 900 W. Georgia St. and dating from 1939, this hotel was built and owned by the Canadian Pacific Railway (CPR), just as the city itself was for many, many years. In return for agreeing in 1885 to make Vancouver its western terminus, the CPR was given 2,428 hectares (6,000 acres) of prime real estate—nearly the whole of today's downtown. The Hotel Vancouver is built in the CPR's signature château style, with a verdigris-green copper roof. Construction took 11 years, halted mid-build by the Great Depression. It's worth stepping inside to see the grand, old-fashioned ambience of the lobby.

Leaving by the Burrard St. exit, turn left. Pass the intersection with Alberni St., and when you reach the corner, turn right, cross Burrard St., and you're on:

2 Robson Street

The shops on this corner are said to get more foot traffic than any others in Canada. But things were different back in the 1950s, when so many German delis and restaurants opened up that for a time the street was sign-posted as "Robsonstrasse." Beginning in the 1980s, the older businesses were replaced with high-end clothiers and new restaurants and gift shops with signs in Japanese. Whether you're into shopping or not, Robson Street is a great place to walk and people-watch. The street has an international cosmopolitan feel to it, and chances are you'll hear Cantonese, Croatian, Japanese, and other tongues as you stroll.

2 blocks farther down Robson St. at Bute St., turn left and walk 2 blocks and through a mini-park to Barclay St., and you've entered:

3 The West End

Beginning in about 1959, this down-at-its-heels neighborhood of once-grand Edwardian houses was transformed by the advent of the concrete high-rise. By 1970, most of the Edwardian houses had been replaced by apartment towers, and the West End was on its way to becoming one of the densest—and simultaneously one of the most livable—inner cities on the continent. The mini-park at Bute and Barclay is one of the things that makes the neighborhood so successful: Traffic is kept to a minimum on the tree-lined West End streets, so that residents—though they live in the city center—can enjoy a neighborhood almost as quiet as a small town. Beautiful landscaping, and plenty of it, adds to the area's appealing allure.

Turn right and walk 3 blocks down Barclay St. to Nicola St. Along the way, you'll see some of the elements that make the West End such a sought-after enclave: the gardens, street trees, and range and variety of buildings—including a few surviving Edwardians, like the Arts and Crafts house at 1351 Barclay St. and the pair of houses on Barclay between Broughton and Nicola sts., otherwise known as:

4 Barclay Square

This beautifully preserved bit of 19th-century Vancouver consists of Barclay Manor, built in the Queen Anne style in 1890, and **Roedde House,** a rare domestic design by Francis Rattenbury, British Columbia's leading 19th-century institutional architect, who designed the Vancouver Courthouse that Arthur Erickson revamped into the Vancouver Art Gallery (p. 123). Roedde House (✆ **604/684-7040;** www.roeddehouse.org) is now a museum, open for guided tours Wednesday through Friday 1 to 4pm; admission is C$5 adults. On Sundays, tea and cookies are served and the admission price is C$1 more.

Turn left and walk south down Nicola St. for 1 block—past Fire Station No. 6—then turn right and go 1 block on Nelson St., then left again onto Cardero St. Just ahead is the tiny Cardero Grocery at 1078 Cardero St. All the grocery needs of the West End were once supplied by little corner stores like this one. Turn right and walk 2 blocks on Comox St. to reach Denman St., the perfect place to:

5 Urban Rush & Delaney's on Denman ☕

If Robson Street is the place Vancouverites go for hyperactive shopping sprees, Denman Street is where they go to sit back, sip a latte, and watch their fellow citizens stroll past. **Urban Rush** (1040 Denman St.; ✆ **604/685-2996**) is a fine spot for coffee and people-watching, particularly if you can nab a table on their outdoor terrace. One block down on the opposite side of the street, **Delaney's on Denman** (1105 Denman St.; ✆ **604/662-3344**) is a favorite coffee hangout for members of the West End's sizable gay community. Everyone's welcome, of course, and the pies and cakes at this little cafe are great.

English Bay beach is a great place to get sunset views.

When you're ready to continue the walking tour, go 2 blocks farther down Denman St. and you're at:

6 English Bay Beach

This is the place to be when the sun is setting or on one of those crystal-clear days when the mountains of Vancouver Island can be seen looming in the distance—or any day at all, really, so long as the sun is shining. Every January 1, shivering Vancouverites in fancy costumes surround the bathhouse here at the very foot of Denman Street (entrance at beach level) to take part in the annual Polar Bear Swim. Check out the Bathhouse where a sign dating to 1931 prohibits "immodest attire"; back then, swimmers would rent wool bathing suits that tended to sag when wet.

Walk southeastward (left, as you're facing the water) on palm-tree lined Beach Ave., and you come to a tiny green space with a band shell known as:

7 Alexandra Park

Back around the turn of the 20th century, a big Bahamian immigrant named Joe Fortes used to make his home in a cottage near this spot—that is, when he wasn't down on the beach teaching local kids to swim. In recognition of his many years of free service, the city finally appointed Fortes its first life-guard. Later, a marble water fountain was erected in his memory by the Beach Avenue entrance to the park.

When you're finished looking around the park, head up Bidwell St. 2 blocks to Davie St., cross the street, turn right, walk 2 blocks farther on Davie St., and on your left at no. 1531, you'll see:

8 The Gabriola

This was the finest mansion in the West End when it was built in 1900 for sugar magnate B. T. Rogers. Its name comes from the rough sandstone cladding, quarried on Gabriola Island in the Strait of Georgia. Unfortunately for Rogers, the Shaughnessy neighborhood soon opened up across False Creek, and the West End just wasn't a place a millionaire could afford to be seen anymore. By 1925, the mansion had been sold off and subdivided into apartments. Since 1975, it's been a restaurant of one sort or another although at press time the building sat vacant and the gardens gated.

If it's open, cut through the garden and walk up through the Nicola St. mini-park, turning right on:

9 Pendrell Street

A few interesting bits of architecture reside on this street. One block farther, at the corner of Broughton Street, is the **Thomas Fee house** (1119 Broughton St.), where one of the city's leading turn-of-the-20th-century developer-architects made his home. Farther along, at the southeast corner of Pendrell and Jervis streets, is **St. Paul's Anglican Church,** a 1905 Gothic Revival church built entirely of wood. Next door at 1254 Pendrell, is the **Pendrellis**—a piece of architecture so unbelievably awful, one gets a perverse delight just looking at it. Built as a seniors' home at the height of the 1970s craze for concrete, the multistory tower is one great concrete block, with nary a window in sight.

At Bute St., turn left and walk 1 block to Comox St., and you're at:

10 Mole Hill

These two dozen or so preserved Edwardian homes provide a rare view of what the West End looked like in, say, 1925. That they exist at all is more or less a fluke. The city began purchasing buildings here in the 1950s but continued renting them out, thinking one day to tear them down for a park. By the 1990s, however, heritage had become important. The residents of the houses waged a sophisticated political campaign, renaming the area Mole Hill and bringing in nationally known architectural experts to plead the case for preservation. The city eventually gave in.

Cut across the park to Nelson St. and continue down Nelson St. past Thurlow St. to 970 Burrard St., where stands:

11 The BC Hydro Building

Built in 1957 by architects Ned Pratt and Ronald Thom, it was one of the first modernist structures erected in Canada and has since become a beloved Vancouver landmark, thanks in no small part to its elegant shape and attention to detail. Note how the windows, the doors, and even the tiles in the lobby and forecourt echo the six-sided lozenge shape of the original structure. In the mid-'90s, the building was converted to condominiums and rechristened the Electra. And contrary to the former-tenant BC Hydro's present-day power-saving messages, lights in the building were once routinely left on with the idea to make the building a city icon.

From here, continue on Nelson St., crossing Burrard St. and Hornby St. to:

12 The Provincial Law Courts

Internationally recognized architect Arthur Erickson has had an undeniable impact on his native city of Vancouver. His 1973 Law Courts complex covers 3 full city blocks, including the Erickson-renovated Vancouver Art Gallery at its north end. Linking the two is Robson Square, which Erickson—and everyone else—envisioned as the city's main civic plaza. As with so many Erickson designs, this one has elements of brilliance—the boldness of the vision itself, the tiered fountains (behind them are the offices of the Crown attorney—the Canadian equivalent of a district attorney), the cathedral-like space of the courthouse atrium—but, raised above street level, the entire ensemble is removed from all the life around it. To reach the courthouse, take the concrete stairway up and follow the elevated pedestrian concourse. The courthouse, with its giant glass-covered atrium, is worth a visit.

When you've seen the Law Courts, backtrack along the concourse, and you'll end up at:

13 Robson Square

As a civic plaza, Robson Square should be grand, but in fact, it's pretty underwhelming. Its basic problem is that it has been sunk 6m (20 ft.) below street level, so it's never exactly appealing or inviting to passersby. Despite the skating rink added for the 2010 Winter Games and a UBC bookstore, Robson Square lacks the throngs of people that add the essential ingredient—life—to a civic plaza. But look across the street, and you'll see the life that Robson Square lacks.

Directly across from Robson Sq., at 750 Hornby St., is the:

14 Vancouver Art Gallery

On sunny days, people bask like seals on the steps of the old courthouse-turned-art-gallery, a great gathering place and the perfect spot to see jugglers and buskers, pick up a game of outdoor speed chess, or listen to an activist haranguing the world at large about the topic du jour. Designed as a courthouse by Francis Rattenbury, architect of Roedde House, described earlier, and the Legislature Buildings (p. 276) and Fairmont Empress hotel in Victoria (p. 239) and renovated into an art gallery by Arthur Erickson, the Vancouver Art Gallery (p. 123) is home to a tremendous collection of works by iconic west coast painter Emily Carr, as well as rotating exhibits ranging from native masks to video installations. Film buffs may remember the entrance steps and inside lobby from the movie *The Accused*. To continue the tour, go around the gallery and proceed down Hornby Street. Note the fountain on the Art Gallery's front lawn. It was installed by a very unpopular provincial government as a way—according to some—of forever blocking protesters from gathering on what was then the courthouse lawn. In 2007, the 2010 Olympic Winter Games countdown clock was placed here. The clock has since been removed.

Cross Georgia St. and have a glance inside the Hong Kong Bank building (885 W. Georgia St.), where a massive pendulum designed by artist Alan Storey slowly swings back and forth. Cross Hornby St. and continue west on Georgia St. to 690 Burrard St., where stands:

15 Christ Church Cathedral

A Gothic Revival sandstone church with a steep gabled roof, buttresses, and arched stained-glass windows, the Anglican Christ Church Cathedral was completed in 1895. It was nearly demolished in 1971, when the church membership voted to build an Erickson-designed high-rise on the corner. But the public outcry overwhelmed the congregation's vote, resulting in the cathedral being named a heritage building in 1976.

The stained glass windows at Christ Church Cathedral date back to 1895.

Backtrack east to Hornby St., turn left, walk half a block, and climb the few steps into:

16 Cathedral Place

Often overlooked by Vancouverites, peaceful Cathedral Place is a charming example of an urban park. The building behind it, at 639 Hornby St., is a postmodern structure with small Art Deco parts melded onto a basically Gothic edifice. Some of the panels on its front were salvaged from the Georgia Medical-Dental building, a much-loved skyscraper that used to stand on this site. As for the Cathedral Place courtyard itself, which although it lacks sunlight, has the formality and calm of a French garden. The garden also adjoins the Bill Reid Gallery (p. 118).

WALKING TOUR 2: **GASTOWN & CHINATOWN**

START:	**Canada Place.**
FINISH:	**Maple Tree Square.**
TIME:	**2 to 4 hours, not including shopping, eating, and sightseeing stops.**
BEST TIME:	**Any day during business hours, but Chinatown is particularly active in the mornings. If you arrive between noon and 2pm, you can enjoy dim sum at many of the restaurants.**
WORST TIME:	**Chinatown's dead after 6pm, except on weekends in the summer, when they close a few streets to traffic and hold a traditional Asian night market from 6:30 to 11pm.**

Chinatown and Gastown are two of Vancouver's most fascinating neighborhoods. Gastown has history and the kind of old-fashioned architecture that no longer exists downtown or in the West End. Chinatown has brightly colored facades, street markets, and the buzz of modern-day Cantonese commerce. One small travel advisory, however: The two neighborhoods border on Vancouver's Downtown Eastside, a skid-row area troubled by alcoholism and drug use. While there's actually little danger for outsiders, there is a good chance you'll cross paths with a down-and-outer here and there, particularly around Pigeon Park at the corner of Carrall and Hastings or outside the Carnegie Community Centre at Hastings and Main streets. The tour route has been designed to avoid these areas.

1 Canada Place

With its five tall Teflon sails and bowsprit jutting out into Burrard Inlet, Canada Place is meant to resemble a giant sailing ship. Inside, it's a convention center and giant cruise-ship terminal, with the Pan Pacific Vancouver (p. 68) perched on top. Around the perimeter is a promenade with plaques at regular intervals explaining the sights or providing mostly shipping-related historical tidbits. During the summer months, this area is jammed with tourists and passengers arriving and departing from Alaskan cruises; the rest of the year, you'll have it pretty much to yourself. A huge expansion, completed in 2009, tripled the available convention space and added additional docking facilities. Look west from Canada Place to see the glassy, new building under its living roof.

To follow the promenade, start by the flag poles, likely flying Canadian flags, and head north along the walkway. On the roof toward the far end of the pier, a pair of leaping metal lions, which are ringed with lights at night, point up and out toward a pair of peaks on the North Shore called the Lions. The mountains are so named for their supposed resemblance to the bronze lions in Trafalgar Square. But rough-minded early settlers called them Sheba's Paps, and later The Sisters. Continue around the promenade, and you'll turn and look back toward the LEGO-block port containers and the city skyline: The low-rise older buildings just beyond the railway tracks are Gastown.

To continue the tour, walk back toward the shore along the promenade, go down the steps, turn left, and curve along the sidewalk until you pass the Aqua Riva restaurant. Then turn left and go up the steps, taking an indoor shortcut to an elevated plaza. You're now at:

2 Granville Square

Had some ill-advised politicians and developers had their way, all of Gastown and Chinatown would have been replaced by towers like the one you see here at 200 Granville Sq. In 1970, the plans were drawn up and the bulldozers were set to move when a coalition of hippies, heritage lovers, and Chinatown merchants took to the barricades in revolt. This undistinguished building was the only one ever built, and the plan was abandoned soon afterward. The Vancouver Harbour Control Tower sits at the top, ushering in buzzing floatplanes.

At the east end of the plaza a doorway leads into:

3 Waterfront Station

Though this Beaux Arts edifice at 601 W. Cordova St. was converted into the SeaBus terminal in the 1970s (SkyTrain service was first added in 1985 with the Canada Line, the newest route, opening in 2009), the building was originally the CPR's Vancouver passenger-rail terminal. Look up high on the walls, and you'll see oil paintings depicting scenes you might encounter if you took the train across Canada (much easier then than now). On the main floor are a Starbucks and some tourist shops. This is also where you can catch the SeaBus over to Lonsdale Quay in North Vancouver.

Leave by the front doors, turn left, and proceed to cobblestoned Water St., Gastown's main thoroughfare. The Landing, at 375 Water St., is home to some high-end retail stores and offices. As you walk along, note the Magasin Building at 332 Water St. Each of the column capitals bears the bronze head of a Gastown notable, among them Ray Saunders, the man who designed the:

4 Steam Clock

A quirky urban timepiece, the Steam Clock at Water and Cambie streets gives a steamy rendition of the Westminster Chimes every 15 minutes, drawing its power from the city's underground steam-heat system. A plaque on the base of the clock explains the mechanics of it all. (*Note:* The chimes can be erratic.)

Continue down Water St., past Hill's Native Art (165 Water St.), where Bill Clinton picked up a little bear statuette as a gift for you-know-who. At Abbott St., cross over to the south side and continue on Water St. until you come to the Gaoler's Mews building (12 Water St.). Duck in through the passageway and cross Carrall St. to reach:

5 The Irish Heather 🍺

This old Vancouver favorite in a new (since 2009) location serves excellent beer and good pub food. Look for its evening Long Table Series dinners, which seat 40 folks at a communal table. 210 Carrall St. ℰ **604/688-9779.**

Once you leave the pub, continue down Carrall St. to:

6 Maple Tree Square

A historic spot, Maple Tree Square is where Vancouver first began. The statue by the maple tree (not the original tree, but a replacement planted in the same spot) is of Gassy Jack Deighton, a riverboat captain and innkeeper who in 1867 erected Vancouver's first significant structure—a saloon built in 24 hours by local mill workers. Deighton got the nickname Gassy because of his propensity to jaw on at length (gassing, as it was known) about

Gassy Jack Deighton built Vancouver's first saloon in 1867.

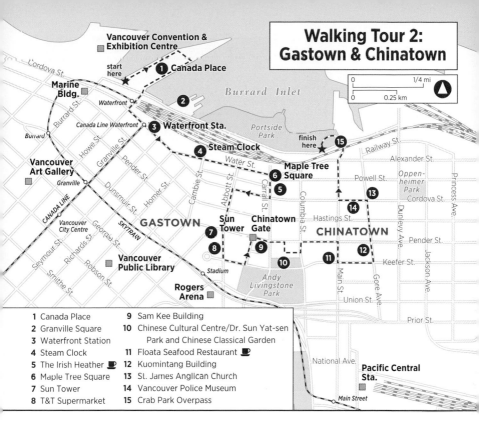

Vancouver Convention &
Exhibition Centre

start
here

1 Canada Place

Cordova St.

**Marine
Bldg.**

Waterfront St.

Burrard Inlet

2

Burrard St.

Canada Line Waterfront

3 Waterfront Sta.

*Portside
Park*

finish
here

15

Railway St.

Burrard

Howe St.

Granville St.

Pender St.

4 Steam Clock

Water St.

**Maple Tree
Square** **6**

Alexander St.

Powell St.

*Oppen-
heimer
Park*

Princess Ave.

**Vancouver
Art Gallery**

Granville

Dunsmuir St.

Homer St.

Cambie St.

Abbott St.

Carrall St.

Columbia St.

5

13

Cordova St.

Dunlevy Ave.

Jackson Ave.

CANADA LINE

SKYTRAIN

George St.

GASTOWN

**Sun
Tower**

**Chinatown
Gate**

Hastings St.

14

CHINATOWN

Pender St.

**Vancouver
City Centre**

Seymour St.

Richards St.

Robson St.

7

8

9

**Vancouver
Public Library**

Stadium

10

11

12

Keefer St.

Main St.

Gore Ave.

Smithe St.

**Rogers
Arena**

*Andy
Livingstone
Park*

Union St.

Prior St.

National Ave.

**Pacific Central
Sta.**

Main Street

1 Canada Place
2 Granville Square
3 Waterfront Station
4 Steam Clock
5 The Irish Heather
6 Maple Tree Square
7 Sun Tower
8 T&T Supermarket

9 Sam Kee Building
10 Chinese Cultural Centre/Dr. Sun Yat-sen
   Park and Chinese Classical Garden
11 Floata Seafood Restaurant
12 Kuomintang Building
13 St. James Anglican Church
14 Vancouver Police Museum
15 Crab Park Overpass

whatever topic happened to spring to mind. In 1870, when the town was officially incorporated as Granville, it was home to exactly six businesses: a hotel, two stores, and three saloons. Most folks called it Gastown, after Jack. More recent history: On August 7, 1971, some 1,500 hippies gathered in the square for the Grasstown Smoke-In & Street Jamboree. There were riots, arrests, and lots of stoned people.

Continue south on Carrall St. to W. Cordova St., turn right, and walk 1 block to Abbott St. Turn left and walk 2 blocks down Abbott St., crossing W. Hastings St. and stopping at W. Pender St., where you get a great view of the:

7 Sun Tower

At 500 Beatty St., it was the tallest building in the British Empire when it was built in 1911 to house the publishing empire of Louis D. Taylor, publisher of *Vancouver World*. Not only was the building tall, but it was also slightly scandalous, thanks to the nine half-nude caryatids that gracefully support the cornice halfway up the building. Three years after the building opened, Louis D. was forced to sell it.

Cross W. Pender St. and continue on Abbott St. until you come to the entrance at 179 Keefer Place of:

T&T Supermarket is a great place to discover unusual Asian fruits.

8 T&T Supermarket

Think you know supermarkets? Unless your hometown is Hong Kong or Singapore, you haven't seen one like this. Just have a gander at the seafood display inside the doors: king crab, scallops, three different kinds of oysters, lobster, and geoducks. Farther in is a host of other wondrous products, including strange Asian fruits like rambutan, lychee, and the pungent durian. Browse, maybe pick up something you don't recognize, and have an impromptu picnic in nearby Andy Livingstone Park.

Outside, walk 1 block east on Keefer St. to Taylor St. Andy Livingstone Park is just ahead to your right, but to continue the tour, turn left on Taylor St. and walk 1 block north to Pender St. Turn right on Pender St. and walk 1 block. Now, you're in one of North America's most populous Chinatowns. Our first Chinatown stop, at 8 W. Pender St., is the:

9 Sam Kee Building

The world's thinnest office building—at its base just shy of 1.5m deep (4 ft. 11 in. to be exact)—was Sam Kee's way of thumbing his nose at both the city and his greedy next-door neighbor. In 1912, the city expropriated most of Kee's land in order to widen Pender Street but refused to compensate him for the tiny leftover strip. Kee's neighbor, meanwhile, hoped to pick up the leftover sliver dirt-cheap. The building was Kee's response. Huge bay windows helped maximize the available space, as did the extension of the basement well out underneath the sidewalk (note the glass blocks in the pavement).

Just behind the Sam Kee Building is the **Shanghai Alley,** which just 40 years ago was jampacked with stores, restaurants, a pawnshop, a theater, rooming houses, and a public bath. It's been semi-revitalized with historical information boards and the hulking West Han Dynasty Bell. More interesting is the **Chinese Freemason's building,** just across the street at 1 W. Pender St. The building could be a metaphor for the Chinese experience in Canada. On predominantly Anglo Carrall Street, the building is the picture of Victorian conformity. On the Pender Street side, on the other hand, the structure is exuberantly Chinese.

Walk 1 block farther (east) on Pender St., and you'll come to the:

10 Chinese Cultural Centre/Dr. Sun Yat-Sen Park & Chinese Classical Garden

A modern building with an impressive traditional gate, the cultural center provides services and programs for the neighborhood's thousands of Chinese-speaking residents. Straight ahead as you enter the courtyard, a door set within a wall leads into the **Dr. Sun Yat-Sen Park,** a small urban park with a pond, walkways, and a nice gift shop selling scaled-down replicas of the ancient terra-cotta warriors unearthed in the tomb of Chinese Emperor Qin Shi Huang. Admission to the park is free. Adjoining the park, and accessible through another small doorway to the right of it, is the **Dr. Sun Yat-Sen Classical Chinese Garden** (p. 123). Modeled after a Ming period (1368–1644) scholar's retreat in the Chinese city of Suzhou, this garden is definitely worth a visit. Dr. Sun Yat-Sen, for whom the park and garden are named, is known as the father of modern China.

Exit the public park by the gate on the east side, turn left on Columbia St., and you'll find the Chinese Cultural Centre Museum and Archives at 555 Columbia St. From here, continue on Columbia St. up to Pender St., turn right and continue east, peeking in here and there to explore Chinese herbalist shops like Vitality Enterprises at 126 E. Pender St. At Main St., turn right and walk south 1 block to Keefer St. and:

11 Floata Seafood Restaurant 💻

Though it's Canada's largest Chinese restaurant, it isn't easy to find. In classic Hong Kong–restaurant style, it's on the third floor of a bright red shopping plaza/parking garage. Time your arrival for midmorning dim sum (a kind of moving Chinese smorgasbord) if you can. Alternatively, you might want to check out the recommended Chinatown restaurants in chapter 6. 180 Keefer St. ℂ **604/602-0368. www.floata.com**.

To continue the tour, stroll east on Keefer St., lined with sometimes pungent sidewalk markets selling fresh fish, fruit, and vegetables. Turn left on Gore Ave., and walk 1 block north to Pender St. On your left, at 296 E. Pender St., is the:

12 Kuomintang Building

Though often a mystery to outsiders, politics was and remains an important part of life in Chinatown. Vancouver was long a stronghold of the Chinese Nationalist League, or Kuomintang (KMT), whose founder, Dr. Sun Yat-Sen, stayed in Vancouver for a time raising funds. In 1920, the party erected this building to serve as its western Canadian headquarters. When the rival Chinese Communist party emerged victorious from the 1949 Chinese civil war, KMT leader Chiang Kai-shek retreated to Taiwan. Note the Taiwanese flag on the roof.

Continue north on Gore Ave. for 2 blocks, crossing Pender and Hastings streets. At the corner of Gore Ave. and Cordova St. (303 E. Cordova St.) stands:

13 St. James Anglican Church

Just before getting this commission, architect Adrian Gilbert Scott had designed a cathedral in Cairo—and it shows. Cater-corner to the church, the Firehall Arts Centre presents a range of performing and visual arts in an old fire station.

Walking a half block farther west on Cordova St. brings you to the:

14 Vancouver Police Museum

Located in the former Coroner's Court at 240 E. Cordova St., the **Vancouver Police Museum** (p. 124) is worth a visit if you're in a macabre mood. Among other displays, the museum has the autopsy report of Errol Flynn, who died in Vancouver in 1959 in the arms of his 17-year-old girlfriend.

Back on Gore Ave., walk north 2 blocks to Alexander St. Turn left and walk 1 block west on Alexander St. to the:

15 Crab Park Overpass

City Hall calls it Portside Park, and that's how it appears on the map. But to everyone else, it's Crab Park. It was created after long and vigorous lobbying by eastside activists, who reasoned that poor downtown residents had as much right to beach access as anyone else. The park is pleasant, though for those on a tight schedule it's not worth the trouble of walking all the way up and over the overpass. What is worthwhile, however, is walking halfway up to where two stone Chinese lions stand guard. From here, you can look back at Canada Place—where the tour started—or at the container port and fish plant to your right.

To bring the tour to an end, return to Alexander St. and walk 2 blocks west back to Maple Tree Sq. (stop 6).

WALKING TOUR 3: YALETOWN, GRANVILLE ISLAND & KITSILANO

START:	**The Vancouver Public Library Central Branch at Homer and Georgia streets.**
FINISH:	**The Capers Building, 2285 W. 4th Ave. (at Vine St.), in Kitsilano.**
TIME:	**2 to 4 hours, not including shopping, eating, and sightseeing stops.**
BEST TIME:	**Any time during business hours.**
WORST TIME:	**After 6pm, when Granville Island's shops have closed.**

This tour takes you through three of Vancouver's most interesting neighborhoods: the trendy warehouse-turned-retail/restaurant district of Yaletown, the industrial-area-turned-public-market called Granville Island, and the laid-back enclave of Kitsilano. The tour includes a brief ferry ride and a stroll along the waterfront and beach.

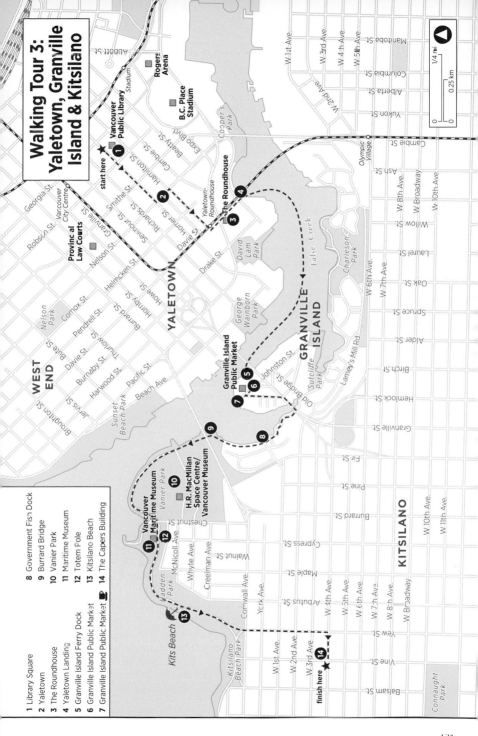

Walking Tour 3: Yaletown, Granville Island & Kitsilano

1 Library Square
2 Yaletown
3 The Roundhouse
4 Yaletown Landing
5 Granville Island Ferry Dock
6 Granville Island Public Market
7 Granville Island Public Market 📌

8 Government Fish Dock
9 Burrard Bridge
10 Vanier Park
11 Maritime Museum
12 Totem Pole
13 Kitsilano Beach
14 The Capers Building

1/4 mi
0.25 km

Abbott St.

Rogers Arena

B.C. Place Stadium

Stadium

start here

① Vancouver Public Library

W. 1st Ave.
W. 3rd Ave.
W. 4th Ave.
W. 5th Ave.

Manitoba St.
Columbia St.
Alberta St.
Yukon St.

W. 2nd Ave.

Cambie St.

Olympic Village
Ash St.

W. 8th Ave.
W. Broadway
W. 10th Ave.

Willow St.

Laurel St.

Oak St.

Spruce St.

Alder St.

Birch St.

Hemlock St.

Granville St.

Fir St.

Pine St.

Burrard St.

Cypress St.

Maple St.

Arbutus St.

Yew St.

Vine St.

Balsam St.

W. 5th Ave.
W. 6th Ave.
W. 7th Ave.
W. 8th Ave.
W. Broadway

W. 10th Ave.
W. 11th Ave.

W. 6th Ave.
W. 7th Ave.

Charleson Park

False Creek

GRANVILLE ISLAND

David Lam Park

George Wainborn Park

Johnston St.

Old Bridge St.

Sutcliffe Park

Lamey's Mill Rd.

② The Roundhouse
③
④

Yaletown-Roundhouse

Expo Blvd.

Beatty St.

Cambie St.

Hamilton St.

Smithe St.

Richards St.

Homer St.

Davie St.

Drake St.

Copper's Park

YALETOWN

Provincial Law Courts

Georgia St.

Robson St.

Nelson St.

Smithe St.

Seymour St.

Richards St.

Granville St.

Howe St.

Hornby St.

Burrard St.

Thurlow St.

Bute St.

Jervis St.

Broughton St.

Comox St.

Pendrell St.

Davie St.

Burnaby St.

Harwood St.

Pacific St.

Beach Ave.

Helmcken St.

Nelson Park

WEST END

Vancouver City Centre

Sunset Beach Park

⑤ Granville Island Public Market
⑥
⑦
⑧
⑨

KITSILANO

Vanier Park

⑩ H.R. MacMillan Space Centre/ Vancouver Museum

⑪ Vancouver Maritime Museum
⑫

Chestnut St.

Walnut St.

McNicoll Ave.

Whyte Ave.

Creelman Ave.

Cornwall Ave.

York Ave.

W. 1st Ave.

W. 2nd Ave.

W. 3rd Ave.

W. 4th Ave.

Connaught Park

Hadden Park

Kits Beach

Kitsilano Beach Park

⑬

⑭

finish here

171

1 Library Square

Designed by architect Moshe Safdie, this branch of the Vancouver Public Library, at 350 W. Georgia St., was enormously controversial when it opened in 1995. Though Safdie denied that the ancient Roman coliseum served as inspiration, the coliseum is exactly what comes to mind when you first see the exterior of this postmodern building. Architectural critics pooh-poohed it as derivative and ignorant of West Coast architectural traditions, but for the public it was love at first sight. The steps out front have become a popular public gathering place, the lofty atrium inside a favored hangout spot and "study-date" locale. Go inside the atrium and then into the high-tech library itself: It's light, airy, and wonderfully accessible.

From the library, walk south down Homer St. and turn left on Nelson St. At Hamilton St. you're in:

2 Yaletown

Vancouver's former meatpacking warehouse district, Yaletown was where roughneck miners from Yale (up the Fraser Valley) used to come to drink and brawl. The city considered leveling the area in the 1970s until someone noticed that the raised loading docks would make great outdoor terraces and the low brick buildings themselves could be renovated into commercial space. Though it's taken years for the neighborhood to really catch on, the result is a funky upscale district of furniture shops, restaurants, multimedia companies, "New York–style" lofts, and lots and lots of clubs. Hamilton Street and Mainland Street are the trendiest arteries in Yaletown. Note the metal canopies over the loading docks on many buildings—they used to keep shipping goods dry; now, they do the same for tourists and craft-beer-sipping computer programmers.

Walk down alleylike Mainland St. and turn left at Davie St. Continue southeast down Davie St. and cross Pacific Blvd. On your right you'll see:

3 The Roundhouse

The Roundhouse is so named because that's exactly what this brick-and-timber frame building was, back when this land was the CPR's switching yard. The structure has since been converted into a community center. It's worth ducking inside to have a look at CPR 372, the locomotive that pulled the first passenger train into Vancouver way back in 1887; you can also see the locomotive from the street, through a giant glass window. The old switching yard is undergoing a revitalization project in 2011, which should see performances and events held in the open space.

Follow Davie St. south to the False Creek waterfront and the:

4 Yaletown Landing (at the Foot of Davie St.)

The forest of high-rises ringing the north shore of False Creek, where you're now standing, is the creation of one company—Concord Pacific, owned by Hong Kong billionaire Li Ka Shing. Formerly a railway switching yard, the area was transformed for the Expo '86 World's Fair. When the fair came to an end, the provincial government sold the land to Li Ka Shing for a song on

Each panel of *Street Light* at Yaletown Landing depicts a seminal event in Vancouver history.

the understanding he would build condominiums. And did he ever. At the landing site, note the large art piece, *Street Light,* designed by Bernie Miller and Alan Tregebov and installed in 1997. The large panels, each of which depicts a seminal event in Vancouver's history, have been arranged so that on the anniversary of that event, the sun will shine directly through the panel, casting a shadowed image on the street.

From here, at the end of the dock, catch a mini-ferry to Granville Island. Both the rainbow-hued **Aquabus** (© **604/689-5858**) and False Creek Ferries (© **604/684-7781**) make the trip every 15 min. through the day; the fare is C$4.50 adults.

The ferry will scoot you across False Creek harbor in about 5 min. and let you off at:

5 Granville Island Ferry Dock

To be topographically honest, Granville Island (p. 115) is not really an island; it's more of a protuberance. But it contains a fascinating collection of shops, restaurants, theaters, artists' workshops, housing, a hotel, and still-functioning heavy industry—one of the few successful examples of 1970s urban renewal. The **Granville Island Information Centre** (1592 Johnston St.; © **604/666-5784**), near the Public Market, has excellent free maps, but they're not really necessary—the place is so compact, the best thing to do is simply wander and explore.

Right at the top of the Aquabus dock is an entrance into the:

6 Granville Island Public Market

This is an amazing place that sells anything and everything that's edible.

The market is a wonderful place to stop and:

7 Granville Island Public Market ☕

If it's edible, this market probably has it, from handmade chocolates and local salmon to artisan bread and strawberries picked that morning out in the Fraser Valley. Those with an immediate hunger gravitate to the far side of the market, where **A La Mode** (✆ **604/685-8335**) sells lattes and fabulous rhubarb-strawberry pie. The most fun way to feed yourself, however, is to roam the market stalls for sandwiches, sausages, or picnic supplies—artichoke hearts, artisan cheese, cold smoked salmon, Indian candy, pepper pâté, freshly baked bread—then head outside for an alfresco feast at one of the tables on the dock overlooking False Creek. The views are great, the slightly salty air invigorating, and if you've brought small children along, it's the perfect place to play that endlessly fascinating (to kids) game of Catch the Seagull.

From Triangle Sq., the small plaza in front of the public market, head south (left) on Duranleau St., where you'll pass enticing shops and marine charter services. At Anderson St., turn right and right again on waterside Island Park Walk, following it north to the:

8 Government Fish Dock

Want to buy fresh from the boat? This is the place to do it. Find fresh salmon in season (summer and early fall), prawns, scallops, and other shellfish much of the rest of the year. Sales take place every day in high season and otherwise on weekend mornings. Hours and availability, of course, depend on the catch. Go Fish (✆ **604/730-5040**), a simple hut serving fish tacos and battered fillets, is within stone-skipping distance of the fish dock.

Continue on the seaside walkway, and eventually you pass beneath the:

9 Burrard Bridge

In 1926, the city fathers commissioned noted urban planner Harland Bartholomew to provide some guidance on how to expand their rather raw seaport city. One of Bartholomew's first injunctions: Build beautiful bridges. The Burrard Bridge is the result, an elegant steel span with two castles guarding the approaches at either end.

Walk beneath the bridge and continue along the pedestrian path in Vanier Park to:

10 Vanier Park

To your left rises the white cone of the **Museum of Vancouver** (p. 129) and **H. R. MacMillan Space Centre** (p. 127). The low building next to that is the **Vancouver Archives** (1150 Chestnut St.; ✆ **604/736-8561**), home to some fascinating panoramic photographs of Vancouver back in the early days. Continuing along the gravel path, watch for artist Alan Chung Hung's massive iron sculpture *Gate to the Northwest Passage*.

Continue on the waterside path until you come to the:

11 Maritime Museum

For centuries, the quest of every European explorer was to find the Northwest Passage, the seagoing shortcut to the riches of the East. The little ship housed inside the **Maritime Museum** (p. 130) is the one that finally did it.

A totem pole in front of the Maritime Museum.

Tours of the RCMP vessel, the *St. Roch,* are available at regular intervals throughout the day. Out back of the museum, the junk on the lawn by the north side all comes from various ships wrecked on the BC coast, while on the waterfront is the enclave of boats docked at Heritage Harbour. Many older wooden vessels find shelter behind the breakwater, including the seiner BCP45 shown on the back of the old C$5 bill.

On the inland side of the museum, you'll see the:

12   Totem Pole

Carved by the exceptional Kwakiutl carver Mungo Martin (who also did many of the poles displayed in the Museum of Anthropology and in Stanley Park), the 10 figures on this 30m-tall (98-ft.) pole each represent an ancestor of the 10 Kwakiutl clans. An identical pole was presented to Queen Elizabeth in 1958 to mark BC's centenary. It now stands in Windsor Great Park in England.

Continue on the waterside pathway to:

13   Kitsilano Beach

Vancouver is blessed with beaches. From here, they stretch almost unbroken to the University of British Columbia, about 8.5km (5¼ miles) west on the tip of the Point Grey peninsula. Each beach has its own distinct personality. Below UBC, Wreck Beach is a semi-wild strand for nudists and nature lovers. Beaches in between cater to dogs, picnicking families, and hikers. Kitsilano Beach (Kits Beach, for short) is home to a spandex-and-testosterone set that loves a fast and furious game on the volleyball courts. But relaxers love Kits, too. The logs lined up on the beach make it a fine place to lay out a blanket and laze the day away. Small children love to play on the nearby swings, while older kids favor the lifeguarded swimming area or the world's largest outdoor saltwater swimming pool. On a clear day, the views of the mountains are tremendous.

About midway down Kits Beach, a sidewalk veers left and takes you up to Yew St. Follow Yew St. uphill to 4th Ave. and turn right. Walk along the restaurant-packed avenue to 2285 W. 4th Ave. and you'll find:

14 The Capers Building

Back in the 1960s, Kitsilano was Canada's Hippie Central, a Haight-Ashbury–like enclave of head shops, communes, and coffeehouses. In the early 1970s, Vancouver's super-square mayor, Tom Campbell, went so far as to propose rounding up all the tie-dyed long-hairs and shipping them off to a detention center. As the years passed, the hippies' waistlines and wallets got thicker, run-down communes and boardinghouses were renovated or replaced with new apartments and condos, and the shops came to reflect Kitsilano's new affluence, though still with a touch of counterculture.

The retail/office/apartment building at 2285 W. 4th Ave. was built according to an innovative energy-efficient design, and now serves as home to **Capers,** an organic supermarket.

The walk ends here. You may want to explore the shopping opportunities along 4th Ave. Or you can catch a no. 4 or 7 bus to take you back to downtown Vancouver.

VANCOUVER SHOPPING

9

Vancouver's a fun place to shop because it's international and cosmopolitan, but hasn't lost its funky, fun-loving edge. There are stores galore, and most of them are not in malls. Blessed with a climate that seems semitropical in comparison to the rest of Canada, Vancouverites never really developed a taste for indoor malls (though there is one—Pacific Centre—right downtown). Below are a few thoughts on where to start your shopping expeditions.

THE SHOPPING SCENE

Outside of malls, stores in Vancouver are generally open Monday through Saturday from 9am to 6pm. A few exceptions: Stores on Robson Street stay open later (usually until 9pm), while stores in Kitsilano open later (around 10am). On Sunday, most stores are open 11am to 6pm, but a few remain closed all day. Malls such as the Pacific Centre are open from 10am to 7pm Monday, Tuesday, and Saturday; 10am to 9pm Wednesday through Friday; and 11am to 6pm on Sunday. During Christmas shopping season, stores extend their hours.

Robson Street

It's been said that the corner of Robson and Burrard streets gets more foot traffic than any other corner in Canada. It's a busy, colorful parade of humanity, with many students, visitors, and residents from Asia (hence the sushi bars and shops with Japanese signs), most with money. Over the past few years, rents have risen so much that Robson Street now mostly offers upscale chain shops and international designer boutiques, though here and there a few local stores survive. Look for high-end clothing and accessories, with a focus on young designer fashions.

South Granville

The 10-block stretch of Granville Street, from 6th Avenue up to 16th Avenue, is where Vancouver's old-money enclave of Shaughnessy comes to shop. Classic and expensive clothiers, and housewares and furniture boutiques, predominate. This is also the heart of the gallery district.

Water Street & Gastown

Though a little too heavy on the souvenir shops, Water Street and Gastown are by no means just a tacky tourist enclave. Look for antiques and cutting-edge furniture, galleries of First Nations art, funky basement retro shops, and up-to-the-minute fashions by local designers.

Main Street

Antiques, and lots of 'em. From about 19th Avenue up to 27th Avenue, Main Street is chockablock with antiques shops. Rather than outbid each other, the stores have evolved so that each covers a particular niche, from Art Deco to

PREVIOUS PAGE: **The Granville Island Public Market is a great place to shop for food and crafts.**

country kitchen to fine Second Empire. It's fun to browse, and if your eyes start to glaze over at the thought of yet another divan, the area also has cafes, bookshops, and clothing stores.

Granville Island

A rehabilitated industrial site beneath the Granville Street Bridge, the Public Market is one of the best places to pick up salmon and other seafood. It's also a great place to browse for crafts and gifts. You can also observe potters, silversmiths, and glass blowers as they work their magic. Particularly interesting is Kids Market, a kind of mini-mall for children, featuring play areas and services for the not-yet-10 demographic. See the Granville Island listing (p. 125).

Asia West: Richmond

If you've never been to Hong Kong, or are just itching to get back, the commercial area on Richmond's No. 3 Road, between Capstan and Alderbridge roads, is the place to shop. Stores in four malls—the Yaohan Centre, President Plaza, Aberdeen Centre, and Parker Place—cater to Vancouver's Asian community by bringing in goods directly from the Far East. If the prices seem a bit high, a simple inquiry is often enough to bring them plummeting by as much as 80%. **Aberdeen Centre** (4151 Hazelbridge Way, at the corner of Hazelbridge Way and Cambie Rd.; ✆ **604/270-1234;** www.aberdeencentre.com) and the adjacent **Yaohan Centre** (3700 No. 3 Rd., btw. Cambie Rd. and Capstan Way; ✆ **604/231-0601;** www.yaohancentre.com) are the best. Both malls have large food courts and specialty shops selling everything from cellphones to candied ginseng.

SHOPPING A TO Z
Antiques

Bakers Dozen Antiques   This charming shop specializes in antique toys, model ships and boats, folk art, and unusual 19th- and early-20th-century furniture. 3520 Main St. ✆ **604/879-3348.**

DoDa Antiques 📖   A colorful and eclectic collection of mid-20th-century pieces—costume and estate jewelry, art glass from Canada, Scandinavia, and Italy, pottery, paintings, and curios—fills this shop. 434 Richards St. ✆ **604/602-0559.** www.dodaantiques.com.

Uno Langmann Limited   Catering to upscale shoppers, Uno Langmann specializes in European and North American paintings, furniture, silver, and objets d'art from the 18th through early 20th centuries. 2117 Granville St. ✆ **604/736-8825.** www.langmann.com.

Books

Blackberry Books   Although this small Granville Island store tends toward general interest and fiction, they have a healthy selection of books about art, architecture, and cuisine. They're right across from the public market. 3–1666 Johnston St. ✆ **866/685-6188** or 604/685-6188. www.bbooks.ca.

Chapters   Chapters chain bookstores stock current titles but seem to be phasing out books in favor of—what else?—gifts and gewgaws. 788 Robson St.; ✆ **604/682-4066.** 2505 Granville St.; ✆ **604/731-7822.** www.chapters.indigo.ca.

Bakers Dozen Antiques specializes in antique toys.

International Travel Maps and Books 🎁 This store has the best selection of travel books, maps, charts, and globes in town, plus an impressive selection of special-interest British Columbia guides. This is the hiker's best source for detailed topographic charts of the entire province. The only problem is that they've closed their handy downtown store and moved out to Richmond. 12300 Bridgeport Rd., Richmond. ✆ **604/273-1400.** www.itmb.com.

Kidsbooks ☺ The largest and most interesting selection of children's literature in the city also has an amazing collection of puppets, games, and toys, and holds regular readings. 3083 W. Broadway; ✆ **604/738-5335.** 3040 Edgemont Blvd., North Vancouver; ✆ **604/986-6190.** www.kidsbooks.ca.

Macleod's Books The kind of dusty, old-fashioned, used bookstore true book-lovers and bibliophiles love to explore, stacked high with reasonably priced books covering every conceivable subject. 455 W. Pender St. ✆ **604/681-7654.**

Ceramics, China, Silver & Crystal

Gallery of BC Ceramics This Granville Island gallery is owned and operated by the Potters Guild of British Columbia and features a collection of sculptural and functional ceramic works from more than 100 BC potters. Closed on Mondays in January. 1359 Cartwright St. ✆ **604/669-3606.** www. bcpotters.com.

The Gallery of BC Ceramics features work from more than 100 BC potters.

A Special Vancouver Experience: Asian Night Markets

Whether you're hoping to sample steamed dumplings, pick up a tin of oolong tea, or just poke around a fascinating scene, visiting one of Vancouver's Asian night markets is great fun. Throughout the summer, Keefer Street between Main and Columbia streets in historic Chinatown closes to make room for the **Chinatown Night Market** (www.vcma.shawbiz.ca). Styled after Asian marketplaces where shopping is personal and haggling is the name of the game, stalls and tables are loaded with bargain-price merchandise, including CDs, garments, novelties, watches, food, and accessories. Enjoy entertainment shows on Fridays and Saturdays, and family fun and games on Sundays. The market runs from mid-May to mid-September every Friday, Saturday, and Sunday from 6:30 to 11pm.

In Richmond, about 30 minutes from downtown Vancouver, the **Richmond Night Market** (12631 Vulcan Way, Richmond; ✆ 604/278-8000; www.summernightmarket.com) is an all-out event that feels like a summer festival with up to 15,000 visitors in 1 night. Vendors sell merchandise from all over the world, and food stalls cook up a storm. Entertainment is also a big part of the market with various performers during the evening. The market runs from mid-May through mid-September every Friday and Saturday night from 7pm until midnight, and Sunday evening from 7 to 11pm.

Martha Sturdy Originals 🛍 Local designer Martha Sturdy—once best known for her collectible, usable, handblown glassware trimmed in gold leaf—is now creating a critically acclaimed line of cast-resin housewares, as well as limited-edition furniture and chairs. Expensive, but, if you've got the dough, the furniture is well worth it. Gallery open by appointment only. 12 W. 5th Ave. ✆ **604/872-5205.** www.marthasturdy.com.

Chinese Goods

Cheung Sing Herbal & Birds Nest Co. 🛍 If you've never been to a Chinese herbalist, this is the one to try: jars, bins, and boxes full of such things as dried sea horse, thinly sliced deer antler, and bird's nest. It's fun to explore and potentially good for what ails you. Chinese remedies can have side effects, however, so before ingesting anything unfamiliar, consult the on-site herbalist. 536 Main St. ✆ **604/899-1123.**

Silk Road Art Trading Co. 🛍 This store, with an entrance on Columbia Street and another within Dr. Sun Yat-Sen Park in the Chinese Cultural Centre, sells reproductions of Chinese art objects, including the ancient terra-cotta warriors unearthed in a Chinese emperor's tomb. 561 Columbia St. ✆ **604/683-8707.**

T&T Supermarket 🛍 This store has racks and racks of goods you won't find at home (unless your home is China), but the real entertainment is in the seafood and produce, where strange and ungainly comestibles lurk: fire-dragon fruit, lily root, and enoki mushrooms. 179 Keefer Place. ✆ **604/899-8836.** www.tnt-supermarket.com.

Ten Ren Tea & Ginseng Co. Whether you prefer the pungent aroma of Chinese black tea or the exotic fragrance of chrysanthemum, jasmine, or ginger flower, you must try the numerous varieties of drinking and medicinal teas in this Chinatown shop. It also carries Korean and American ginseng for a lot less than you might pay elsewhere. 550 Main St. ℭ **604/684-1566.** www.tenren.com.

Cigars & Tobacco

Americans, remember: If they're Cuban, you can't bring them into the U.S.

City Cigar Company Stocking extensive selection of Cubans along with brands from the Dominican Republic, Honduras, Spain, and Jamaica, City Cigar Company claims to be the largest cigar shop in the country. There's also a room purely dedicated to pipes and hookahs. 888 W. 6th Ave. ℭ **604/879-0208.** www. citycigarcompany.com.

La Casa del Habano Casa del Habano has Vancouver's largest walk-in humidor. Cigars range in price from a few dollars to more than a hundred. 402 Hornby St. ℭ **604/609-0511.** www.lacasadelhabano.ca.

Department Stores

The Bay (Hudson's Bay Company) From the establishment of its early trading posts during the 1670s to its modern coast-to-coast department-store chain, The Bay has built its reputation on quality goods. You can still buy a Hudson's Bay woolen "point" blanket (the colorful stripes originally represented how many beaver pelts each blanket was worth in trade), but you'll also find Tommy Hilfiger, Polo, DKNY, and more. 674 Granville St. ℭ **604/681-6211.** www.hbc.com.

Hills of Kerrisdale ♠ This neighborhood department store in central Vancouver is a city landmark. Carrying full lines of quality men's, women's, and children's clothes, as well as furnishings and sporting goods, it's a destination for locals because the prices are often lower than those in the downtown core. 2125 W. 41st Ave. ℭ **604/266-9177.** www.hillsofkerrisdale.com.

Holt Renfrew This high-end trend-stocker can be accessed through Pacific Centre shopping mall and features all the hot designers in a department store setting. 737 Dunsmuir St. ℭ **604/681-3121.** www.holtrenfrew.com.

Discount Shopping

The strips of West 4th Avenue between Cypress and Yew streets and West Broadway from MacDonald to Blenheim streets offer a solid sampling of consignment-clothing shopping.

In-Again Clothing ♠ This shop has a good variety of seasonal consignment clothing, and the selection keeps up with fashion trends. Don't miss the collection of purses, scarves, and belts. 1962 W. 4th Ave. ℭ **604/738-2782.**

Second Suit for Men & Women ♠ This resale- and sample-clothing store has the best in men's and women's fashions, including Hugo Boss, Armani, Donna Karan, Nautica, Calvin Klein, and Alfred Sung. The inventory changes rapidly. 2036 W. 4th Ave. ℭ **604/732-0338.**

Turnabout Turnabout has three stores, each catering to its own shopping neighborhood. This Kitsilano location stocks modern, upbeat designs from BCBG, Banana Republic, and Bebe, while the storefronts on South Granville and in White Rock have a more upscale bent. 3112 W. Broadway. ℭ **604/731-7762.** www.turnaboutclothing.com.

Fashion

FOR CHILDREN

Isola Bella ☺ This store imports an exclusive collection of rather expensive, high-fashion newborn and children's clothing from mostly European designers like Bonpoint, Tartine et Chocolat, and Mann. 5692 Yew St. ✆ **604/266-8808.** www.isolabella.ca.

Please Mum ☺ This Kitsilano store sells attractive Canadian-designed toddler's and children's cotton clothing. 2951 W. Broadway. ✆ **604/732-4574.** www.please mum.com.

FOR MEN & WOMEN

Vancouver has the Pacific Northwest's best collection of clothes from Paris, London, Milan, and Rome, in addition to a great assortment of locally made, cutting-edge fashions. It seems that almost every week a new designer or independent boutique opens in Yaletown, Kitsilano, Gastown, or on Main Street. International designer outlets include **Chanel Boutique** (inside Holt Renfrew at 737 Dunsmuir St.; ✆ 604/682-0522), **Salvatore Ferragamo** (918 Robson St.; ✆ 604/669-4495), and **Gianni Versace Boutique** (Sinclair Centre, 757 W. Hastings St.; ✆ 604/683-1131).

Dream Apparel Big-name designs can be found anywhere, but this little shop is one of the few places to show early collections—clothing and jewelry—of local designers. 311 W. Cordova St. ✆ **604/683-7326.**

Leone Shop where the stars shop. Versace, Donna Karan, Byblos, Armani, and fabulous Italian and French accessories are sold in this very elegant building; valet parking is provided, as well as private after-hours shopping by appointment for VIPs. Sinclair Centre, 757 W. Hastings St. ✆ **604/683-1133.** www.leone.ca.

Obakki Visit this great new fashion boutique in Gastown for original garments created by talented new Canadian designers; high-quality fabrics and attention to design are the hallmarks. 44 Water St. ✆ **604/669-9727.** www.obakki.com.

Roots Canada Proudly Canadian, this chain features sturdy casual clothing, including leather jackets and bags, footwear, outerwear, and athletic wear for the whole family. 1001 Robson St. (corner of Burrard St.). ✆ **604/683-4305.** www. roots.com.

Swimco Located near Kitsilano Beach, this store sells a large variety of bikinis and other bathing suits in the latest styles for men, women, and children. 2166 W. 4th Ave. ✆ **604/732-7946.** www.swimco.com.

Venus & Mars 🎁 Add some drama to your life. This Gastown boutique features Vancouver designer Sanné Lambert's work, specializing in one-of-a-kind handmade gowns, corsets, and velvet robes. Some plus sizes also available. 315 Cambie St. ✆ **604/687-1908.** www.venusandmars.biz.

Zonda Nellis Design Ltd. 🎁 Rich colors and intricate patterns highlight this Vancouver designer's imaginative hand-woven separates, pleated silks, sweaters, vests, and soft knits. Nellis has also introduced a line of hand-painted silks and sumptuous, sheer, hand-painted evening wear. 2203 Granville St. ✆ **604/736-5668.** www.zondanellis.com.

VINTAGE CLOTHING

Deluxe Junk Co. The name fits—there's tons of junk here. However, some real bargains have been known to pop up among the polyester jackets and worn-out dress shirts. 310 W. Cordova St. ℂ **604/685-4871.** www.deluxejunk.com.

True Value Vintage Clothing This shop has a collection of funky fashions from the 1930s through the 1990s, including tons of fake furs, leather jackets, denim, soccer jerseys, vintage bathing suits, formal wear, smoking jackets, sweaters, and accessories. 4578 Main St. ℂ **604/685-5403.**

Woo Clothing With an online store perfect for browsing and a rack-packed store in Mount Pleasant, Woo Clothing offers shoppers an exciting hunt. Expect lots of ranch wear, denim, and a few Hawaiian prints, along with Asian, swing, and rockabilly designs. 4366 Main St. ℂ **604/687-8200.** www.woovintage.com.

First Nations Art & Crafts

You don't have to purchase a pricey antique to acquire original Coast Salish or Haida work. As the experts at the **Museum of Anthropology** explain, if an item is crafted by any of the indigenous Pacific Northwest artisans, it's a real First Nations piece of art. Galleries will tell you about the artist, and explain how to identify and care for these beautifully carved, worked, and woven pieces. Bold, traditional, and innovative geometric designs, intricate carvings, strong primary colors, and rich wood tones are just a few of the elements you'll find in First Nations crafts.

Even if you're not in the market, go gallery-hopping to see works by Haida artists **Bill Reid** (the province's best-known native artist) and **Richard Davidson,** and by Kwakwaka'wakw artist and photographer **David Neel.**

Coastal Peoples Fine Arts Gallery This Yaletown boutique showcases an extensive collection of fine First Nations jewelry. The motifs—Bear, Salmon, Whale, Raven, and others—are drawn from local myths and translated into 14-karat or 18-karat gold and sterling silver creations. Inuit sculptures and items made of glass or wood are also worth a look. Custom orders can be filled quickly and shipped worldwide. There is also a Gastown location at 312 Water St. (ℂ **604/684-9222**) and the two are a short Canada Line trip apart. 1024 Mainland St. ℂ **604/685-9298.** www.coastalpeoples.com.

Hill's Native Art ★ In a re-creation of a trading post interior, this shop, established in 1946 and claiming to be North America's largest Northwest Coast native art gallery, sells ceremonial masks, Cowichan sweaters, moccasins, wood sculptures, totem poles, silk-screen prints, soapstone sculptures, and gold, silver, and argillite jewelry. 165 Water St. ℂ **604/685-4249.** www.hills nativeart.com.

Inuit Gallery of Vancouver This store is home to one of Canada's foremost collections of Inuit and First Nations art. Prices are for serious buyers, but it's worth a visit. 206 Cambie St. ℂ **604/688-7323.** www.inuit.com.

Khot-La-Cha Art Gallery & Gift Shop 🎁 Hand-tanned moose-hide crafts; woodcarvings; Cowichan sweaters; porcupine-quill jewelry; and bone, silver, gold, and turquoise accessories are just a few of the selections at this Coast Salish crafts shop. 270 Whonoak St., North Vancouver. ℂ **604/987-3339.** www.khot-la-cha. com. Turn south on Capilano Rd. (off Marine Dr.) and make the first left (Whonoak St. is parallel to Capilano Rd.).

The Marion Scott Gallery shows traditional and contemporary art by Inuit and First Nations artists.

Lattimer Gallery 🎁   This beautiful gallery showcases museum-quality Pacific Northwest First Nations art, including ceremonial masks, totem poles, limited-edition silk-screen prints, argillite sculptures, and expensive gold and silver jewelry. 1590 2nd Ave. ℂ **604/732-4556.** www.lattimergallery.com.

Marion Scott Gallery/Kardosh Projects   For more than 30 years, this gallery has been well regarded for its Inuit and First Nations art collections and recently shifted to showcase more contemporary works by northern artists. 2423 Granville St. ℂ **604/685-1934.** www.marionscottgallery.com.

Museum of Anthropology   The new and expanded museum gift shop features excellent and elegant works by contemporary First Nations artisans, as well as books about the culture and publications on identifying and caring for Pacific Northwest crafts. University of British Columbia, 6393 NW Marine Dr. ℂ **604/822-5087.** www.moa.ubc.ca.

Food

You'll find **salmon** everywhere in Vancouver. Many shops package whole, fresh salmon with ice packs for visitors to take home. Shops also carry delectable smoked salmon in travel-safe, vacuum-packed containers. Some offer decorative cedar gift boxes; most offer overnight air transport. Try other salmon treats such as salmon jerky and Indian candy (chunks of marinated smoked salmon), which are available at public markets such as **Granville Island Public Market** (p. 187) and **Lonsdale Quay Market** (p. 187).

Chocolate Arts 🎁   The works at this chocolatier are made with exquisite craftsmanship. Seasonal treats include pumpkin truffles around Halloween or eggnog truffles for Christmas. They've even made chocolate toolboxes filled with tiny chocolate tools. Look for the all-chocolate diorama in the window—it changes every month or so. 1620 W. 3rd Ave. ℂ **604/739-0475.** www.chocolatearts.com.

The Lobsterman   Live lobsters, Dungeness crabs, oysters, mussels, clams, geoducks, and scallops are just a few of the varieties of seafood swimming in the saltwater tanks at this Granville Island fish store. The staff steams the food fresh on the spot, free. Salmon and other seafood can also be packed for air travel. 1807 Mast Tower Rd. ℂ **604/687-4531.** www.lobsterman.com.

Murchie's Tea & Coffee   This Vancouver institution has been the city's main tea and coffee purveyor for more than a century. You'll find everything from Jamaican Blue Mountain and Kona coffees to Lapsang Souchong and Kemun teas. The knowledgeable staff will help you decide which flavors and blends fit your taste. A fine selection of bone china and crystal serving ware, as well as coffeemakers and teapots, are also on sale. 825 W. Pender St. ℭ **604/669-0783.** www.murchies.com.

South China Seas Trading Company   The South Seas have always been a source of intrigue. This shop re-creates a bit of that wonder, with a remarkable collection of rare spices and hard-to-find sauces. Look for fresh Kaffir lime leaves, Thai basil, sprigs of curry plant, young ginger, sweet Thai chile sauce, and occasional exotic produce like mangosteens and rambutans. Pick up recipes and ideas from the knowledgeable staff. 1689 Johnston St., Granville Island Public Market. ℭ **604/681-5402.** www.southchinaseas.ca.

Galleries

On the first Thursday of every month, many galleries host free openings from 5 to 8pm. Check the *Georgia Straight* or *Vancouver* magazine for listings, or visit **www.art-bc.com** for more details on Vancouver's art scene.

Buschlen Mowatt   This is the city's leading "establishment" gallery. Look for paintings, sculptures, and prints from well-known Canadian and international artists. 111-1445 W. Georgia St. ℭ **604/682-1234.** www.buschlenmowatt.com.

Monte Clark Gallery ✦   This cutting-edge gallery—in the otherwise slightly staid confines of south Granville's gallery row—is one of the best spots to look for that rising superstar without the rising prices. 2339 Granville St. ℭ **604/730-5000.** www.monteclarkgallery.com.

Home Furnishings & Accessories

Inform Interiors ▮▮   Chances are you won't be lugging a sofa back home, but this classy interior-design store in Gastown has contemporary lighting, home accessories, and design books, in addition to furniture. A second showroom is right across the street at 97 Water St. 50 Water St. ℭ **604/682-3868.** www.informinteriors.com.

Parliament Interiors ✦   The store is filled with crisp whites, glimmering metals, and punchy color accents. From bed frames to cushions to jewelry, Parliament stocks a regularly changing rotation of items for all budgets (and luggage restrictions). 115 Water St. ℭ **604/689-0800.** www.parliamentinteriors.com.

Jewelry

Costen Catbalue ▮▮   One-of-a-kind pieces in platinum and gold are made on the premises here by a team of metalsmiths and artists Mary Ann Buis and Andrew Costen. The two artists' styles complement each other; Buis favors contemporary and clean lines, and Costen's designs tend toward a more ornate Renaissance style. 1832 W. 1st Ave. ℭ **604/734-3259.** www.costencatbalue.com.

Forge & Form   Master Granville Island metal designer Jürgen Schönheit specializes in customized gold and silver jewelry. Renowned for their gold and silver bow ties, he also creates unique "tension set" rings, which hold a stone in place without a setting The studio (open by appointment) is located just past the False Creek Community Centre. 1334 Cartwright St. © **604/684-6298.**

The Raven and the Bear If you've never seen west coast native jewelry, it's worth making a trip here. Deeply inscribed with stylized creatures from North-west mythology, these rings, bangles, and earrings are unforgettable. (See also "First Nations Art & Crafts," above.) 1528 Duranleau St. © **604/669-3990.**

Markets

Granville Island Public Market ★★★ This 3,902-sq.-m (42,000-sq.-ft.) public market features produce, meats, fish, wines, cheeses, arts and crafts, and lots of unique fast-food counters offering a little of everything. The market is open daily 9am to 6pm. From mid-June to October, the Granville Island Farmers' Market operates here Thursday from 10am to 7pm. For more information, see p. 125. 1669 Johnston St. © **604/666-6477.** www.granvilleisland.com.

Lonsdale Quay Market ★ ☺ Located alongside the SeaBus terminal, this public market is filled with produce, meats, fish, specialty fashions, gift and book shops, food counters, coffee bars, a hotel, and Kids' Alley (a section dedicated to children's shops and a play area). 123 Carrie Cates Court, North Vancouver. © **604/985-6261.** www.lonsdalequay.com.

River Market at Westminster Quay A smaller version of the Granville Island Public Market, this market is located 25 minutes away by SkyTrain from downtown Vancouver. Here, you'll find a variety of gift shops, specialty stores, a food court, a delicatessen, and produce stands. Once you're finished browsing, make sure to have a gander at the neighboring Fraser River. A walkway extends along the river and allows great views of the waterfront, the busy boat traffic, and the occasional seal or sea lion. 810 Quayside Dr., New Westminster. © **604/520-3881.** www.rivermarket.ca.

Vancouver Flea Market 🎯 Near the central train/bus terminal, Vancouver's largest flea market is filled with more than 350 stalls. Go early, or the savvy shop-pers will have already cleaned out the gems. Open weekends and holidays 9am to 5pm. 703 Terminal Ave. © **604/685-0666.** www.vancouverfleamarket.com.

Music

Zulu Records 🎁 Zulu Records specializes in alternative music, local and import, new and used. You'll also find a good selection of vinyl and magazines. The staff is happy to make recommendations and bring you up to speed on what's hot in the local music scene. They often sell event tickets for indie shows. 1972 W. 4th Ave. © **604/738-3232.** www.zulurecords.com.

Shoes

John Fluevog Boots & Shoes Ltd. This native Vancouverite has a growing international cult following of designers and models clamoring for his under-C$300 urban and funky creations. You'll find outrageous platforms and clogs, Angelic Sole work boots, and a few bizarre experiments for the daring footwear fetishist. You may even meet the designer, who often spends his time at this flagship store on Granville. A second Vancouver store opened in Gastown at 65 Water St. (© **604/688-6228**). 837 Granville St. © **604/688-2828.** www.fluevog.com.

Specialty

Buddha Supply Centre 🎁 Want money to burn? At Chinese funerals, people burn *joss*—paper replicas of earthly belongings—to help make the afterlife for the deceased more comfortable. This shop has more than 500 combustible products to choose from, including $1-million notes (drawn on the bank of hell), luxury penthouse condos, and that all-important cellphone. 4158 Main St. ✆ **604/873-8169.**

Cookworks This attractive downtown store stocks a finely tuned selection of high-quality, well-designed kitchenware and accessories for the table. 377 Howe St. ✆ **604/662-4918.** www.cookworks.ca.

Escents Beautifully displayed, the large collection of soaps, bath oils, shampoos, and other body products here come in a variety of scents, such as the fresh ginger-citrus twist or the relaxing lavender. Locally produced and made with minimal packaging, the all-natural, environmentally friendly products come in convenient sizes and prices and can be individually blended to fit your mood. An additional store is at 1744 Commercial Dr. (✆ **604/255-4505**). 2579 W. Broadway. ✆ **604/736-7761.** www.escentsaromatherapy.com.

Lush Lush has the look of an old-fashioned deli with big wheels of cheese, slabs of sweets, and vats of dips and sauces, but all those displays are really soaps (custom cut from a block), shampoos, skin treatments, massage oils, and bath bombs made from all-natural ingredients. 1020 Robson St. ✆ **604/687-5874.** www.lush.ca.

The Market Kitchen Store This store has everything you'd like to have (or could even imagine) on your kitchen counters or in your drawers—gourmet kitchen accessories, baking utensils, gadgets, and the like. 2-1666 Johnston St. (Net Loft, Granville Island). ✆ **604/681-7399.**

The Ocean Floor If you want to bring home a few gifts from the sea, then select from this Granville Island shop's collection of seashells, ship models, lamps, chimes, coral, shell jewelry, stained glass, and marine brass. 1522 Duranleau St. ✆ **604/681-5014.**

Three Dog Bakery Beagle Bagels, Scottie Biscotti, or Gracie's Rollovers. Canines will have a hard time deciding on a favorite treat from this gone-to-the-dogs bakery. The store also has leashes, collars, greeting cards, and other dog paraphernalia. 4548 W. 10th Ave. ✆ **604/737-3647.** www.threedog.com.

The Umbrella Shop ★ 🎁 A family business since 1935, this shop carries an amazing assortment of quality umbrellas in every size, shape, and color. 526 W. Pender St.; ✆ **604/669-1707.** 1106 W. Broadway (factory store); ✆ **604/669-9444.** www.theumbrellashop.com.

Sporting Goods

A 2-block area near the Mountain Equipment Co-Op (see below) has become "outdoor central," with at least a half-dozen stores such as **Valhalla Pure Outfitters** (222 W. Broadway; ✆ **604/872-8872;** www.vpo.ca) and **AJ Brooks** (147 W. Broadway; ✆ **604/874-1117;** www.ajbrooks.com). Just down the street, you'll find **Taiga** (301 W. Broadway; ✆ **604/875-8388;** www.taigaworks.ca), which carries inexpensive fleece and other quality outdoor gear.

In the past few years, the corner of 4th Avenue and Burrard Street has become the spot for high-quality snow/skate/surfboard gear, as well as the place

Shopping A to Z

VANCOUVER SHOPPING

to see top level boarders and their groupies hanging out. Shops here include **Pacific Boarder** (1793 W. 4th Ave.; ☏ **604/734-7245;** www.pacificboarder. com), **Showcase** (1766 W. 4th Ave.; ☏ **604/731-6449;** www.showcases nowboards.com), and **Westbeach** (1758 W. 4th Ave.; ☏ **604/734-7252;** www. westbeach.com). **Thriller** (617 Kingsway; ☏ **604/736-5651;** www.thriller shop.com) is another well-known shop carrying independent labels and accessories for surfers and boarders, real and wannabe.

Comor Sports "Go play outside" is Comor's motto, and they certainly have the goods to get you out there. Pick up some skateboard garb, swimwear, hiking shoes, in-line skates, skis, boards, and snow toys. 1980 Burrard St. ☏ **604/736-7547.** www.comorsports.com.

Mountain Equipment Co-Op A true west coast institution and an outdoor-lover's dream come true, this block-long store houses the best selection of top-quality outdoor equipment: rain gear, clothing, hiking shoes, climbing gear, backpacks, sleeping bags, tents, and more. Memorize the MEC label; you're sure to see it later—at the beach, the bar, or the concert hall. 130 W. Broadway (btw. Manitoba & Columbia sts.). ☏ **604/872-7858.** www.mec.ca.

Toys

Kids Market ☺ Probably the only mall in North America dedicated to kids, the Kids Market on Granville Island features a Lilliputian entryway; toy, craft, and book stores; play areas; and services for the younger set, including a "fun hair-dresser." 1496 Cartwright St. (on Granville Island). ☏ **604/689-8447.** www.kidsmarket.ca.

Kites on Clouds ☺ This little Gastown shop has every type of kite. Prices range from C$10 to C$20 for nylon or Mylar dragon kites to around C$200 for more elaborate ghost clippers and nylon hang-glider kites. The Courtyard, 131 Water St. ☏ **604/669-5677.**

Wine

Ten years of restructuring, reblending, and careful tending by French and German master vintners have won the province's vineyards world recognition. When buying BC wine, look for the VQA (Vintner Quality Alliance) seal on the label; it's a guarantee that all grapes used are grown in British Columbia and meet European standards for growing and processing.

Summerhill, Cedar Creek, Mission Hill, and Okanagan Vineyards are just a few of the more than 50 local estates producing hearty cabernet sauvignons, honey-rich icewines, and oaky merlots. These wines can be found at any government-owned BC liquor store, such as the one at 1716 Robson St. (☏ 604/660-9031) and at some privately owned wine stores.

Marquis Wine Cellars If you're looking for a particular BC vintage, try this place first. The owner and staff of this West End wine shop are dedicated to educating their patrons about wines. They conduct evening wine tastings, featuring selections from their special purchases. They also publish monthly newsletters. In addition to carrying a full range of British Columbian wines, the shop also has a large international selection. 1034 Davie St. ☏ **604/684-0445.** www.marquis-wines.com.

The Okanagan Estate Wine Cellar This department store annex, located in the Pacific Centre Shopping Mall, sells a great selection of British Columbian wines by the bottle and the case. The Bay, 674 Granville St. ☏ **604/689-2323.**

10

VANCOUVER AFTER DARK

Vancouver's evening social calendar is filled with a variety of events. Local theater ranges from productions by cutting-edge companies to a Shakespeare festival. There's also top-notch opera, a popular symphony, and folk, film, and jazz festivals that draw people from all over the world. For a late-night crowd, there are the bars, lounges, pubs, clubs, and cafes—lots of them— for every taste, budget, and fetish.

Dining out at a fine restaurant is considered an evening out; at a restaurant like Coast or Hawksworth in the Rosewood Hotel Georgia (both reviewed in chapter 5), the presentation is theater on a plate; in a restaurant-lounge like Yaletown's glowbal, the room transitions from dining to drinks and beats.

For the best overview of Vancouver's nightlife, pick up a copy of the weekly **Georgia Straight** (www.straight.com). The Thursday edition of the *Vancouver Sun* contains the weekly tabloid-format entertainment section **Westcoast Life.** The monthly **Vancouver** magazine (www.vanmag.com) is filled with listings and strong views about what's really hot in the city. Or get a copy of **Xtra! West** (www.xtra.ca), the free gay and lesbian biweekly tabloid, available throughout the West End.

The **Alliance for Arts and Culture** (100-938 Howe St.; ☎ **604/681-3535**; www.allianceforarts.com) is a great information source for all performing arts, literary events, and art films. The office is open Monday through Thursday from 9am to 5pm.

Ticketmaster (☎ **855/985-5000**; www.ticketmaster.ca) has outlets at the Tickets Tonight booth in the Tourism Vancouver Visitor Centre (200 Burrard St.), Rogers Arena (Gate 10-800 Griffiths Way), and the Chan Centre for the Performing Arts (6265 Crescent Rd., UBC).

Half-price tickets for same-day shows and events are available at the **Tickets Tonight** (www.ticketstonight.ca) kiosk (daily 10am–6pm) in the **Tourism Vancouver Information Centre** (200 Burrard St.; ☎ **604/684-2787** for recorded events info). The Touristinfo Centre is open daily from 8:30am to 6pm.

THE PERFORMING ARTS

Three major theaters in Vancouver regularly host touring performances. The **Orpheum Theatre** (801 Granville St.; ☎ **604/665-3050**; www.vancouver.ca/theatres) is a 1927 theater that originally hosted the Chicago-based Orpheum vaudeville circuit. The theater now hosts the Vancouver Symphony and pop, rock, and variety shows. The Orpheum got a much-needed interior makeover for the 2010 Winter Games. The Queen Elizabeth Theatre and the Vancouver Playhouse comprise the **Queen Elizabeth Complex** (630 Hamilton St., btw. Georgia and Dunsmuir sts.; ☎ **604/665-3050**; www.vancouver.ca/theatres), home

PREVIOUS PAGE: **The Vancouver Playhouse puts on a diverse mix of performances.**

to the Vancouver Opera and Ballet British Columbia. The 668-seat Vancouver Playhouse presents chamber-music performances and recitals. Located in a converted turn-of-the-20th-century church, the **Vancouver East Cultural Centre** (the "Cultch" to locals; 1895 Venables St.; ℂ **604/251-1363;** www.thecultch. com) coordinates an impressive program that includes avant-garde theater productions, performances by international musical groups, and children's programs.

On the UBC campus, the **Chan Centre for the Performing Arts** (6265 Crescent Rd.; ℂ **604/822-2697;** www.chancentre.com) showcases the work of the UBC music students and local choirs, and hosts various concert series. Designed by local architectural luminary Bing Thom, the Chan Centre's crystal-clear acoustics are the best in town.

Theater

An annual summertime Shakespeare series, **Bard on the Beach,** is presented in Vanier Park (ℂ **604/739-0559;** www.bardonthebeach.org). You can also bring a picnic dinner to Stanley Park and watch **Theatre Under the Stars** (see below), which features popular musicals and light comedies.

Arts Club Theatre Company The 450-seat **Granville Island Stage** presents dramas, comedies, and musicals, with post-performance live music in the Backstage Lounge (p. 197). The Arts Club **Revue Stage** is an intimate, cabaret-style showcase for small productions and musical revues. The Art Deco **Stanley Industrial Alliance Theatre** plays host to longer-running plays and musicals. Granville Island Stage: 1585 Johnston St. Stanley Industrial Alliance Stage: 2750 Granville St. ℂ **604/687-1644.** www.artsclub.com. Tickets C$29–C$74.

Frederic Wood Theatre 🔥 Some students at UBC are actors in training, and their productions are extremely high caliber. For the price, they're a steal. Presentations range from classic dramatic works to new plays by Canadian playwrights. All shows start at 7:30pm. The theater goes dark during the summer. 6354 Crescent Rd., University of British Columbia. ℂ **604/822-2678.** www.theatre.ubc.ca. Tickets C$22 adults, C$15 seniors, C$10 students.

Theatre Under the Stars From mid-July to mid-August, favorite musicals like *Annie, Singin' in the Rain,* and *Bye Bye Birdie* are performed outdoors by a mixed cast of amateur and professional actors. Bring a blanket (it gets chilly once the sun sets) and a picnic for a relaxing evening. Malkin Bowl, Stanley Park. ℂ **877/ 840-0457** or 604/734-1917. www.tuts.ca. Tickets C$29–C$44 adults, C$27–C$42 children 5–15.

Vancouver Playhouse The company here presents a program of six plays each season, usually a mix of the internationally known, nationally recognized, and locally promising. 601 Hamilton St. (btw. Georgia and Dunsmuir sts. in the Queen Elizabeth complex). ℂ **604/873-3311.** www.vancouverplayhouse.com. Tickets C$33–C$74.

Classical Music & Opera

Vancouver Bach Choir ★★ Vancouver's international, award-winning amateur choir, a 150-voice ensemble, presents five major concerts a year at the Orpheum Theatre. Specializing in symphonic choral music, the choir's singalong performance of Handel's *Messiah* during the Christmas season is a favorite. 304-3102 Main St. ℂ **604/872-8789.** www.vancouverbachchoir.com. Tickets up to C$55.

Vancouver Cantata Singers ★ This semiprofessional, 40-person choir specializes in works by Bach, Brahms, Monteverdi, Stravinsky, and Handel, as well as Eastern European choral music. Seasons can include up to six programs, all at various locations, with a popular Christmas concert at the Holy Rosary Cathedral. 1254 W. 7th Ave. ✆ **604/730-8856.** www.vancouvercantatasingers.com. Tickets C$20-C$25.

Vancouver Chamber Choir ★★★ Western Canada's only professional choral ensemble presents an annual concert series at the Orpheum Theatre, the Chan Centre, and Ryerson United Church. Under conductor Jon Washburn, the choir has gained an international reputation. 1254 W. 7th Ave. ✆ **604/738-6822.** www. vancouverchamberchoir.com. Mainstage tickets C$23-C$47 adults, C$20-C$47 seniors and students. Church performances C$25-C$28 adults. C$10 rush tickets for students.

Vancouver Opera ★★★ I've always been impressed with the quality of the stagings and performances at the Vancouver Opera. The company produces both concert versions and fully staged operas, often sung by international stars. The season runs October through April, with performances in the Queen Elizabeth Theatre (p. 191). 835 Cambie St. ✆ **604/683-0222.** www.vancouveropera.ca. Tickets C$29-C$184.

Vancouver Symphony ★★★ At its home in the Orpheum Theatre during the fall, winter, and spring, Vancouver's excellent orchestra, under the baton of maestro Bramwell Tovey, presents a variety of year-round concerts. The box office is open from 6pm until showtime. 601 Smithe St. ✆ **604/876-3434.** www.vancouver symphony.ca. Tickets C$27-C$165; discounts available for seniors and students.

Dance

The **Scotiabank Dance Centre,** 677 Davie St., provides a focal point for the Vancouver dance community. Renovated by Arthur Erickson, the former bank building now offers studio and rehearsal space to local dance companies, and is open to the general public for events, workshops, and classes. For more information, call ✆ **604/606-6400** or check www.thedancecentre.ca.

For fans of modern dance, the time to be here is early July, when the **Dancing on the Edge Festival** (✆ **604/689-0926;** www.dancingontheedge.org) presents about 30 original pieces over a 10-day period. For more information about other festivals and dance companies around the city, contact the **Dance Centre** at ✆ **604/606-6400** or www.thedancecentre.ca.

Ballet British Columbia ★ This established company strives to present innovative works, such as those by choreographers William Forsythe, Jean Grande-Maître, and artistic director Emily Molnar, along with more productions by visiting companies from Alberta and Winnipeg. Performances are usually at the Queen Elizabeth Theatre, at 630 Hamilton St. (p. 191). 677 Davie St., 6th Fl. ✆ **604/732-5003.** www.balletbc.com. Tickets C$48-C$70.

LAUGHTER & MUSIC
Comedy Club/Improv Show

Vancouver TheatreSports League ★★ Part comedy, part theater, and partly a take-no-prisoners test of an actor's ability to think extemporaneously, TheatreSports involves actors taking suggestions from the audience and spinning

The Ballet British Columbia presents innovative work alongside more traditional productions by visiting companies.

them into short skits or full plays, often with hilarious results. Shows are Wednesday and Thursday at 7:30 and 9pm; Friday and Saturday at 8, 10, and 11:45pm; and Sunday at 7:30pm. The Improv Centre, 1502 Duranleau St. ℂ **604/738-7013.** www.vtsl.com. Tickets C$16–C$21.

Strictly Live

The **Vancouver International Jazz Festival** (ℂ **604/872-5200;** www.coastaljazz.ca) takes over many venues and outdoor stages around town every June. The festival includes a number of free concerts.

The **Vancouver Folk Music Festival** (ℂ **604/602-9798;** www.thefestival.bc.ca) is one of the big ones on the west coast. It takes place outdoors in July on the beach at Jericho Park.

The Cellar Jazz Club   A hidden basement club run by musician Cory Weeds, the Cellar Jazz Club features live performances from Tuesday to Sunday. Shows at the small 75-seat venue are often reserved well in advance. 3611 W. Broadway. ℂ **604/738-1959.** www.cellarjazz.com. Cover C$15.

The Commodore Ballroom ★   Every town should have one, but sadly very few do: a huge old-time dance hall, complete with a suspended hardwood dance floor. And though the room and floor date back to the Jazz Age, the lineup nowadays includes many of the best modern bands coming through town. In fact, the Commodore is one of the best places to catch a midsize band. 868 Granville St. ℂ **604/739-4550.** Tickets C$20–C$50.

O'Doul's Restaurant & Bar ★★   Thursday to Saturday, the restaurant for the Listel Hotel (p. 77) becomes the venue for Vancouver's top jazz performers. You can dine on West Coast cuisine by candlelight or enjoy a drink while listening to the mellow sounds. During the Vancouver International Jazz Festival in late June, O'Doul's becomes the scene of late-night jam sessions with world-renowned musicians. 1300 Robson St. (at Jervis St.). ℂ **604/661-1400.** www.odoulsrestaurant.com.

The Roxy Live bands play every day of the week in this no-holds-barred club, which also features bartenders with Tom Cruise *Cocktail*-style moves. Theme nights—Extreme Karaoke, '80s Only, Sunday Country Night (with two-step)—and other events add to the entertainment and the sometimes pretty raucous scene. On weekends, the lines are long, the patrons often soused. Dress code: No bags, backpacks, track suits, or ripped jeans; everything else is okay. 932 Granville St. © **604/331-7999.** www.roxyvan.com. Cover C$5–C$13.

Yale Hotel This century-old tavern on the bridge-end of Granville is Vancouver's one-and-only home of the blues. Visiting heavyweights have included Stevie Ray Vaughan and Jeff Healey. When outside talent's not available, the Yale features the homegrown, including William Van Eyes and the party band Brickhouse. Shows on most nights start at 9pm. Saturdays, see an open-stage blues jam from 3 to 7pm. 1300 Granville St. © **604/681-9253.** www.theyale.ca. Cover Thurs–Sat C$5–C$15.

BARS, PUBS & WATERING HOLES

Vancouver has loosened up a great deal in the past few years. Until recently, patrons in a restaurant could drink only if they were eating or *had the intention of eating*. Nowadays, Vancouver drinkers can stand tall and order that beer with no fear of being forced to purchase a token cookie or french fries. Even better, bars can now stay open until 2am, and as late as 4am in peak summer months.

That said, officialdom in the city still doesn't love the late-night crowd. They seem to look on drinkers and revelers as an unfortunate byproduct of urbanism and bars as a necessary evil. City policy has been to concentrate the city's pubs and clubs into two ghettos—er, *entertainment zones*—one along **Granville Street** and the other along **Water and Pender streets** in Gastown. **Yaletown** is a third, more upscale, bar/lounge/club zone. Pubs and clubs can be found in other places, and many are listed below, but if you just want to wander out for a serendipitous pub-crawl, the Granville or Water Street strips are best with reasonable options also in Kitsilano and along Main Street in Mount Pleasant. Granville Street tends more to Top 40 discos and upscale lounges, while down in Gastown, it's dark cellars spinning hip-hop and house. Yaletown is the newest late-night entertainment/drinking area, a place where martinis reign and some of the restaurants turn into cocktail lounges at 11pm.

One holdover from the bad old days of the liquor license drought is the relatively large number of restaurants that look suspiciously like pubs. You can order food in these places. Indeed, it used to be a condition of drinking (wink, wink), but most patrons stick to a liquid diet.

Gastown Crawl

The Alibi Room This high-end, trendy restaurant/bar pours a huge selection of craft beers to complement its modern-British-pub style yet locally sourced menu. The room tends toward a revelrous crowd that amplifies as the night goes on. Located on the eastern edge of Gastown. 157 Alexander St. (at Main St.). © **604/623-3383.** www.alibi.ca.

Guilt & Co. Besides having an admirable selection of mocktails, it's the board games like giant Jenga that draw patrons into this basement bar. Guilt & Co. is also a hub for music and art experiments. Basement, 1 Alexander St. © **604/288-1704.** www.guiltandcompany.com.

The Irish Heather A bright, pleasant Irish pub in the dark heart of Gastown, the Heather boasts numerous nooks and crannies, some of the best beer in town, and a menu that does a lot with the traditional Emerald Isle spud. Long-table dinners serve up meat-and-potatoes with a gastropub flair. The clientele is from all over the map, from artsy types to urban pioneers. 210 Carrall St. ☎ **604/688-9779.** www.irishheather.com.

Peckinpah Although this convivial spot operates as a cafe and late-night takeout window, it's the selection of more than 20 bourbons that distinguish Peckinpah from other Gastown drink-and-eat places. However, the bar snacks are undeniably intriguing, especially the corndogs served with "ballpark" mustard. 2 Water St. ☎ **604/681-5411.** www.peckinpahbbq.com.

The Lennox Pub features an extensive beer list.

Granville Crawl

The Lennox Pub Part of the renewal of Granville Street, this pub fills a big void in the neighborhood; it's a comfortable spot for a drink without having to deal with lines or ordering food. The beer list is extensive, featuring such hard-to-find favorites as Belgian Kriek, Hoegaarden, and Leffe, along with a great selection of single-malt Scotches, too. The menu covers all the pub-food basics. 800 Granville St. ☎ **604/408-0881.**

The Morrissey This pub on the street-level of the Ramada Inn and Suites is usually crammed elbow-to-elbow with a relaxed crowd who comes for the beers and occasional celebrity rocker sightings. 1227 Granville St. ☎ **604/682-0909.**

Main Street Crawl

The Cascade Room This low-lit, Main-Street lounge combines premium spirits, hand-pressed juices, and custom cordials into classic cocktails, such as the Algonquin with fresh pineapple juice or the Clover Club with raspberry syrup and egg white. The crowd is 20- and early 30-somethings huddled around booth tables. 2616 Main St. ☎ **604/709-8650.** www.thecascade.ca.

The Whip Beer drinkers will love the 10 casks on draught at this two-level, off-Main St. bar. Other libations include a wide selection of single-malt whiskeys, premium spirits, and virtue-themed sangria (you pick btw. prudence, courage, and temperance). 209 E. 6th Ave. ☎ **604/874-4687.** www.thewhiprestaurant.com.

A Sports Bar

The Shark Club Bar and Grill The city's premier sports bar, the Shark Club—in the Sandman Inn—features lots of wood and brass, TVs everywhere, and on weekend evenings, lots of young women who don't look very interested in sports. 180 W. Georgia St. (at Beatty St.). ℂ **604/687-4275.** www.sharkclubs.com. Cover varies on sporting-event nights.

Bars with Views

You're in Vancouver. Odds are you're aware that this is a city renowned for its views. The entire population could make more money living in a dull flat place like Toronto, but they stay here because of the seductive scenery. As long as that's your raison d'être, you may as well drink in style at one of the places below. Also check out the view at restaurant **Lift** (p. 96) and at the nearby **Westin Bayshore** resort (p. 76).

Cardero's Marine Pub   On the water at the foot of Cardero Street, this Coal Harbour pub and restaurant offers a great view of Stanley Park, the harbor, and the North Shore. Overhead heaters take away the chill when the sun goes down. 1583 Coal Harbour Quay. ℂ **604/669-7666.** www.vancouverdine.com.

Cloud Nine   As this sleek hotel-top lounge rotates 6 degrees a minute, your vantage point circles from volcanic Mount Baker, the Fraser estuary, and English Bay to Stanley Park, the towers of downtown, the harbor, and East Vancouver. Live entertainment Friday and Saturday nights. 1400 Robson St. (42nd floor of the Empire Landmark Hotel, p. 78). ℂ **604/687-0511.** www.cloud9restaurant.ca. Cover Fri–Sat C$7 after 8pm.

The Dockside Brewing Company   The Dockside is located in the Granville Island Hotel (p. 80) and looks out across False Creek to Yaletown and Burnaby Mountain far in the distance. The grub's based on classic seafood, cooked up in a kitchen wrapped by a 15m (50 ft.) aquarium, and the beer is among the best in town—brewed-on-the-premises lagers, ales, and porters. Even with the overhead gas heaters on chillier evenings, it's a good idea not to arrive too late: An hour or two after the sun goes down, the mostly 30-something patrons remember that they have homes to go to. 1253 Johnson St. ℂ **604/685-7070.** www.docksidebrewing.com.

The Flying Beaver Bar 🔷   Located beneath the flyway of Vancouver International, the Beaver offers nonflyers great views of incoming jets, along with views of mountains, bush planes, and river craft—and truly fine brewpub beer. 4760 Inglis Dr., Richmond. ℂ **604/273-0278.** www.markjamesgroup.com.

Lounges

Afterglow   Intimate couches and a soft soundtrack (which gets cranked up to deafening decibels as the evening wears on) make for candlelit dessert to a meal at glowbal grill (p. 93); you can also stay in the low-slung love seats for a long evening's cuddle. 1082 Hamilton St. ℂ **604/602-0835.**

The Arts Club Backstage Lounge   The Arts Club Lounge has a fabulous location under the Granville Bridge by the water on the edge of False Creek. The crowd is a mix of tourists, theater patrons from the neighboring Arts Club, and art school students from Emily Carr University. A live band plays most evenings (cover charge). If the sun's out, the waterfront patio is packed. 1585 Johnston St. ℂ **604/687-1354.** www.thebackstagelounge.com. Cover C$5–C$15.

Bacchus Lounge ★   This luxuriously comfy hot spot in the tony Wedgewood Hotel (p. 70) stages a powerhouse cocktail hour for mostly well-to-do professionals, then becomes an irony-free piano bar. In the Wedgewood Hotel, 845 Hornby St. ℭ **604/608-5319.** www.wedgewoodhotel.com.

George Ultra Lounge ★   Small, loud, crowded, and hedonistic. Look for local glitterati and primo cocktails made by the friendly, showy mixologists, who draw their ingredients from the well-stocked bar. 1137 Hamilton St. ℭ **604/628-5555.** www.georgelounge.com.

Ginger Sixty-Two   A mix of lounge, restaurant, and club, Ginger is the darling of the fashion-industry trendsetters who love to be spotted here Thursday to Saturday. The room is funky warehouse-chic-meets-adult-rec-room, decorated in red, orange, pink, and gold. Comfy crash pads are strategically placed throughout the room, and plenty of pillows help prop up those less-than-young in the joints. 1219 Granville St. ℭ **604/688-5494.** www.ginger62.com.

Gotham Cocktail Bar   A clear case of the law of unintended consequences: The lounge adjoining this new steakhouse was designed for a male clientele— thick leather benches and a mural of sensuous women in Jazz Age fashions. Men do show up—well-off suits in their 30s and 40s, particularly—but you'll also find gaggles of dolled-up women. There's live music Monday to Saturday. 615 Seymour St. (btw. Dunsmuir and Georgia sts.). ℭ **604/605-8282.** www.gothamsteakhouse.com.

Opus Bar ★   Supertrendy decor, great drinks, and a succulent small-plates menu have helped the Opus Bar in the lobby of the cool Opus Hotel (p. 68) become a Yaletown hot spot for a pre-dinner martini or an extended evening schmooze. In the Opus Hotel, 350 Davie St. ℭ **604/642-0557.** www.opusbar.ca.

Brewpubs

Don't forget the **Dockside Brewing Company** (1253 Johnson St.; ℭ **604/685-7070**), in the Granville Island Hotel, listed under "Bars with Views," above.

Steamworks Pub & Brewery   Winding your way from room to room in this brewery verging on Gastown and Downtown is almost as much fun as drinking. Upstairs, by the doors, it's a London city pub where stockbrokers ogle every new female entrant. Farther in by the staircase, it's a refined old-world club, with wood paneling, leather chairs, and great glass windows overlooking the harbor. Down in the basement, it's a Bavarian drinking hall with long lines of benches, set up parallel to the enormous copper vats. Fortunately, the beer's good. Choose from a half-dozen in-house beers. 375 Water St. ℭ **604/689-2739.** www.steamworks.com.

Yaletown Brewing Company   Every Sunday, all pints of brewed-on-the-premises beer are C$4.50 and pizzas are C$8. The excellent beer is complemented by an extremely cozy room, a great summertime patio, and a good appetizer menu. 1111 Mainland St. (at Helmcken St.). ℭ **604/681-2739.** www.markjamesgroup.com.

DANCE CLUBS

Generally, clubs are open until 2am every day but Sunday, when they close at midnight. In the summer months (mid-June through Labour Day), open hours at some clubs extend to 4am. The city's clubs and discos are concentrated around two "entertainment zones," downtown around Granville Street, and along Water and Pender streets in Gastown.

The popular AuBAR is packed most nights.

AuBAR   An address is unnecessary for AuBAR; the long Seymour Street line of those not-quite-beautiful-enough for expedited entry immediately gives it away. Inside, this downtown bar is packed with beautiful people milling from bar to dance floor to the table nooks and back again. Observing them is like watching a nature documentary on the Discovery Channel: Doelike women prance and jiggle while predatory men roam in packs, flexing pecs and biceps. 674 Seymour St. ℭ **604/648-2227.** www.aubarnightclub.com. Cover C$12–C$16.

Caprice   Upstairs, it's the Lounge, with dark wood, a fireplace, and couches. Downstairs, it's the Nightclub, a large room with a funky semicircular glowing blue bar, big comfy wall banquettes, a secluded circular passion pit in one corner, and a medium-size dance floor. Earlier in the week, the DJ spins house, but on weekends, when the older, richer 25-and-overs come out to play, the cover goes up and the DJ retreats to the safety of Top 40. 967 Granville St. ℭ **604/685-3288.** www.capricenightclub.com. Cover up to C$15.

The Cellar   The Cellar inhabits that netherworld between dance club, bar, meat market, and personals ads. Dance-club characteristics include a cover charge, small dance floor, and a DJ who mostly spins Top 40. But Cellar patrons are far less interested in groovin' than they are in meeting other Cellar dwellers, a process facilitated by a wall-length message board upon which pickup lines are posted. 1006 Granville St. ℭ **604/605-4350.** www.cellarvan.com. Cover C$6–C$12.

Fabric Nightclub   Located in the heart of Gastown, one of Vancouver's biggest and most legendary rooms (it was formerly Sonar) has been revitalized and reborn as Fabric Nightclub. With a 500-plus capacity, couches, a VIP balcony section overlooking the giant dance floor, plus big-name DJs from around the world, this doesn't disappoint. 66 Water St. ℭ **604/683-6695.** www.fabricvancouver.com. Cover C$20.

The Red Room   This basement warren has two bars, numerous intimate cubby holes, and a DJ that does progressive house and hip-hop, plus a live band sometimes on the weekend. And if that weren't enough, there are also two pool tables. 398 Richards St. ℭ **604/687-5007.** www.redroomonrichards.com. Cover C$12–C$20.

Shine This downstairs cellar in Gastown plays house and hip-hop, with occasional forays into other genres such as reggae. 364 Water St. ☎ **604/408-4321.** www.shinenightclub.com. Cover C$10–C$20.

GAY & LESBIAN BARS

BC's enlightened attitude—remember, same-sex couples can wed in Canada—has had a curious effect on Vancouver's queer dance-club scene: It's so laid-back and attitude-free that it's often hard to tell straight from gay, male go-go dancers and naked men in showers notwithstanding. The "Gay Village" is in the West End, particularly on Davie and Denman streets. Many clubs feature theme nights and dance parties, drag shows are ever popular, and every year in early August, as Gay Pride nears, the scene goes into overdrive. **QMUNITY**—BC's Queer Resource Centre (1170 Bute St.; ☎ **604/684-5307;** www.qmunity.ca) has information on the current hot spots, but it's easier just to pick up a free copy of *Xtra West!*, available in most downtown cafes.

The Fountainhead Pub Reflecting the graying and—gasp!—mellowing of Vancouver's boomer-age gay crowd, the hottest hangout for gays is the Fountainhead, a pub located in the heart of the city's gay ghetto on Davie Street. The Head offers excellent micro-brewed draft, good pub munchies, and a pleasant humming atmosphere until the morning's wee hours. 1025 Davie St. ☎ **604/687-2222.** www.thefountainhead pub.com.

Numbers A multilevel dance club with five floors and three bars, Numbers hasn't changed much over the years. Extroverts hog the dance floor while admirers look on from the bar above. On the third floor, carpets, wood paneling, pool tables, darts, and a lower volume of music give it a neighborhood-pub feel. 1042 Davie St. ☎ **604/685-4077.** www.numbers.ca. Cover Fri–Sat C$6.

The Fountainhead Pub is one of the city's most popular gay bars.

CINEMA

Thanks to the number of resident moviemakers (both studio and independent), Vancouver is quite a film town. First-run theaters show the same Hollywood junk seen everywhere in the world, but for those with something more adventurous in mind, plenty of options can be found.

Attendance at the **Vancouver International Film Festival** (☎ **604/685-0260;** www.viff.org) reaches about 150,000, plus the celebs who drop in. At this highly respected October event, nearly 250 new feature-length films and 150 films under 1 hour are shown, representing filmmakers from 80 countries. Asian films are particularly well represented.

Specialty Theaters

Since 1972, the **Pacific Cinematheque** (1131 Howe St.; ℭ **604/688-FILM** [604/688-3456]; www.cinematheque.bc.ca) has featured classic and contemporary films from around the world. Screenings are organized into themes, such as "Jean-Luc Godard's Early Efforts," film noir, or the "Hong Kong Action Flick: A Retrospective." Schedules are available in hipper cafes, record shops, and video stores around town, and on the website. Admission is C$11 adults, and C$9 seniors and students; double features cost C$2 extra. Annual membership, required to purchase tickets, is C$3.

A gargantuan screen at the **OMNIMAX** Theatre at Science World (ℭ **604/443-7443;** www.scienceworld.ca) features flicks about empty, wide-open spaces, space, colorful coral reefs, and the like. See the Science World at TELUS World of Science listing under "The Top Attractions," in chapter 7.

Way off in the strip-mall lands of farthest Kingsway stands the **Raja** (3215 Kingsway; ℭ **604/436-1545** or 604/879-7252; www.rajacinema.com), a modest single-screen movie house dedicated to bringing in the best Bollywood flicks from Bombay, the world's moviemaking capital. Expect unbelievable plots mixed with big-production musical numbers. Some have English subtitles, though strictly speaking, they're not necessary.

WHISTLER

ne of the world's greatest ski resorts, **Whistler Blackcomb** hosted the 2010 Olympic and Paralympic Winter Games—no small achievement for a ski resort that's barely 40 years old. This favored spot, less than 2 hours by car from Vancouver, has more vertical runs, lifts, and varied ski terrain than any other ski resort in North America. Winter sports rule from December through April: Downhill, backcountry, cross-country and heli-skiing, snowboarding, sledding, and sleigh riding are just the tip of the glacier.

In the summer, Whistler is a mecca for mountain bikers, with a world-class mountain bike park to match its world-class winter skiing. If you're not a fan of biking, you can spend your summer days rafting, hiking, golfing, wildlife-watching, and horseback riding. Or, for some wonderful low-tech, eco-friendly fun, try zipping across Fitzsimmons Creek on Ziptrek (p. 224) and exploring the sublime coastal rainforest between Whistler and Blackcomb mountains.

The focus for all the action is **Whistler Village.** This resort community is sophisticated and international, but so new that at first glance it might strike you as a bit like Disneyland, or a huge mall with hotels (what the retail industry calls a "lifestyle center"). Back in the 1970s, a few visionary planners made the decision to build a resort town and set about creating a carefully planned infrastructure and aesthetic. The results are impressive—a compact resort, at the base of two mountains, arranged around a stroll-able, in parts ski-able, and completely carless village street lined with upscale shopping, great restaurants, lots of pubs and cafes with outdoor patios, and plenty of plazas. What was sacrificed in this drive to become the perfectly planned community was space for the odd, the funky, the quaint, and the nonconforming. It's just too new and too affluent (at least, in the winter; in the summer season, it becomes more family oriented). When word went out in 2003 that the 2010 Olympic Winter Games were to be held here, real estate prices skyrocketed and more luxury hotels went up.

ESSENTIALS

128km (80 miles) N of Vancouver

Prices for hotels jump considerably during the high season from December through April, and that's also—not surprisingly—when Whistler is at its most seductive, blanketed with snow and twinkling with lights. July, August, and September are the best months for summer recreation on the mountains. During the shoulder seasons—May, June, October, and November—you can expect rain; the area is, after all, a coastal rainforest.

PREVIOUS PAGE: **Whistler Blackcomb has many great runs for powder skiing.**

Getting There

BY BUS **Perimeter Whistler Express** (8695 Barnard St.; ✆ **888/717-6606** or 604/717-6600; www.perimeterbus.com) operates bus service from Vancouver International Airport and downtown Vancouver hotels to Squamish and the Whistler Bus Loop, as well as drop off service at most Whistler hotels and properties. In summer, there are five daily departures; in winter, there are nine. The trip takes 2½ to 3 hours; round-trip fares from Whistler Village are C$118 adults, C$60 children 2 to 12, and free for children under 2. Children under 1.25m (4 ft.) require a car seat. Reservations are required year-round.

SnowBus (✆ **888/794-5511;** www.snowbus.ca) is a luxury coach featuring hosts, movies, snacks, and drinks for early-morning departures from Vancouver during the winter ski season. They can also arrange lift tickets and rentals. Round-trip adult fare is C$60. **Whistler Direct Shuttle** (✆ **888/405-2410;** www.whistlerdirectshuttle.com) operates year-round deluxe highway coach service between Vancouver and Whistler. The service is by reservation only and picks up from the airport and all downtown Vancouver hotels. Adult one-way fare from a Vancouver hotel is C$49; the fare from the airport is C$65.

Greyhound (Pacific Central Station, 1150 Station St.; ✆ **800/661-8747** or 604/683-8133; www.greyhound.ca), operates daily bus service (seven to eight trips a day, staggered btw. 5:15am–7pm) from the downtown bus depot to the Whistler Village and Whistler Creekside bus stops. The trip takes about 2½ hours; round-trip fares are C$56 to C$63 adults, C$42 to C$48 children 2 to 11, and free for children 1 and under.

BY CAR Whistler is about a 2-hour drive from Vancouver along **Highway 99,** also called the **Sea-to-Sky Highway.** The spectacular drive winds first along the edge of Howe Sound before climbing through the mountains. In preparation for the 2010 Winter Games, the highway was completely overhauled. Ample pay parking is available for day skiers and visitors at C$14 for a full day in summer and C$9 in winter. The result of an unpopular move by the resort council in 2010, the pay system replaced free parking in the village day lots. Most hotels in Whistler Village and Upper Village charge a minimum of C$20 for underground parking.

BY PLANE From mid-May through September, **Whistler Air** (✆ **888/806-2299;** www.whistlerair.ca) offers two daily flights from Vancouver's Coal Harbour to the Whistler area. Fares are C$169 round-trip.

BY TRAIN From May through September, **Rocky Mountaineer** (✆ **877/460-3200** or 604/606-7245; www.rockymountaineer.com) offers Thursday to Monday service between North Vancouver

The Whistler Mountaineer train features vintage dome observation cars.

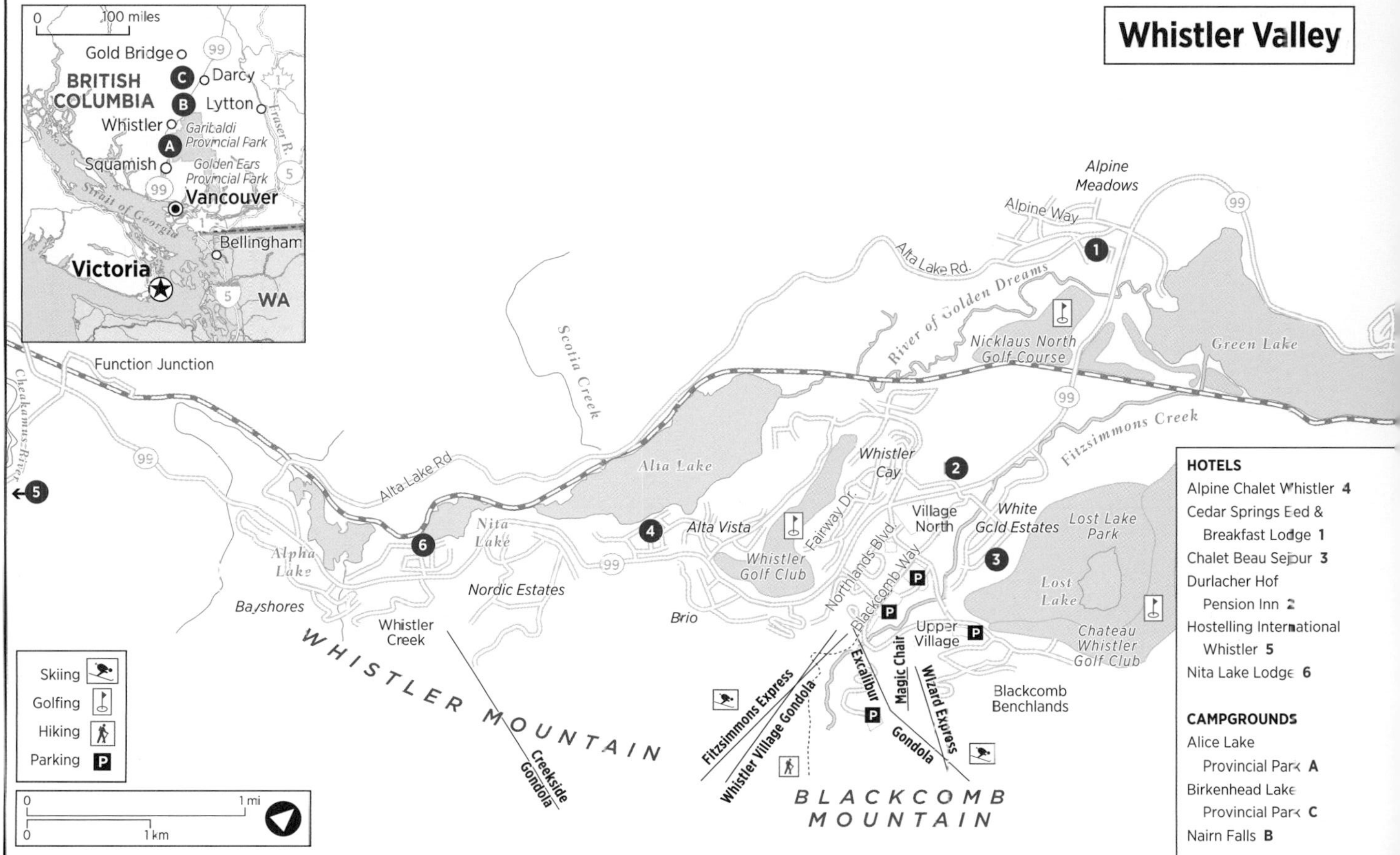

Whistler Valley

HOTELS

Alpine Chalet Whistler **4**
Cedar Springs Bed &
Breakfast Lodge **1**
Chalet Beau Sejour **3**
Durlacher Hof
Pension Inn **2**
Hostelling International
Whistler **5**
Nita Lake Lodge **6**

CAMPGROUNDS

Alice Lake
Provincial Park **A**
Birkenhead Lake
Provincial Park **C**
Nairn Falls **B**

Green Lake

Alpine Meadows

Alpine Way

Alta Lake Rd.

River of Golden Dreams

Nicklaus North Golf Course

Fitzsimmons Creek

Lost Lake Park

Lost Lake

Chateau Whistler Golf Club

White Gold Estates

Village North

Whistler Cay

Blackcomb Benchlands

Upper Village

Wizard Express

Magic Chair

Gondola

Blackcomb Way

Northlands Blvd.

Excalibur

BLACKCOMB MOUNTAIN

Whistler Village Gondola

Fitzsimmons Express

Fairway Dr.

Whistler Golf Club

Alta Vista

Brio

Alta Lake

Scotia Creek

Nordic Estates

Nita Lake

Creekside Gondola

Whistler Creek

WHISTLER MOUNTAIN

Alta Lake Rd.

Alpha Lake

Bayshores

Function Junction

Cheakamus River

Legend

Skiing
Golfing
Hiking
Parking

0 — 1 mi
0 — 1 km

Gold Bridge

Darcy

Lytton

Fraser R.

Garibaldi Provincial Park

Golden Ears Provincial Park

Whistler **C**

Squamish **B** **A**

BRITISH COLUMBIA

Vancouver

Bellingham

WA

Strait of Georgia

Victoria

0 — 100 miles

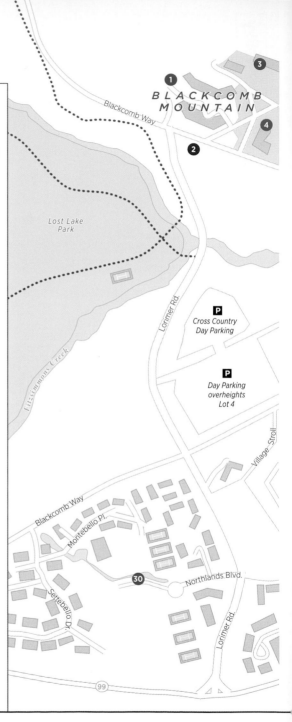

ATTRACTIONS

Blackcomb Gondola **8**
Maurice Young Millennium Place **14**
Squamish Lil'Wat Cultural Centre **2**
Tourism Whistler Information Center **18**
Whistler Museum **32**
Whistler Village Gondola **9**

HOTELS

Delta Whistler Village Suites **33**
The Fairmont Chateau Whistler **3**
Four Seasons Resort Whistler **1**
The Listel Hotel **28**
Pan Pacific Whistler Mountainside **5**
Pan Pacific Whistler Village Centre **17**
Summit Lodge & Spa **31**
The Westin Resort & Spa Whistler **11**

RESTAURANTS

Araxi **20**
Bearfoot Bistro **27**
Caramba! Restaurant **15**
Ciao-Thyme Bistro and Fitz Pub **4**
Citta Bistro **23**
Dubh Linn Gate Old Irish Pub **6**
Hy's Steakhouse **34**
Ingrid's Village Café **21**
Rimrock Cafe and Oyster Bar **35**
Trattoria di Umberto **10**
Whistler BrewHouse **12**
Wild Wood Bistro & Bar **30**

NIGHTLIFE

Buffalo Bills **26**
Cinnamon Bear Bar **29**
Dubh Linn Gate Old Irish Pub **7**
Garfinkel's **16**
Maxx Fish **22**
Moe Joe's **25**
Tapley's **24**
Tommy Africa's **19**
Whistler BrewHouse **13**

Whistler Village

WHISTLER MOUNTAIN

Wizard Express

Magic Chair

Blackcomb Base

Glacier Drive

Blackcomb Way

Fitzsimmons Trail

Fitzsimmons Creek

Excalibur Gondola

Whistler Village Gondola

Day Parking Lot 1 P

Day Parking Lot 2 P

Day Parking Lot 3 P

5 **6** **8**

7

Village Gondola Base

9

Skiers Plaza

Mountain Square

11

10

Sundial Place

Village Common

Blackcomb Way

Skier's Approach

Village Lane

Village Stroll

Springs Lane

Mountain Lane

Whistler Way

21

22

29

14

12 **13**

17

19

20

18

23

26

28

27

24

25

Village Square

Golfer's Approach

15

16

Town Plaza

Gateway Dr.

Visitor Centre Bus Loop (To Vancouver)

Gateway Loop Way

Village Gate Blvd.

Whistler door Way

P

P

P

Driving Range

33

34

Main Street

Main Street

31

32

Northlands Blvd.

Whistler Way

99

P

35→

99

Main Street

Whistler Golf Club

Skiing	
Golfing	
Hiking	
Par	P
Tennis Court	

and Whistler on the **Whistler Mountaineer** ★★★, which are refurbished trains with vintage dome observation cars. Trains depart North Vancouver at about 8am (transportation to the train station is provided by most Vancouver hotels) and arrive at 11:30am; departure time from Whistler is 3pm, arriving back in North Vancouver at 7pm. Breakfast is served on the way up, and a light meal on the return. Standard adult round-trip "Classic" fare is C$235 for adults, C$165 for children 2–11.

Visitor Information

The **Whistler Visitor Info Centre** (4230 Gateway Dr., off Village Gate Blvd. from Hwy. 99; ✆ **877/991-9988** or 604/935-3357; www.whistlerchamber.com) is open daily from 8am to 10pm (8pm during spring and fall), and can answer questions about the area, as well as help you find accommodations. For planning and accommodations deals, contact **Tourism Whistler** (✆ **800/WHISTLER** [944-7853] or 604/932-0606; www.whistler.com).

Another good website for general information and mountain updates is **www.whistlerblackcomb.com**.

Getting Around

Compact and pedestrian-oriented, Whistler Village has signed trails and pathways linking hotels, shops, and restaurants with the gondolas up to Whistler and Blackcomb mountains. If you're staying in the Village, you can park and leave your car for the duration of your stay.

The resort is divided into **Whistler Village** (where you get gondolas for both Whistler and Blackcomb mountains) and the **Upper Village** (where you get the gondola for Blackcomb); it takes about 5 minutes to walk between the villages, and 11 minutes to hop between mountains on the Peak to the Peak gondola (p. 219). At some of the hotels, you can ski from the front entrance directly to the gondolas.

BY BUS **Whistler and Valley Express** (WAVE; ✆ **604/932-4020**; www.bctransit.com), a year-round public transit service, runs from the Gondola Transit Exchange to the neighboring districts of Whistler Creekside, Alpine Meadows, and Emerald Estates. Service from the Village to Village North and Upper Village accommodations is free; on other routes, one-way fares are C$2.50 adults, C$2 seniors and students, and free for children 4 and under.

BY CAB **Whistler Taxi** (✆ **800/203-5322** or 604/932-3333) runs 24 hours.

BY CAR Rental cars are available from **Avis** (4315 Northlands Blvd.; ✆ **800/230-4898** or 604/932-1236).

Special Events

Non-Olympic downhill **ski competitions** are held December through May. Contact Tourism Whistler (see "Visitor Information," above) for event listings.

Cornucopia (www.whistlercornucopia.com) is Whistler's premier wine-and-food festival. Held in November, the CRUSH Grand Gala showcases 75 top wineries, many from the Pacific region. Other events include a winemakers' dinners, food and wine seminars, and wine tastings.

For other month-by-month event listings, visit www.whistler.com.

WHERE TO STAY

The first and biggest decision to make is whether to stay in or outside of Whistler Village. If you stay in the Village, you can forget about your car for the duration of your visit and walk along paved pathways from hotel to ski lift to restaurant to pub. If you stay outside the Village, you'll have a short drive to the parking lots on the perimeter of Whistler Village (many hotels outside the Village offer shuttle service). Accommodations within the Village are top quality, while outside the Village affords a bit more variety, including some fine European-style inns.

To get the best rates on the hotels listed below, check the hotel's website to see if special packages are available or promotions are going on. In some cases, you can nab incredible ski/hotel packages.

Whistler Accommodation Reservations (✆ 800/944-7853; www. whistler.com) can book a wide range of rooms, suites, and vacation rentals in the Whistler area and provide a customized package with lift tickets and transportation from and to Vancouver.

In the Village
VERY EXPENSIVE

The Fairmont Chateau Whistler ★★   The Fairmont Chateau Whistler in the Upper Village at the foot of Blackcomb Mountain is absolutely enormous and built in the style of the great old Canadian Pacific lodge hotels. The elegantly styled rooms and suites are quite large (the mountainview suites, in fact, are huge), very quiet, and have good-size bathrooms with a separate soaker tub and shower. Rooms on the Fairmont Gold floor have cozy fireplaces. The heated outdoor pool and

Jacuzzis look out over the base of the ski hill, and the property is the only hotel where you can ski up to the back door. Massive wooden beams, double-sided stone fireplaces, and an on-site spa help create a truly resortlike ambience.

4599 Chateau Blvd., Whistler, BC V0N 1B4. www. fairmont.com. ✆ **800/606-8244** or 604/938-8000. Fax 604/938-2291. 550 units. Spring–fall C$240–C$330 double, C$320–C$1,400 suite; winter C$360–C$800 double, C$440–C$1,460 suite; holidays C$360–C$800 double, C$440–C$3,160 suite. AE, MC, V. Underground valet parking C$35, self-parking C$30. **Amenities:** 4 restaurants; bar; babysitting; children's programs; concierge; health club; Jacuzzi; 2 heated outdoor pools; room service; sauna; spa; 2 tennis courts; golf course. *In room:* A/C, TV w/pay movies, fridge, hair dryer, Internet (C$15).

Four Seasons Resort Whistler ★★★
If you want the best, this is it. In the Upper Village, the Four Seasons has set a standard for luxury and service in Whistler. The guest rooms, suites, and town houses are the largest in Whistler. All

The Four Seasons Resort Whistler has some of the largest rooms in town.

feature beautifully detailed wood-trimmed interiors, gas fireplaces, and views of the mountains, forest, valley, pool, or courtyard from step-out balconies. The decor is an updated version of a 1920s grand mountain lodge, with a rustic note added to the elegant, modern style. You won't find larger or more luxurious bathrooms anywhere in Whistler; each one has a deep soaker tub, a separate glass-enclosed shower, and two sinks. Every amenity you can think of is available, including valet ski service. Pets are welcomed at no additional charge.

4591 Blackcomb Way, Whistler, BC V0N 1B4. www.fourseasons.com. © **888/935-2460** or 604/935-3400. Fax 604/935-3455. 273 units and 37 residences. Spring, summer, and fall C$305–C$465 double, C$525 suite; winter C$405–C$650 double, from C$720 suite. AE, DC, DISC, MC, V. Underground valet parking C$33. **Amenities:** Restaurant; bar; babysitting; concierge; executive-level rooms; health club; Jacuzzi; heated outdoor pool; room service; sauna; spa. *In room:* A/C, TV w/pay movies, DVD/CD player, hair dryer, minibar, Wi-Fi (free).

EXPENSIVE

Delta Whistler Village Suites ★ ☺   Just minutes from all the major attractions in Whistler, the Delta offers a variety of comfortable, unpretentious, one- and two-bedroom suites with gas fireplaces, balconies, living rooms, fully equipped kitchens, and washer-dryers. They have standard double rooms as well. The beds are firm and comfortable, and the bathrooms are plain but adequate. You won't find the fine finishes and furnishings of a luxury hotel, but you will get great service and the use of a large heated pool with three Jacuzzis (two outdoor, one indoor). **Hy's Steakhouse** (p. 216) and the **Elephant & Castle** are in the same building. The hotel has special kids' programs.

4308 Main St., Whistler, BC V0N 1B4. www.deltahotels.com. © **888/299-3987** or 604/905-3987. Fax 604/938-6335. 205 units. May–Dec 15 C$110–C$210 double, C$130–C$400 suite; Dec 16–Apr C$190–C$500 double, C$300–C$1,000 suite. AE, MC, V. Underground valet parking C$26, self-parking C$22. **Amenities:** 2 restaurants; babysitting; children's programs; concierge; health club; indoor and outdoor Jacuzzis; heated outdoor pool; room service; sauna; ski rental. *In room:* A/C, TV w/pay movies, hair dryer, Internet (C$12/day), kitchen.

The Listel Hotel   The Listel is a basic option in a fantastic location, close to dining and nightlife. The rooms with two queen beds have ample space, despite feeling a tad motel-like. All rooms have the comfort factors of refrigerators, down duvets, and large flatscreen TVs. The lobby, where the Whistler tones of wood and stone create a warm, slick focal point, is the most stylish area of the hotel, complete with a high-top table laid out for chess and checker games. The highlight of the property, however, is the **Bearfoot Bistro** (p. 215) and its more casual **Champagne Lounge.** The lounge has Canada's first vodka tasting room complete with walls made from stacked ice blocks.

4121 Village Green, Whistler, BC V0N 1B4. www.listelhotel.com. © **800/663-5472** or 604/932-1133. Fax 604/932-8383. 98 units. Spring, summer, and fall C$100–C$190. Winter C$140–C$250. AE, DC, DISC, MC, V. Children 18 and under stay free in parent's room. Underground self-parking C$18. **Amenities:** Restaurant; bar; Jacuzzi; sauna. *In room:* TV w/pay movies, hair dryer, Wi-Fi (free).

Pan Pacific Whistler Mountainside ★★   The Pan Pacific's location, overlooking the Whistler gondola and ski slopes, puts this hotel right in the center of the action. You can literally ski out the door straight to the gondola. The look here is contemporary lodge-style, sophisticated, and very comfortable, with lots of warm wood in the rooms. Every suite has a fully equipped kitchenette and balcony. The studio suites, with fold-down Murphy beds, are the smallest units available but still don't skimp on the living area; the one- and two-bedroom suites are quite roomy. One of the best features is the huge heated outdoor pool and Jacuzzi deck overlooking the snowy slopes. The hotel's **Dubh Linn Gate Old Irish Pub** (p. 215) is a popular après-ski rendezvous point and has a new covered patio with fire pits.

The **Pan Pacific Whistler Village Centre** (4299 Blackcomb Way; ℭ **888/966-5575** or 604/966-5500; www.panpacificwhistler.com), run by the same company, is an all-suite, boutique hotel with fine amenities and a village location. A full breakfast is included with the room rate. Spring-to-fall rates for a one-bedroom suite are C$160 to C$270; winter rates for a one-bedroom suite are C$220 to C$850.

4320 Sundial Crescent, Whistler, BC V0N 1B4. www.panpacificwhistler.com. ℭ **888/905-9995** or 604/905-2999. Fax 604/905-2995. 121 units. Spring–fall C$140–C$230 studio, C$190–C$360 suite; winter C$200–C$770 studio, C$250–C$1,170 suite. AE, MC, V. Underground valet parking C$25. **Amenities:** Restaurant; pub; concierge; fitness center; Jacuzzi; heated outdoor pool; room service. *In room:* A/C, TV, DVD, CD player, hair dryer, Internet (free), kitchen.

Summit Lodge & Spa ★★ Quiet and harmony reign at this classy boutique hotel located just a short stroll from the slopes and featuring a unique, full-service spa. All of the guest rooms are suites with kitchenettes, fireplaces, and balconies, some of which look out onto the private-feeling screen of a treescape. All the units showcase granite countertops, custom-designed cherry-wood furnishings, original artwork, and oversize beds with down-filled duvets and pillows. The bathrooms feature soaker tubs. Staff give an extra friendly welcome to pets, with no added fee (past furry guests have included dogs, cats, and ferrets). Pet-free rooms also available. The hotel's dining spot, Elements Urban Tapas Lounge, offers upscale tapas, fresh seafood, infused martinis, and rare wines. The hotel's on-site Taman Sari Royal Heritage Spa features traditional Javanese spa treatments.

4359 Main St., Whistler, BC V0N 1B4. www.summitlodge.com. ℭ **888/913-8811** or 604/932-2778. Fax 604/932-2716. 81 units. C$90–C$405 suite. AE, MC, V. Underground parking C$20. **Amenities:** Restaurant; Jacuzzi; heated outdoor pool; sauna; full-service spa. *In room:* A/C, TV, hair dryer, Internet (free), kitchenette.

The Westin Resort & Spa Whistler ★★★ Located just a few hundred meters from the Whistler gondola and built into the slope of the mountain, this two-tower hotel provides outstanding service and luxury-level amenities. All 419 generously sized suites include upscale kitchens and gas fireplaces, and most have balconies—and all were refurbished in 2009. The bathrooms are roomy, with separate bathtubs and showers in most units. Some rooms in the back have lovely mountain views, but you can hear distant traffic noise from Highway 99, so ask about this when booking. Little luxuries include ski valet, boot-warming services, and the full-service spa, Avello, one of the best in Canada, offering more than 75 treatments. There's also an award-winning restaurant, Aubergine Grille, for patio and fine dining, as well as a village-level shopping plaza.

4090 Whistler Way, Whistler, BC V0N 1B4. www.westinwhistler.com. ℭ **888/634-5577** or 604/905-5000. Fax 604/905-5640. 419 units. C$160–C$900 junior suite; C$210–C$1,100 1-bedroom suite. Children 17 and under stay free in parent's room. AE, MC, V. Underground valet parking C$32. **Amenities:** 2 restaurants; bar; babysitting; concierge; health club; indoor and outdoor Jacuzzi; indoor-outdoor pool; room service; sauna; spa; ski rentals. *In room:* A/C, TV w/ pay movies, hair dryer, kitchenette, Wi-Fi (C$15/day).

Outside the Village

VERY EXPENSIVE

Nita Lake Lodge ★★　Close to the restaurants and lifts at Whistler Creekside, Nita Lake Lodge has a woodsy feel without giving up a note of luxury. From the deep soaker tubs with adjacent rain showers in the spa-style bathrooms to fireplaces and covered balconies, the overall feel here is pure coziness, snuggled up with finery. The lakeside rooms provide the best views—the property is the only lakefront hotel in Whistler. An on-site spa offers Ayurvedic treatments that tie in with restaurant dining options and yoga programs. **Aura Restaurant** is a burgeoning dining spot and with Chef Tim Cuff at the helm. There's an on-site charcuterie, and **Cure Lounge** serves tasting platters of sausages, pates, and dry-cured meats. The **Whistler Mountaineer** (p. 208) ends its Sea-to-Sky run at the station next door.

2131 Lake Placid Rd., Whistler, BC V0N 1B2. www.nitalakelodge.com. ✆ **888/755-6482** or 604/966-5700. 77 units. C$230–$600 studio. C$270–C$650 1-bedroom. AE, MC, V. Valet parking C$30; self-parking C$20. **Amenities:** Restaurants; bar; cafe; concierge; health club; room service; Jacuzzi; sauna; spa; bikes; fishing rods. *In room:* A/C, TV, DVD, hair dryer, MP3 docking station, kitchenette, Wi-Fi (free).

EXPENSIVE

Alpine Chalet Whistler ★　This elegant chalet hosts guests seeking an enhanced level of nutrition and wellness, offering daily yoga classes and an allergen-reduced retreat. The common room is a dream, with comfy chairs and a big fireplace. The adjoining dining area is flooded with natural light from the overhead skylights. Rooms are named after trees and come in essentially two configurations: Standard rooms are comfortable but not huge, with two twins or a queen-size bed, bathrooms with heated floors, and a functional tub/shower combo; signature rooms are larger, with vaulted ceilings, queen- or king-size beds but with Italian linen, as well as a gas fireplace and comfy leather armchairs. Several of these rooms also have pocket balconies, and although the views are of nothing much, the chalet is close to a quiet lakeside park. Breakfasts are a top-quality feast prepared by an in-house chef.

3012 Alpine Crescent, Whistler, BC V0N 1B3. www.alpinechaletwhistler.com. ✆ **800/736-9967** or 604/935-3003. Fax 604/935-3008. 8 units. C$150–C$400 double. Rates include full breakfast. MC, V. Free parking. Take Hwy. 99 2km (1¼ miles) past Whistler Creekside (before Whistler Village), turn left onto Alta Vista and Hillcrest Dr., then a quick right onto Alpine Crescent; the chalet is on the left side about a block away. **Amenities:** Hot tub; small steam room; yoga room. *In room:* TV, DVD, MP3 docking station, Wi-Fi (free).

Durlacher Hof Pension Inn ★ 🎒　This lovely inn has an Austrian feel and a wonderfully sociable atmosphere. Both are the result of the exceptional care and service shown by owners Peter and Erika Durlacher. The guest rooms in this two-story chalet-style property vary in size from comfortable to spacious and come with goose-down duvets and Ralph Lauren linens on extra-long twin-, queen-, or king-size beds; private bathrooms (some with jetted tubs) come with deluxe

The downstairs lounge at the Durlacher Hof Pension Inn has complimentary après-ski appetizers prepared by the innkeeper.

toiletries. The private balconies give way to incredible mountain views. Better still is the downstairs lounge, with a fireplace and complementary après-ski appetizers baked by innkeeper Erika, who also provides a substantial gourmet breakfast. On select evenings, the inn hosts musicians in the gardens, winemaker dinners, or guest chefs.

7055 Nesters Rd., Whistler, BC V0N 1B7. www.durlacherhof.com. (**C**) **877/932-1924** or 604/932-1924. Fax 604/938-1980. 8 units. C$140–C$280 double. Additional adult C$35. Rates include full breakfast and afternoon tea. MC, V. Free parking. Take Hwy. 99 .8km (½ mile) north of Whistler Village to Nesters Rd. and turn left; the inn is immediately on the right. **Amenities:** Sauna; shared guest fridges. *In room:* Hair dryer, no phone, Wi-Fi (free).

MODERATE

Cedar Springs Bed & Breakfast Lodge ☺   This is one of Whistler's few B&Bs that welcomes children. Guests at this charming lodge have a choice of king-, queen-, or twin-size beds in comfortably modern surroundings. The largest room (no. 4) features a wood-burning fireplace and balcony, though the bathroom is shower only. Room no. 8 has a queen-size bed, two twins, and a big soaker tub, while room no. 7 has two queen-size beds and a shower only. The guest sitting room has a fireplace, TV, DVD, and movie library; a sauna and hot tub on the sun deck (overlooking the gardens) fill out the list of amenities. An excellent breakfast is served by the fireplace in the dining room, and guests are welcome to enjoy afternoon tea. A complimentary shuttle service takes you to and from the ski lifts.

8106 Camino Dr., Whistler, BC V0N 1B8. www.whistlerbb.com. (**C**) **800/727-7547** or 604/938-8007. Fax 604/938-8023. 8 units (6 with private bathroom;). Winter C$85–C$135 single, C$110–C$280 double; off season C$70–C$80 single, C$95–C$175 double. Rates include full breakfast. AE, MC, V. Free parking. Take Hwy. 99 north toward Pemberton 4km (2½ miles) past Whistler Village; turn left onto Alpine Way, go a block to Rainbow Dr. and turn left; go a block to Camino St. and turn left; the lodge is a block down at the corner of Camino St. and Cedar Springs Rd. **Amenities:** Bikes; hot tub; sauna. *In room:* Hair dryer, no phone, Wi-Fi (free).

Chalet Beau Sejour ✦ The standout feature of the Beau Sejour is a large common room with a fireplace and a fine view of Whistler Mountain and the valley. The medium-size rooms are comfortable and clean, with two single beds that can be joined together to make a king-size. Of the four units, one is a self-contained suite with a queen-size bed and its own fireplace and full kitchen, although all units provide the best value you're likely to find in a Whistler B&B. There is a large indoor hot tub for guests' use. The B&B is on a public bus route, and located only about a 15-minute walk from the Village via pedestrian paths. Guests are provided with locker space in Whistler Village for the duration of their stay, plus a shuttle to/from the Chalet on their first/last day (so you can drop off/pick up your ski gear).

7414 Ambassador Crescent, Whistler, BC V0N 1B7. www.beausejourwhistler.com. © **604/938-4966.** Fax 604/938-6296. 4 units. Summer C$120–C$130 double; winter C$140–C$175 double. Rates include full breakfast. AE, MC, V. Free parking. Take Hwy. 99 north toward Pemberton about 1km (½ mile) past Whistler Village; turn right onto Nancy Green Dr., and 3 blocks to Ambassador Crescent; turn right. Children by arrangement. **Amenities:** Jacuzzi. *In room:* No phone, Wi-Fi (free).

INEXPENSIVE

Hostelling International Whistler ✦ One of the few inexpensive spots in Whistler, this brand-new purpose-built hostel served as part of the athletes' village during the 2010 Winter Games before opening to the public as a hostel in July 2010. Located 30 minutes from the ski slopes by bus, it features an on-site cafe, lounge with a fireplace, common kitchen, TV lounge and game room, and storage for bikes, boards, and skis. In the summer, guests have use of a barbecue and outdoor patio. As with all hostels, most rooms and facilities are shared, but several private rooms with en suite bathrooms (with showers) and TVs are available. Book by September at the latest for the winter ski season.

1035 Legacy Way, Whistler, BC V0N 1B1. www.hihostels.ca. © **866/762-4122** or 604/962-0025. 180 beds (in 14 private rooms and 4-bed dorms). C$85–C$145 private room (IYHA members), C$95–C$155 private room (nonmembers); C$30–C$35 shared room (members), C$35–C$40 shared room (nonmembers). 2-year adult membership C$35. MC, V. Free parking. Drive North along Hwy. 99 and turn right on Cheakamus Lake Rd. at Function Junction (first traffic light in Whistler), cross the bridge and continue on to Legacy Way; the hostel is the first building on your right side. **Amenities:** Wi-Fi (free).

Campgrounds

You can reserve spots for the campgrounds listed here through **Discover Camping** (© **800/689-9025;** www.discovercamping.ca). Reservation fees are uniformly C$6 per night, with a maximum of C$18 for 3 nights. South of Whistler on the Sea-to-Sky corridor is the very popular **Alice Lake Provincial Park.** Free hot showers, flush toilets, and a sani-station are among the available facilities. Hiking trails, picnic areas, sandy beaches, swimming areas, and fishing spots are also on the grounds.

WHERE TO EAT

Whistler overflows with dining choices, and a stroll through the Village will take you past 30 or more restaurants. Some serve overpriced resort food, but a number of them stand out for either atmosphere or the quality of their meals. For those willing to spend a bit more, Whistler has some outstanding fine-dining options.

On the Village Square, **Ingrid's Village Cafe** (✆ **604/932 7000;** www. ingridswhistler.com), open daily 7am to 6pm, is a local favorite for quality and price; it's been around for over 20 years, making it one of Whistler's oldest businesses. A large bowl of Ingrid's daily soup costs C$4.50; a veggie burger, C$7. Right across from Ingrid's, **Citta Bistro** (✆ **604/932-4177;** www.cittabistro. com) is a favorite dining and night spot, open daily 11am to 1am. It serves thin-crust pizzas, gourmet burgers, and various appetizers. Besides having good food and good prices (main courses are C$12–C$17), it has a terrace, with heat lamps, and serves as a perfect spot for people-watching.

For good beer and stick-to-your-ribs and interesting grub (think veal goulash and spit-roasted chicken), try the family-friendly **Whistler BrewHouse** (4355 Blackcomb Way; ✆ **604/905-2739;** www.drinkfreshbeer.com), located just over the creek in Village North. It's open Sunday to Thursday 11:30am to midnight (Fri–Sat 11:30am–1am). Shared plates run from C$9 to C$15; dinner entree prices are C$16 to C$37. Equally fun indoor dining can be had at the **Dubh Linn Gate Old Irish Pub** (✆ **604/905-4047;** www.dubhlinngate. com) in the Pan Pacific Mountainside hotel (p. 210). The Gate offers pub classics like Irish corned beef and shepherd's pie in an atmosphere evoking the Emerald Isle. Open Monday through Saturday 8am to 1am, Sundays 8am to midnight; main courses cost C$13 to C$24.

Very Expensive

Bearfoot Bistro ★★★ FRENCH   What began as a fairly simple bistro has become Whistler's most elegant French restaurant. The kitchen procures the finest wild and cultivated products, and almost everything is prepared "a la minute" with an emphasis on the quality of the ingredients without over-complication. Diners create their own tasting menus from selections that change daily. For an appetizer, you might choose the Vancouver Island black cod or local Pemberton beets and carrots roasted with Agassiz hazelnuts. Your main course might be Alberta elk or a selection of lobster, scallops, and Dungeness crab. The wine list at Bearfoot Bistro is outstanding, and the expert sommelier can help you with wine pairings. The frozen-walled Belvedere ice room is the setting for vodka tastings (C$36). For the proper experience, allot at least 2 hours to dine here and be prepared for wonderful and unpretentious service.

4121 Village Green. ✆ **604/932-3433.** www.bearfootbistro.com. Reservations essential. Tasting menus C$49–C$159. AE, DISC, MC, V. Daily 5–10pm.

Expensive

Araxi ★★★ PACIFIC NORTHWEST   If you're looking for sublime food and an atmosphere of relaxed but sophisticated elegance, Araxi is as good as it gets. The haute spot of Whistler cuisine, this Village restaurant is consistently voted "Best Restaurant in Whistler" by *Vancouver* magazine. The menu is nominally Italian but with a Pacific Northwest bent that emphasizes fresh regional products, and especially seafood. The raw bar is extraordinary, with appetizers such as fresh oysters and a Dungeness crab roll. Many of the offerings are certified sustainable under the Vancouver Aquarium's Ocean Wise program. Mains might include almond- and roasted garlic-crusted halibut; tagliatelle pasta with local clams, mussels and scallops; loin of lamb with parmesan polenta and a slow-cooked ragout; or prime beef tenderloin. Araxi's always-changing wine list has

Araxi is consistently voted Best Restaurant in Whistler.

reached an awe-inspiring 27 pages long and offers a great selection of wines by the glass. Dinner is served in a warm, woody, beautifully designed space that looks out on the main village street; they also have a newly expanded outdoor patio.

4222 Village Sq. (𝒞 **604/932-4540.** www.araxi.com. Reservations recommended. Main courses C$23–C$39; small plates C$13–C$20. AE, MC, V. Daily 11am–3pm and 5–11pm.

Hy's Steakhouse ★ NORTH AMERICAN   This is the place to go if you're hungering for a big slab of roast beef served with garlic mashed potatoes and Yorkshire puddings or a juicy steak (Hy's is famous for the quality of its beef). The menu also has seafood and even a vegetarian dish. The baby back ribs are deliciously tender and basted with a tangy, housemade barbecue sauce. Service is friendly and prompt, and the wood and leather dining room provides a very masculine setting.

In the Delta Whistler Village Suites (p. 210), 4308 Main St. (𝒞 **604/905-5555.** www.hyssteak house.com. Main courses C$27–C$55. AE, DC, MC, V. Daily 5–10pm.

Rimrock Cafe ★★ SEAFOOD/CONTEMPORARY   Rimrock is outside the village center but worth the visit for the service, consistent food, and atmosphere—a long, narrow room, high ceiling, and a great stone fireplace. It's not really the atmosphere that draws folks in, though; it's the superlative kitchen creations. The first order of business should be a plate of oysters. The chef serves them up in half a dozen ways, from raw with champagne to Rasputin with vodka and caviar. Entrees are seafood-oriented but also include steak and fresh game (venison, anyone?). Look for wild salmon grilled with miso and served with a dollop of lobster mash potatoes, or halibut piri piri, grilled with baby leeks and oysters. The accompanying wine list has a number of fine vintages from BC, California, New Zealand, and Australia.

2117 Whistler Rd. (𝒞 **877/932-5589** or 604/932-5565. www.rimrockwhistler.com. Reservations recommended. Prix-fixe menus C$49–C$68; main courses C$39–C$54. AE, MC, V. Daily 6–9:30pm (call ahead May, June and Sept–Nov).

Trattoria di Umberto ★ ITALIAN   The Mediterranean tones shine through in this ground-level dining room that looks out on the pool deck of the Mountainside Lodge. In the Vancouver area, Umberto—as in chef and restaurateur Umberto Menghi—is synonymous with Italian. Trattoria serves rustic Tuscan cuisine from a lively, open kitchen. An extensive wine menu, focusing on Italian reds, keeps patrons buzzing. Beyond pastas and gnocchi, look for venison chops with a blackberry reduction or roast pheasant with wild mushrooms. Service is friendly and families are welcomed. Umberto's other Whistler restaurant, **Il Caminetto** (🕾 **604/932-4442**), is on the Village Stroll.

4417 Sundial Place. 🕾 **604/932-5858.** www.umberto.com. Reservations recommended. Mains C$20–C$39. MC, V. Daily 5:30–10pm (call ahead for seasonal lunch hours).

Moderate

Caramba! Restaurante ☺ MEDITERRANEAN   The food here won't win any awards, but Caramba! remains a good spot for casual dining; parents can bring their kids and not feel like they're "eating down." The nominally Mediterranean menu is something of an anomaly when it comes to culinary influences. Try the pasta, free-range chicken, or whole trout. If you're into sharing, order a whole-wheat crust pizza or two and a plate of calamari or flatbread with eggplant tapenade.

12-4314 Main St., Town Plaza. 🕾 **604/938-1879.** www.caramba-restaurante.com. Main courses C$13–C$39. AE, MC, V. Summer daily 11:30am–10:30pm; winter Mon–Thurs 5–10pm, Fri–Sun 11:30am–10pm.

Ciao-Thyme Bistro and Fitz Pub ★ ☺ 🎁 CASUAL/PACIFIC NORTHWEST   This popular spot in the Upper Village is a favorite with locals and a dream come true for visitors who want to eat well on a limited budget. The space is small, and the lines can be long (reserve if you're coming for dinner), but the fresh, delicious food is worth the wait. The bistro is a great spot for breakfast (until 3pm), lunch, or dinner (the only meal they serve in the winter), with a simple menu that reaches from free-range egg omelets to hearty soups (like the rich seafood chowder) and delicious sandwiches (try the pulled pork). The special kids' menu features standards like grilled cheese sandwiches and pasta. Dinner options are a tad more upscale, with lobster tail risotto and roasted elk with barley. The menu is the same in both the bistro and the pub next door.

2-4573 Chateau Blvd., Upper Village. 🕾 **604/932-7051.** www.ciaothymebistro.com. Main courses C$13–C$26. AE, MC, V. Spring–fall daily 8am–4pm and 6–10pm (closed Mon–Tues in May); winter daily 6–10pm.

Wild Wood Bistro & Bar ★★ 🎁 PACIFIC NORTHWEST   More locals than visitors line up at Wild Wood, but only because of its off-the-stroll location at the Whistler Racquet Club. The menu offers such interesting fusions as banana bread French toast for breakfast, a Halifax donair wrap (a Nova Scotia specialty) for lunch, and Sambucca jumbo prawns for dinner. Floor-to-ceiling windows have tennis-court and mountain views, while the large patio makes for fabulous summer lounging.

4500 Northlands Blvd. (Village North). 🕾 **604/935-4077.** www.wildwoodrestaurants.ca. Main courses C$15–C$25. MC, V. Daily 7am–3pm and 5–9pm.

WHAT TO SEE & DO OUTDOORS

Whistler and Blackcomb Mountains ★★★ ☺   Both mountain resorts are operated by Intrawest, so your pass gives you access to both ski areas. Whistler is generally considered better for beginners and middle-range skiers, while steeper Blackcomb is geared to the experienced. A new gondola—the longest in the world—now links the two mountains (see "A Peak to Peak Experience: The Intermountain Ski Lift," below). **Whistler Mountain** has 1,530m (5,020 ft.) of vertical (and more than 100 marked runs) serviced by two high-speed gondolas and seven high-speed chairlifts, plus 10 other lifts and tows. Helicopter service from the top of the mountain provides access to another nearly 500 runs on nearby glaciers. The peak has cafeterias, gift shops, and a restaurant. **Blackcomb Mountain** has 1,609m (5,279 ft.) of vertical (and more than 100 marked) runs serviced by one high-speed gondola, nine high-speed chairlifts, plus seven other lifts and tows. The cafeteria, restaurant, and gift shop aren't far from the peak. Both mountains also have bowls and glade skiing, with Blackcomb Mountain offering glacier skiing well into July. A family-friendly Tube Park, located at Base II on Blackcomb, offers a 305m (1,000-ft.) run with eight lanes, accessed by a carpet-style lift. *Note:* You can save about 20% on your multiday lift tickets by booking online. All lift tickets include the Peak to Peak Gondola between Whistler and Blackcomb.

4545 Blackcomb Way, Whistler, BC V0N 1B4. ☎ **800/766-0449** in North America or 0800/587-1743 in the U.K.; 604/687-7507 snow report in Vancouver, 604/932-4211 snow report in Whistler. www.whistlerblackcomb.com. Winter lift tickets C$95 adults, C$81 seniors and children 13–18, C$48 children 7–12, free for children 6 and under. A variety of multiday passes are available. Tube park per hour C$16 adults, C$12 children 13–18, C$10 children 12 and under. Children must be at least .90m (3 ft.). Lifts daily noon–6pm (depending on weather and conditions).

The Peak to Peak Gondola is the longest free-span lift in the world.

The gondola links the peaks of Whistler (elev. 2,182m/7,159 ft.) and Blackcomb (elev. 2,284m/7,493 ft.) mountains, and opened in December 2008. The longest free-span lift in the world, at 3km (1¾ miles), and with a total length of 4.4km (2¾ miles), the **Peak to Peak Gondola** is also the highest detachable lift in the world, at 436m (1,427 ft.) above the valley floor. The gondola has 28 cars, each carrying up to 28 passengers, and leaves about once every minute. The lift takes 11 minutes to travel from peak to peak. The new gondola offers skiers greater flexibility for skiing the highest runs of both mountains and provides summer visitors with one of the most thrilling gondola rides in the world. The price for a gondola ride is included in your winter lift ticket; if you want to skip the skiing (or summer mountain biking) and just ride on the gondola, the cost is C$45 adults, C$38 seniors and children 13 to 18, and C$21 children 7 to 12. To reach the Peak to Peak gondola, you must take either the Whistler or Blackcomb gondola up to the new boarding area.

The Lowdown on Skiing in Whistler

Whistler Blackcomb offers **ski** and **snowboarding lessons** and **ski guides** for all levels and interests. Phone **Guest Relations** at ✆ **800/766-0449** for details.

You can **rent ski and snowboard gear** at the base of both Whistler and Blackcomb Villages just prior to purchasing your lift pass. No appointment is necessary (or accepted), and the system is first-come, first-served. Arrive at 8am, and you'll be on the gondola by 8:15. Arrive at 8:30am, and you won't be up until 9:15 at the earliest.

Summit Ski (✆ **866/608-6225** or 604/932-6225; www.summitsport. com), at various locations including the Delta Whistler Village Suites and Hilton Whistler Resort & Spa, rents high-performance and regular skis and snowboards.

BACKCOUNTRY SKIING The **Spearhead Traverse,** which starts at Whistler and finishes at Blackcomb, is a well-marked backcountry route that has become a local classic.

Garibaldi Provincial Park (✆ **604/898-3678**) maintains marked backcountry trails at **Diamond Head,** with additional trails at **Singing Pass,** and **Garibaldi Lake.** These are ungroomed and unpatrolled rugged trails, and you have to be at least an intermediate skier and bring (and know how to use) appropriate clothing and avalanche gear. Several access points to the trails are along Highway 99 between Squamish and Whistler. If you're not sure of yourself off-*piste,* hire a guide through **Whistler Alpine Guides Bureau** (✆ **604/938-9242**; www.whistlerguides.com).

CROSS-COUNTRY SKIING Well-marked, fully groomed cross-country trails run throughout the area. The 32km (20 miles) of easy-to-very-difficult marked trails at **Lost Lake** start a block away from the Blackcomb Mountain parking lot. These trails are groomed for track skiing and ski-skating, patrolled by Whistler employees, and at their best from mid-December to mid-March. Passes are C$20 per day; a 1-hour cross-country lesson, including pass and equipment rental, runs about C$79 and can be booked at the same station where you buy your trail pass. For more information, contact **Lost Lake Cross Country Connection** (✆ **604/905-0071;** www.crosscountry connection.ca). **Whistler Olympic Park** (4910 Glacier Lane [turn off Hwy. 99 about 12km/7½ miles south of Whistler Village]; ✆ **877/764-2455** or 604/964-0060; www.whistlerolympicpark.com) in the **Callaghan Valley** hosted Nordic events during the Winter Games, and has more than 90km (56 miles) of groomed cross-country trails. Day passes cost C$20 for adults. The **Valley Trail System** in the village becomes a well-marked cross-country ski trail during winter.

HELI-SKIING   For intermediate and advanced skiers who can't get enough fresh powder or vertical on the regular slopes, there's always heli-skiing. **Whistler Heli-Skiing** (✆ **888/435-4754** or 604/905-3337; www.whistlerheli skiing.com) offers a three-run day, with 1,400 to 2,300m (4,593–7,546 ft.) of vertical helicopter lift, for C$815 per person. A four-run day for expert skiers and riders only, with 1,800 to 3,500m (5,906–11,483 ft.) of vertical helicopter lift, is also available.

Other Winter Pursuits

SLEIGHING & DOG SLEDDING   For a horse-drawn sleigh ride, contact **Blackcomb Horsedrawn Sleigh Rides** (✆ **604/932-7631;** www.blackcomb sleighrides.com). In winter, tours go out every evening from base 2 on Blackcomb Mountain and cost C$55 adults, C$35 children 3 to 12, children 2 and under ride free. Other options include daylight, romantic, and dinner sleigh rides.

From mid-December through March, **Canadian Snowmobile Adventures Ltd.** (Carleton Lodge, 4290 Mountain Sq.; ✆ **604/938-1616;** www.canadiansnowmobile.com) gives 3-hour dog-sled tours for C$175 per person, based on two adults per sled.

SNOWMOBILING & ATVS   Year-round, hop on either an ATV or a snowmobile for a tour of mountain trails with **Canadian Snowmobile Adventures Ltd.** (Carleton Lodge, 4290 Mountain Sq.; ✆ **604/938-1616;** www.canadian snowmobile.com). All tours are weather and snow conditions permitting. Drivers on both the snowmobile and the ATV must have a valid driver's license. A 3-hour Mountain Safari on Blackcomb Mountain costs C$159 for a driver and C$125 for a passenger. A 2-hour Mountain Explorer ATV tour costs C$99 for the driver and C$59 for a passenger.

Blackcomb Snowmobile (✆ **604/932-8484;** www.blackcomb snowmobile.com) offers a variety of guided snowmobile tours, including family tours on Blackcomb Mountain. A 2-hour wilderness adventure tour costs C$149 for one adult, or C$119 each for two adults sharing. Family tours and slower-speed scenic tours are also available.

SNOWSHOEING   Snowshoeing is the world's easiest and most environmentally friendly form of snow-commotion; it requires none of the training and motor skills of skiing or boarding, and it's quiet, so it lets you appreciate nature in a different way. You can wear your own shoes or boots, provided they're warm and waterproof, strap on your snowshoes, and off you go. Rentals are available at the ski-and-board rental companies listed above. One of the best rental and trail companies is **Lost Lake Cross Country Connection** (✆ **604/905-0071;** www.crosscountryconnection.ca), which rents snowshoes for C$20 per day. **Whistler Olympic Park** (☎ 877/764-2455 or 604/964-0060; www.whistlerolympicpark.com) in the **Callaghan Valley** also maintains snowshoeing trails and rents equipment. A day pass costs C$10 and renting a pair of snowshoes costs C$20.

Summer Pursuits

CANOEING & KAYAKING The 3-hour River of Golden Dreams Kayak & Canoe Tour is a great way for novices, intermediates, and experts to get acquainted with the beautiful stretch of slow-moving glacial water running between Green Lake and Alta Lake behind the village of Whistler. Contact the **Whistler Visitor Information Centre** (☎ 877/991-9988) for information. Packages begin at C$49 per person, unguided, and include all gear and return transportation to the village center. The information center can also assist with booking lessons and clinics, as well as windsurfing rentals.

GOLFING Robert Trent Jones, Jr.'s, **Fairmont Chateau Golf Club,** at the base of Blackcomb Mountain (☎ 877/938-2092, or 604/938-2097 for the pro shop; www.golfwhistler.com), is an 18-hole, par-72 course. With an elevation gain of more than 120m (394 ft.), this course traverses mountain ledges and crosses cascading creeks. A panoramic view of the Coast Mountains unfolds midcourse. Greens fees range from C$109 to C$159, including power-cart rental.

    Nicklaus North at Whistler (☎ 800/386-9898 or 604/938-9898; www.nicklausnorth.com or www.golfwhistler.com) is a 5-minute drive north of the Village on the shores of Green Lake. The par-71 course's mountain views are spectacular. It was the second Canadian course designed by Nicklaus. Greens fees are C$39 to C$149.

The Fairmont Chateau Golf Club is located at the base of Blackcomb Mountain.

Lost Lake Trail winds through lush cedar groves.

Whistler Golf Club (✆ **800/376-1777** or 604/932-3280; www.whistlergolf.com or www.golfwhistler.com), designed by Arnold Palmer, features nine lakes, two creeks, and magnificent vistas. This 18-hole, par-71 course offers a driving range, putting green, sand bunker, and pitching area. Greens fees are C$59 to C$129.

A-1 Last Minute Golf Hotline (✆ **800/684-6344** or 604/878-1833) can arrange a next-day, last-minute tee time at Whistler golf courses and elsewhere in BC at more than 30 courses. Savings can be as much as 40%. No membership is necessary. Call between 3 and 9pm for the next day or before noon for the same day. The hotline also arranges group and advanced bookings (up to a year ahead).

HIKING   Numerous easy hiking trails can be found in and around Whistler. Besides taking a lift up to Whistler and Blackcomb mountains' high mountain trails (you can somewhat easily hike to the foot of a glacier) during summer, you have a number of other choices.

Lost Lake Trail starts at the northern end of the Day Skier Parking Lot at Blackcomb Mountain. The lake is less than a mile from the entry. The 32km (20 miles) of marked trails that wind around creeks, beaver dams, blueberry patches, and lush cedar groves are ideal for biking, cross-country skiing, or just strolling and picnicking. The **Valley Trail System** is a well-marked paved trail that connects parts of Whistler. A trail access-point is on the west side of Highway 99, adjacent to the Whistler Golf Course. From there, the trail winds through quiet residential areas, as well as golf courses and parks.

Garibaldi Provincial Park's **Singing Pass Trail** is a 4-hour hike of moderate difficulty. The fun way is to take the Whistler Mountain gondola to the top and walk down the well-marked path that ends on an access road in the Village. Winding down from above the tree line, the trail takes you through stunted alpine forest into Fitzsimmons Valley. Along Highway 99 between Squamish and Whistler are several access points into the park.

Nairn Falls Provincial Park ★★, about 32km (20 miles) north of Whistler on Highway 99, features a 1.6km-long (1 mile) trail that leads you to a stupendous view of the glacial Green River as it plunges 60m (197 ft.)

over a rocky cliff into a narrow gorge on its way downstream. You will also spy an incredible view of Mount Currie peeking over the treetops.

On Highway 99 north of Mount Currie, **Joffre Lakes Provincial Park** has an intermediate-level hike that leads past several brilliant blue glacial lakes up to the very foot of a glacier.

The **Ancient Cedars** area of Cougar Mountain, near the north end of Green Lake, is an awe-inspiring grove of towering cedars and Douglas firs. (Some of the trees are more than 1,000 years old and measure 3m/9¾ ft. in diameter.)

Guided nature hikes provide an excellent opportunity to learn more about the ecology of the region. Contact the **Whistler Visitor Information Centre** (✆ **877/991-9988** or 604/938-2769; www.tourismwhistler. com) for guided hikes and interpretive tours available through various Whistler operators.

HORSEBACK RIDING **Adventure Ranch** (1641 Airport Rd., Pemberton; ✆ **604/894-5200;** www.adventureranch.net) offers 2-hour trail rides along the Green River, through the forest, and across the Pemberton Valley from its 4-hectare (10-acre) riverside facility, a 35-minute drive north of Whistler. The 2-hour ride costs C$69 per person; longer rides can be arranged.

JET BOATING **Whistler Jet Boating** (✆ **604/905-9455;** www.whistlerjet boating.com) takes guests up the Green River just below Nairn Falls, where moose, deer, and bear sightings are common in the canyon (although the noise of the jet boat might scare them away). Three-hour tours cost C$109 for adults and C$99 for children 5 to 15.

MOUNTAIN BIKING A rumor is afloat that mountain biking at Whistler will eventually be bigger than skiing. **Whistler Mountain Bike Park** ★★★ (✆ **866/218-9688;** www.whistlerblackcomb.com/bike) offers some of the best mountain-biking trails, skill centers, and jump parks in the world. When the snow melts, the slope is reconfigured for biking—with more than 200km

The world-class Whistler Mountain Bike Park offers more than 200km (124 miles) of marked trails.

ZIPPING WITH ziptrek ★★★

One of Whistler's most exciting year-round adventures is offered by **Ziptrek Ecotours** (☎ **866/935-0001** or 604/935-0001; www.ziptrek.com)—the same folks who set up a zipline over Vancouver's Robson Square during the 2010 Winter Games. On guided 3-hour tours, you're taken through Whistler's ancient temperate rainforest on a network of up to 10 zipline rides joined by canopy bridges, boardwalks, and trails. Along the way, you're harnessed into a safety contraption that lets you whiz out on cables suspended hundreds of feet above glacier-fed Fitzsimmons Creek. It sounds hair-raising, but it's completely safe for all ages and abilities, and you'll never forget the experience. Individual Ziptrekkers must be 6 or older and weigh between 30 and 125kg (66–276 lb.); children can ride tandem with one of the guides. Choose from two five-line tours, which cost C$99 to C$119 adults, C$79 to C$99 for seniors 65 and older and children 14

and under. If you don't want to zip, consider the **Treetrek,** which explores the rare and ancient temperate rainforest along a network of suspension bridges, boardwalks, and treetop viewing platforms (C$39 adults, C$29 seniors and children 14 and under). The sales desk is located in the Carleton Lodge right across from the Whistler Village Gondolas.

(124 miles) of marked trails, open mid-May to early October from 10am to 5pm, with extended hours of 10am to 8pm from mid-June to early September. The variety of trails can accommodate almost all ages and experience levels. Single-day ticket prices with gondola are C$55 adults, C$49 seniors and children 13 to 18, and C$30 children 7 to 12. *Note:* Children 12 and under are not permitted in the bike park unless accompanied by a parent.

You can rent the best mountain bikes (about C$65 for 4 hr. or C$100 for a full day) and body armor (C$20) right next to the bike park. **Lost Lake Cross Country Connection** (☎ **604/905-0071;** www.crosscountry connection.ca) offers bike rentals and guided tours for levels from beginner to expert.

RAFTING For first-timers, **Wedge Rafting** (Carleton Lodge, Whistler Village; ☎ **888/932-5899** or 604/932-7171; www.wedgerafting.com) offers Green River, Elaho and Squamish Rivers, and Cheakamus River tours. For the Green River trip, about 2½ hours, the shuttle picks up rafters in Whistler and takes them to the wilderness launch area for briefing and equipping. It's an exciting hour or more on the icy rapids. Tours cost C$89, with up to six daily departures. The tour down the Elaho and Squamish rivers takes about 8 hours, includes snacks and a barbecue lunch, and costs C$165. Discounts are available for children 10 to 16; however, they must weigh at least 41kg (90 lb.).

Located in the gorgeous Squamish valley, **Sun Wolf Outdoor Centre** (℡ 877/806-8046; www.sunwolf.net) leads family float trips as well as summer rafting trips on the Elaho and Squamish rivers and winter eagle-viewing trips on the Cheakamus and Squamish rivers. Full-day summer rafting trips cost C$155 per person, and the winter eagle trips cost C$100 per person.

ROCK CLIMBING The **Core** (4010 Whistler Way; ℡ 604/905-7625; www.whistlercore.com) has a year-round indoor climbing center, as well as guided climbs and instruction. An adult day pass is C$18.

TENNIS The **Whistler Racquet Club** (4500 Northlands Blvd.; ℡ 604/932-1991; www.whistlertennis.com) has three covered courts, seven outdoor courts, and a practice cage. Indoor courts are C$16 per hour, outdoor courts C$10 per hour. Adult and junior tennis camps are offered in summer. Camp prices run C$315 to C$340 for a 3-day adult camp. Kids' camps cost C$225 for a week.

The **Fairmont Chateau Whistler Resort** (Fairmont Chateau Whistler Hotel, Upper Village; ℡ 604/938-8000) also offer courts to drop-in players. Prices run about C$20 per hour per court; racquet rentals are available for C$5 per hour.

Free public courts (℡ 604/935-7529) are located at Alpha Lake, Meadow, Millar's Pond, Brio, Balsam, and White Gold parks.

Indoor Pursuits

For **performing arts,** from classical and choral to folk and blues, check out the **Maurice Young Millennium Place** (℡ 604/935-8410; www.myplacewhistler.org).

A HISTORY MUSEUM To learn more about Whistler, visit the **Whistler Museum** (4333 Main St., off Northlands Blvd.; ℡ 604/932-2019; www.whistlermuseum.com). The museum exhibits reveal the life and culture of the First Nations tribes that have lived in the lush Whistler and Pemberton

---

A New First Nations Cultural Center

The **Squamish Lil'wat Cultural Centre** (℡ 866/441-7522; www.slcc.ca) is an architecturally stunning showcase of soaring glass and stone, designed to celebrate the joint history and living cultures of the Squamish and Lil'wat Nations. Anchored by a monumental Great Hall with traditional artifacts and 67m (220-ft.) glass walls revealing spectacular mountain and forest views, the center also features a gallery of Squamish and Lil'wat sacred cultural treasures and icons, plus a shop for First Nations art. Outdoors, you'll find a longhouse, which was the traditional dwelling of the Squamish people, and a replica Lil'wat "ístken" or "Pit House," the traditional dwelling of the Lil'wat people. The cultural center is located at the entrance to the Upper Village, along Lorimer Road, on a wedge of land near the Four Seasons Resort and the Fairmont Chateau Whistler. The Centre is open daily year-round from 9:30am or 10am to 5pm. Admission is C$18 adults, C$14 seniors, C$11 children 13 to 18, and C$8 children 6 to 12. To get the best value, allow enough time to take a guided tour.

valleys for thousands of years. There are also re-creations of the village's early settlement by British immigrants during the late 1800s and early 1900s, and a heavy emphasis on the athletes and Olympians who have skied Whistler's slopes in recent decades. The museum is open daily from 11am to 5pm. Admission is C$7 adults, C$5 seniors and students, C$4 children 7 to 18, and free for children 6 and under.

SHOPPING   The **Whistler Marketplace** (in the center of Whistler Village) and the area surrounding the **Blackcomb Mountain lift** brim with clothing, jewelry, crafts, specialty, and equipment shops that are generally open daily from 10am to 6pm. **Escape Route** (✆ 604/938-3228), at Whistler Marketplace and Crystal Lodge, has a great line of outdoor clothing and equipment.

For some of the finer things in life, visit the **Whistler Village Art Gallery** (✆ 604/938-3001; www.whistlerart.com) and **Adele Campbell Gallery** (✆ 604/938-0887; www.adelecampbell.com). Their collections include fine art, sculpture, and glass. **Keir Fine Jewellery** (Village Gate House; ✆ 604/932-2944; www.keirfinejewellery.com) sells Italian gold, Swiss watches, and handmade Canadian jewelry. For a list and map of all the galleries in town, as well as information on events, contact the **Whistler Community Arts Council** (✆ 604/935-8410; www.whistlerartscouncil.com).

SPAS   The **Taman Sari Royal Heritage Spa** (✆ 888/913-8811; www.tamansarispa.com) offers an unusual array of Javanese and European spa treatments. The Westin's **Avello** (✆ 877/935-7111; www.whistlerspa.com) has a variety of signature treatments, including hot rock, Thai, and Satago massage. The **Vida Wellness Spa** at **Fairmont Chateau Whistler Resort** (✆ 604/938-2086) provides massage therapy, skin care, and body wraps.

The Whistler Village Art Gallery features sculpture and fine art.

A Finnish Indulgence at Scandinavie Spa

Drawing on Finnish traditions of hydro-therapy, **Scadinavie Spa** (8010 Mons Rd.; *𝒞* **604/935-2424**; www.scandinave.com) is an inviting post-slope stop with outdoor baths set in a coniferous forest. Spa-goers first warm up in the cedar sauna, steam room, or hot pool, then refresh themselves under a cold waterfall or shower. A terrace, hammocks, and solarium provide a more tempered relaxation spot. Bath-only access costs C$58, with add-on Swedish, hot stone, and deep tissue massages available. The spa opens daily year-round from 10am to 9pm.

If something didn't quite go right on the slopes or on the trails, **Whistler Physiotherapy** (www.whistlerphysio.com) specializes in sports therapy. There are two locations: 339-4370 Lorimer Rd., at Marketplace (*𝒞* **604/932-4001**) and 202-2011 Innsbruck Dr., next to Boston Pizza in Creekside (*𝒞* **604/938-9001**).

Especially for Kids

Whistler Village and the Upper Village sponsor daily activities for kids of all ages near the base of the mountains. Mountain-bike races; an in-line skating park; trapeze, trampoline, and wall-climbing lessons; summer skiing; snowboarding; snowshoeing; bungee jumping; and a first-run multiplex movie theater are just a few of the options.

Based at Blackcomb Mountain, the **Dave Murray Summer Ski and Snowboard Camp** (*𝒞* **604/902-2600;** www.skiandsnowboard.com) is North America's longest-running summer ski camp. Junior programs cost C$2,195 for 8 days or C$1,195 for a 5-day package; both are available from mid-June to mid-July. Packages include food; lodging (day-camp packages without the hotel are also available); lift passes; and tennis, trapeze, and mountain biking options. Days are spent skiing, boarding, or free-riding on the excellent terrain parks and half-pipes. Camps accommodate a range of abilities, from beginners to champion-level skiers and riders; the age group is 7 to 18 years. The comprehensive instruction and adult supervision at this activity-oriented camp are excellent.

WHISTLER AFTER DARK

For a town of just 10,000, Whistler has a pretty good nightlife scene. Of course, it *is* considered the preeminent ski resort in North America and attracts millions of year-round visitors. Bands touring through Vancouver regularly make the trip up the Sea to Sky Highway; some even make Whistler their Canadian debut. Concert listings can be found in *Pique*, a free paper available at cafes and food stores.

Tommy Africa's (*𝒞* **604/932-6090;** www.tommyafricas.com), beneath the Rexall at the entrance to the Main Village, and the dark and cavernous **Maxx Fish** (*𝒞* **604/932-1904;** www.maxxfish.moonfruit.com), in the Village Square below the Amsterdam Cafe, caters to the 19- to-22-year-old crowd: lots of beat and not much light. The crowds at **Garfinkel's** (*𝒞* **604/932-2323;** www.garfswhistler.com), at the entrance to Village North, and **Moe Joe's** (*𝒞* **604/935-1152;** www.moejoes.com) on Golfer's Approach are similar, though the

Après-Ski

"Après-ski" refers to that delicious hour after a hard day on the slopes, when you sit back with a cold or hot drink and nurse the sore spots in your muscles. On the Whistler side, the many loud and kicky beer bars will be in your face the moment your skis cease to schuss. On the Blackcomb side, **Merlin's Bar** (© 604/938-7700) is almost as obvious and equally young and lubricated. However, **The Mallard Lounge and Terrace ★** (© 604/938-8000), inside the Fairmont Chateau Whistler (p. 209), is one of the most civilized après-ski bars on Earth.

cutoff age can reach a little higher. The **Cinnamon Bear Bar** in the Hilton (© **604/966-5060**), **Buffalo Bills** (© **604/932-6613**; www.buffalobills.ca) across from the Whistler Gondola, and sports bar **Tapleys** (© **604/932-4011**; www.tapleyspub.com), off the Village Square, cater to the 30-something crowd. Bills is bigger, with a pool table, video ski machine, a small dance floor, and music straight from the 1980s, Tapleys has multiple screens for airing hockey games, and the Cinnamon Bear is a slick, tranquil spot.

For a short visit, try the four- or five-bar **Whistler Club Crawl** (© **604/722-2633;** www.whistler clubcrawl.com) to skip the lines and save on cover. Guided tours run on Thursday and Saturday nights. The C$50 per person cost covers dinner, five drinks, and cover.

The Whistler BrewHouse offers great dining along with its strong selection of beers.

If all you want to do is savor a beer and swap ski stories, try the **Whistler BrewHouse** (© **604/905-2739**) in Village North or the fun and very Irish **Dubh Linn Gate Old Irish Pub** (© **604/905-4047**) in the Pan Pacific Whistler Mountainside hotel (p. 210), which often features live musicians.

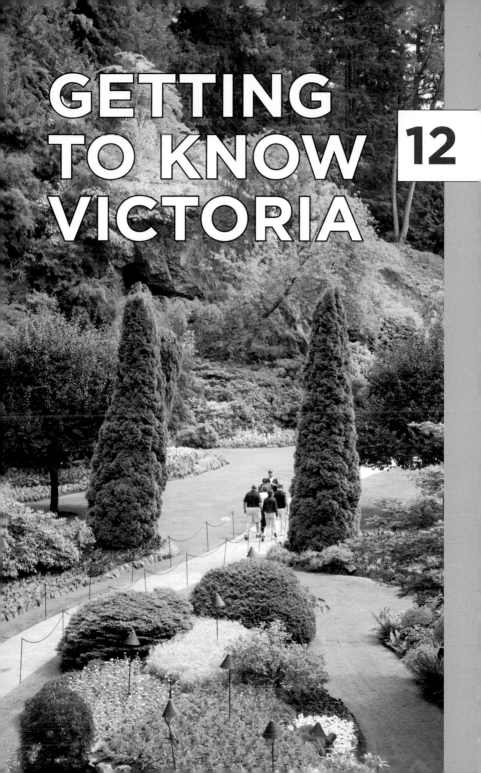

GETTING TO KNOW VICTORIA

12

O nce a far flung vestige of the British Empire, Victoria is one of those heritage cities that has kept the best of the old, smartened it up with snazzy new, and flavored the scene with a dash of island culture. Add to this a spectacular dose of wilderness beauty, and you have a one-of-a-kind island destination, geared to the 21st century.

ORIENTATION

Victoria is on the southeastern tip of Vancouver Island, which lies southwest of the city of Vancouver across the Strait of Georgia and Haro Strait. BC's island capital looks south across the Strait of Juan de Fuca to Port Angeles, Washington, and Washington's snowcapped Olympic peninsula. Many people arrive in Victoria by ferry (see "Getting to Victoria," in chapter 20): The ferry from Port Angeles is the only one that arrives in the Inner Harbour downtown; the ferries from Vancouver and Anacortes arrive in Swartz Bay or Sidney, about 20 minutes north of Victoria.

Getting into Town from the Airport

Several **car-rental** firms have desks at the airport, including **Avis** (✆ 800/879-2847 or 250/656-6033; www.avis.ca), **Budget** (✆ 800/668-9833 or 250/953-5300; www.budgetvictoria.com), **Hertz** (✆ 800/654-3131 or 250/656-2312; www.hertz.com), and **National** (✆ 800/227-7368 or 250/656-2541; www.nationalcar.com). If you're driving from the airport, take Highway 17 south to Victoria; it becomes Douglas Street as you enter downtown.

The **Akal Airporter shuttle bus** (✆ 250/386-2525; www.victoriaairportshuttle.com or victoriaairporter.com) has a ticket counter at the airport and makes the trip downtown in about a half-hour. Buses leave every 30 minutes daily from 4:30am to midnight; the fare is C$18 one-way. Drop-offs are made at most hotels and bed-and-breakfasts, and pickups can be arranged, as well. A limited number of hotel courtesy buses also serve the airport. A cab ride into downtown Victoria costs about C$50, plus tip. **Empress Cabs** and **Blue Bird Cabs** (p. 234) make airport runs.

Visitor Information

Tourism Victoria Visitor Centre (812 Wharf St.; ✆ 250/953-2033; www.tourismvictoria.com) is located on the Inner Harbour, across from the Fairmont Empress hotel (p. 239). The center is open daily September through April from 9am to 5pm, and May through August from 9am to 8:30pm. It also operates a **Reservations Hotline** at ✆ 800/663-3883.

If you want to explore the rest of the 459km-long (285-mile) Vancouver Island (it's roughly the size of Holland), this office will help put you on the right

PREVIOUS PAGE: **The famous Butchart Gardens are just a short distance from downtown.**

track; you'll find a list of all the **regional tourism offices** on Vancouver Island at **www.vancouverisland.travel.**

For details on the after-dark scene, pick up a copy of *Monday Magazine,* available free in cafes around the city; it's an excellent guide to Victoria's nightlife and has also driven at least one mayor from office with its award-winning muck-raking journalism. The online version (www.mondaymag.com) has detailed entertainment listings.

City Layout

Victoria was born at the edge of the Inner Harbour in the 1840s and spread outward from there. The areas of most interest to visitors, including **downtown** and **Old Town,** lie along the eastern edge of the **Inner Harbour.** (North of the Johnson St. Bridge is the **Upper Harbour,** which is largely industrial but taking on new life as old buildings are redeveloped.) A little farther east, the **Ross Bay** and **Oak Bay** residential areas around Dallas Road and Beach Drive reach the beaches along the open waters of the Strait of Juan de Fuca.

Victoria's central landmark is the **Fairmont Empress** hotel on Government Street, right across from the Inner Harbour. If you turn your back to the hotel, downtown and Old Town are on your right, while the **Provincial Legislature Buildings** and the **Royal BC Museum** are on your immediate left. Next to them is the dock for the **Seattle–Port Angeles ferries,** and beyond that the residential community of **James Bay,** the first neighborhood in the city to be developed.

MAIN ARTERIES & STREETS   Three main **north-south arteries** intersect just about every destination you may want to reach in Victoria.

Government Street goes through Victoria's main downtown shopping-and-dining district. Wharf Street, edging the harbor, merges with Government Street at the Fairmont Empress. **Douglas Street,** running parallel to Government Street, is the main business thoroughfare, as well as the road to Nanaimo and the rest of the island. It's also Trans-Canada Highway 1. The "Mile 0" marker sits at the corner of Douglas Street and Dallas Road. Also running parallel to Government and Douglas streets is **Blanshard Street** (Hwy. 17), the route to the Saanich Peninsula—including the Sidney-Vancouver ferry terminal—and Butchart Gardens.

Important **east-west streets** include the following: **Johnson Street** lies at the northern end of downtown and the Old Town, where the small E&N Station sits opposite Swans Hotel at the corner of Wharf Street. The Johnson Street Bridge is the demarcation line between the Upper Harbour and the Inner Harbour. **Belleville Street** is the Inner Harbour's southern edge. The Legislative Buildings and the ferry terminal are here. Belleville Street loops around westward toward Victoria Harbour before heading south, becoming **Dallas Road.** Dallas Road follows the water's edge past residential areas and beaches before it winds northward up to Oak Bay.

FINDING AN ADDRESS   Victoria addresses are written like those in Vancouver: The suite or room number precedes the building number. For instance, 100-1250 Government St. refers to suite 100 at 1250 Government St.

Victoria's streets are numbered from the city's southwest corner and increase in increments of 100 per block as you go north and east. (1000 Douglas St., for example, is 2 blocks north of 800 Douglas St.) Addresses for all the east-west streets (Fort, Yates, Johnson, and so on) downtown start at 500 at Wharf Street; thus, all buildings between Wharf and Government streets fall between 500 and 599, while all buildings between Government and Douglas streets fall between 600 and 699, and so on.

STREET MAPS   Street maps are available free at the **Tourism Victoria Visitor Centre** (see "Visitor Information," above). The best map of the surrounding area is the **BC Provincial Parks** map of Vancouver Island, also available at the Info Centre.

Neighborhoods in Brief

INNER HARBOUR   For most visitors, this is where it's at, and it's what those glossy tourism brochures depict. Framed by the Parliament Buildings on one side and the Fairmont Empress on another, the Inner Harbour is where to find cabs, horse-drawn carriage rides, double-decker tour buses, ferries, floatplanes, whale-watching outfitters, kayaking tours, fish and chips, and the main Visitor Information Centre. The BC Royal Museum, IMAX, and the Undersea Gardens are among the top attractions, as is a waterside stroll around the harbor to Fisherman's Wharf, its small community of fish boats selling their catch of the day, and floating homes. In summer, the place fills up with a myriad of artist-vendors who add to the entertainment value of your meanderings.

DOWNTOWN & OLD TOWN   These areas have been the city's social and commercial focal points since the mid-1800s, when settlers first arrived by ship. This is also the area of the city most popular with visitors, filled with shops, museums, heritage buildings, and lots of restaurants. The area's fascinating Barbary Coast history—which includes rum smuggling, opium manufacturing, gold prospecting, whaling, fur trading, and shipping—is reflected in the hundreds of heritage buildings, once home to chandleries, warehouses, factories, whorehouses, and gambling dens.

The two neighborhoods are usually listed together because it's difficult to say where one leaves off and the other begins. The Old Town consists of the pre-1900 commercial sections of the city that grew up around the original Fort Victoria at View and Government streets. Roughly speaking, it extends from Fort Street north to Pandora Street and from Wharf Street east to Douglas Street. Downtown is everything outside of that, from the Inner Harbour to Quadra Street in the east and from Belleville Street in the south up to Herald Street at the northern edge of downtown.

CHINATOWN   Victoria's Chinatown is tiny—only 2 square blocks—but venerable. In fact, it's the oldest Chinese community in North America. At one time, legal opium manufacturing took place in the hidden courtyard buildings flanking the 1.2m-wide (4-ft.) Fan Tan Alley, Canada's narrowest commercial street.

JAMES BAY, ROSS BAY & OAK BAY   When Victoria was a busy port and trading post, the local aristocracy would retire to homes in these neighborhoods to escape the hustle and bustle in the city center. Today, they remain beautiful residential communities. Houses are perched on hills overlooking the straits or nestled amid lushly landscaped gardens. Golf courses, marinas, and cozy inns edge the waters, where you can stroll the beaches or take a dip if you don't mind a chill.

GETTING AROUND
By Public Transportation

BY BUS   The **Victoria Regional Transit System** (**BC Transit;** 📞 **250/382-6161;** www.bctransit.com) operates 40 bus routes through greater Victoria, as well as the nearby towns of Sooke and Sidney. Buses run to both the Butchart Gardens and the Vancouver Ferry Terminal at Sidney. Regular service on the main routes runs daily from 6am to just past midnight.

Schedules and route maps are available at the Tourism Victoria Visitor Centre (see "Visitor Information," above), where you can pick up a copy of the *Victoria Rider's Guide* or *Discover Vancouver on Transit: Including Victoria.* Popular Victoria bus routes include **no. 2** (Oak Bay), **no. 5** and no. 11 (downtown, James Bay, Beacon Hill Park), **no. 14** (Victoria Art Gallery, Craigdarroch Castle, University of Victoria), **no. 61** (Sooke), **no. 70** (Sidney, Swartz Bay), and **no. 75** (Butchart Gardens).

Fares are good throughout the Greater Victoria area. One-way fares are C$2.55 adults, C$1.65 seniors and students, and free for children 5 and under. Transfers are good for travel in one direction only, with no stopovers. A **DayPass**—C$7.75 adults, C$5.50 seniors and students—covers unlimited travel throughout the day. You can buy passes at the Tourism Victoria Visitor Centre (see "Visitor Information," above), convenience stores, and ticket outlets throughout Victoria displaying the FAREDEALER sign.

BY FERRY   Crossing the Inner, Upper, and Victoria harbors by one of the blue 12-passenger **Victoria Harbour Ferries** (📞 **250/708-0201;** www.victoriaharbourferry.com) is cheap and fun. May through September, the ferries to the Fairmont Empress, Coast Harbourside Hotel, and Ocean Pointe Resort hotel run about every 15 minutes daily from 9am to 9pm. In March, April, and October, ferry service runs daily 11am to 5pm, weather permitting so call ahead to confirm. November through February, the ferries run only on sunny weekends 11am to 5pm. The cost per hop is C$5 adults and C$2.50 children.

Instead of just taking the ferry for a short hop across, try the 45-minute **Harbour tour** ★ or the 55-minute **Gorge tour** ★; both cost C$22 adults, C$20 seniors, and C$12 children 12 and under.

 The Ferry Ballet

Starting at 9:45am every Sunday during summer, the ferries gather in front of the Fairmont Empress to perform a **ferry "ballet"**—it looks a bit like the hippo dance in Disney's *Fantasia.*

By Car

You can easily explore the downtown area of Victoria on foot. If you're planning out-of-town activities, you can rent a car in town or bring your own on one of the car-passenger ferries from Vancouver, Port Angeles, or Anacortes. Traffic is light in Victoria, largely because the downtown core is so walkable.

RENTALS   Car-rental agencies in Victoria include the following: **Avis** (1001 Douglas St.; 📞 **800/879-2847** or 250/386-8468; www.avis.ca; bus no. 5 to Broughton St.), **Budget** (757 Douglas St.; 📞 **800/268-8900** or 250/953-5300; www.budgetvictoria.com), **Hertz** (2634 Douglas St.,

© **800/263-0600** or 250/385-4440; www.hertz.com), and **National** (767 Douglas St.; © **800/387-4747** or 250/386-1213; www.national victoria.com).

PARKING Metered **street parking** is available downtown, but be sure to feed the meter because rules are strictly enforced. Many meters have a centralized location (that is, not by every spot as in Vancouver), so make a note of your space number before you head to the machine. Unmetered parking on side streets is rare. All major downtown hotels have guest parking. Parking lots can be found at **View Street** between Douglas and Blanshard streets, **Johnson Street** off Blanshard Street, **Yates Street** north of Bastion Square, and **The Bay** on Fisgard at Blanshard Street.

DRIVING RULES Some of the best places on Vancouver Island can be reached only via gravel logging roads, on which logging trucks have absolute right of way. If you're on a logging road and see a logging truck coming from either direction, pull over to the side of the road and stop to let it pass.

By Bike

Biking is the easiest way to get around the downtown and beach areas. The city has numerous bike lanes and paved paths in parks and along beaches. Helmets are mandatory, and riding on sidewalks is illegal, except where bike paths are indicated. You can rent bikes starting at C$7 per hour and C$28 per day (lock and helmet included) from **Cycle BC** (685 Humboldt St.; © **866/380-2453** or 250/380-2453; www.cyclebc.ca).

By Taxi

Within the downtown area, you can expect to travel for less than C$10, plus tip. It's best to call for a cab; you won't have much luck if you try to flag one down on the street. Drivers don't always stop, especially when it's raining. Call for a pickup from **Yellow Cabs** (© **250/381-2222**) or **Blue Bird Cabs** (© **250/382-2222**).

By Peddle-Cab

You get to sit while an avid bicyclist with thighs of steel peddles you anywhere you want to go for C$1 per minute for a 2-person cab (C$2 per min. if there are four of you). You'll see these two- and four-seater bike cabs along the Inner Harbour at the base of Bastion Square, or you can call **Kabuki Kabs** (© **250/385-4243;** www.kabukikabs.com) for 24-hour service.

[Fast FACTS] VICTORIA

Business Hours Victoria **banks** are open Monday through Thursday 10am to 3pm and Friday 10am to 6pm. **Stores** are generally open Monday through Saturday 10am to 6pm. Some establishments are open later, as well as on Sundays, in summer.

Last call at the city's **bars** and **cocktail lounges** is 2am.

Currency Exchange
The best exchange rates in town can be found at banks and by using ATMs. **Royal Bank** (1079 Douglas St., at Fort St.) is in the heart of downtown. Take bus no. 5 to Fort Street.

Dentist Most major hotels have a dentist on call. **Cresta Dental Centre** (3170 Tillicum Rd., at Burnside St. in the Tillicum Mall; ☏ **250/384-7711;** bus no. 10) is open Monday through Friday 8am to 9pm, Saturday 9am to 5pm, and Sunday 11am to 5pm.

Doctor Hotels usually have doctors on call. The **Tillicum Mall Medical Clinic** (3170 Tillicum Rd., at Burnside St.; ☏ **250/381-8112;** bus no. 10 to Tillicum Mall), accepts walk-in patients daily 9am to 9pm. **The Downtown Medical Clinic** (622 Courtney St., ☏ **250/380-2210**) also accepts walk-in patients, Monday to Friday 8am to 4:30pm.

Hospitals Local hospitals include the **Royal Jubilee Hospital** (1900 Fort St.; ☏ **250/370-8000,** or 250/370-8212 for an emergency) and the **Victoria General Hospital** (1 Hospital Way; ☏ **250/727-4212,** or 250/727-4181 for an emergency). You can get to both hospitals on bus no. 14.

Internet Access In the heart of Old Town, **Stain Internet Café** (609 Yates St.; ☏ **250/382-3352**) is open daily 10am to 2am (C$4 per hour). Closer to the Legislature, try **James Bay Coffee and Books** (143 Menzies St.; ☏ **250/386-4700**), open daily 7:30am to 10pm (C$1 per 10 min.). Most hotels have Internet access, as does the Victoria Public Library; see below.

Library The **Greater Victoria Public Library** (☏ **250/382-7241;** bus no. 5 to Broughton St.) is at 735 Broughton St., near the corner of Fort and Douglas streets.

Luggage Storage & Lockers Coin lockers are available outside the bus station (behind the Fairmont Empress). Take bus no. 5 to the Convention Centre.

Pharmacies **Shopper's Drug Mart** (1222 Douglas St.; ☏ **250/381-4321;** bus no. 5 to View St.) is open Monday through Friday 7am to 8pm, Saturday 9am to 7pm, and Sunday 9am to 6pm.

Police Dial ☏ **911.** This is a free call. The **Victoria City Police** can also be reached by calling ☏ **250/995-7654.**

Post Office The **main post office** is at 714 Yates St. (☏ **250/953-1352;** bus no. 5 to Yates St.). There are also postal outlets in **Shopper's Drug Mart** (see "Pharmacies," above) and in other stores displaying the CANADA POST postal outlet sign. Supermarkets and many souvenir and gift shops also sell stamps.

13

WHERE TO STAY IN VICTORIA

ictoria has a wide choice of fine accommodations in all price ranges, most in the Old Town, in downtown, or around the Inner Harbour and within easy walking distance of the city's main attractions. As in Vancouver, you'll find a disarming friendliness when you check into a Victoria hotel.

BEST VICTORIA HOTEL BETS

- o **Best Historic Hotel:** She's a grande dame, no doubt about it, and she sits on Victoria's Inner Harbour like an Empress on her throne. For sheer showoffy splendor, the **Fairmont Empress** has no peers. See p. 239.

- o **Best for Business Travelers: The Magnolia** stands conveniently right downtown and features business-friendly amenities. The views are nothing to write home about, but the rooms are comfortable and the bathrooms surprisingly luxe. See p. 246.

- o **Best Hotel Lobby:** The two-story, plate-glass windows in the lobby of the **Delta Victoria Ocean Pointe Resort and Spa** provide the best vantage in Victoria for watching the lights on the Legislature switch on. The comfy chairs and fireplaces also make this a great place to warm up, though the decor feels a bit outdated. See p. 239.

- o **Best for Families:** Honest, thrifty, and down-to-earth, the **Royal Scot Hotel & Suites** is great if you have kids in tow, thanks to the in-suite kitchens, communal pool, and games room. The staff is exceptionally child-friendly, providing advice and kindness. See p. 243.

- o **Best B&B:** With rooms double the size of those in other B&Bs and every possible need taken care of, the friendly innkeepers at the **Haterleigh Heritage Inn** do themselves proud. See p. 240. **Abigails** is a strong runner-up. See p. 245.

- o **Best Inexpensive Hotel:** While the rooms in the main hotel are just okay, the next-door suites and cottage operated by the **James Bay Inn** are a veritable steal. See p. 245.

price CATEGORIES

Very Expensive	C$275 and up
Expensive	C$175–C$274
Moderate	C$100–C$174
Inexpensive	Under C$100

PREVIOUS PAGE: **The Fairmont Empress Hotel has outstanding views of the harbor.**

WHAT YOU'LL really PAY

Hotel listings below provide the rack rates, or the rates you would receive if you walked in off the street and requested a room. The highest prices tend to be during high season from June to September. It is advised to make reservations well ahead for summer travel, but note that even stretches of April and May can be busy.

By checking the hotel's website, you'll almost always find lower rates, including special "romance packages" and weekend-getaway specials.

Prices quoted here don't include the 12% harmonized sales tax (HST).

o **Most Romantic Hotel: Brentwood Bay Lodge & Spa** is a small luxury resort overlooking a pristine fjord. Every detail in the rooms and bathrooms is perfect, from fabrics to fireplace, and couples can have side-by-side treatments in the lovely spa. See p. 250.

o **Most Environmentally Conscious Hotel: Sooke Harbour House** wins hands down in the go-green department: It has its own bioreactor to reprocess wastewater, which is then used to water its gardens, and it has a green parking lot. This hotel also has the **best hotel restaurant** and the **best ocean-side location.** See p. 251.

o **Best Boutique Hotel Makeover:** Hands down, the transformation of a former heritage (run-down) hotel into the chic and hip **Hotel Rialto** takes the crown. See p. 249.

o **Best Alternative Accommodations: The Boathouse** is a real (converted) boathouse, with a private dock and a rowing dinghy. Built in a secluded cove, the tiny cottage is a perfect spot for those seeking privacy and a glorious outlook right on the water. See p. 250.

o **Best Location:** The **Fairmont Empress** sits right on the Inner Harbour and is minutes away from the sightseeing and shopping in and around downtown Victoria. See p. 239.

o **Best Spa:** Three spas share top billing, depending on what you're looking for. The Willow Stream spa at the **Fairmont Empress** offers about 20 different types of European spa treatments, all of which include time in the sauna, steam room, and Hungarian mineral pool (p. 239). The Essence of Life spa at **Brentwood Bay Lodge & Spa** has the most impressive hydro-bath in British Columbia and provides massage treatments for couples (p. 250). Aveda enthusiasts should check out Spa Magnolia at the **Magnolia Hotel,** which does the Aveda concept proud (p. 246).

o **Best View:** Score a redesigned and redecorated suite in the South Wing of the **Inn at Laurel Point** facing the harbor, and you may never want to leave (p. 240). Outside of town, the best view on Vancouver Island goes to **The Wickaninnish Inn** in Tofino; it has no peers (p. 332).

THE INNER HARBOUR & NEARBY

BEST FOR: Travelers who like to stay in the thick of all the action. Almost everything you would want to see and do is within easy walking distance so leave the car at home.

DRAWBACKS: This is Victoria's prime real estate so hotels fill up quickly and rates climb sky-high, especially in the summer. Parking is not always included so it can become an expensive extra.

Very Expensive

Delta Victoria Ocean Pointe Resort and Spa ★★ ☺

The "OPR," located across the Johnson Street Bridge on the Inner Harbour's north shore, is a big, bright, modern hotel with commanding harbor views of downtown, the Legislature, and the Fairmont Empress. Rooms and bathrooms are big; many have floor-to-ceiling windows to take advantage of the stunning scenery. Perhaps that's why the decor leans to a clutter-free feel. A few extra dollars buys a few extra perks, like breakfast and evening hors d'oeuvres in the third-floor Signature Lounge. All guests have use of the big (family-friendly) indoor ozonated pool, a really good whirlpool, and a fully equipped gym with racquetball and tennis courts. Lots of guests come for the spa, one of the best in Victoria, and for the romantic views and great food at **Lure Seafood Restaurant.** Kids receive a free welcome kit of goodies.

45 Songhees Rd., Victoria, BC V9A 6T3. www.deltavictoria.com. ℭ **800/667-4677** or 250/360-2999. 250 units. C$130–C$400 double; C$450–C$800 suite. Children 18 and under stay free in parent's room. AE, DC, DISC, MC, V. Underground valet parking C$15. Pets accepted (C$35 per stay). Bus: 24 to Colville. **Amenities:** Restaurant/lounge; babysitting; executive-level rooms; health club; Jacuzzi; indoor pool; room service; sauna; spa; 2 night-lit outdoor tennis courts; indoor racquetball and squash court. *In room:* A/C, TV w/pay movies, hair dryer, minibar, Wi-Fi (free).

The Fairmont Empress ★★★ ☺

Staying at this full-service landmark hotel makes for a memorable experience. But to get the most out of your stay, book the Gold level which comes with larger rooms, a dedicated concierge, breakfast, and evening hors d'oeuvres; it's like a smaller hotel within the hotel. Otherwise, expect a standard room to offer cozy quarters and little in the way of a view. Deluxe rooms or a Signature corner suite have more space plus high ceilings and harbor views. Furnishings throughout the hotel are beautifully traditional (some might say old-fashioned), but its fabulous location and first-class amenities—including a kid-friendly indoor pool and luxurious Willow Stream spa—are all part of the Empress experience. If you stay elsewhere, at least come for the famous afternoon tea (see "Taking Afternoon Tea," in chapter 14), a spa visit, or a cocktail in the wood-paneled, Colonial-styled Bengal Lounge.

721 Government St., Victoria, BC V8W 1W5. www.fairmont.com/empress. ℭ **866/540-4429** or 250/384-8111. 477 units. C$250–C$800 double; C$430–C$1,500 suite, C$400–C$1,500 Fairmont Gold. Children 11 and under stay free in parent's room. AE, DC, DISC, MC, V. Underground valet parking C$29. Small pets accepted (C$25). Bus: 5. **Amenities:** 2 restaurants; bar/lounge; tearoom; babysitting; concierge; executive-level rooms; health club; indoor lap pool; room service; spa. *In room:* A/C, TV w/pay movies, hair dryer, minibar, MP3 docking station, Wi-Fi (free).

Expensive

The Haterleigh Heritage Inn ★ This exceptional, adult-oriented B&B captures the essence of Victoria's romance with a combination of antique furniture, original stained-glass windows, and attentive personal service. The rooms feature high arched ceilings, large windows, sitting areas, and large bathrooms, some with hand-painted tiles and Jacuzzi tubs. On the top floor, the cozy Angel's Reach room features a big four-poster bed. The second-floor Secret Garden room has a small balcony with views of the Olympic mountain range. A full gourmet breakfast with organic produce is served, and complimentary sherry is available in the drawing room each evening.

243 Kingston St., Victoria, BC V8V 1V5. www.haterleigh.com. © **866/234-2244** or 250/384-9995. 7 units. C$165–C$250 double. Rates include full breakfast. MC, V. Free parking. Bus: 30 to Superior and Montreal sts. **Amenities:** Jacuzzi; Wi-Fi (free). *In room:* Hair dryer.

Hotel Grand Pacific ★★ Sitting directly across the street from the Port Angeles–Victoria ferry dock, the Grand Pacific is grand in name and nature: more luxurious than the Delta Ocean Pointe (p. 239) and with more spacious rooms than most at the Fairmont Empress (p. 239). Amenities here include a spa and a newly expanded health club as well as a huge ozonated indoor pool. All rooms have balconies and are attractively and comfortably furnished. Suites provide the best views, overlooking the harbor and the Empress. Well-equipped bathrooms offset their slightly small size. Dining options include the informal Pacific Restaurant and the **Mark** (p. 257), one of the city's finest and most intimate fine-dining restaurants.

463 Belleville St., Victoria, BC V8V 1X3. www.hotelgrandpacific.com. © **800/663-7550** or 250/386-0450. 304 units. C$200–C$390 double; C$250–C$500 suite. Children 17 and under stay free in parent's room. AE, DC, DISC, MC, V. Self-parking C$15; valet parking C$24. Bus: 30 to Superior and Oswego sts. **Amenities:** 2 restaurants; lounge; concierge; babysitting; superior health club; Jacuzzi; indoor ozone-filtered pool; room service; spa; squash courts. *In room:* A/C, TV w/pay movies, hair dryer, minibar, Wi-Fi (free).

Inn at Laurel Point ★★★ This art-filled, resortlike hotel occupies a pretty, landscaped promontory jutting out into the Inner Harbour. It consists of the Laurel Wing, which contain rooms and family suites, and the Erickson Wing, which is where you want to be. For here's where you'll find suites with particularly au courant furnishings, Asian artwork, balconies overlooking a Japanese garden, shoji-style sliding doors, and luxurious marble bathrooms with deep soaker tubs

---

THE BEST bed & breakfast REGISTRY

If you prefer to stay at a B&B other than those listed in this chapter, check out **www.BCsBestBnBs.com,** which lists some great inns in Victoria as well as inns throughout the province, just in case travel plans take you farther afield. **Canada-West Accommodations Bed &**

Breakfast Registry (P.O. Box 86607, North Vancouver, BC V7L 4L2; © **800/561-3223** or 604/990-6730; www.b-b.com) is another, much smaller outfit, which strives to match guests to the B&Bs that best suit their needs.

Victoria Hotels

Abbeymoore Manor Inn 31
Abigail's Hotel 27
Admiral Inn 13
Andersen House B&B 18
The Beaconsfield Inn 28
The Bedford Regency Hotel 10
Best Western Carlton Plaza 8
Chateau Victoria Hotel & Suites 25
Coast Victoria Harbourside
   Hotel & Marina 11
Dashwood Manor 30
Days Inn on the Harbour 21
Delta Victoria Ocean Point
   Resort & Spa 2
The Fairmont Empress 23
The Gatsby Mansion
   Boutique Hotel 14
Harbour Towers Hotel & Suites 16
The Haterleigh Heritage Inn 17
Hotel Grand Pacific 2
Hotel Rialto 7
Huntingdon Hotel & Suites 15
Inn at Laurel Point 12
Isabella's Guest Suites 4
The James Bay Inn 29
The Magnolia Hotel 24
Ocean Island Backpackers Inn 9
The Oswego Hotel 19
Paul's Motor Inn 6
Royal Scot Hotel & Suites 20
Spinnakers Guest House 1
Swans Suite Hotel 5
Victoria Marriott Inner Harbour 26
The Victoria Regent Hotel 3
Villa Marco Polo 32

241

and glassed-in showers. The overall Japanese-influenced design is a refreshing change from the chintz and florals found in so many Victoria hotels. Rooms in the Laurel Wing come with pocket balconies (every room in the hotel has a water view) and nice bathrooms. The hotel's restaurant, **Aura** (p. 256), is a new dining hot spot and the patio scores high marks.

680 Montreal St., Victoria, BC V8V 1Z8. www.laurelpoint.com. (℗ **800/663-7667** or 250/386-8721. 200 units. C$200–C$270 double; C$250–C$370 suite. Additional adult C$25. Children 18 and under stay free in parent's room. AE, DC, MC, V. Secure parking C$18. Small pets accepted (C$50). Bus: 30 to Montreal and Superior sts. **Amenities:** Restaurant; bar; babysitting; concierge; small fitness center; indoor pool; room service. *In room:* A/C, TV w/pay movies, hair dryer, MP3 docking station, Wi-Fi (free).

Moderate

Andersen House   The art and furnishings in Andersen House are drawn from the whole of the old British Empire and a good section of the modern world beyond. The 1891 house has the high ceilings, stained-glass windows, and ornate fireplaces typical of the Queen Anne period, but the art and decorations are far more eclectic. Each room is unique: The sun-drenched Casablanca room on the top floor, for example, boasts Persian rugs, a four-poster queen-size bed, and a boxed window seat. All rooms have private entrances and come with two-person Jacuzzis, books, CD players and CDs. Although rates no longer include breakfast, there are plenty of early-morning dining options nearby.

301 Kingston St., Victoria, BC V8V 1V5. www.andersenhouse.com. (℗ **877/264-9988** or 250/388-4565. 3 units. C$205–C$235 double. AE, MC, V. Free off-street parking. Bus: 30 to Superior and Oswego sts. Children 11 and under not allowed. *In room:* TV/DVD player, hair dryer, Wi-Fi (free).

The Gatsby Mansion Boutique Hotel and Restaurant   Built in 1897, this white clapboard Victorian across from the Seattle–Port Angeles ferry terminal has been fully restored and now serves as a B&B-style inn, along with two other heritage houses. With its hand-painted ceramic-tiled fireplace, rich wood paneling, stained-glass windows, frescoed ceilings, and crystal chandeliers, it evokes a turn-of-the-20th-century elegance with a dash of kitsch. The spacious, sometimes quirky, rooms feature down duvets, fine linens, and lots of Victorian antiques. Some rooms have views of the Inner Harbour, while others have private parlors. The landscaped complex also includes the Huntingdon Hotel and Suites (p. 244).

309 Belleville St., Victoria, BC V8V 1X2. www.gatsbymansion.com. (℗ **800/563-9656** or 250/388-9191. 20 units. C$160–C$350 double. Rates include breakfast. AE, DC, MC, V. Free underground parking. Bus: 30 or 31 to Belleville and Government sts. **Amenities:** 2 restaurants; bikes; Jacuzzi; room service; sauna; spa. *In room:* TV w/pay movies, hair dryer, Wi-Fi (free).

The Oswego Hotel ★★   The contemporary and eco-friendly Oswego, which looks and feels like a small apartment building, opened in 2009 as Victoria's first purpose-built boutique hotel. It's located in the quiet James Bay neighborhood, 2 blocks from the Inner Harbour. All the studios, one-bedroom, and two-bedroom suites have fully equipped designer kitchens and floor-to-ceiling windows; most have balconies, too. For the absolute best here, book one of the penthouse suites with enormous balconies and fabulous views. The O Bistro is one of Victoria's urban-hip restaurants and is often the evening venue for Jazz ensembles.

500 Oswego St., Victoria, BC V8V 5C1. www.oswegovictoria.com. (℗ **877/767-9346** or 250/294-7500. 90 units. C$180–C$290 double; C$230–C$450 suite; C$600 penthouse. Additional adult

C$25. Children 18 and under stay free in parent's room. AE, DC, MC, V. Self parking C$10. Pets accepted (C$25). Bus: 31 to Oswego and Kingston sts. **Amenities:** Restaurant; lounge; small exercise room; room service. *In room:* HD satellite TV, hair dryer, kitchen, Wi-Fi (free).

Royal Scot Hotel & Suites 😊 🍴   A block from the Inner Harbour, the Royal Scot provides friendly service and good value, particularly if you opt for a studio or one-bedroom suite. Originally an apartment building, the rooms are larger than average. Each studio suite has a divider separating the bedroom from the living room, while one-bedroom suites have separate bedrooms. All suites have lots of closet space, fully equipped kitchens, complimentary refreshments, and sofa beds in the living rooms. The decor is comfortable but uninspired, and bathrooms tend to be on the small side. In summer, the Royal Scot fills up with families. Kids make heavy use of the pool.

425 Quebec St., Victoria, BC V8V 1W7. www.royalscot.com. 📞 **800/663-7515** or 250/388-5463. 176 units. C$165–C$250 double; C$185–C$425 suite. Weekly and monthly rates available. AE, DC, MC, V. Parking C$10. Bus: 30 to Superior and Oswego sts. or bus 5 to Belleville and Government sts. **Amenities:** Restaurant; babysitting; exercise room; Jacuzzi; indoor pool; room service; sauna. *In room:* TV, hair dryer, kitchen, Wi-Fi (free).

Spinnakers Guest House ★ 🍴   This bed-and-breakfast guesthouse offers good accommodations at a moderate price. The two separate buildings are owned and operated by the same local entrepreneur who runs Spinnakers Brewpub (p. 258). The 1884 heritage building on Catherine Street is the more luxurious. Rooms feature queen-size beds, lovely furnishings, in-room Jacuzzis, fireplaces, high ceilings, and lots of natural light. The four Garden Suites units on Mary Street are really self-contained apartments, with separate bedrooms and full kitchens, perfect for longer stays or for families. Guests at both buildings get an in-room breakfast. The waterfront location is a 10- to 20-minute walk from downtown; the harbor ferry stops nearby.

308 Catherine St., Victoria, BC V9A 3S8. www.spinnakers.com. 📞 **877/838-2739** or 250/384-2739. 11 units. C$179–C$280 double. Rates include breakfast. AE, DC, MC, V. Free parking. Bus: 24 to Catherine St. **Amenities:** Brewpub. *In room:* TV, hair dryer, kitchen (some units), Wi-Fi.

Inexpensive

Admiral Inn 😊 🍴   The family-operated Admiral is in a three-story building on the Inner Harbour, near the Port Angeles–bound ferry terminal and close to restaurants and shopping. The combination of clean, comfortable rooms and reasonable rates attracts young couples, families, seniors, and other travelers in search of a harbor view at a moderate price. The rooms are pleasant and comfortably furnished, a bit motel-like, with small bathrooms and balconies or terraces. The more expensive rooms come with a kitchenette with a small fridge and stove. The suites come with full kitchens. Some units can sleep up to six (on two double beds and a double sofa bed). The owners provide sightseeing advice, as well as free bicycles, cots and cribs, free local calls, and free parking—a bonus anywhere near the city's core.

257 Belleville St., Victoria, BC V8V 1X1. www.admiralinnhotel.com. 📞 **888/823-6472** or tel/fax 250/388-6267. 33 units. C$150–C$230 double; C$140–C$230 suite. Third and additional adults C$15 each. Children 11 and under stay free in parent's room. Rates include continental breakfast. AE, DC, MC, V. Free parking. Pets allowed (C$15). Bus: 5 to Belleville and Government sts. **Amenities:** Complimentary bikes. *In room:* A/C, TV, hair dryer, kitchen/kitchenette, Wi-Fi.

Coast Victoria Harbourside Hotel & Marina ★ 🥢 With its harbor-side location, fine-dining restaurant, and amenities, this hotel is a really good value, giving it a special edge over all others in this price range. Spring for a Premium room on the 10th floor, and you'll be looking out over the Inner Harbour from a balcony. The rooms are not overly fancy, but they are comfortable and nicely appointed with contemporary decor; they all have balconies or sliding windows that open wide. The least expensive rooms have a city rather than water view. The **Blue Crab Bar & Grill** (p. 256) is one of Victoria's best seafood restaurants. The path in front of the hotel winds around the entire harbor; downtown is a 10-minute walk. Any day in the summer or on weekends year-round, you can take one of the little harbor ferries to the hotel's marina dock.

146 Kingston St., Victoria, BC V8V 1V4. www.coasthotels.com. 📞 **800/716-6199** or 250/360-1211. 132 units. C$150–C$220 double. AE, DC, MC, V. Free parking. Harbor ferry. **Amenities:** Restaurant; small exercise room; Jacuzzi; indoor-outdoor pool; marina; room service. *In room:* TV w/pay movies, fridge, hair dryer, Wi-Fi.

Days Inn on the Harbour This hotel across from the MV *Coho* ferry terminal on the Inner Harbour has small, motel-like rooms that aren't very distinguished but put you in a great location. Half the rooms face the Inner Harbour; the other half of the rooms have views of the nearby residential area. View rooms cost a little more. The rooms come with queen-size, king-size, or two double beds, and are outfitted with standard furnishings and step-up bathtubs. Eighteen rooms are equipped with kitchenettes. A small outdoor pool is in back, and a patio overlooking the harbor is in front.

427 Belleville St., Victoria, BC V8V 1X3. www.daysinnvictoria.com. 📞 **800/665-3024** or 250/386-3451. 71 units. C$125–C$175 double. Additional adult C$10. Children 11 and under stay free in parent's room. AE, DC, MC, V. Free parking. Bus: 5 to Belleville and Government sts. **Amenities:** Restaurant; bar; Jacuzzi; seasonal heated outdoor pool. *In room:* TV, hair dryer, kitchenettes (in some units), Wi-Fi.

Harbour Towers Hotel & Suites ★ ☺ Though this 12-story tower by the Inner Harbour has a few standard rooms, the one- and two-bedroom suites with fully equipped kitchens are a better value. In recent years, the hotel has added some great features, such as an impressively upscale lobby, a day spa, and an improved fitness center with indoor pool. The rooms also received a complete overhaul, but the traditional-looking decor, though comfy, is fairly mundane. Most units feature floor-to-ceiling windows opening onto private balconies, some with spectacular harbor views. The larger suites are great for families, and the gym has a kids' play area. Vic's Steakhouse attracts locals and visitors alike; it's always crammed with seniors and families, which is evidence of its value.

345 Quebec St., Victoria, BC V8V 1W4. www.harbourtowers.com. 📞 **800/663-5896** or 250/385-2405. 196 units. C$160–C$305 standard double or suite; C$400 penthouse suite. Additional adult C$19. Children 16 and under stay free in parent's room. AE, DC, MC, V. Underground parking C$12. Bus: 30 or 31 to Superior and Oswego sts. **Amenities:** Restaurant; bar; babysitting; fitness center; indoor pool; room service; sauna; spa. *In room:* TV w/pay movies, hair dryer, Wi-Fi.

Huntingdon Hotel and Suites ☺ 🥢 Set within a stone's throw of the Inner Harbour, the Huntingdon Hotel and the adjacent Gatsby Mansion Inn (owned by the same company) are set on a landscaped block with a courtyard, cafes, and shops. Built in 1981, the three-story Huntingdon is a pleasant low-key hotel that's particularly good if you're traveling with children. The standard rooms are fairly large, and all rooms come equipped with fridges. The prime rooms are the split-level gallery rooms or lofts on the third floor, which have a sitting room with TV, a pullout double bed on the ground floor, and a master bedroom (and second TV) upstairs; all sleep four comfortably; some accommodate six. Some units have fully equipped kitchens, but you have to pay an additional C$10 charge to use them.

330 Quebec St., Victoria, BC V8V 1W3. *(C)* **800/663-7557** or 250/381-3456. www.bellevillepark. com. 116 units. C$90–C$190 double; C$125–C$225 suite. AE, DC, MC, V. Parking C$5. Bus: 5, 28, or 30. **Amenities:** 2 restaurants; bar; Jacuzzi; room service; sauna, spa. *In room:* A/C (3rd-floor gallery suites only), TV, fridge, hair dryer, kitchen (in some units), Wi-Fi.

The James Bay Inn *⚲* The Inner Harbour/James Bay area isn't especially blessed with cheap digs, but this Edwardian manor on the edge of Beacon Hill Park is one of the few. Built in 1907, it still offers one of Victoria's best accommodations deals. The standard rooms in the main building of this four-story walk-up are small and simply furnished. The real bargains: the adjacent cottage and four suites located next door in a renovated heritage property. The two studios are on the small side but come with a full-size kitchen; the larger one-bedroom suites also feature a full kitchen, a bedroom with queen-size bed, and a separate living room area. The cottage is a fully furnished, two-bedroom house cater-cornered to the James Bay Inn. With space for eight people and a peak-season price of C$240, it's a steal.

270 Government St., Victoria, BC V8V 2L2. www.jamesbayinn.bc.ca. *(C)* **800/836-2649** or 250/ 384-7151. 45 units. C$125–C$225 double; C$145–C$240 cottage. Additional adult C$15. Children 16 and under stay free in parent's room. AE, MC, V. Free limited parking. Bus: 5 or 30 to Niagara St. **Amenities:** Restaurant; bar. *In room:* TV, hair dryer, Wi-Fi.

DOWNTOWN, OLD TOWN & NEARBY

BEST FOR: Getting a flavor of Victoria's neighborhoods without feeling totally overrun with tourists. Parking is usually free.

DRAWBACKS: Bearing in mind that Victoria isn't exactly a late-night city, some locations are near noisy pubs and on busy thoroughfares; many are a 10-minute walk to the city's core.

Expensive

Abigail's Hotel ★★ Located in a residential neighborhood just east of downtown, Abigail's began life in the 1920s as a luxury apartment house before being converted to a boutique hotel. If you like small, personalized bed-and-gourmet-breakfast hotels, you'll enjoy this impeccably maintained property. Everything is done well here, and the quality is high throughout. In the original building, some of the 16 rooms are bright and sunny, and beautifully furnished with pedestal sinks and goose-down duvets. Others feature soaker tubs and double-sided fireplaces, so you can relax in the tub by the light of the fire. The six Celebration Suites in the Coach House are even more luxurious; they have Italian-marble bathrooms with snazzy fixtures. There's also a tiny spa.

906 McClure St., Victoria, BC V8V 3E7. www.abigailshotel.com. *(C)* **800/561-6565** or 250/388-5363. 23 units. C$250–C$410 double. Rates include full breakfast. AE, MC, V. Free parking. Some pets accepted (C$25). Bus: 1 to Cook and McClure sts. **Amenities:** Concierge; lounge; spa. *In room:* A/C, TV/DVD player, hair dryer, Wi-Fi.

The Beaconsfield Inn ★ Built in 1905, this elegantly restored Edwardian mansion is located just a few blocks from Beacon Hill Park and the Inner Harbour. The inn features fir paneling, mahogany floors, antique furnishings, and stained-glass windows. The nine guest rooms are prettily decorated and filled with fresh flowers from the garden. Some suites have skylights and French doors that open onto the garden. For couples who want to get away from it all, book the cozy Beaconsfield Suite. Located on the third floor, this room has a four-poster canopy bed, a sitting area in front of a wood-burning fireplace, a jetted tub, and a window seat. A full hot breakfast is served in the sunroom or the dining room, and afternoon refreshments are served in the library. Children 12 and under, pets, and smoking are not permitted.

998 Humboldt St., Victoria, BC V8V 2Z8. www.beaconsfieldinn.com. ℂ **888/884-4044** or 250/384-4044. Fax 250/384-4052. 9 units. C$170–C$300 double. Rates include full breakfast, afternoon tea and sherry hour. AE, MC, V. Free parking. Bus: 1 or 2 to Humboldt and Quadra sts. Children 12 and under not allowed. **Amenities:** Access to nearby health club; Jacuzzi. *In room:* TV, Wi-Fi (free).

Isabella's Guest Suites ★ 👜 These two suites are a real find. Located above Willy's bakery, they provide affordable, fun, and surprisingly stylish accommodations in the heart of the city. The front suite is a large studio with a bed/sitting room that opens into a dining room and full kitchen. Bright colors and cheerful accents, upscale rustic furniture, high ceilings, large windows, and plenty of space make this a great home base for exploring Victoria. The second unit, a one-bedroom suite, overlooks the alley and patio of the hotel's restaurant, **Il Terrazzo** (p. 260). Both units have hardwood floors, funky furniture, king-size beds, and are nonsmoking. Rates include a $20 credit to breakfast or lunch in the bakery downstairs—Willy's being one of the best breakfast places in town. Parking is free, and you have your own entrance.

537 Johnson St., Victoria, BC V8W 1M2. www.isabellasbb.com. ℂ **250/812-9216.** 2 units. C$175–C$195 double. Rates include continental breakfast. MC, V. Free parking. Bus: 5. *In room:* A/C, TV, hair dryer, kitchen.

The Magnolia ★★ Celebrities and quasi celebs, such as Elton John's florist, love the discreet, European ambience of this centrally located hotel, which is all about luxe comfort at a reasonable price. Room decor manages to be traditional without feeling frumpy, with high-quality linens, down duvets, and quality furnishings. The large marble bathrooms feature walk-in showers and deep soaker tubs. The windows extend floor to ceiling, letting in lots of light, but the hotel really does not have any great views. For business travelers, there are large, well-lit work desks with high-speed Internet access. Local calls are complimentary. The Diamond Suites on the sixth and seventh floors feature a sitting room with fireplace. The hotel's steakhouse, **Prime** (p. 260), has since garnered many kudos, and the excellent, full-service Aveda concept spa is a destination unto itself.

623 Courtney St., Victoria, BC V8W 1B8. www.magnoliahotel.com. ℂ **877/624-6654** or 250/381-0999. 64 units. C$210–C$350 double. Rates include continental breakfast. Additional adult C$30. Children 11 and under stay free in parent's room. AE, DC, MC, V. Valet parking C$15. Small pets accepted (C$60). Bus: 5. **Amenities:** Restaurant; bar; concierge; executive-level rooms; access to nearby health club; room service; spa. *In room:* A/C, TV w/pay movies, fridge, hair dryer, minibar, MP3 docking station, Wi-Fi.

Swans Suite Hotel ★★ ☺ In 1988, this heritage building was turned into a hotel, restaurant, brewpub, and nightclub. Located near the Johnson Street

Bridge, it's just minutes from Bastion Square, Chinatown, and downtown. Like any good boutique hotel, Swans is small, friendly, and charming. The suites are large, and many are split-level, featuring open lofts and huge exposed beams. All come with fully equipped kitchens, dining areas, living rooms, queen-size beds, and original artwork. The two-bedroom suites are like little town houses; they're great for families, accommodating up to six comfortably. Swan's Brewpub is one of the most popular in the city and features nightly entertainment. The one potential drawback to this otherwise fine hotel is that a homeless shelter is located across the street.

506 Pandora St., Victoria, BC V8W 1N6. www.swanshotel.com. 📞 **800/668-7926** or 250/361-331030 units. C$200 studio; C$290–C$360 suite. Weekly and monthly rates available. Additional adult C$35. Up to 2 children 12 and under stay free in parent's room. AE, DC, MC, V. Parking C$9. Bus: 23 or 24 to Pandora Ave. **Amenities:** Restaurant; wine bar; brewpub; babysitting; access to nearby health club; room service. *In room:* TV, hair dryer, kitchen, Wi-Fi.

The Victoria Regent Hotel ☺ An outside upgrade freshened the exterior of this hotel, which sits right on the Inner Harbour, closer to the water than any other hotel in Victoria. Rooms are fairly large and comfortable, though the decor is not very inspired. The 10 large one-bedroom suites feature king-size beds, small balconies (with big views), and standard serviceable bathrooms. The 35 two-bedroom suites have larger bathrooms and great views of the harbor (you're right on it). All the suites have full kitchens, so the hotel is popular with families. Rates include a good continental breakfast.

1234 Wharf St., Victoria, BC V8W 3H9. www.victoriaregent.com. 📞 **800/663-7472** or 250/386-2211. 45 units. C$210 double; C$290–C$450 suite. Additional adult C$20. Rates include continental breakfast. Children 15 and under stay free in parent's room. AE, DC, DISC, MC, V. Free underground parking. Bus: 6, 24, or 25 to Wharf St. **Amenities:** Restaurant; babysitting; concierge; access to nearby health club. *In room:* TV/DVD player, CD player, hair dryer, minibar, Wi-Fi.

Villa Marco Polo ★★★ With the Lieutenant Governor's residence in the neighborhood, you know this place has got to be classy. More than that, everything about this Italian Renaissance mansion is true to its well-traveled namesake whether it's the Chinese antiquities in the lounge, the handmade books in the library, or the Italian crystal chandelier in the dining room. Each room is themed to a country: Zanzibar, Turkey, Persia, and the Silk Road with enchanting, hand-painted Tuscan murals. The loft is a tiny spa and yoga retreat overlooking ornamental gardens. Rates include afternoon tea, early evening hors d'oeuvres, and breakfast that is a veritable feast.

1524 Shasta Place, Victoria, BC V8S 1X9. www.villamarcopolo.com. 📞 **877/601-1524** or 250/370-1524. 4 units. C$295–C$355 double. Rates include breakfast, afternoon tea, and hors d'oeuvres. 2-night minimum July and Aug. AE, MC, V. Free parking. **Amenities:** Lounge; spa. *In room:* TV/CD/DVD player, hair dryer, MP3 docking station, Wi-Fi.

Moderate

Abbeymoore Manor Inn ★★ 📷 This impressive 1912 mansion is in Rockland, an area of "Old Victoria" where grand homes were built by Victoria's elite. It's one of the best B&Bs you'll find, with large, attractive rooms, lots of period antiques and finishes, and an overall charm that's hard to beat. All the rooms are individually decorated and have private bathrooms and beds fitted with fine linens. Two ground-floor garden suites have separate entrances and fully equipped kitchens; the penthouse suite has views of the ocean. A delicious gourmet breakfast is served, and complimentary beverages are available throughout the day.

1470 Rockland Ave., Victoria, BC V8S 1W2. www.abbeymoore.com. ☏ **888/801-1811** or 250/370-1470. 7 units. C$190–C$240 double; C$219–C$240 suite. Additional adult C$40. Rates include full breakfast. MC, V. Free street parking. Bus: 11 or 14. Children 12 and under not accepted. **Amenities:** Lounge; CD/DVD library. *In room:* TV (in suites), CD/DVD player, MP3 docking station, Wi-Fi.

Best Western Carlton Plaza ☺   In the heart of Victoria's shopping and entertainment district, the Best Western Carlton is ideally located for those who like to step right into the hustle and bustle of downtown. Rooms are comfortably furnished. Almost half the units come with a fully equipped kitchen, and even the standard rooms are pretty large. Perfect for families, the junior suites have two double beds, a sitting area with a pullout couch, a dining-room table, and full kitchen. The Best Western prides itself on being a child-friendly hotel, and pets are also welcome. There's an onsite fitness center, although the hotel's complimentary bikes make for a better option, especially as you'll be able to explore Victoria with pedal power. If this Best Western is full, try for the **Best Western Plus** (☏ **888/383-2378**) near the Parliament Buildings.

642 Johnson St., Victoria, BC V8W 1M6. www.bestwesterncarlton.com. ☏ **800/663-7241** or 250/388-5513. 103 units. C$115–C$200 double; C$155–C$250 suite. Additional adult C$20. Children 17 and under stay free in parent's room. Small pets welcome (C$10). AE, MC, V. Free parking winter; May–Oct C$9. Bus: 5 to Douglas and Johnson sts. **Amenities:** Restaurant; concierge; bicycles (free); exercise room; room service. *In room:* A/C, TV w/pay movies, hair dryer, Wi-Fi.

Chateau Victoria Hotel 🏊   This 18-story hotel was built in 1975 as a high-rise apartment building, so the hotel's rooms and one-bedroom suites are unusually spacious; many suites have kitchenettes, and all have balconies. Prices are higher for the 5th through 15th floors, where the views are better; if you can, get one of the corner 09 rooms with windows on two sides. Thankfully, the hotel has finally shed its '70s look with more up-to-date decor and has been hyping up its image by being the locale for Clives Classic Lounge—*the* place for new and happening cocktails. The Vista 18 Rooftop Lounge still has a '70s vibe, though, but with one of the best views of downtown Victoria, it's barely noticeable.

740 Burdett Ave., Victoria, BC V8W 1B2. www.chateauvictoria.com. ☏ **800/663-5891** or 250/382-4221. 177 units. C$129–C$185 double; C$135–C$289 suite. Children 18 and under stay free in parent's room. AE, DC, DISC, MC, V. Free parking. Bus: 2 to Burdett Ave. **Amenities:** Rooftop restaurant; bar; babysitting; concierge; small exercise room; Jacuzzi; indoor pool; room service. *In room:* A/C, TV w/pay movies, fridge, hair dryer, Internet (free).

Dashwood Manor ★   Overlooking the bluff of the Pacific Ocean at the edge of Beacon Hill Park, this lovely old Elizabethan-style, half-timbered manor is a landmark heritage property. Upgrades have turned it into a comfortable, but far from pretentious, inn with large, bright rooms appointed with carefully chosen furniture and wood-paneled walls. Bathrooms have been updated with new tile and fixtures, including deep-jetted tubs, and several of the rooms have large Jacuzzis. All of the rooms offer excellent ocean views; some have balconies. Complimentary sherry, port, and wine are laid out in the lobby in the evenings; a gourmet breakfast is served each morning, including a stash of extra home-baked cookies or muffins to take on the road.

1 Cook St., Victoria, BC V8V 3W6. www.dashwoodmanor.com. ☏ **800/667-5517** or 250/385-5517. 11 units. C$169–C$279 suite. Additional adults C$45. Children 11 and under not accepted.

Rates include breakfast. MC, V. Free parking. Bus: 5 to Dallas Rd. and Cook St. **Amenities:** Lounge. *In room:* TV/DVD player, hair dryer, Wi-Fi.

Hotel Rialto Like a phoenix from the ashes, the Rialto has risen out of a has-been hotel to become the city's hippest new boutique hotel. Rooms are modern with dark wood furnishings, granite countertops, an in-room wine bar, flatscreen plasma TVs, and superior queen- or king-size beds. It's in the heart of downtown's busiest commercial district so if you like to shop 'til you drop, this is your spot. Especially at Veneto Tapas Lounge, the *in* gathering place for local trendies. Hotel Rialto is named after the famous Rialto Bridge in Venice, and the widespread use of marble throughout the lobby and dining areas are typical of northern Italy, though most of this marble is quarried locally.

653 Pandora Ave., Victoria, BC V8W 1N8. www.hotelrialto.ca. © **800/332-9981.** 39 units. C$165–C$229 double. Additional adult C$25. Children 11 and under stay free in parent's room. AE, MC, V. Parking C$10. **Amenities:** Restaurant; bar. *In room:* TV w/pay movies, DVD player, fridge, hair dryer, MP3 docking station, Wi-Fi.

Victoria Marriott Inner Harbour The Marriott is a high-rise hotel with lots of marble in the lobby, and all the usual Marriott amenities, including an added-price concierge level that offers a pleasant lounge with breakfast and evening hors d'oeuvres. But there isn't a whole lot of personality. The rooms are nice enough, especially the concierge-level suites on the 16th floor, but decor is somewhat indefinable and doesn't convey much beyond a cookie-cutter corporate aesthetic. The hotel has a good workout room and a nice big indoor pool, and the service here is friendly and efficient. If you're a fan of Marriott, you'll find it all to your liking.

728 Humboldt St., Victoria, BC V8W 3Z5. www.marriottvictoria.com. © **866/306-5451** or 250/480-3800. 236 units. C$130–C$300 double. AE, DC, MC, V. Valet parking C$20, or self-parking C$16. Bus: 2 to the Convention Center. **Amenities:** Restaurant; lounge; babysitting; executive-level and concierge-level rooms; health club; Jacuzzi; indoor pool; room service; sauna. *In room:* A/C, TV, fridge, hair dryer, minibar, Wi-Fi.

Inexpensive

The Bedford Regency Hotel 🗲 If you're looking for a budget hotel right smack-dab in the middle of downtown, this heritage property is it. The Bedford Regency occupies the oldest building in Victoria (dating from 1869); it's not glamorous, but it's well maintained and has some surprising features, such as wood-burning fireplaces, harbor views, and spa-type bathrooms in the Superior rooms. The furnishings here are decidedly old-fashioned, but not without a certain charm. Caffè Artigiano (a favorite coffee bar chain in Vancouver and Victoria; p. 262) operates next door, and the hotel also houses Garrick's Head, the oldest pub in Victoria, where pub food and microbrews are served.

1140 Government St., Victoria, BC V8W 1Y2. www.bedfordregency.com. © **800/665-6500** or 250/384-6835. 49 units. C$170–C$230 double. AE, MC, V. Parking C$10. Bus 5 to Douglas and Johnson sts. **Amenities:** Coffee bar; lounge; pub. *In room:* A/C, TV, fridge, Wi-Fi.

Ocean Island Backpackers Inn ★ 🗲 All sorts of travelers make their way to this inexpensive, centrally located hostel (an alternative to the Hostelling International network), from families with children to on-the-go seniors and young adults with global wanderlust. The big, comfy lounge/common area always has all kinds of stuff going on, including live music and open-mic evenings. You can buy cheap meals and snacks, use the kitchen, or kick back with a beer or glass of wine. In addition to the dorm rooms, there are 60 private rooms, in various configurations, including some with their own bathrooms. The staff here goes out of its way to help guests make the most of their time in Victoria and on Vancouver Island, including arranging day trips to out-of-the-ordinary places.

791 Pandora Ave., Victoria, BC V8W 1N9. www.oceanisland.com. 🕾 **888/888-4180** or 250/385-1788. 50 units. C$20–C$29 dorm bed; C$28–C$86 private room (some with private bathroom). MC, V. Parking C$8. Bus: 70 to Pandora Ave. and Douglas St. **Amenities:** Restaurant; lounge. *In room:* TV (in some rooms), Wi-Fi (C$3/hr.).

Paul's Motor Inn 🐾 Sometimes nothing but an inexpensive motor inn or motel will do, and that's where Paul's comes in. It's been around for ages, it's very well maintained, and it's within a 15-minute walking distance to downtown. The rooms are pleasant for what they are and much nicer than those in many motel chains. The staff here is friendly and helpful, and there's an above-average restaurant. Clean and cheerful all around.

1900 Douglas St., Victoria, BC V8T 4K8. www.paulsmotorinn.com. 🕾 **866/333-7285** or 250/382-9231. 75 units. C$69–C$124 double. AE, DISC, MC, V. Free parking. Bus: 30 to Douglas and Chatham sts. **Amenities:** Restaurant. *In room:* TV, fridge, Wi-Fi.

OUTSIDE THE CENTRAL AREA

BEST FOR: Relaxing away from the downtown core. These surprisingly easy-to-reach urban escapes that feel like another world. Getting there is half the fun.

DRAWBACKS: With effort, transit will get you there but you really need a car to reach these out-of-the-way locales.

Expensive

The Boathouse ★★★ 🎁 Vancouver Island has nothing else like it, and it's almost guaranteed that you'll fall in love with this tiny, secluded cottage—a former boathouse—set on pilings over Saanich Inlet on Brentwood Bay. The only passersby you're likely to encounter are seals, bald eagles, otters, herons, and raccoons, plus the occasional floatplane flying in. The converted boathouse is at the end of a very long flight of stairs (if you have mobility issues, this is not the place for you). Outside, there's a waterside porch you may never want to leave; inside are a queen-size bed, a dining table, a kitchen area with a small refrigerator and toaster oven, an electric heater, and a reading alcove. Toilet and shower facilities are in a separate bathhouse, 17 steps back uphill. A small dinghy is reserved exclusively for guests' use. It's wonderful.

746 Sea Dr., Brentwood Bay, Victoria, BC V8M 1B1. www.accommodationsbc.com/boathouse. html. 🕾 **866/654-9370** or 250/652-9370. 1 unit. C$250 double with continental breakfast; C$215 double without breakfast. 2-night minimum. AE, MC, V. Free parking. Closed Oct–Feb. Bus: 75 to Wallace Dr. and Benvenuto Ave. Children 17 and under not allowed. No pets. *In room:* Fridge, hair dryer, Wi-Fi (free).

Brentwood Bay Lodge & Spa ★★★ 🎁 Located on a pristine inlet about 20 minutes north of downtown Victoria, this West Coast timber-and-glass lodge offers the best of everything, including a fabulous spa, boat shuttle to Butchart Gardens, and all manner of eco-adventures, including kayaking, scuba diving, fishing, and boat trips through the surrounding waters. The rooms are beautifully outfitted with handcrafted furnishings, gas fireplaces, luxurious bathrooms with soaker tubs and body massage showers, balconies, and king size beds fitted with the highest quality Italian linens. The **SeaGrille** dining room and pub (p. 265) offers fine seasonal menus and great pub food. The hotel has its own marina and is a licensed PADI (Professional Association of Diving Instructors) dive center—the fjord on which it sits is considered one of the best diving spots in the world.

849 Verdier Ave. on Brentwood Bay, Victoria, BC V8M 1C5. www.brentwoodbaylodge.com. ℂ **888/544-2079** or 250/544-2079. 39 units. C$330–C$360 double; C$590 suite. AE, MC, V. Free parking. Take Pat Bay Hwy. north to Keating Crossroads, turn left (west) to Saanich Rd., turn right (south) to Verdier Ave. **Amenities:** Restaurant; pub; concierge; Jacuzzi; heated outdoor pool; room service; spa. *In room:* A/C, TV/DVD player, fridge, hair dryer, minibar, MP3 docking station, Wi-Fi.

Poets Cove Resort & Spa ★   To reach Pender Island, one of the Gulf Islands between the mainland and Vancouver Island, you have to take a ferry or water taxi from Sidney, north of Victoria; you can also skipper your own boat and dock it at the 110-slip marina (with a Customs clearance checkpoint). Overlooking Bedwell Harbour and its own marina, Poets Cove comprises a 22-room lodge with 15 seaside cottages and 9 villas, all built with a contemporary Craftsman-style Pacific Northwest look and ambience. All the accommodations feature ocean or forest-and-water views, fireplaces, big bathtubs for soaking, and all the amenities of an upscale resort. You can dine on fresh Pacific Northwest cuisine at the Aurora Restaurant in the lodge, or enjoy snacks and comfort food in the lounge. Susurrus Spa offers tons of relaxation and aesthetic treatments, including those for couples.

9801 Spalding Rd., Pender Island, BC V0N 2M3. www.poetscove.com. ℂ **888/512-7638** or 250/629-2100. 22 lodge units, 9 villas, 15 cottages. C$190–C$300 double in lodge; C$240–C$530 villa; C$359–C$699 cottage. Children 17 and under stay free in parent's room. AE, DC, MC, V. Free parking. Pets accepted (C$50 per stay). Ferry from Sidney to Pender Island (www.bcferries.com), then take Island Hwy. from the ferry terminal. **Amenities:** Restaurant; pub; concierge; eco-adventure tours; fitness center; 2 hot tubs (seasonal); 2 heated outdoor pools (seasonal); 2 tennis courts, spa. *In room:* TV/DVD/CD player, player, fridge, hair dryer, kitchen (in villas and cottages), Wi-Fi.

Sidney Pier Hotel & Spa ★★ ☺ ⛨   This seaside boutique hotel has brought a splash of stylish (but low-key) glamour to Sidney's waterfront. (The Vancouver and Anacortes ferry terminals are less than 5 min. away.) The guest rooms are well designed and comfortable, with calm, minimalist interiors and a refreshing lack of froufrou. Most of the rooms have ocean views; the suites have balconies and fireplaces, and connect with adjoining rooms, making them very family-friendly. Bathrooms are equally well designed, some with showers only, others with soaker tubs and walk-in showers. Haro's, the hotel's restaurant, serves fresh area specialties, including salads, fish, and lamb. At Haven Spa, all manner of rejuvenating and refreshing treatments are available.

9805 Seaport Place, Sidney, BC V8L 4X3. www.sidneypier.com. ℂ **866/659-9445** or 250/655-9445. 55 units. C$180–C$250 double; C$260–C$490 suite. AE, MC, V. Underground parking C$5. Pets accepted (C$30) one-time charge plus C$15/night. From Victoria, drive north on Patricia Bay Hwy. (Hwy. 17) to Sidney, turn right (east) on Beacon Ave. and continue toward the waterfront; turn left (north) on Seaport Place. **Amenities:** 2 restaurants; bar; airport shuttle; concierge; small fitness center; spa. *In room:* A/C, TV/DVD player, fridge, hair dryer, kitchen (in suites), Wi-Fi.

Sooke Harbour House ★★★   This artsy, distinctive inn, located right on the ocean at the end of a sand spit about 30km (19 miles) west of Victoria, has earned an international reputation for its sumptuous rooms, each furnished and decorated according to a particular Northwest theme, and its outstanding restaurant (p. 266), which makes use of fragrant herbs and edible flowers from the inn's magnificent seaside gardens. Thanks to some clever architecture, all the rooms are awash in natural light and have fabulous ocean views. All have wood-burning fireplaces and sitting areas, and most have sun decks and Jacuzzis or soaker tubs. Breakfast (served in your room) is included in the room rate. It's also very eco-conscious, incorporating many green practices into the business, such as water reclamation and composting programs long before green was vogue.

1528 Whiffen Spit Rd., Sooke, BC V9Z 0T4. www.sookeharbourhouse.com. © **800/889-9688** or 250/642-3421. 28 units. C$400–C$600 double. Rates include full breakfast. MC, V. Free parking. Take the Island Hwy. (Hwy. 1) to the Sooke/Colwood turnoff (junction Hwy. 14); follow Hwy. 14 to Sooke; about 1.6km (1 mile) past the town's only traffic light, turn left onto Whiffen Spit Rd. **Amenities:** Restaurant; babysitting; nearby golf course; access to nearby health club; room service; sauna; spa. *In room:* CD player, fridge, hair dryer, minibar, Wi-Fi.

Westin Bear Mountain Victoria Golf Resort & Spa ★★★   This resort hotel sits between two, 18-hole mountaintop golf courses designed by Jack Nicklaus and his son. Part of a high-end resort-community development covering some 486 hectares (1,201 acres), the hotel is big and handsomely crafted, with fine natural finishes of wood and stone, and the overall ambience of a giant west coast mountain lodge. Rooms (in two separate buildings) are spacious, well designed, and furnished in a way that's both luxurious and comfortable; each has a balcony. The extra-large bathrooms feature soaker tubs and separate showers. The gym is the best on Vancouver Island, as is the Sante Spa. Dining options include the Copper Rock Grill, open for breakfast, lunch, and dinner, and the more exclusive Panache, with its gallery kitchen serving both traditional and fusion-inspired fare.

1999 Country Club Way, Victoria, BC V9B 6R3. www.bearmountain.ca. © **888/533-2327** or 250/391-7160. 156 units. C$230–C$460 double. Additional adult C$30. AE, MC, V. Resort fee (C$15) includes parking, Wi-Fi, fitness club access, golf bag valet, and storage. Take the Island Hwy. (Hwy. 1) to exit 14, then take Millstream Rd. to Bear Mountain Pkwy. and follow the signs. **Amenities:** 4 restaurants; sports bar; 2 golf courses; driving range; health club; room service; saltwater pool; spa; mountain-bike rentals; *In room:* TV w/pay movies, hair dryer, kitchen, Wi-Fi

Moderate

Birds of a Feather Oceanfront Bed & Breakfast   Located on an ocean-front lagoon 20 minutes west of Victoria, this quiet, eco-friendly B&B run by birding enthusiasts so is super for fellow bird-watchers and nature lovers. The lagoon is on the Pacific Flyway and attracts thousands of migratory birds and other wildlife. The three guest rooms, in their own separate wing, are furnished with Arts and Crafts–styled beds and comfy leather chairs; they all have a good-size bathroom, kitchen, gas fireplace, and patio area with views of the water. The Honeymoon Suite is flooded with light on two sides; the family room has two levels with a spiral staircase.

206 Portsmouth Dr., Victoria, BC V9C 1R9. www.victorialodging.com. © **800/730-4790** or 250/391-8889. 3 units. C$165–C$215 double. Rates include full breakfast. AE, MC, V. From Victoria, take Hwy. 1 to exit 10 (Colwood/View Royal), turn left on Ocean Blvd., right on Lagoon Rd., right on Heatherbell Rd., and right on Portsmouth Dr. **Amenities:** Complimentary bikes; complimentary canoes and kayaks. *In room:* TV/DVD player, hair dryer, kitchen, Wi-Fi.

Inexpensive

Point-No-Point Resort ★ 🎁 Away from it all in your own snug cabin, you'll have 16 hectares (40 acres) of wilderness around you and a wide rugged beach in front of you, with nothing to do but laze away the day in your hot tub. Or stroll along the beach. Or roam in the forest. Or watch the flight of an eagle. This oceanfront resort has been welcoming guests since 1950. Cabins vary, depending on when they were built. All have fireplaces, full kitchens, and bathrooms; newer ones have hot tubs on their private decks. Lunch and afternoon tea are available daily in the small, sunny central dining room. Dinner is served Wednesday through Sunday. The dining room tables are conveniently equipped with binoculars, so you won't miss a bald eagle as you dine.

10829 West Coast Rd., Shirley, BC V9Z 1G9. www.pointnopointresort.com. ✆ **250/646-2020.** Fax 250/646-2294. 25 units. C$180–C$280 cabin. 2-night minimum stay on weekends; 3-night minimum stay July and Aug holiday weekends and Christmas holidays. Small pets accepted (C$10). AE, MC, V. Free parking. No public transit. Take Hwy. 14 to exit 10 (Sooke); resort is 20 min. past Sooke. **Amenities:** Restaurant; Jacuzzi. *In room:* Kitchen, no phone, Wi-Fi.

PRACTICAL INFORMATION
The Big Picture

Victoria has been welcoming visitors and adventurers for more than a century, so it knows how to do so with style. You'll find most of the accommodations downtown, Old Town, and the Inner Harbour. However, if you choose to stay farther afield, a half-hour drive takes you to all manner of marvelous resorts and inns, some on the ocean, some next to quiet bays and harbors, and some perched on mountaintops.

Getting the Best Deal

Hotels in Victoria fill up during the high season (June–Sept), with rates in the city fluctuating with the seasons. Most properties offer package deals outside the busy season; these are usually advertised on hotel websites. Spas are now an almost essential part of big hotels in Victoria—so much so that the Inner Harbour has been dubbed Spa Harbour, with major spas at the Fairmont Empress, the Delta Ocean Pointe, the Hotel Grand Pacific, the Magnolia, and others throughout the city. Be sure to check the hotel websites for special packages, and promotional or seasonal rates cheaper than the summer rack rates listed here.

Reservation Services

You'll save big time if you schedule your holiday from October to May. When the high summer season starts in June, rates tend to skyrocket, especially at the finer hotels. Reservations are essential in Victoria June through September. If you arrive without a reservation and have trouble finding a room, **Tourism Victoria** (✆ **800/663-3883** or 250/953-2033; www.tourismvictoria.com) can make reservations for you at hotels, inns, and B&Bs.

Alternative Accommodations

The majority of properties listed in this chapter are hotels and bed-and-breakfasts. Bed-and-breakfasts especially can vary widely (from fussy frills to sleek and urban) and can be ideal for leisure travelers. For a list of quality local accommodations, check out the **BC Bed & Breakfast Innkeepers Guild** (www.bcsbestbnbs.com).

WHERE TO EAT IN VICTORIA

14

V ictoria has jumped on the foodie bandwagon and offers a cornucopia of culinary styles from around the world. With its strong "eat local" ethos—more so than in Vancouver—Victoria's 700 restaurants offer fresh creativity for every taste and wallet.

BEST VICTORIA DINING BETS

- **Best Spot for a Romantic Dinner: Camille's** offers a quiet, intimate, candlelit room and a wine list with a bottle or glass for every occasion. See p. 260.

- **Best Pacific Northwest:** Much of the menu at **Sooke Harbour House** is picked fresh from the adjacent garden, a treasure-trove of edible beauty. You'll find unique seasonal flavors, inventive cooking, and a superlative wine cellar. See p. 266.

- **Best Local Crowd: Café Brio,** one of Victoria's top dining spots, is a consistent local fave. See p. 259. **Superior,** though, is a strong contender. See p. 258.

- **Best for Kids: rebar** offers large portions, terrific quality, and a funky laid-back atmosphere. See p. 263.

- **Best Burgers & Beer: Six Mile Pub** offers 10 house brews, juicy burgers (even veggie burgers), and loads of British pub-style atmosphere. See p. 267.

- **Best Afternoon or High Tea:** How can you brag about your trip to Victoria if you don't include tea at the **Fairmont Empress?** It's more than a tradition—it's a legendary experience and the closest you'll come to reliving a bygone era, albeit as a mass-production. See p. 261.

- **Best Patio:** Located on the waterfront walkway between the Inner Harbour and Fisherman's Wharf, the views, food, and martinis make **Aura** a must-stop. See p. 256.

- **Best Steaks: Prime Steakhouse & Lounge,** in the Magnolia Hotel, serves up the best steaks and prime rib in the city. See p. 260.

- **Best Small Plates: Stage,** an always busy bistro in the Fernwood neighborhood, serves a full menu of small plates that are big on taste. See p. 265.

- **Best Pizza: Pizzeria Prima Strada** delivers authentic Neapolitan, wood-fired pizzas in a stylish bistro atmosphere. A second location is at 2960 Bridge St. See p. 264.

- **Best Eco-Eats:** At the busy take-out stand at **Red Fish/Blue Fish,** the seafood is delicious and comes only from sustainable sources, and every plate and container is biodegradable and/or recyclable. It even has a rooftop garden. See p. 259.

WHERE TO EAT IN VICTORIA

Best Victoria Dining Bets

PREVIOUS PAGE: The Blue Crab Bar & Grill is one of Victoria's best bets for seafood.

255

price CATEGORIES

Very Expensive	Entrees C$30 and up
Expensive	C$20–C$29
Moderate	C$12–C$19
Inexpensive	Under C$12

- **Best Take-Out: Foo** puts gourmet Asian-inspired cuisine into a take-away box. Exotic. Delicious. And street-wise. See p. 258.
- **Best Hang-Out for Under-30s:** With its busy Bastion Square location, views of the Inner Harbour, great beers and cocktails, and casual menu, **The Local Kitchen** draws a big crowd, especially on warm days, when you can sit outside at a sidewalk table. See p. 259.

THE INNER HARBOUR

Expensive

Aura Restaurant REGIONAL   World Culinary Olympic chefs make this place sizzle with terrific food, artisan wines, and dishes that earn kudos from local foodies. Lunch favorites include a snow crab quesadilla, while dinner highlights such creations as a sour cherry glazed duck breast served with cauliflower ricotta gnocchi. Every item has a recommended wine pairing, so it's a real opportunity to educate and titillate the palate. Aura's contemporary style includes floor-to-ceiling windows, through which you can take in breathtaking harbor views. The patio's one of the best in the city; located on the waterfront path between downtown and Fisherman's Wharf, Aura is a perfect stop-off point to savor much of what Victoria has to offer.

In the Inn at Laurel Point (p. 240), 680 Montreal St. ℂ **250/414-6739.** www.aurarestaurant.ca. Reservations recommended. Main courses lunch C$12–C$18, dinner C$26–C$32. AE, DC, MC, V. Daily 7am–10pm.

The Blue Crab Bar and Grill ★★★ SEAFOOD   One of Victoria's best bets for seafood, the Blue Crab combines excellent fresh ingredients and a fairly uncomplicated preparation. Sitting right on the Inner Harbour, it has a wonderful view across the water. Like other top-end restaurants in town, the Crab sources most of its ingredients locally, and it's a member of Ocean Wise, a group dedicated to sustainable fishing practices. For lunch, tuck in to Pacific seafood chowder or a grilled arctic char sandwich; at dinner, try the fresh oysters, a Cortes Island clam and mussel pot, fresh halibut with pasta, or the signature hot pot of local seafood prepared with ginger and lemon grass broth. The award-winning wine list (several *Wine Spectator* Awards of Excellence) features midrange and top-end vintages, drawn mostly from BC, Washington, and California. The service is deft and obliging.

In the Coast Victoria Harbourside Hotel (p. 244), 146 Kingston St. ℂ **250/480-1999.** www.bluecrab.ca. Reservations recommended. Main courses lunch C$12–C$25, dinner C$20–C$35. AE, DC, MC, V. Daily 6:30am–10pm.

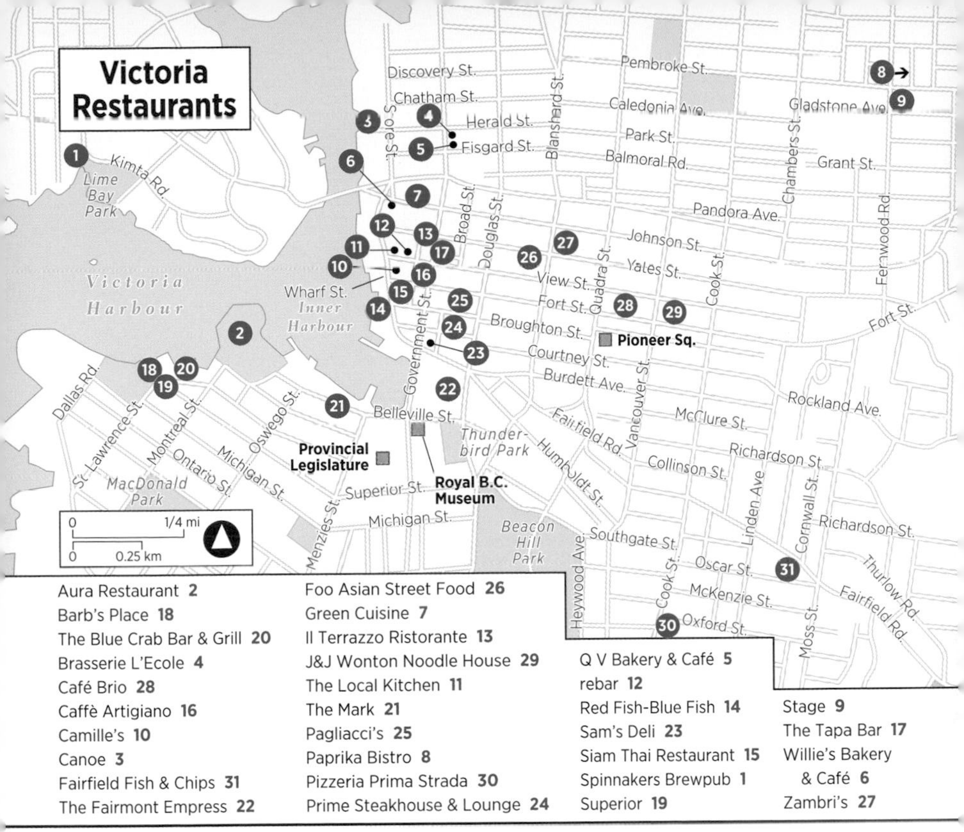
Victoria Restaurants
Discovery St.
Chatham St.
Herald St.
Fisgard St.
Store St.
Blanshard St.
Pembroke St.
Caledonia Ave.
Park St.
Balmoral Rd.
Gladstone Ave.
Grant St.
Chambers St.
Pandora Ave.
Fernwood Rd.
Johnson St.
Yates St.
View St.
Fort St.
Broughton St.
Courtney St.
Burdett Ave.
Broad St.
Douglas St.
Quadra St.
Cook St.
Pioneer Sq.
Kimta Rd.
Lime Bay Park
Victoria Harbour
Wharf St.
Inner Harbour
Government St.
Belleville St.
Dallas Rd.
St. Lawrence St.
Montreal St.
Ontario St.
Michigan St.
Oswego St.
MacDonald Park
Provincial Legislature
Thunderbird Park
Royal B.C. Museum
Superior St.
Michigan St.
Menzies St.
Fairfield Rd.
Humboldt St.
Vancouver St.
McClure St.
Rockland Ave.
Richardson St.
Collinson St.
Linden Ave.
Cornwall St.
Beacon Hill Park
Heywood Ave.
Southgate St.
Oscar St.
McKenzie St.
Oxford St.
Moss St.
Thurlow Rd.
Fairfield Rd.
0 1/4 mi
0 0.25 km
Aura Restaurant 2
Barb's Place 18
The Blue Crab Bar & Grill 20
Brasserie L'Ecole 4
Café Brio 28
Caffè Artigiano 16
Camille's 10
Canoe 3
Fairfield Fish & Chips 31
The Fairmont Empress 22
Foo Asian Street Food 26
Green Cuisine 7
Il Terrazzo Ristorante 13
J&J Wonton Noodle House 29
The Local Kitchen 11
The Mark 21
Pagliacci's 25
Paprika Bistro 8
Pizzeria Prima Strada 30
Prime Steakhouse & Lounge 24
Q V Bakery & Café 5
rebar 12
Red Fish-Blue Fish 14
Sam's Deli 23
Siam Thai Restaurant 15
Spinnakers Brewpub 1
Superior 19
Stage 9
The Tapa Bar 17
Willie's Bakery & Café 6
Zambri's 27

The Mark ★★ PACIFIC NORTHWEST The fine dining room at the Hotel Grand Pacific (p. 240) is a small, candlelit haven. Here, you can enjoy highly personalized service, delicious food prepared with locally grown ingredients, and fine wines chosen by an astute sommelier. To sample the best of everything, try the seasonal tasting menu, priced at C$70, or C$110 with wine pairings. The menu might start with Kushi oysters and poached Qualicum Bay scallops, and continue with basil-scented squab breast followed by loin of venison with cannellini bean gnocchi. The hotel's casual **Pacific Restaurant** is a good choice for lunch or dinner, with nicely done dishes such as west coast–seafood linguine, vegetarian pizzas, and high-quality steak and lamb. The Pacific has a great outdoor patio overlooking the harbor.

In the Hotel Grand Pacific, 463 Belleville St. ✆ **250/380-4487.** www.themark.ca. Reservations required for the Mark, recommended for Pacific Restaurant. The Mark main courses C$30–C$43; Pacific Restaurant main courses C$16–C$30. AE, DC, MC, V. The Mark daily 5–9:30pm; Pacific Restaurant daily 6:30am–10pm.

Moderate

Canoe ★ PUB FARE/PACIFIC NORTHWEST What was once a Victorian power station is now one of Victoria's loveliest and liveliest brewpub restaurants, with an outdoor patio overlooking the harbor toward the Johnson Street Bridge and an industrial-inspired interior with massive masonry walls and heavy timber crossbeams. Canoe is popular because it has something tasty for every palate, all made with local ingredients whenever possible. The kitchen offers intriguing variations on standard pub fare and bar snacks, including thin-crust pizzas, classic burgers, and their signature potpie. Head upstairs for finer fare such as premium top sirloin steak, seafood curry, or the day's fresh fish. The beer is excellent, and the award-winning wine list is small but select. A gluten-free menu is available.

450 Swift St. ℭ **250/361-1940.** www.canoebrewpub.com. Reservations recommended for weekend dinner and Sun brunch. Main courses C$13–C$26; pub fare and bar snacks C$9–C$17; lunch special C$12. AE, MC, V. Sun–Wed 11:30am–11pm; Thurs 11:30am–midnight; Fri–Sat 11:30am–1am.

Spinnakers Brewpub PUB FARE/PACIFIC NORTHWEST   Spinnakers is Canada's oldest, licensed brewpub, and has always been at the forefront of crafting rich ales, stouts, and lagers, all of which are brewed on premises. The cuisine has changed over the years and evolved into above-average gastro-pub fare with some adventurous fresh west coast seafood, all served in a fun, bustling pub atmosphere with great Inner Harbour views. It's hard to go wrong with the burgers, steamed mussels, or fish and chips.

308 Catherine St. ℭ **250/384-2739.** www.spinnakers.com. Main courses C$7–C$20. AE, MC, V. Daily 11am–11pm.

Superior ★★ 🏠 BISTRO   Located in a residential neighborhood, Superior sits a block from the water, a spot tourists tend to bypass. The restaurant has a comfortable and slightly quirky vibe, with its blend of surrealist art and antiques; you can sit inside near the fireplace or outside on the lovely, two-level brick patio. Menu items include traditional chicken potpie, charcuterie, and grilled salmon atop a Caesar salad. The entertainment changes nightly, from jazz to R&B. On Friday and Saturday nights, non-diners can expect a cover charge after 7:30pm; on other nights, a bucket is passed, New Orleans–style.

106 Superior St. ℭ **250/380-9515.** Reservations recommended. Main courses C$11–C$17. MC, V. Tues–Sun 11am–3pm and 5–11pm. Closed Mon.

Inexpensive

Barb's Place ☺ FISH & CHIPS   Barb's was the first no-frills harbor-side "chippie" stand, and has since become somewhat of a legend. It serves lightly breaded halibut (and other locally caught fish) and hand-hewn chips, plus a good seafood chowder, seafood specialties, and burgers. Picnic tables are nearby at Fisherman's Wharf, as is a floating dessert shop that sells whimsically iced cupcakes.

Fisherman's Wharf, Erie St. ℭ **250/384-6515.** www.barbsplace.ca. Menu items C$2–C$7; meals C$11–C$19. MC, V. Daily 11am–sunset.

Foo Asian Street Food ASIAN   If there's an iota of adventure in your heart, then let your taste buds travel most of Asia—in a box! Because this tiny street-side kitchen (actually located in a parking lot) has no fancy linens or service staff—all its efforts focus on food. Inspirations include a Thai red coconut curry, Indian butter chicken, Vietnamese Ginger caramel chicken, Malaysian papaya salad, crispy pakoras, and paneer cheese dumplings. There's a small sit down counter overlooking all the culinary action, and an outside deck.

769 Yates St. (C) **250/383-3111.** www.foofood.ca. Menu items C$9–C$12. MC, V. Mon–Fri 11:30am–10pm; Sat–Sun 5–9:30pm.

The Local Kitchen PACIFIC NORTHWEST Located right at the base of Bastion Square, with outdoor sidewalk seating in good weather, the Local Kitchen is a great place to hang out for a couple of hours with a beer, a cocktail, a shared mix of small plates, or a more substantial meal. For main courses, try the lamb curry, barbecued pork ribs, or the seafood linguine. Smaller plates include seafood chowder and Dungeness crab cakes. It's a favorite spot for the 30-somethings and the generation that came after, who come here for the crowd more than anything else. Summer Sunday brunch is very popular.

1205 Wharf St. (at Bastion Sq.). (C) **250/385-1999.** www.thelocalkitchen.ca. Small plates C$4–C$15; main courses C$16–C$30. MC, V. Mon–Sat 11:30am–11pm; Sun 9:30am–6pm.

Red Fish/Blue Fish ★ ♨ FISH & CHIPS/SEAFOOD Locals and tourists alike flock to this former waterside container-cum-kitchen for fresh, fast, sustainably harvested seafood delights. Wild Pacific fish and chips, oyster or wild salmon tacos, and fresh fish sandwiches are generally on the menu, as well as fish chowder and an organic vegetarian salad. Every paper plate and container used here is recycled. If the weather's nice, you can sit at wooden tree stumps posing as tables—a successful way of getting around city bylaws that don't permit dining on a dock. This popular spot is located on the pier next to the floatplane terminal right on the Inner Harbour, below the landmark "pink building."

1006 Wharf St. (C) **250/298-6877.** www.redfish-bluefish.com. Menu items C$5–C$17. AE, MC, V. Daily 11:30am–5pm (7pm in summer).

DOWNTOWN & OLD TOWN
Expensive

Brasserie L'Ecole ★★ FRENCH In the overheated world of food fashion, it's so refreshing to find simple French bistro fare deftly prepared and served at reasonable prices. L'Ecole's menu changes daily, depending entirely on what comes in fresh from Victoria's hinterland farms. Because honesty is what's on offer at this warm, comfortable restaurant, preparation is simple, no big reductions or complicated *jus,* just shellfish, local fish, meats with red-wine sauces, and fresh vegetables with vinaigrettes. The wine list is small, with no hugely expensive vintages, but has good straightforward wine to match the excellent food. Very satisfying in every way.

1715 Government St. (C) **250/475-6260.** www.lecole.ca. Reservations recommended. Main courses C$21–C$29. AE, MC, V. Tues–Sat 5:30–11pm.

Café Brio ★★★ PACIFIC NORTHWEST/ITALIAN Café Brio is one of Victoria's best and buzziest spots for casual but top-flight dining. The Tuscan-influenced cuisine strongly reflects the seasons, fresh local meats and produce, and Pacific seafood. The menu changes daily, but appetizers always include locally harvested oysters, a wonderful house-made paprika sausage, and a delicious charcuterie plate (the chef makes all his charcuterie on the premises). For entrees, choose from handmade pasta (such as fresh herb-ricotta *agnolotti*), or roasted or poached wild fish. The wine list is excellent, with an impressive selection of BC and international reds and whites. The service is deft, friendly, and knowledgeable, and the kitchen stays open as long as guests keep ordering. An all-around winner.

944 Fort St. ✆ **250/383-0009.** www.cafe-brio.com. Reservations recommended. Main courses C$16–C$36. AE, MC, V. Daily 5:30–10pm.

Camille's ★★★ PACIFIC NORTHWEST For quiet romance, with discreetly attentive service, Camille's is one of Victoria's very best. Tucked away in two rooms beneath the old Law Chambers, its decor contrasts white linen with century-old exposed brick, stained-glass lamps, and candlelight. Chef and owner David Mincey was one of the founders of a Vancouver Island farm cooperative that brings local farmers together with local restaurants, so you're usually dining on foods found within a 100-mile radius of the restaurant. The ever-changing menu displays Mincey's love for cheeky invention and the seasonal bounty of Vancouver Island. To sample a bit of everything, try the five-course tasting menu, a fantastic bargain at C$50, or C$75 with wine pairings. The reasonable and extensive wine list comes with liner notes that are amusing and informative.

45 Bastion Sq. ✆ **250/381-3433.** www.camillesrestaurant.com. Reservations recommended. Main courses C$26–C$37. AE, MC, V. Tues–Sat 5:30–10pm.

Il Terrazzo Ristorante ★★ ITALIAN This charming spot in a converted heritage building off Waddington Alley is always a top contender for Victoria's best Italian restaurant. You can be assured of a good meal here. The northern Italian cooking includes wood-oven-roasted meats, fish, and pizzas, as well as homemade pastas. An emphasis on fresh produce and local seafood sets the tone for the menu, with appetizers such as artichokes stuffed with salmon and crabmeat drizzled with a light lemon-cream sauce, and entrees like salmon crusted with almond and black pepper, and then baked in the wood-burning oven, or a fabulous rack of lamb. The mood is bustling and upbeat, complete with an atmospheric courtyard furnished with flowers, marble tables, wrought-iron chairs, and heaters. The wine list is enormous, with some 1,200 vintages. Service is friendly and helpful.

555 Johnson St. (off Waddington Alley). ✆ **250/361-0028.** www.ilterrazzo.com. Reservations recommended. Main courses lunch C$9–C$23; dinner C$15–C$38. AE, MC, V. Mon–Sat 11:30am–3pm; daily 5–10pm.

Prime Steakhouse & Lounge ★★ STEAK When Prime opened in 2009, it quickly established itself as Victoria's best steakhouse. And it still is. They dry age their New York steak to preserve its full flavor and succulence. Thick, juicy prime rib, another house specialty, is served with a great Yorkshire pudding and fresh horseradish. For lunch, you can get a spiced lamb burger, fresh fish, or pasta. If you like oysters, start your meal with those. They have a good and reasonably priced wine list that features BC and international vintages.

In the Magnolia Hotel, 621 Courtney St. ✆ **250/386-2010.** www.primesteak.ca. Reservations recommended. Main courses lunch C$12–C$24, dinner C$21–C$42. AE, MC, V. Daily 11:30am–11pm.

Moderate

Pagliacci's ☺ ITALIAN Victoria's night owls used to come here when Pagliacci's was one of the few places to offer late-night dining. Though the city's evening

TAKING AFTERNOON tea

Far from a simple cup of hot water with a Lipton tea bag in it, a proper afternoon tea is both a meal and a ritual.

Any number of places in Victoria serve afternoon tea; some refer to it as high tea. Both come with sandwiches, berries, and tarts, but high tea usually includes some more substantial savory fare such as a meat-and-vegetable-filled turnover. Though the caloric intake can be hefty, it's really more about the ritual. For that reason, you don't want to go to any old teahouse. Note that in summer, it's a good idea to book *at least* a week ahead.

If you want, and can afford, the best (and overrated) experience, head to the **Fairmont Empress** ★★ (721 Government St.; ✆ **250/384-8111;** p. 239), where tea is served in the Tea Lobby, a busy and beautifully ornate room at the front of the hotel. Price depends on the time and season, and runs from C$47 to C$58. For that, you and hundreds of tea-taking compatriots will be pampered with fresh berries and cream or a fruit compote; sandwiches of smoked salmon, cucumber, and curried chicken; scones with strawberry preserves and thick Jersey cream; and an assortment of tarts and chocolates. The menu even accommodates special diets with gluten-free and diabetic choices. Seatings are every 15 minutes four times a day starting at noon, until 3:45pm; reservations are essential and a "smart casual" dress code is in effect (no torn jeans, short shorts, or flip-flops).

More affordable, less crowded, and just as historic is tea on the lawn of **Point Ellice House** (2616 Pleasant St.; ✆ **250/ 380-6506;** www.pointellicehouse.ca), where the cream of Victoria society used to gather in the early 1900s. On the Gorge waterway, Point Ellice is just a 5-minute trip by ferry from the Inner Harbour, or take bus no. 14 to Pleasant

Street. Afternoon tea costs C$23 and includes a half-hour tour of the mansion and gardens, plus the opportunity to play a game of croquet. Open daily 11am to 5pm (tea served noon–4pm) May through the first Monday of September (weather permitting); phone ahead for reservations and Christmas hours.

If you want your tea in a historic garden setting, head over to **Abkhazi Garden** (1964 Fairfield Rd.; ✆ **250/598-8096;** by car or bus no. 1 from downtown), where tea is served daily in the small, modernist house built by Russian Prince and Princess Abkhazi; see p. 270 for a description of the garden.

Set in impeccably maintained gardens, "Afternoon Tea at the Gardens" at the **Butchart Gardens Dining Room Restaurant** ★★★ (800 Benvenuto Ave.; ✆ **250/652-8222;** www.butchart gardens.com; bus no. 75) is a memorable experience. Sitting inside the Butchart mansion and looking out over the flowers, you can savor this fine tradition for C$27 per person. Tea is served daily year-round noon to 3pm; reservations recommended. Call ahead for winter hours.

What the **White Heather Tea Room** ★★ (1885 Oak Bay Rd.; ✆ **250/ 595-8020;** www.whiteheather-tearoom. com; bus nos. 7 and 2) lacks in old-time atmosphere it makes up for with the sheer quality and value of the tea and the charm of proprietress and tea mistress Agnes. For those feeling not so peckish, try the Wee Tea at C$16; for those a little hungrier, the Not So Wee Tea at C$20. If you feel like going the whole hog, try the Big Muckle Great Tea for Two at C$45. Open Tuesday through Saturday 10am to 5pm, tea served from 11:30am. Call for reservations.

scene has improved since expatriate New Yorker Howie Siegal opened the restaurant in 1979, Pagliacci's can still boast an un-Victoria kind of big-city energy. Tables jostle against one another as guests ogle each other's food and eavesdrop on conversations. The menu is southern Italian—veal *parmigiana,* tortellini, and 19 or 20 other a la carte pastas, all fresh and made by hand, many quite inventive. Live jazz, swing, blues, or Celtic music starts at 8:30pm, Sunday through Wednesday. Howie hosts a very good brunch on Sunday. Children are welcome and enjoy this fun, laid-back environment.

1011 Broad St. ✆ **250/386-1662.** Reservations not accepted. Main courses lunch C$7–C$12; dinner C$12–C$26; brunch C$10–C$15. AE, MC, V. Mon–Thurs 11:30am–11pm; Fri–Sat 11:30am–midnight; Sun 11am–11pm.

The Tapa Bar 🎁 TAPAS   The perfect meal for the commitment-shy, tapas are small and flavorful plates that you combine together to make a meal. Tapas to be sampled in this warm and welcoming spot include fried calamari, hearts of palm, and grilled portobello mushrooms. However, don't pass up on the *gambas al ajillo*—shrimp in a rich broth of garlic. The martini list is likely longer than the list of wines, but between the two, there's plenty to keep the room buzzing.

620 Trounce Alley. ✆ **250/383-0013.** www.tapabar.ca. Tapas plates C$7–C$15. AE, MC, V. Mon–Thurs 11:30am–11pm; Fri–Sat 11:30am–midnight; Sun noon–10pm.

FINDING HIGH-OCTANE coffee

Good coffee is one of the great joys of life. Fortunately, Victoria's tea-party Englishness hasn't stopped it from buzzing into the same coffee-cuckoo-ness that's engulfed Vancouver and the rest of the Pacific Northwest. Some to savor:

- On a sunny day, head for **Willie's** (537 Johnson St.; ✆ **250/381-8414**). Order your brew from the counter and take a seat on the patio. This bakery serves up excellent sweets and great hot breakfasts. It's open Monday to Friday 7am to 5pm, Saturday 8am to 5pm, and Sunday 8:30am to 4:30pm.

- Out in Oak Bay, **Ottavio** ★ (2272 Oak Bay Ave.; ✆ **250/592-4080;** www.ottaviovictoria.com) is a charming cafe, bakery, and deli with great Italian pastries, snacks, and coffee. It's open Tuesday to Saturday from 8am to 6pm. Take bus no. 2 Oak Bay to Oak Bay Avenue and Monterey Street.

- Some of the best all-round coffees in Victoria are served at the **Caffè**

Artigiano (1140 Government St.; ✆ **250/388-4147**), beside the lobby of the Bedford Regency Hotel (p. 249) in Victoria's oldest (1867) building. It's open Monday through Friday from 6am to 6pm, Saturday and Sunday from 7am to 6pm.

- It's not a glamorous place, but **Habit** (552 Pandora Ave.; ✆ **250/294-1127;** www.habitcoffee.com) is for coffee purists looking for hand-crafted java from seed to cup. Coffee here is custom-roasted using a 1918 vintage, cast-iron Royal #7 roaster! There's a newer, less bohemian, location in The Atrium (808 Yates St., ✆ 250/590-5953).

Zambri's ★ 🍴 ITALIAN   This upscale deli-restaurant relocated into the city's swish new Atrium building in 2010, and continues to earn accolades for its fresh Italian cuisine served in an unpretentious, no-nonsense style. The lunch menu includes daily pasta specials and a handful of entrees such as fresh rockfish or salmon. In the evenings, the atmosphere is slightly more formal with table service and a regularly changing a la carte menu. Menu items veer from penne with sausage and tomato to pasta with chicken liver pâté or peas and Gorgonzola. There is a nice patio for summer dining, and pizzas have been added to the menu.

800 Yates St., Atrium Building. ✆ **250/360-1171.** www.zambris.ca. Reservations not accepted. Main courses lunch C$12–C$17, dinner C$18–C$30. MC, V. Tues–Sat 11:30am–2:30pm and 5–9pm.

Inexpensive

Green Cuisine 🌱 VEGETARIAN   In addition to being undeniably healthy, Victoria's only fully vegan eatery offers remarkably tasty choices, with a self-serve salad bar, hot buffet, dessert bar, and full bakery. Available dishes range from pasta primavera salad to pumpkin tofu cheesecake, not to mention a wide selection of freshly baked breads. They also have a large selection of freshly squeezed organic juices, smoothies, and shakes, plus organic coffees and teas.

560 Johnson St. (in Market Sq.). ✆ **250/385-1809.** www.greencuisine.com. Main courses C$4–C$10. AE, MC, V. Daily 10am–8pm (Sun 10am–5pm in winter).

J&J Wonton Noodle House ★ 🍴 CHINESE   This tiny cafe doesn't go overboard on the atmosphere, but it's perfectly pleasant and, more importantly, you won't find better noodles anywhere in Victoria. The kitchen is glassed in, so you can watch the chefs spinning out noodles. Lunch specials—which feature different fresh seafood every day—are good and cheap, so expect a line of locals at the door. If you miss the specials, noodle soups, wontons, and other dishes are also quick, delicious, and inexpensive. Dinner is pricier.

1012 Fort St. ✆ **250/383-0680.** www.jjnoodlehouse.com. Main courses C$11–C$20; lunch specials C$7–C$15. MC, V. Tues–Sat 11am–2pm and 4:30–8:30pm. Bus: 5.

Q V Bakery & Café BAKERY   The main attraction of this diner on the edge of downtown isn't so much its quality—though the coffee, muffins, cookies, and light meals like lasagnas and salads are all good—as its availability. On weekends, Q V is open 24 hours, which in Victoria is enough to make it very special indeed.

1701 Government St. ✆ **250/384-8831.** Main courses C$4–C$10. MC, V. Sun–Thurs 6am–3am; Fri–Sat 24 hr.

rebar 😊 VEGETARIAN   Even if you're not hungry, it's worth dropping in here for a juice blend—say grapefruit, banana, melon, and pear with bee pollen or blue-green algae for added oomph. If you're hungry, rejoice: rebar is the city's premier purveyor of vegetarian comfort food. Disturbingly wholesome as that may sound, rebar is not only tasty, but fun, and a great spot to take the kids for brunch or breakfast. The room—in the basement of an 1890s heritage building—is bright and funky; the service is friendly and casual; and the food tends toward the simple and healthy. The menu features quesadillas, omelets, and crisp salads. Juices are still the crown jewels, with more than 80 blends on the menu.

50 Bastion Sq. ✆ **250/361-9223.** www.rebarmodernfood.com. Main courses C$10–C$18. AE, MC, V. Mon–Thurs 8:30am–9pm; Fri–Sat 8:30am–10pm; Sun 8:30am–3:30pm. Reduced hours in winter.

Sam's Deli DELI If you don't like lines, avoid the lunch hour, for Sam's is *the* lunchtime soup-and-sandwich spot in Victoria. Sandwiches come in all tastes and sizes (mostly large), but the shrimp and avocado is the one to get. The home-made soups are excellent, as is the chili. And Sam's is right across the street from the harbor, making it unbeatably convenient.

805 Government St. ☏ **250/382-8424.** www.samsdeli.com. Main courses C$5–C$10. MC, V. Summer Mon–Fri 7:30am–10pm, Sat–Sun 8am–10pm; winter Mon–Fri 7:30am–5pm.

Siam Thai Restaurant ☏ THAI Tucked away just half a block from the waterfront, this little local favorite offers good-quality Thai cooking. Menu items are starred from mild to spicy, and include many signature Thai dishes such as pad Thai noodles and a variety of curries. The lunch specials are a great deal.

512 Fort St. ☏ **250/383-9911.** www.siamthaivictoria.com. Main courses C$10–C$20. MC, V. Tues–Sun 11:30am–2pm; daily 5–9:30pm.

EDGING DOWNTOWN

Expensive

Paprika Bistro ★★ EASTERN EUROPEAN Veteran chef George Szasz does the cooking, and his wife Linda does the welcoming. It's a winning combo, and it's dedicated to the concept of "slow food." Paprika, a short walk from Willows Beach in Estevan Village, is housed in an attractive old building updated with a warm contemporary interior. The menu is classic bistro with Hungarian underpinnings. Start with some house-made sausage, then try the crispy, slow-braised pork belly; or potato strudel with duck confit and a sauce made from sour cherries and ginger. In summer, menu items are lighter, such as a superbly house-smoked chicken breast and a simple pan-fried halibut with caper parsley. All the produce is local and organic. This is a place to go for a memorable meal just a bit off the beaten track.

2524 Estevan Ave. ☏ **250/592-7424.** www.paprika-bistro.com. Reservations recommended. Main courses C$22–C$34. AE, MC, V. Daily 5–10pm. Bus: 11.

Moderate

Pizzeria Prima Strada ★★ PIZZA Located just on the other side of Beacon Hill Park (a 15-min. walk from the Inner Harbour), this bistro-style pizza parlor has terrific atmosphere and the best wood-fired, Neopolitan pies in the city. There are plenty of choices, but to test for the best, go for the margherita with Italian plum tomatoes, fresh herbs, and mozzarella. Start with a homemade anti-pasti selection, and save room for homemade gelato. A second location at 2960 Bridge St. (☏ **250/590-4380**) is a bit more casual.

230 Cook St. ☏ **250/590-4380.** www.pizzeriaprimastrada.com. Main courses C$11–C$15. MC, V. Daily 11:30am–9:30pm. Bus: 3.

Inexpensive

Fairfield Fish and Chips ☏ FISH & CHIPS A colorful storefront sit-down restaurant on Fairfield Road welcomes budget-minded diners to this great neighborhood "chipper." The menu is limited to fish (halibut, haddock, cod, rockfish) burgers and hand cut chips, all excellent. The halibut burger is a scrumptious treat; so is the oyster burger. You can order your fish lightly or richly battered.

1277 Fairfield Rd. ☎ **250/380-6880.** http://members.shaw.ca/fairfieldfishandchips. Main courses C$4–C$9. AE, MC, V. Tues–Sat 11:30am–7:30pm. Bus: 7.

Stage ★ BISTRO/PACIFIC NORTHWEST   Just a few minutes from downtown, in the funky Fernwood neighborhood, this smart, bustling new bistro and wine bar takes its name from the nearby Belfry Theatre (p. 317). Stage serves excellent and reasonably priced small plates that you can share. Choose from charcuterie, cheese, fish, meat, and vegetarian selections, all of them fresh and flavorful. There's a great selection of wines by the glass, as well.

1307 Gladstone Ave. (at Fernwood Rd.). ☎ **250/388-4222.** Small plates C$3.50–C$12. AE, MC, V. Tues–Sat 5pm–midnight; Sun–Mon 5–10pm. Bus: 22.

OUTSIDE THE CENTRAL AREA
Very Expensive

Deep Cove Chalet ★★ FRENCH   Perched on a grassy bank overlooking a beautiful inlet, Deep Cove is where to come for a classic fine-dining experience, particularly for special occasions. Top-notch service makes the superb menu even more memorable, and if you have any leanings for oenophilia, the cellar boasts some 18,000 bottles in its reserve. The a la carte menu selections can add up to be pricey (duck bouillon en croute is C$25); four-course prix-fixe dinners, though, won't break the bank and feature items such as roast venison, Dungeness crab, and curried scallops.

11190 Chalet Drive Rd., Sidney ☎ **250/656-3541.** Reservations recommended. Main courses brunch C$30, lunch C$23, dinner C$26–C$38; prix-fixe dinner C$58–C$75. AE, MC, V. Wed–Sun noon–2:30pm; Tues–Sun 5:30–9:30pm. Take Pat Bay Hwy. (Hwy. 17) north to Wain Rd., turn left and continue to West Saanich Rd. Turn right and then take an immediate left onto Birch Rd., which leads to Chalet Rd. Turn left.

SeaGrille ★★ PACIFIC NORTHWEST   The dining room of beautiful Brentwood Bay Lodge (p. 250), about a 20-minute drive north of Victoria, is all warm wood with giant windows overlooking Saanich Inlet. The food prepared here emphasizes fresh, seasonal, sustainable seafood such as BC salmon, arctic char, halibut, and sablefish. You can also choose from sushi, steaks, chops, and chicken breast, plus a vegetarian special, or order from the more casual pub menu, which includes thin-crust pizzas and staples such as fish and chips and a great halibut burger. To sample the best of what's on offer, go for the reasonably priced Chef's Menu. SeaGrille is a lovely place to dress up and dine well, but you won't feel out of place if you're in casual garb.

In Brentwood Bay Lodge and Spa, 849 Verdier Ave., Brentwood Bay. ☎ **888/544-2079** or 250/544-5100. www.brentwoodbaylodge.com. Reservations recommended. Main courses C$22–C$36; Chef's Menu C$59; C$93 with pairings. AE, DC, MC, V. Sun–Thurs 7:30am–10pm; Fri–Sat 7:30am–midnight. From Victoria, take Pat Bay Hwy. north to Keating Crossroads, turn left (west) to Saanich Rd., turn right (south) to Verdier Ave.

Sooke Harbour House ★★★ PACIFIC NORTHWEST   The dining room of this celebrated restaurant/inn offers spectacular views of Sooke Harbour, a relaxed atmosphere, and some of Canada's best and most inventive food. Dishes on the daily changing, seasonally adjusted menu are prepared with care, imagination, and panache. Ingredients are resolutely local: Many come from the inn's own organic garden or from the ocean at the Harbour House's doorstep. Depending on the season, dishes might include pan-seared rockfish on a sweet-and-sour arugula salad with bok choy, carrot-butternut squash-fennel, and smoked sablefish tortellini, or roasted rack of lamb served with spicy Savoy cabbage, a chickpea-oregano filo roll, and carrot–pumpkin seed flan. The wine cellar is one of the best in Canada. A four-course set menu or a seven-course Gastronomical Menu is offered nightly. You need to make your dinner reservations 3 days in advance (3 weeks in advance in the summer).

In the Sooke Harbour House Hotel (p. 251), 1528 Whiffen Spit Rd., Sooke. ℂ **800/889-9688** or 250/642-3421. www.sookeharbourhouse.com. Reservations required. Set menus C$50–C$125. MC, V. June–mid Sept daily 5–9:30pm; mid Sept–mid June Thurs–Mon 5–9pm. Take the Island Hwy. to the Sooke/Colwood turnoff (Junction Hwy. 14); continue on Hwy. 14 to Sooke; 2km (1¼ miles) past the town's only traffic light, turn left onto Whiffen Spit Rd.

Expensive

Markus' Wharfside Restaurant PACIFIC NORTHWEST   When locals keep coming back for more, you know you're onto a good thing. And because the restaurant's small, all the emphasis goes on the food whether it's on freshly caught seafood such as sautéed spot prawns with a white wine, lemon, and garlic butter sauce, or a flat iron steak, grilled to perfection. The risotto is always different and oh-so-tasty. For a real treat, have the co-owner/sommelier pair wines with every course, including dessert, the must-choice for which is the Chef's Trio that comprises whatever three signature dishes are "on show" that day.

1831 Maple Ave., Sooke. ℂ **250/642-3596.** www.markuswharfsiderestaurant.com. Main courses C$14–C$34. MC, V. Tues–Sat 5:30–10pm. Take the Island Hwy. to the Sooke/Colwood turnoff (Junction Hwy. 14); continue on Hwy. 14 (West Coast Rd.) to Sooke; 1km (½ mile) past the town's only traffic light, turn left onto Maple Ave.

Moderate

Smoken Bones Cookshack ★★★ 🔥 CAJUN/CREOLE   This boxlike restaurant, located in a small roadside strip mall belies all expectations. The food here is plentiful, tasty, and prepared with a superlative southern flair, in large part because of the in-house natural wood-smoking techniques that see pork ribs spending hours in the smoker. Southerners themselves have high praise for the Cookshack's spicy Gumbo, fresh-baked cornbread, braised collard greens, and butter-fried cabbage. And you can't get much better than that! Kids' portions and sharing plates make it a great find for family dining.

101–721 Station St. ℂ **250/391-6328.** www.smokenbones.ca. Reservations recommended. Main courses C$12–C$20. MC, V. Mon–Sat 11:30am–9pm; Sun noon–9pm. From Victoria, take Hwy. 1 (Douglas St.) west to the Millstream Rd turnoff south. Station Ave. is on your right, just past Goldstream Ave.

Inexpensive

Six Mile Pub PUB FARE   This pub dates from 1855 and has a rich history. Originally named the Parson's Bridge Hotel, it was filled with sailors when the Esquimalt Naval Base opened nearby in 1864. When Victoria elected to continue Prohibition until 1952, the Six Mile Pub became the hub for provincial bootleggers. Loyal locals still come for the atmosphere and the dinner specials. You can enjoy the warm ambience of the fireside room, or sit on the outdoor patio. Start with one of the 10 house brews on tap, then enjoy a hearty Cornish pasty, steak-and-mushroom pie, or juicy prime rib. If meat isn't part of your diet, try a veggie burger. They've recently gone "international," too, and serve various tapas, pot stickers, and more adventuresome seafood dishes. Just don't bring the kids—you must be at least 19 years old to enter.

494 Island Hwy. ✆ **250/478-3121.** www.sixmilepub.com. Main courses C$7–C$15. MC, V. Mon–Thurs 11am–11pm; Fri–Sat 11am–1am; Sun 10am–11pm.

PRACTICAL INFORMATION

The Big Picture

The touristy restaurants along Wharf Street serve mediocre food for folks they know they'll never have to see again, so avoid them. The canny visitor knows to head inland (even a block is enough), where the proportion of tourists to locals drops sharply and the quality jumps by leaps and bounds.

The one time-honored aspect of English cuisine that Victoria is still known for is the custom of afternoon tea. For the best places, see "Taking Afternoon Tea," earlier in this chapter.

Note: Because Victoria is so compact, most of the restaurants listed in this chapter are in downtown or Old Town, and no more than a 10-minute walk from most hotels. Thus, public transit information is listed only for those spots that are a bit farther out.

Complement your dining experience with one of BC's award-winning wines. Vineyards in the Okanagan Valley in eastern BC and the Cowichan Valley on Vancouver Island produce some remarkable reds and a couple of delicious sparkling whites. Ask your sommelier or server to steer you in the right direction.

Reservations

Reservations are strongly recommended for prime sunset seating during summer, especially on weekends.

Dining Hours

Victoria is not the kind of late-night, show-off, see-and-be-seen dining city that Vancouver is. Most restaurants in Victoria close around 10pm.

Tipping

The base-line tip in Victoria calculates as 15%, with more offered for exceptional service. Groups of six or more can anticipate an automatic added service charge of 15% to 18% percent—this serves as the tip and diners are not expected to leave an additional amount unless service was outstanding. Keep in mind that restaurants in British Columbia add the **12% harmonized sales tax (HST) to the bill.**

RESTAURANTS BY CUISINE

ASIAN
Foo Asian Street Food ($, p. 258)

BAKERY
Caffè Artigiano (p. 262)
Habit ($, p. 262)
Ottavio ★ ($, p. 262)
Q V Bakery & Café ($, p. 263)
Willie's ($, p. 262)

BISTRO
Stage ★ ($, p. 265)
Superior ($$, p. 258)

CAJUN/CREOLE
Smoken Bones Cookshack ★★★
($$, p. 266)

CHINESE
J&J Wonton Noodle House ★
($, p. 263)

DELI
Sam's Deli ($, p. 264)

EASTERN EUROPEAN
Paprika Bistro ★★ ($$$, p. 264)

FISH & CHIPS
Barb's Place ($, p. 258)
Fairfield Fish and Chips ($, p. 264)
Red Fish/Blue Fish ★ ($, p. 259)

FRENCH
Brasserie L'Ecole ★★ ($$$, p. 259)
Deep Cove Chalet ★★
($$$$, p. 265)

ITALIAN/PIZZA
Café Brio ★★★ ($$$, p. 259)
Il Terrazzo Ristorante ★★
($$$, p. 260)
Pagliacci's ($$, p. 260)
Pizzeria Prima Strada ($$, p. 264)
Zambri's ★ ($$, p. 263)

PACIFIC NORTHWEST
Café Brio ★★★ ($$$, p. 259)
Camille's ★★★ ($$$, p. 260)
Canoe ★ ($$, p. 257)
The Local Kitchen ($, p. 259)
The Mark ★★ ($$$, p. 257)
Markus' Wharfside Restaurant
($$$, p. 266)
SeaGrille ★★★ ($$$$, p. 265)
Sooke Harbour House ★★★
($$$$, p. 266)
Spinnakers Brewpub ($$, p. 258)
Stage ★ ($, p. 265)

PUB FARE
Canoe ★ ($$, p. 257)
Six Mile Pub ($, p. 267)
Spinnakers Brewpub ($$, p. 258)

SEAFOOD
The Blue Crab Bar and Grill ★★★
($$$, p. 256)
Red Fish/Blue Fish ★ ($, p. 259)

STEAK
Prime Steakhouse & Lounge ★★
($$$, p. 260)

TAPAS
The Tapa Bar ($$, p. 262)

TEA
Abkhazi Garden ($, p. 261)
Butchart Gardens Dining Room
Restaurant ★★★ ($$$, p. 261)
The Fairmont Empress ★★
($$$$, p. 261)
Point Ellice House ($$, p. 261)
White Heather Tea Room ★★
($, p. 261)

THAI
Siam Thai Restaurant ($, p. 264)

VEGETARIAN
Green Cuisine ($, p. 263)
rebar ($, p. 263)

KEY TO ABBREVIATIONS:
$$$$** = Very Expensive   **$$$** = Expensive   **$$** = Moderate   **$ = Inexpensive

15

EXPLORING
VICTORIA

V ictoria's top draws are its waterfront—the beautiful view created by the Fairmont Empress and the Provincial Legislature Buildings on the edge of the Inner Harbour—and its historic Old Town. Two must-see attractions are the Butchart Gardens, about a 20-minute drive from downtown, and the Royal BC Museum on the Inner Harbour.

So attractive and civilized is this small capital city, though, that folks sometimes forget what a beautiful and wild part of the world it's set in. If you have time, step out of town and see some nature: Sail out to see killer whales, beachcomb for crabs, kayak along the ocean shorelines, or hike into the hills for fabulous views and scenery. Pacific Rim National Park, a wild and wonderful wonderland on the west coast of Vancouver Island, is covered in Chapter 19.

SEEING THE SIGHTS
The Top Attractions

Abkhazi Garden ★ 🎁 It's a bit out of the way, about 5 minutes east of downtown by car, but if you're a nature lover, you'll love discovering this .4-hectare (1-acre) jewel box of a garden and the romantic story behind its creation. The wealthy Marjorie (Peggy) Pemberton-Carter met Russian Prince Nicholas Abkhazi in Paris in the 1920s, but they didn't meet again until 1946, by which time both had endured incarceration in prisoner-of-war camps (she in Shanghai as a British national, he in Germany). They wed, moved to Victoria, and set about creating a

The Abkhazi Garden is beautifully landscaped; PREVIOUS PAGE: Getting to know the animals at Beacon Hill Children's Farm.

Attractions in Downtown Victoria

Abkhazi Garden **12**
Art Gallery of
  Greater Victoria **10**
Craigdarroch Castle **11**
Emily Carr House **9**
The Fairmont Empress **4**
Helmcken House **5**
Maritime Museum of
  British Columbia **1**
Miniature World **3**
Pacific Undersea Gardens **8**
Provincial Legislature
  (Parliament Buildings) **7**
Royal BC Museum **6**
Victoria Bug Zoo **2**

landscape garden that takes full advantage of a dramatic site that contains quiet woodland, rocky slopes, and lovely vistas. The Abkhazis' modernist summerhouse has been lovingly restored, as has the small, charming house where they eventually lived. The house is used as a tearoom and gift shop. Allow 1 hour.

1964 Fairfield Rd. ✆ **250/598-8096.** www.abkhazi.com. Admission Mar–Sept C$10 adults, C$7.50 seniors and students, free for children 12 and under; Oct–Feb free admission (donation required). Garden daily Mar–Sept 11am–5pm, Oct–Dec 23 and Feb 11am–3pm, closed Dec 24–Jan; tearoom daily Mar–Sept 11:30am–4pm, Oct–Feb 11am–3pm. Bus: 1 to Fairfield Rd. and Foul Bay.

Art Gallery of Greater Victoria ★★　Housed in a combination of contemporary exhibition space and historic 19th-century mansion called Gyppeswick, the Art Gallery of Greater Victoria features a permanent collection of more than 15,000 objets d'art, drawn from Asia, Europe, and North America, though the gallery's primary emphasis is on Canada and Japan. The permanent exhibit **Emily Carr and Her Contemporaries ★★** integrates Carr's works—from her earliest British-style watercolors to her compelling BC-coast paintings to her final landscapes—with the works of her contemporaries in BC and Canada. (For more on Emily Carr, see "Emily Carr: Visionary from Victoria," in chapter 2.) There is also a gallery devoted to contemporary Canadian art. This museum is beautifully integrated into the neighborhood around it and can be seen in about an hour.

1040 Moss St. ✆ **250/384-4101.** www.aggv.bc.ca. Admission C$13 adults, C$11 seniors and students, C$2.50 children 6–17. Tues, Wed, Fri and Sat 10am–5pm; Thurs 10am–9pm; Sun noon–5pm. Bus: 11, 14, or 22.

British Columbia Aviation Museum　Located adjacent to Victoria International Airport, this small hangar is crammed with a score of original, rebuilt, and replica airplanes. The collection ranges from the first Canadian-designed craft ever to fly (a bizarre kitelike contraption) to slightly more modern water bombers and helicopters. Thursdays, you can watch the all-volunteer crew in the restoration hangar working to bring these old aircraft back to life.

The British Columbia Aviation Museum has original, rebuilt, and replica airplanes.

The 39-room Craigdarroch Castle is filled with Victorian opulence.

1910 Norseman Rd., Sidney. (𝄢 **250/655-3300.** www.bcam.net. Admission C$7 adults, C$5 seniors, free for children 12 and under. Daily summer 10am–4pm; winter 11am–3pm. Closed Dec 25 and Jan 1. Bus: Airport.

Butchart Gardens ★★★   These internationally acclaimed gardens were created after Robert Butchart exhausted the limestone quarry near his Tod Inlet home, about 22km (14 miles) from Victoria. His wife, Jenny, gradually landscaped the deserted eyesore into the resplendent Sunken Garden, opening it for public display in 1904. Over the years, a Rose Garden, Italian Garden, and Japanese Garden were added. The gardens—still in the family—now display more than a million plants throughout the year. On one stroll, passing through all of them, you'll be amazed at the gardeners' painstaking care and the beauty of the plantings.

On summer evenings, the gardens are illuminated with a variety of softly colored lights. June through September, musical entertainment is provided free Monday through Saturday evenings. You can even watch **fireworks displays** ★★★ on Saturdays in July and August. A very good lunch, dinner, and afternoon tea are offered in the Dining Room Restaurant (p. 261) in the historic residence; afternoon and high teas are also served in the Italian Garden (reservations recommended). Allow 2 to 3 hours; in peak summer months you'll encounter less congestion in the garden if you come very early or after 3pm. Admission prices vary according to season.

800 Benvenuto Ave., Brentwood Bay. (𝄢 **866/652-4422** or 250/652-4422; dining reservations 250/652-8222. www.butchartgardens.com. Admission C$17–C$29 adults, C$10–C$15 children 13–17, C$2–C$3 children 5–12, free for children 4 and under. Daily 9am–sundown (call or visit website for seasonal closing times); visitors can remain in gardens for 1 hr. after gate closes. Bus: 75. Take Blanshard St. (Hwy. 17) north toward the ferry terminal in Saanich, then turn left on Keating Crossroads, which leads directly to the gardens—about 20 min. from downtown Victoria.

Craigdarroch Castle ★★   What do you do when you've scraped, clawed, and bullied your way up from indentured servant to coal baron and richest man in British Columbia? You build a castle, of course, to show the other buggers what you're worth. Located in the highlands above Oak Bay, Robert Dunsmuir's home, built to cement his status and please his socially ambitious wife in the 1880s, is a stunner. The four-story, 39-room Highland-style castle is topped with stone turrets and chimneys and filled with opulent Victorian splendor: detailed woodwork, Persian carpets, stained-glass windows, paintings, and sculptures. The nonprofit society that runs Craigdarroch does an excellent job showcasing the castle. You're provided with a self-tour booklet; several volunteer docents are happy to provide further information. The castle also hosts many events throughout the year, including theater performances, concerts, and dinner tours. Allow 30 minutes to 1 hour for the castle tour. After visiting Craigdarroch, you might want to visit Hatley Park (see below), the castle built by Dunsmuir's son in 1910.

1050 Joan Crescent (off Fort St.). ✆ **250/592-5323.** www.craigdarrochcastle.com. Admission C$14 adults, C$13 seniors, C$9 students, C$5 children 6–12, free for children 5 and under. Daily June 15 to Labour Day 9am–7pm; day after Labour Day to June 14 10am–4:30pm. Closed Dec 25, Dec 26, and Jan 1. Bus: 11 or 14 to Joan Crescent. Take Fort St. out of downtown just past Cook St. and turn right on Joan Crescent.

Emily Carr House ★   The house where the great artist and writer Emily Carr was born (see "Emily Carr: Visionary from Victoria," p. 21) has been restored to the condition it would have been in when Carr lived there. Many of the rooms have also been hung with reproductions of her art or quotations from her writings, providing a good introduction to this true BC original. On selected days throughout the year, Molly Raher Newman, a local actress, portrays Emily Carr and regales visitors with Carr family stories; call ahead to see if she is performing.

207 Government St. ✆ **250/383-5843.** www.emilycarr.com. Admission C$6 adults, C$5 seniors and students, C$4 children 6–18; C$15 families. May–Sept Tues–Sat 11am–4pm.

Fort Rodd Hill & Fisgard Lighthouse   Perched on an outcrop of volcanic rock, the **Fisgard Lighthouse** has guided ships toward Victoria's sheltered harbor since 1873. The light no longer has a keeper (the beacon has long been automated), but the site itself has been restored to its 1873 appearance. Two floors of exhibits in the light keeper's house recount stories of the lighthouse, its keepers, and the shipwrecks that gave this coastline its ominous moniker "the graveyard of the Pacific."

Adjoining the lighthouse, **Fort Rodd Hill** is a preserved 1890s coastal artillery fort sporting camouflaged searchlights, underground magazines, and its original guns. Audiovisual exhibits bring the fort to life with the voices and faces of the men who served at the outpost. Displays of artifacts, room re-creations, and historic film footage add to the experience. Allow 1 to 2 hours.

603 Fort Rodd Hill Rd. ✆ **250/478-5849.** www.fortroddhill.com. Admission C$4 adults, C$3.50 seniors, C$2 children 6–16, free for children 5 and under; C$10 families. Daily Feb 15–Oct 10am–5:30pm; Nov–Feb 14 9am–4:30pm. Head north on Douglas St. until it turns into Hwy. 1. Stay on Hwy. 1 for 5km (3 miles), then take the Colwood exit (exit 10). Follow Hwy. 1A for 2km (1¼ miles), then turn left at the 3rd traffic light onto Ocean Blvd.; follow the signs to the site.

Hatley Park National Historic Site ★   Craigdarroch Castle (see above) was built during the 1880s to serve as Scottish coal-mining magnate Robert Dunsmuir's home. In 1908, Dunsmuir's son, James, after a bitter inheritance battle with his mother, built his own palatial manse, Hatley Castle, on a 226-hectare (559-acre) waterfront estate about 25 minutes from Victoria. The younger Dunsmuir reportedly commissioned architect Samuel Maclure with the words, "Money doesn't matter, just build what I want." The bill came to more than C$1 million (equivalent to about US$40 million today). The impressive castle, built of local stone in a hybrid Norman-Tudor fantasy style, is open to visitors on guided tours on the weekend or on weekdays by appointment; the admission price is way too high, but Hatley does make for an interesting excursion. As you're shown around the castle, you have to use your imagination, since all the furniture was sold in 1937 (much of it is now in Craigdarroch Castle), and the rooms are either empty or filled with office modules and equipment. The paneling and wood floors are truly remarkable, though. The surrounding estate features several heritage gardens, including the tranquil Japanese Garden, designed almost a century ago by the Japanese architect Isaburo Kishida, who also designed the Japanese Gardens at Butchart Gardens (p. 273). Allow 1 to 2 hours.

Royal Roads University, 200 Sooke Rd., Colwood. (*) **866/241-0674** or 250/391-2666. www.hatley park.ca. 1-hr. castle tour and garden access C$18 adults, C$16 seniors, C$11 children 6–17, free for children 5 and under; gardens only C$4.75 adults, C$4.25 seniors, C$3.25 children 6–17, free for children 5 and under. Castle tours weekends 10am–4pm, weekdays by appointment; gardens and museum daily 10am–4pm. From Victoria, take Government St. north for about 2km (1¼ miles), turn left onto Gorge Rd. (Hwy. 1A) and follow about 20km (12 miles); turn left onto Sooke Rd. (Hwy. 14A) and look for signs to Royal Roads University or Hatley Park National Historic Site.

Maritime Museum of British Columbia   Housed in the former provincial courthouse, this museum is dedicated to recalling BC's rich maritime heritage. The displays do a good job of illustrating maritime history, from the early explorers to the grand ocean liners. An impressive collection of ship models and paraphernalia—uniforms, weapons, and gear—is complemented by photographs and journals. The museum also shows films in its Vice Admiralty Theatre. Allow 1 hour.

28 Bastion Sq. (*) **250/385-4222.** www.mmbc.bc.ca. Admission C$12 adults, C$10 seniors and students, C$5 children 6–11, free for children 5 and under; C$25 families. Daily 9:30am–4:30pm. Closed Dec 25. Bus: 5 to View St.

Miniature World ☺   It sounds cheesy—hundreds of dolls, miniatures, and scenes from old fairy tales, but Miniature World, inside the Fairmont Empress (the entrance is around the corner), is actually kinda cool, and kids love it. You

Kids love the scenes at Miniature World.

Something Fishy in Sidney

The **Shaw Ocean Discovery Centre** (☎ **250/665-7511;** www.oceandiscovery.ca) in Sidney, 25 minutes north of Victoria, is Vancouver Island's most creative way to learn about ocean ecology and explore British Columbia's unique sea life. Opened in 2009, the center features 17 giant aquarium habitats that house hundreds of fish, invertebrates, and plant life—including giant Pacific octopus, wolf eels, rock fish, and colorful anemones. With floor-to-ceiling viewing panels highlighting the breathtaking array of local marine life, visitors are transported to the ocean depths and coastal environments. The center promotes environmental awareness and conservation of the ocean environment, and has a multimedia classroom designed to engage and inspire students from pre-school to high school about human connectivity to the ocean. The Ocean Discovery Centre is located in the Sidney Pier Building at the end of Beacon Street. Hours are 10am to 4:30pm daily. Admission is C$12 adults, C$6 children 7 to 17, C$3 children 3 to 6, and free for children 2 and under. Bus 70.

walk in, and you're plunged into darkness, except for a moon, some planets, and a tiny spaceship flying up to rendezvous with an orbiting mother ship. This is the most up-to-date display. Farther in are re-creations of battle scenes, a miniature Canadian Pacific Railway running all the way across a miniature Canada, Victorian dollhouses, and a three-ring circus and midway. Better yet, most of these displays do something: The train moves at the punch of a button, and the circus rides whirl around and light up as simulated darkness falls. Allow about 30 minutes to see it all.

649 Humboldt St. ☎ **250/385-9731.** www.miniatureworld.com. Admission C$13 adults, C$10 children 12–17, C$8 children 4–11, free for children 3 and under. Daily summer 9am–9pm; fall and winter 9am–5pm; spring 9am–7pm. Bus: 5, 27, 28, 30, or 31.

Pacific Undersea Gardens   Locals aren't very keen on the sight of this conspicuous white structure floating in the Inner Harbour, and those with some knowledge of Vancouver Island's marine environment will tell you that many of the creatures on display here are not indigenous to these waters. But your kids might enjoy a visit—or they might not, since the place is dark and kind of scary for little ones. A gently sloping walkway leads down to a glass-enclosed viewing area. One of the star attractions is a remarkably photogenic octopus (reputedly the largest in captivity). Injured seals and orphaned seal pups are cared for in holding pens alongside the observatory as part of a provincial marine-mammal rescue program. Allow 1 hour.

490 Belleville St. ☎ **250/382-5717.** www.pacificunderseagardens.com. Admission C$10 adults, C$9 seniors, C$8 children 12–17, C$6 children 5–11, free for children 4 and under. Oct–May daily 10am–5pm; June–Sept daily 9am–8pm. Bus: 5, 27, 28, or 30.

Provincial Legislature Buildings (Parliament Buildings) ★★   Designed by a 25-year-old Francis Rattenbury (see "Francis Rattenbury: Famous Architect and Murder Victim," in chapter 2) and built between 1893 and 1898 at a cost of nearly C$1 million, the Provincial Legislature Buildings (which some diehard Anglophiles insist on calling "the Parliament buildings") are one of the most noteworthy landmarks on Victoria's Inner Harbour. The 40-minute tour comes across at times like an eighth-grade civics lesson, but it's worth it to see the fine mosaics, marble, woodwork, and stained glass.

501 Belleville St. ⓒ **250/387-3046.** www.leg.bc.ca. Free admission. Victoria Day (late May) to Labour Day Mon–Thurs 9am–5pm, Fri–Sun 9am–6pm; Sept to late May Mon–Fri 9am–4pm. Tours summer every 20–30 min.; winter call ahead for tour schedules. Bus: 5, 27, 28, or 30.

Royal BC Museum ★★★ ☺   One of North America's best regional museums, the Royal BC has a mandate to present the land and the people of coastal British Columbia. The second-floor **Natural History Gallery** showcases the coastal flora, fauna, and geography from the Ice Age to the present; it includes dioramas of a temperate rainforest, a seacoast, and (particularly appealing to kids) a life-size woolly mastodon. The third-floor **Modern History Gallery** presents the recent past, including historically faithful re-creations of Victoria's downtown and Chinatown. On the same floor, the **First Peoples Gallery** ★★★ is an incredible showpiece of First Nations art and culture with rare artifacts used in day-to-day native life, a full-size re-creation of a longhouse, and a hauntingly wonderful gallery with totem poles, masks, and artifacts. The museum also has an **IMAX theater** showing an ever-changing variety of large-screen movies. On the way out (or in), be sure to stop by **Thunderbird Park,** beside the museum, where a cedar longhouse (Mungo Martin House, named after a famous Kwakiutl artist) houses a workshop where native carvers work on new totem poles. Seeing and experiencing everything takes at least 2 hours.

675 Belleville St. ⓒ **888/447-7977** or 250/356-7226. www.royalbcmuseum.bc.ca. Admission C$15 adults; C$9.50 seniors, students and children 6–18; free for children 5 and under; C$40 families. IMAX C$11 adults; C$9 seniors, students and children 6–18; C$5 children 5 and under. Museum daily 10am–5pm IMAX daily 10am–8pm. Closed Dec 25 and Jan 1. Bus: 5, 28, or 30.

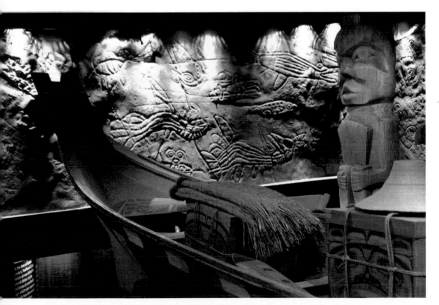

The Royal BC Museum is considered one of the best regional museums in North America.

ON THE lookout: VICTORIA'S BEST VIEWS

In town, the best view of the Fairmont Empress and the Legislature comes from walking along the pedestrian path in front of the **Delta Ocean Pointe Resort,** off the Johnson Street Bridge. In summer, sit and enjoy a coffee or glass of wine with the view from the patio.

When the fishing fleets come in early in the morning, head over to **Fisherman's Wharf,** at St. Lawrence and Erie streets, to watch as the fishermen unload their catches beside a small community of floating homes. Stroll back to town along the waterfront promenade, stopping by to enjoy a cappuccino or craft beer on another stellar patio at **Laurel Point Inn.** Later on, you can enjoy the sunset from the wharf along the eastern edge of the Inner Harbour or from the 18th floor of the **Vista 18 Restaurant** (740 Burdett Ave.; ☎ **250/382-9258**).

Just south of downtown, you can see across the Strait of Juan de Fuca and the San Juan Islands to the mountains of the Olympic Peninsula from the **Ogden Point** breakwater, the top of the hill in **Beacon Hill Park,** or the walking path above the beach along **Dallas Road.** Farther afield, **Fort Rodd Hill** and **Fisgard Lighthouse** offer equally good views of the mountains, as well as a view of the ships in Esquimalt Harbour.

Mount Douglas ★, a 15-minute drive north of the city on Shelbourne Street, affords a panoramic view of the entire Saanich Peninsula, with a parking lot just a 2-minute walk from the summit. To the east, **Mount Work** also offers a good view, but the walk up takes about 45 minutes. At the top of Little Saanich Mountain (about 16km/10 miles north of Victoria) stands the **Dominion Astrophysical Observatory** (5071 W. Saanich Rd.; ☎ **250/363-8262**) and its **Centre of the Universe** interpretive center, which offers guided tours of the observatory from May to mid-June Monday through Friday from 1 to 4:30pm; cost is C$9 adults, C$8 seniors and students, C$5 children 5 to 12. Mid-June through August, hours are Tuesday through Saturday from 3 to 11pm; prices are C$12 adults, C$10 seniors and students, and C$7 children 5 to 12. The observatory is closed to the public from September to May. There is no public transportation to the observatory, so you'll have to take a cab or drive.

Victoria Butterfly Gardens ★ ☺ This is a great spot for kids, nature buffs, or anyone who just likes butterflies. An ID chart allows you to identify the hundreds of exotic, colorful butterflies fluttering freely through this lush tropical greenhouse. Species range from the Central American Julia (a brilliant orange butterfly about 7.6cm/3 in. across) to the Southeast Asian Giant Atlas Moth (mottled brown and red, with a wingspan approaching 1 ft.). Naturalists are on hand to explain butterfly biology, and a display allows you to see the beautiful creatures emerge from their cocoons. You'll also see tropical birds, fish, and exotic plants, including an orchid collection. Allow 1 hour.

The Victoria Butterfly Gardens has a wide range of species to look at.

1461 Benvenuto Ave. (P.O. Box 190), Brentwood Bay. ✆ **877/722-0272** or 250/652 3822. www. butterflygardens.com. Admission C$13 adults, C$12 seniors and students, C$6.50 children 5–12, free for children 4 and under. Daily Mar–May and Oct 9am–4:30pm; June–Sept 9am–5:30pm. Closed Nov-Feb. Bus: 75.

Architectural Highlights & Historic Homes

First a trading post, and then a gold-rush town, a naval base, and a sleepy provincial capital, Victoria bears architectural witness to all these eras. What Vancouver mostly demolished, Victoria saved, so you really do have a feast of heritage buildings to enjoy. The best of Victoria's buildings date from the pre–World War I years, when gold poured in from the Fraser and Klondike rivers, fueling a building boom responsible for most of downtown.

Perhaps the most intriguing downtown edifice isn't a building but a work of art. The walls of **Fort Victoria,** which once spanned much of downtown, have been demarcated in the sidewalk with bricks bearing the names of original settlers and traders. Look on the sidewalk on the corner of Government and Fort streets.

Most of the retail establishments in Victoria's Old Town area are housed in 19th-century shipping warehouses that have been carefully restored as part of a heritage-reclamation program. You can take a **self-guided tour** of the buildings, most of which were erected between the 1870s and 1890s; their history is recounted on easy-to-read outdoor plaques. The majority of the restored buildings are between Douglas and Government streets from Wharf Street to Johnson Street. The most impressive structure once housed a number of shipping offices and warehouses, and is now the home of a 45-shop complex known as **Market Square** (560 Johnson St./255 Market Sq.; ✆ **250/386-2441**).

Some of the British immigrants who settled Vancouver Island during the 19th century built magnificent estates and mansions. In addition to architect Francis Rattenbury's crowning turn-of-the-20th-century achievements—the **Provincial Legislature Buildings** (501 Belleville St.; completed in 1898), and the opulent **Fairmont Empress** (721 Government St.; completed in 1908)—you'll find a number of other magnificent historic architectural sites.

Helmcken House (Royal BC Museum; ✆ **250/356-7226**) is the oldest house in BC still standing on its original site. Dr. John Sebastian Helmcken, a surgeon with the Hudson's Bay Company, set up house here in 1852 when he married the daughter of Governor Sir James Douglas. Originally a three-room log cabin, the house

Helmcken House is the oldest home in BC still standing on its original site.

A PROVINCIAL PARK, A native village & A FEW WINERIES

A short drive north from Victoria along the Island Highway takes you to the spots discussed below. The drive—along the ocean, up over the Malahat mountains, and then through the beautiful Cowichan Valley—can be completed in one leisurely day.

Goldstream Provincial Park

This quiet little valley overflowed with prospectors during the 1860s gold-rush days. Trails take you past abandoned mine shafts and tunnels, as well as 600-year-old stands of towering Douglas fir, lodgepole pine, red cedar, indigenous yew, and arbutus trees. The **Gold Mine Trail** leads to Niagara Creek and the abandoned mine that was operated by Lt. Peter Leech, a royal engineer who discovered gold in the creek in 1858. **The Goldstream Trail** leads to the salmon spawning areas. (You might also catch sight of mink and river otters racing along this path.)

For general information on Goldstream Provincial Park and all other provincial parks on the South Island, contact **BC Parks** at (✆ 250/391-2300 or check www.bcparks.ca. Throughout the year, Goldstream Park's **Freeman King Visitor Centre** (✆ 250/478-9414) offers guided walks, talks, displays, and programs geared toward kids but interesting for adults, too. Open daily 9am to 4:30pm. Take Highway 1 about 30 minutes north of Victoria. *Note:* BC government cutbacks have significantly reduced the number of events and services in most provincial parks. There is a C$3 day-use parking fee at Goldstream.

Three species of salmon (chum, chinook, and steelhead) make **annual salmon runs** up the Goldstream River during October, November, December, and February. You can easily observe this natural wonder along the riverbanks. Contact the park's visitor center for details.

Quw'utsun' Cultural & Conference Centre ★

The main reason for visiting the town of Duncan is to see the Quw'utsun' Cultural and Conference Centre (200 Cowichan Way; ✆ 877/746-8119 or 250/746-8119; www.quwutsun.ca). Created by the Cowichan People, the center brings First Nations culture to visitors in a way that's commercially successful yet still respectful of native traditions.

Longhouses along the crystal-clear Cowichan River give you an idea of the lodgings and ceremonial structures built by the aboriginal tribes who have lived in the area for thousands of years. Totem poles placed throughout the grounds represent traditional stories and legends. Master and apprentice carvers create poles, masks, and feasting bowls in workshops open to the public; the traditional Cowichan art of knitting sweaters is also demonstrated. Original tools, clothing, and pictures are on display and a film presents an oral history of the Cowichan culture. A large gift shop in the complex sells native-made carvings, crafts, jewelry, clothing, silk-screen prints, and other items. You can enjoy authentic native foods (salmon, oysters, and venison) at the **River Walk Café.** The center, gift shops, and River Walk Café are open June through September, Monday

was built by Helmcken and expanded as both the prosperity and size of the family grew. It still contains its original furnishings, imported from England. Helmcken went on to become a statesman and helped negotiate the entry of through Saturday, 10am to 4pm. Admission is C$13 adults, C$10 seniors and children 13 to 18, and C$8 children 5 to 12.

The **Duncan-Cowichan Visitor Info Centre** is at 381 Trans-Canada Hwy., Duncan (☏ **888/303-3337**). During July and August, it's open daily from 9am to 6pm; September through June, hours are Monday through Saturday 9am to 3pm.

The Cowichan Valley Wineries

The vintners of gorgeous agricultural Cowichan Valley have gained a solid reputation for producing fine wines. Several of the wineries offer 1-hour tours—a great introduction for novices. They usually include a tasting of the vintner's art, as well as a chance to purchase bottles or cases of your favorites. (A great gift idea because you will not find any of these wines outside British Columbia.)

Cherry Point Vineyards (840 Cherry Point Rd., Cowichan; ☏ **250/743-1272;** www.cherrypointvineyards.com), looks like a slice of California's Napa Valley (pictured below). The wine-tasting room and gift shop are open year round,

daily from 10am to 5pm. From May through September, you can have lunch at the on-site bistro (main courses about C$15). **Blue Grouse Estate Winery** (4365 Blue Grouse Rd., Duncan; ☏ **250/743-3834;** www.bluegrousevineyards.com) is a smaller winery that began as a hobby. April through September, it's open for tastings and on-site purchases Wednesday through Sunday (Oct–Dec Wed–Sat, Jan–Mar Sat only) 11am to 5pm. **Merridale Ciderworks,** located just south of Cowichan Bay at 1230 Merridale Rd. (☏ **250/743-4293;** www.merridalecider.com), is worth a stop to taste their artisan ciders or for lunch at their bistro. Be sure to stroll the orchard (especially in Apr when blossoms are in their full glory), and watch for wood nymphs and fairies along the way. Open daily 10:30am to 4:30pm; bistro is Wednesday through Sunday, noon to 3pm.

Cowichan Bay (off Hwy. 1, south of Duncan) is a pleasant half-hour drive from the wine country. Just southeast of Duncan, Cowichan Bay is a pretty little seaside town with a view of the ocean and a few attractions such as a glass-blowing studio and the acclaimed gallery of First Nations artist Arthur Vickers (his brother Roy Vickers has a gallery in Tofino). The **Cowichan Bay Maritime Centre** (1761 Cowichan Bay Rd., Cowichan Bay; ☏ **250/746-4955;** www.classicboats.org) is a unique museum where boats are displayed in special pods seen from atop an old, picturesque pier that stretches out into the bay. It's open daily 9am to dusk; admission is by donation.

British Columbia as a province into Canada. Helmcken House is open daily May through September from noon to 4pm. Admission is by donation (C$5 suggested) though it is included in admission to the Royal BC Museum.

Cemeteries

Ross Bay Cemetery (1495 Fairfield Rd.) has to be one of the finest locations in all creation to spend eternity. Luminaries interred here include the first governor of the island, James Douglas; frontier judge Matthew Begbie; and west coast painter Emily Carr. *An Historic Guide to Ross Bay Cemetery* (Sono Nis Press), available in Munro's Books (p. 311), as well as other bookstores, gives details on people buried here and directions to grave sites.

Pioneer Square, on the corner of Meares and Quadra streets beside Christ Church, is one of British Columbia's oldest cemeteries. Hudson's Bay Company fur traders, ship captains, sailors, fishermen, and crew members from British Royal Navy vessels lie beneath the worn sandstone markers. Contact the **Old Cemeteries Society** (℡ **250/598-8870;** www.oldcem. bc.ca) for more information on tours of both of these graveyards.

Neighborhoods of Note

From the time the Hudson's Bay Company settled here in the mid-1800s, the historic **Old Town** was the center of the city's bustling business in shipping, fur trading, and legal opium manufacturing. Market Square and the surrounding warehouses once brimmed with exports like tinned salmon, furs, and timber bound for England and the United States. Now part of the downtown core, this is still a terrific place to find British, Scottish, and Irish imports (a surprising number of these shops date back to the early 1900s), souvenirs of all sorts, and even outdoor equipment for modern-day adventurers. Just a block north on Fisgard Street is **Chinatown.** Founded in 1858, it's the oldest Chinatown in Canada.

The **James Bay** area on the southern shores of the Inner Harbour is a quiet, middle-class, residential community. As you walk along its tree-lined streets, you'll find many older private homes that have maintained their original Victorian flavor.

Beautiful residential communities such as **Ross Bay** and **Oak Bay** have a more modern West Coast appearance, with houses and apartments perched on hills overlooking the beaches amid lush, landscaped gardens. Private marinas in these areas are filled with perfectly maintained sailing craft.

Parks & Gardens

With the mildest climate in Canada, Victoria's gardens are in bloom year-round. In addition to the world-renowned **Butchart Gardens ★★★** (p. 273) the **Abkhazi Garden ★** (p. 270), and the gardens at **Hatley Park National Historic Site ★** (p. 274), several city parks attract strollers and picnickers. The 61-hectare (151-acre), 128-year-old **Beacon Hill Park ★** stretches from Southgate Street to Dallas Road between Douglas and Cook streets. In 1882, the Hudson's Bay Company gave this property to the city. Stands of indigenous Garry oaks (found only on Vancouver, Hornby, and Salt Spring islands) and manicured lawns are interspersed with floral gardens and ponds. Hike up Beacon Hill to get a clear view of the Strait of Georgia, Haro Strait, and Washington's Olympic Mountains. The children's farm (see "Especially for Kids," below), aviary, tennis courts, lawn-bowling green, putting green, cricket pitch, wading pool, and playground make this a wonderful place to spend a few hours with the family. The **Trans-Canada Highway's "Mile 0" marker** stands at the edge of the park on Dallas Road.

Government House, the official residence of the lieutenant governor, is at 1401 Rockland Ave., in the Fairfield residential district. Around back, the hillside of Garry Oaks is one of the last places to see what the area's natural fauna looked like before European settlers arrived. The rose garden at the front is quite sumptuous.

Just outside downtown, **Mount Douglas Park** has great views of the area, several hiking trails, and—down at the waterline—a picnic/play area with a trail leading to a good walking beach.

About 45 minutes southwest of town, **East Sooke Park ★** is a 1,400-hectare (3,460-acre) microcosm of the west coast wilderness: jagged seacoast, native petroglyphs, and hiking trails up to a 270m (886-ft.) hilltop. Access is via the Old Island Highway and East Sooke Road.

ESPECIALLY FOR KIDS

Victoria offers unique opportunities for kids to view creatures, from whales and butterflies to sea anemones and hermit crabs. The oldest of petting zoos is the **Beacon Hill Children's Farm** (Circle Dr., Beacon Hill Park; ✆ **250/381-2532;** www.beaconhillpark.ca), where kids can ride ponies; pet goats, rabbits, and other barnyard animals; and cool off in the wading pool. May to early September, the farm is open daily 10am to 5pm (11am–4pm mid-Sept to Oct; 10am–4pm Apr). Admission is by donation.

To see and touch (or be touched by) even smaller creatures, visit the **Victoria Butterfly Gardens** (p. 278). Closer to town is the **Victoria Bug Zoo** (631 Courtney St.; ✆ **250/384-BUGS** [250/384-2847]; www.bugzoo.bc.ca), home to praying mantises, stick insects, and African cockroaches. Admission is C$9 adults, C$8 seniors, C$7 students 13 to 16, C$6 children 3 to 15, and free for children 2 and under; open Monday to Saturday 10am to 5pm, Sunday 11am to 5pm.

Beacon Hill Children's Farm has a wide variety of barnyard animals.

For energy-burning activities, head over to **WildPlay Elements Park** (1767 Island Hwy., ✆ **250/590-7528;** www.wildplay.com) and its tree-to-tree obstacle course. Located near Bear Mountain, about 20 minutes north of downtown, the course is packed with ziplines, bridges, scramble nets, and swing logs, many of which are 18m (59 ft.) above ground. Children must be 7 years or older. Admission is C$40 for the full course; C$20 for the kids course; open daily, 9am to 5pm.

The **Pacific Undersea Gardens** (p. 276) give you a face-to-face introduction to some of the sea creatures of the Pacific coast. Better still, take the kids out to explore any of the tide pools on the coast. **Botanical Beach Provincial Park ★★★**, near Port Renfrew, is excellent, though the 60km (37-mile) drive west along Highway 14A may make it a bit far for some. Closer to town, try **French Beach ★** or **China Beach ★** (also along Hwy. 14A), or even the beach in **Mount Douglas Park** (p. 283). Find a good spot, bend down over a tide pool, and look—or else pick up a rock to see crabs scuttle away. Remember to put the rocks back where you found them.

In **Goldstream Provincial Park** (p. 280), the Visitor Centre (✆ **250/478-9414**) has nature programs and activities geared especially for children. The **Swan Lake Christmas Hill Nature Sanctuary** (3873 Swan Lake Rd.; ✆ **250/479-0211;** www.swanlake.bc.ca) offers a number of nature-themed drop-in programs over the summer, including Insectmania and Reptile Day.

Back in the city, the **Royal BC Museum ★★★** (p. 277) has many displays geared toward kids, including a rather dramatic and amazing life-size reconstruction of a woolly mastodon.

Miniature World (p. 275), with its huge collection of dolls and dollhouses, model trains, and diminutive circus displays, is a favorite with kids of all ages.

Located in Elk and Beaver Lake Regional Park (p. 287), **Beaver Lake** is a great freshwater spot where kids can enjoy a day of watersports and swimming in safe, lifeguard-attended waters.

ORGANIZED TOURS

Bus Tours

Gray Line of Victoria (4196 Glanford Ave.; ✆ **800/663-8390** or 250/388-6539; www.graylinewest.com) conducts a number of tours of Victoria and Butchart Gardens. The 1½-hour "Grand City Tour" costs C$29 adults and C$18 children 5 to 11. This is a hop on-hop off affair and tickets are valid for 2 days. There are daily departures throughout the year, usually at 11am or 1pm. For other tours, check the website.

Specialty Tours

Victoria Harbour Ferries (1234 Wharf St.; ✆ **250/708-0201;** www.victoriaharbourferry.com) offers a terrific 45-minute **harbor tour ★** for C$22 adults, C$20 seniors, and C$12 children under 12. Harbor tours depart from seven stops around the Inner Harbour every 15 or 20 minutes daily 10am to 4pm (longer hours May–Sept). If you wish to stop for food or a stroll, you can get a token good for reboarding at any time during the same day. A 50-minute **Gorge Tour ★** takes you to the gorge opposite the Johnson

Victoria Harbour Ferries offers a terrific 45-minute harbor tour.

Street Bridge, where tidal falls reverse with each change of the tide. The price is the same as for the harbor tour; June through September, gorge tours depart from the dock in front of the Fairmont Empress every half-hour 9am to 8:15pm; at other times, the tours operate less frequently, depending on the weather. The ferries are 12-person, fully enclosed boats, and every seat is a window seat.

Heritage Tours and Daimler Limousine Service (713 Bexhill Rd.; ℭ **250/474-4332**) guides you through the city, Butchart Gardens, and Craigdarroch Castle in a six-passenger British Daimler limousine. Rates start at C$90 for the Daimler per hour per vehicle (not per person).

The bicycle-rickshaws operated by **Kabuki Kabs** (649 Pembroke St.; ℭ **250/385-4243;** www.kabukikabs.com) can usually be found on the causeway in front of the Fairmont Empress or hailed in the downtown area. Prices for a tour are C$1 per minute for a two-person cab; C$1.75 per minute for a four-person cab.

Tally-Ho Carriage Tours (Veyaness St., Saanichton; ℭ **250/383-5067;** www.tallyhotours.com) has conducted tours of Victoria in horse-drawn carriages and trolleys since 1903. Horse-drawn trolley and carriage excursions start at the corner of Belleville and Menzies streets. Fares for the trolley (which hold up to 20 passengers) are C$15 adults, C$12 seniors, C$9 students, and C$7 children 17 and under. Trolley tours operate daily every 30 minutes 9am to 3pm during summer. An assortment of private carriage tours (maximum six people) is available throughout the year from Tally-Ho and competing operators. Competition keeps prices in line so you can expect to pay about C$50 for 15 minutes to C$240 for 2 hours.

To get a bird's-eye view of Victoria, take a 20-minute flight tour with **Harbour Air Seaplanes** (1234 Wharf St.; ℭ **800/665-0212** or 250/384-2215; www.harbour-air.com). Rates are C$99 per person. For a romantic evening, try the "Fly and Dine" to Butchart Gardens deal; C$239 per person, including the flight to the gardens, admission, dinner, and a limousine ride back to Victoria. **Hyack Air** (ℭ **250/384-2499;** www.hyackair.ca) offer similar excursions.

Walking Tours

Chapter 16 has two self-guided walking tours around Victoria. If you'd prefer to have a guide, **Victoria Bobby Walking Tours** (ℭ **250/995-0233;** www.walkvictoria.com) offers a leisurely story-filled walk around Old Town. Tours depart at 11am daily, May through September 15, from the Visitor Centre on the Inner Harbour; cost is C$15 per person.

Discover the Past (ℭ **250/384-6698;** www.discoverthepast.com) organizes interesting walks year-round. In the summer, **Ghostly Walks** explores Victoria's haunted Old Town, Chinatown, and historic waterfront; tours depart from the front of the Visitor Info Centre May through October nightly at 7:30pm, November through February Saturdays at 7:30pm, and March and April Fridays and Saturdays at 7:30pm. The cost is C$15 adults, C$11 seniors and students, C$8 children 6 to 12, and C$35 families. Cash only. Check the website for other walks.

The name says it all for **Walkabouts Historical Tours** (ℭ **250/592-9255;** www.walkabouts.ca). Charming guides lead tours of the Fairmont Empress, Victoria's Chinatown, Antique Row, and Old Town Victoria, or will help you with your own itinerary. The Empress Tour costs C$10 and begins at 10am daily in the Empress Tea Lobby. Other tours have different prices and starting points.

Victoria's Cemetery Tours

The **Old Cemetery Society of Victoria** (*©* **250/598-8870; www.oldcem.bc.ca**) runs regular cemetery tours throughout the year. Particularly popular are the **Lantern Tours of the Old Burying Ground ★**, which begin at the Cherry Bank Hotel (845 Burdett Ave.) at 9pm nightly in July and August. The tour lasts about 1 hour. On Sundays throughout the year, the Society offers historically focused tours of **Ross Bay Cemetery.** Tours depart promptly at 2pm from Starbucks in the Fairfield Plaza (1594 Fairfield Rd.), across from the cemetery gate. Both tours are C$5 per person. Call first to make certain the tour is on.

The **Victoria Heritage Foundation** (No. 1 Centennial Sq.; *©* **250/383-4546**) offers the excellent free pamphlet *James Bay Heritage Walking Tour*. The well-researched pamphlet (also available at the Visitor Info Centre) describes a self-guided walking tour through the historic James Bay neighborhood.

Hosted by foodie expert Kathy McAree, **Travel with Taste** (*©* **250/385-1527; www.travelwithtaste.com**) is an urban grazing experience—sample a Dutch pastry here, a truffle there, and even take a sip or two of local wine. Four-hour excursions are C$89 per person; call for reservations.

Ecotours

The 2-hour **wilderness cruise ★★★**, departing from the marina at **Brentwood Bay Lodge & Spa** (*©* **888/544-2079** or 250/544-2079; p. 250), provides an extremely informative and enjoyable exploration of Finlayson Inlet, a deep fjord with a fascinating history. On the cruise, it's not uncommon to spot eagles, seals, and sometimes whales. Cost is C$69 per person; cruises are available from mid-May through mid-October; call to reserve.

OUTDOOR ACTIVITIES

Sports Rent (1950 Government St.; *©* **250/385-7368;** www.sportsrentbc. com) is a great general outdoors equipment and watersports rental outlet. The inventory is impressive, containing everything from roller blades to gear for mountaineering and camping.

Beaches

The most popular beach is Oak Bay's **Willows Beach,** at Beach and Dalhousie roads along the esplanade. The park, playground, and snack bar make it a great place to spend the day building a sand castle. **Gyro Beach Park,** at Beach Road on Cadboro Bay, is another good spot for winding down. At the **Ross Bay Beaches,** below Beacon Hill Park, you can stroll or bike along the promenade at the water's edge.

For a taste of the wild and rocky west coast, hike the ocean side trails in beautiful **East Sooke Regional Park ★**. Take Highway 14A west, turn south on Gillespie Road, and then take East Sooke Road.

Two inland lakes give you the option of swimming in fresh water. **Elk and Beaver Lake Regional Park,** on Patricia Bay Road, is 11km (6¾ miles) north of downtown Victoria; to the west is **Thetis Lake,** about 10km (6¼ miles; Hwy. 1 to exit 10 or 1A onto Old Island Hwy. 14, turn right at Six Mile Pub and follow the signs), where locals shed all their clothes but none of their civility.

Biking

Biking is one of the best ways to get around Victoria. The 13km (8-mile) **Scenic Marine Drive bike path ★★** begins at Dallas Road and Douglas Street, at the base of Beacon Hill Park. The paved path follows the walkway along the beaches before winding up through the residential district on Beach Drive. It eventually turns left and heads south toward downtown Victoria on Oak Bay Avenue. The **Inner Harbour pedestrian path** has a bike lane for cyclists who want to take a leisurely ride around the entire city seawall. The popular **Galloping Goose Trail** (www.gallopinggoosetrail.com) is part of the Trans-Canada Trail, and runs from Victoria west through Colwood and Sooke all the way up to Leechtown. If you don't want to bike the whole thing, you can park at numerous places along the way, as well as at several places where the trail intersects with public transit. Contact **BC Transit** (✆ **250/382-6161;** www.bctransit.com) to find out which bus routes take bikes. Bikes and child trailers are available at **Cycle BC Rentals** (685 Humboldt St.; ✆ **250/380-2453;** www.cyclebc.ca), open year round. Rentals run C$7 per hour and C$28 per day; helmets and locks included. They also rent out scooters (C$16 per hour) and Harley-Davidsons (from C$58 per hour).

The popular Galloping Goose Trail is part of the Trans-Canada trail.

Birding

The **Victoria Natural History Society** (www.vicnhs.bc.ca) runs regular weekend birding excursions but, as a volunteer-run group, organizers change frequently. Check the website for contact numbers; usually any one of those listed will point you in the right direction of an upcoming event. **Goldstream Provincial Park** (p. 280) and the village of **Malahat**—both off Highway 1 about 40 minutes north of Victoria—are filled with dozens of varieties of migratory and local birds, including eagles. **Elk and Beaver Lake Regional Park,** off Highway 17, has some rare species such as the rose-breasted grosbeak and Hutton's vireo. Ospreys also nest there. **Cowichan Bay,** off Highway 1, is the perfect place to observe ospreys, bald eagles, great egrets, and purple martins.

Boating, Canoeing & Kayaking

Ocean River Sports (1824 Store St.; ✆ **800/909-4233** or 250/381-4233; www.oceanriver.com) can equip you with everything from a single or double kayak or a canoe to life jackets, tents, and dry-storage camping gear. Rental costs for a single kayak range from C$35 for 2 hours to C$55 per day. Multiday and weekly rates are also available. The company also offers numerous **guided tours ★** of the Gulf Islands and the coast. For beginners, try the guided 5½-hour Explorer Tour of the coast around Victoria or Sooke for C$125 per person. They also offer a guided 3-day/2-night trip to the nearby Gulf Islands for C$635 per person.

Rowboats, kayaks, canoes, and power boats are available for hourly or daily rental from **Great Pacific Adventures** (811 Wharf St.; ✆ **877/733-6722** or 250/386-2277; www.greatpacificadventures.com).

Blackfish Wilderness Expeditions (✆ **250/216-2389**; www.blackfish wilderness.com) offers a number of interesting kayak-based tours such as the kayak/boat/hike combo, where you boat to the protected waters of the Discovery Islands, hike one of the islands, and kayak to see the pods of resident killer whales that roam the waters around Victoria. Bird-watching is a specialty. Day tours start at C$70 per person.

Diving

The coastline of **Pacific Rim National Park** (see chapter 19) is known as "the graveyard of the Pacific." Submerged in the water are dozens of 19th- and 20th-century shipwrecks and the marine life that has taken up residence in them. Underwater interpretive trails help identify what you see in the artificial reefs. If you want to take a look for yourself, contact the **Ogden Point Dive Centre** (199 Dallas Rd.; ✆ **888/701-1177** or 250/380-9119; www.divevictoria.com), which offers a 2-day Race Rocks and Shipwreck Tour package that starts at C$209 per person, including all equipment and transportation. The **Saanich Inlet,** about a 20-minute drive north of Victoria, is a pristine fjord considered one of the top cold-water diving areas in the world (glass sponges are a rarity found only here). Classes and underwater scuba adventures can be arranged through **Brentwood Bay Lodge & Spa** (p. 250), Canada's only luxury PADI (Professional Association of Diving Instructors) dive resort.

Fishing

Saltwater fishing's the thing out here, but unless you know the area, it's best to take a guide. **Adam's Fishing Charters** (✆ **250/370-2326**;

www.adamsfishingcharters.com) is located on the Inner Harbour down below the Visitor Info Centre. Chartering a boat and guide starts at C$95 per hour per boat, with a minimum of 5 hours.

To fish, you need a saltwater fishing license. Licenses (including the salmon surcharge) for nonresidents cost C$20 for 1 day, and C$50 for 8 days. Tackle shops sell licenses, have details on current restrictions, and often carry copies of the *BC Tidal Waters Sport Fishing Guide* and *BC Sport Fishing Regulations Synopsis for Non-Tidal Waters*. Independent anglers should also pick up the *BC Fishing Directory and Atlas*. **Robinson's Sporting Goods Ltd.** (1307 Broad St.; © **250/385-3429**) is a reliable source for information, recommendations, lures, licenses, and gear. For the latest fishing hot spots and recommendations on tackle and lures, check out **www.sportfishingbc.com**. You'll find official fishing information at the Fisheries and Oceans Canada website, **www. pac.dfo-mpo.gc.ca**.

Golfing

Victoria's Scottish heritage doesn't stop at the tartan shops. The greens here are as beautiful as those at St. Andrews. The **Cedar Hill Municipal Golf Course** (1400 Derby Rd.; © **250/475-7151;** www.golfcedarhill.com), the busiest course in Canada, is an 18-hole, par-67 public course 3km (1¾ miles) from downtown Victoria. It's open on a first-come, first-served basis; daytime weekday greens fees are C$40 to C$48 and twilight fees (after 3pm) are C$25 to C$35. Golf clubs can be rented for C$20. The **Cordova Bay Golf Course** (5333 Cordova Bay Rd.; © **250/658-4444;** www.cordovabaygolf.com) is northeast of the downtown area. Designed by Bill Robinson, the par-71, 18-hole course features 66 sand traps and some tight fairways as well as short practice and driving range facilities. Greens fees are C$69 to C$89, depending on day and season; twilight fees range from C$49 to C$62.

The star of Vancouver Island golf courses, and the most expensive to play, is Canada's only 36-hole Nicklaus-designed golf course, located in the foothills of Mount Finlayson: **Westin Bear Mountain Golf Resort & Spa** (1999 Country Club Way; © **888/533-2327,** or 250/744-2327 for tee time bookings). GPS-equipped carts (included with fee) and collared shirts (blue jeans not permitted) are mandatory on this upscale course, which features breathtaking views and a spectacular 19th hole for recreational betting. Nonmember greens fees, depending on when you reserve and the time you play, range from C$69 to C$150.

You can call **A-1 Last Minute Golf Hot Line** at © **800/684-6344** or 604/878-1833 (www.lastminutegolfbc.com) for substantial discounts and short-notice tee times.

Hiking

Goldstream Provincial Park (30 min. west of downtown along Hwy. 1; p. 280) is a tranquil site for a short hike through towering cedars and past clear, rushing waters.

The hour-long hike up **Mount Work** provides excellent views of the Saanich Peninsula and a good view of Finlayson Arm. The trail head is a 30- to 45-minute drive. Take Highway 17 north to Saanich, then take Highway 17A (W. Saanich Rd.) to Wallace Drive, turn onto Wallace Drive and turn right on Willis

Goldstream Provincial Park offers tranquil hiking trails a half-hour outside of town.

Point Drive, and right again on Ross-Durrance Road, looking for the parking lot on the right. Signs are posted along the way. Equally good, though more of a scramble, is the hour-plus climb up **Mount Finlayson** in Gowland-Tod Provincial Park (take Hwy. 1 west, get off at the Millstream Rd. exit, and follow Millstream Rd. north to the very end).

The very popular **Sooke Potholes** trail wanders up beside a river to an abandoned mountain lodge. Take Highway 1A west to Colwood, then Highway 14A (Sooke Rd.). At Sooke, turn north on Sooke River Road and follow it to the park.

For a taste of the wild and rocky west coast, hike the ocean-side trails in beautiful **East Sooke Regional Park ★★**. Take Highway 14A west, turn south on Gillespie Road, and then take East Sooke Road.

For serious backpacking, go 104km (65 miles) west of Victoria on Highway 14A to Port Renfrew and the challenging **West Coast Trail ★★★**, extending 77km (48 miles) from Port Renfrew to Bamfield in a portion of **Pacific Rim National Park ★★★** (p. 323). The trail was originally a lifesaving trail for shipwrecked sailors. Plan a 7-day trek for the entire route; reservations are required, so call ✆ **800/435-5622** or 250/387-1642. The trail is rugged and often wet, but the scenery changes from old-growth forest to magnificent secluded sand beaches, making it worth every step. You may even spot a few whales along the way. **Robinson's Outdoor Store** (1307 Broad St.; ✆ **250/385-3429;** www.robinsonsoutdoors.com) is a good place to gear up before you go. At Robinson's, ask about the newer, less challenging 48km-long (30-mile) **Juan de Fuca Marine Trail ★★** connecting Port Renfrew and the Jordan River.

For something less strenuous but still scenic, try the **Swan Lake Christmas Hill Nature Sanctuary** (3873 Swan Lake Rd.; ✆ **250/479-0211;** www.swanlake.bc.ca). A floating boardwalk winds its way through this 40-hectare (99-acre) wetland past resident swans; the adjacent Nature House supplies feeding grain on request.

Paragliding

Vancouver Island Paragliding (☎ **250/ 514-8595;** www.viparagliding.com) offers tandem paraglide flights for C$185. The pilot steers; you hang on and enjoy the adrenaline rush. Flights last around 25 minutes. They also offer 1-day training courses (C$365) that allow you to take off on your own.

Sailing

One of the most exciting ways to explore the Strait of Juan de Fuca is aboard the **Thane,** on a **3-hour sail tour ★★** for C$69 per person. The multi-mast vessel is a replica of a late 1800s sailing ship, and is moored in front of the Fairmont Empress. Daily summer sailings leave at 9am, 1, and 5pm. Guests are welcome to bring a picnic. Contact the **SV Thane** (☎ **877/788-4263** or 250/885-2311).

A trained pilot steers while you enjoy the views at Vancouver Island Paragliding.

Skiing

Mount Washington Alpine Resort (Courtenay, BC; ☎ **888/231-1499,** 250/ 338-1386, or 250/338-1515 for snow report; www.mountwashington.ca), in the Comox Valley, is British Columbia's third-largest ski area, a 5-hour drive from Victoria, and open year-round (for hiking or skiing, depending on the season). A 480m (1,575-ft.) vertical drop and 50 groomed runs are serviced by four chairlifts and a beginners' tow. The terrain is popular among snowboarders and well suited to intermediate skiers. For cross-country skiers, 31km (19 miles) of track-set Nordic trails connect to Strathcona Provincial Park. Full-day rates are C$62 adults, C$50 seniors and students, C$32 children 6 to 12, and free for children 5 and under. Equipment rentals are available. The resort is located 100km (62 miles) north of Nanaimo; take Highway 19 to exit 130.

Watersports

The **Crystal Pool & Fitness Centre** (2275 Quadra St.; ☎ **250/361-0732**) is Victoria's main aquatic facility. The 50m (164-ft.) lap pool; children's pool; diving pool; sauna; whirlpool; and steam, weight, and aerobics rooms are open Monday through Thursday 5:30am to 11pm, Friday 5:30am to 10pm, Saturday 6am to 6pm, and Sunday 8:30am to 6pm. Drop-in admission is C$4.75 adults, C$4.25 seniors, C$3.75 students, C$2.75 children 6 to 12, and free for children 5 and under. **Beaver Lake** in Elk and Beaver Lake Regional Park (see "Birding," above) has lifeguards on duty, as well as picnicking facilities along the shore.

    Surfing has recently taken off on the island. The best surf is along the west coast at **China, French,** and **Mystic beaches ★**. To get there, take Blanshard Street north from downtown, turn left onto Highway 1 (the Trans-Canada Hwy.), then after about 10km (6¼ miles), take the turnoff onto Highway 14A (Sooke Rd.). Follow Highway 14A north along the coast. The beaches are well signposted.

EXPLORING VICTORIA | Outdoor Activities

Windsurfers skim along outside the Inner Harbour and on Elk Lake when the breezes are right. Though French Beach, off Sooke Road on the way to Sooke Harbour, has no specific facilities, it is a popular local windsurfing spot.

Whale-Watching

The waters surrounding the southern tip of Vancouver Island teem with orcas (killer whales), harbor seals, sea lions, harbor and Dall porpoises, and bald eagles. All whale-watching companies offer basically the same tour; the main difference comes in the equipment they use: Some use a 12-person Zodiac, where the jolting ride is almost as exciting as seeing the whales, whereas others take a larger, more leisurely craft. Both crafts offer excellent platforms for seeing whales. In high season (June to Labour Day), most companies offer several trips a day. Always ask if the outfitter is a "responsible whale-watcher"—that is, doesn't go too close to disturb or harass the whales.

Seafun Safaris Whale Watching (950 Wharf St.; ℂ **877/360-1233** or 250/360-1200; www.seafun.com) is just one of many outfits offering whale-watching tours in Zodiacs and covered boats. Adults and kids will learn a lot from the naturalist guides, who explain the behavior and nature of the orcas, gray whales, sea lions, porpoises, cormorants, eagles, and harbor seals encountered along the way. Fares for the Zodiac tour are C$129 adults and C$79 children.

Other reputable companies include **Prince of Whales** (812 Wharf St.; ℂ **888/383-4884** or 250/383-4884; www.princeofwhales.com), just below the Visitor Info Centre, which offers a variety of Zodiacs and larger, more leisurely craft, and **Orca Spirit Adventures** (ℂ **888/672-ORCA** [6722] or 250/383-8411; www.orcaspirit.com), which departs from the Coast Harbourside Hotel dock.

A ride on a Zodiac boat is almost as exciting as seeing the whales.

Ziplining

Adrenaline Zip Adventures (5128 Sooke Rd.; ☎ **866/947-9145** or 250/642-1933; www.adrenalinezip.com) leads exhilarating zips through the rainforest from one treetop to another. Riding the wires is a great family excursion, albeit at 46m (151 ft.) off the ground. Rides are C$79 adults and C$69 children 5 to 17 years old. The company provides shuttle service to and from downtown Victoria and has teamed up with **Sooke Coastal Explorations** (☎ **250/642-2343;** www.sooke whalewatching.com) for whale-watching, and **Rush Adventures** (☎ **250/642-2159;** www.ruch-adventures.com) for ocean-kayaking. **WildPlay Elements Park** (p. 283) also offers ziplining as part of its tree-to-tree obstacle course.

VICTORIA STROLLS & BIKING TOUR

V ictoria's ambience is made for the wanderer, its pavements picture-perfect for perambulation. Victoria, in short, is a great place to walk, bike, in-line skate, skateboard, or scooter. The tours below work, no matter what your favored form of transportation.

WALKING TOUR 1: **THE INNER HARBOUR**

START & FINISH:	**The Visitor Centre (812 Wharf St.) on the Inner Harbour.**
TIME:	**2 hours, not including shopping, museum, and pub breaks.**
BEST TIME:	**Late afternoon, when the golden summer sunlight shines on the Fairmont Empress.**
WORST TIME:	**Late in the evening, when the shops close and the streets empty.**

Victoria was born on the Inner Harbour. When the Hudson's Bay Company's west coast head of operations, James Douglas, happened across this sheltered inlet in 1843 while searching for a new corporate HQ, it was love at first sight. "The place appears a perfect Eden," he wrote to a friend. High praise indeed, although as Douglas was pretty deep into local real estate, his words should be taken with a wee pinch of salt. His confidence in the location certainly paid off, however, for less than 20 years after Douglas set foot onshore, the native stands of Garry oak had been supplanted by small farms, the town was choked with miners and mariners, and the harbor was full of ships, many of which had circled the globe. This tour circumnavigates the Inner Harbour, showing some of its lesser-known nooks and crannies while providing an opportunity to enjoy the same view seen by many a Victorian sailor.

1 Victoria Visitor Centre

At 812 Wharf St., this is without a doubt one of the finest-looking visitor centers in the world—a masterful Art Deco pavilion topped with a shining white obelisk rising high above the Inner Harbour. It would be a tribute to the taste and vision of city tourism officials, except that it started out life as a gas station.

From the Visitor Centre, thread your way south through the jugglers and musicians on the causeway until you're opposite 721 Government St., where stands:

The Art Deco style Victoria Visitor Centre; PREVIOUS PAGE: **Fan Tan Alley is known as the world's narrowest street.**

2 The Fairmont Empress

"There is a view, when the morning mists peel off the harbor, where the steamers tie up, of the Houses of Parliament on one hand, and a huge hotel on the other, which is an example of cunningly fitted-in waterfronts and facades worth a very long journey." Thus spoke Rudyard Kipling during a visit to the city in 1908. If he'd come only 5 years earlier, he would've been looking at a nasty, garbage-choked swamp. The causeway was then a narrow bridge over the tidal inlet, and as Victorians made a habit of pitching their refuse over the rail, the bay was, not surprisingly, a stinking cesspit of slime. In 1900, the ever-shrewd Canadian Pacific Railway made an offer to the city—we'll build a causeway and fill in the stinky bay if you let us keep the land. The city jumped at the offer. Little was expected—the land was swamp, after all. But taking their cue from the good folks in Amsterdam, the CPR drove long pilings down through the muck to provide a solid foundation. And on top of that, they built the Fairmont Empress. The architect was Francis Rattenbury, and his design was masterful, complementing his own Provincial Legislature Buildings to create the view that has defined the city ever since.

Around the south side of the Fairmont Empress is a formal rose garden—worth putting your nose in for a sniff. Cut through the garden, cross over Belleville St. and continue another half-block east to the corner of Douglas St., where you'll find:

3 Thunderbird Park

The park is instantly recognizable by its forest of totem poles. Even if you've overdosed on the ubiquitous 15cm (6-in.) souvenir totem, take a second look at these. The original poles on this site had been collected in the early 1900s from various villages up and down the coast. Some decades later, when officials decided the severely weathered poles needed restoring, they discovered the art of native carving had eroded even more than their collection of poles. From all the thousands of carvers on the coast, only one man still carried on the craft. In 1952, Kwakiutl artist Mungo Martin set up a carving shed on the park grounds and began the work of restoration. Martin replaced or repaired all the existing poles while teaching his son and step-grandson-in-law to carve. Seeing them at work renewed public interest in the form. Other young artists came to learn and train, which led to a revival of totem carving and native artistry among coastal natives.

All poles have a purpose; most tell a story. The stories associated with the poles in Thunderbird Park have unfortunately been lost, but many of the figures are easily recognized, including Thunderbird (look for the outstretched wings and curly horns on the head), Raven, Bear, and Killer Whale. On the edge of the park is the shed where Martin carved many of the poles. Feel free to poke your head in to take a look and ask the carvers what they're up to. The artists generally welcome questions and enjoy sharing their stories.

Farther back in the park, at 638 Elliott St. Sq., stands the:

4 Helmcken House

This simple woodframe house, the oldest house in BC still standing in its original position, was built by Dr. John Sebastian Helmcken in 1852. A surgeon with the Hudson's Bay Company, Helmcken married the daughter of

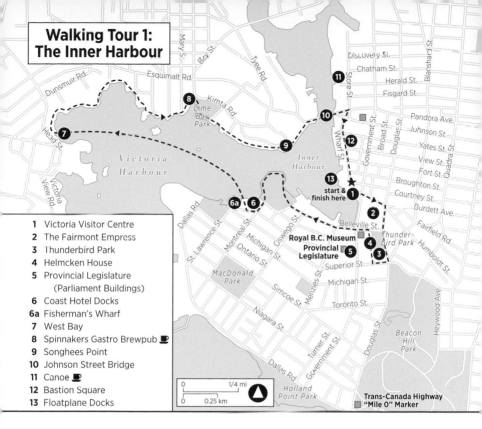

**Walking Tour 1:
The Inner Harbour**

1 Victoria Visitor Centre
2 The Fairmont Empress
3 Thunderbird Park
4 Helmcken House
5 Provincial Legislature
   (Parliament Buildings)
6 Coast Hotel Docks
6a Fisherman's Wharf
7 West Bay
8 Spinnakers Gastro Brewpub ☕
9 Songhees Point
10 Johnson Street Bridge
11 Canoe ☕
12 Bastion Square
13 Floatplane Docks

Governor James Douglas and went on to become a statesman and an important figure in the negotiations to allow British Columbia to become a province of Canada. The house, originally a three-room log cabin, is open daily
from May through September noon to 4pm; admission is by donation (C$5
suggested).

Walk west along Belleville past the modern-looking Carillon Tower (a gift from the
Dutch people who settled in BC) and the not-to-be-missed Royal BC Museum
(p. 277); cross Government St. You're now standing in front of 501 Belleville St.
at the:

5 Provincial Legislature Buildings (Parliament)

In 1892, a 25-year old Yorkshireman arrived on the west coast just as an
architectural competition for a new Legislature Building in Victoria was
announced. Francis Mawson Rattenbury had no professional credentials
but was blessed with both talent and ambition. He submitted a set of draw-
ings and, to the surprise of all, beat out 65 other entries from around the
continent. For more about Rattenbury, who was murdered in 1935, see
"Francis Rattenbury: Famous Architect and Murder Victim," in chapter 2.
The Provincial Legislature Buildings are open for tours 9am to 5pm. In
summer, the 40-minute tours start every 20 minutes (p. 276).

From the Legislature lawn, make your way past the horse-drawn calèches parked on Menzies St. and walk west on Belleville St. for 2 blocks to Pendray St. The road takes a sharp right, but follow the path leading down to a waterfront walkway as it curves around Laurel Point. Continuing around the pathway past the first few jetties takes you to the:

6 Coast Hotel Docks

Here is one of several ports of call for the **Victoria Harbour Ferries** (✆ **250/708-0201;** p. 284). From here, the official Frommer's route is to take the ferry all the way across the harbor to West Bay (the next stop on this tour). If the weather's clear, you'll enjoy views of the Olympic Mountains to the south and possibly spot a seal or bald eagle. You have several options here: You can take a short hop out to **Fisherman's Wharf** (6A on the map on p. 297), where just-caught fish is sold when in season; go directly across to Spinnakers Brewpub (stop 8) on the far shore; take the ferry across to Songhees Point (stop 9); or go directly to Canoe (stop 11). You can even give up on your feet entirely and take the full Harbour Ferries tour.

If you stick with the program, however, the next stop is:

7 West Bay

While a pleasant little residential neighborhood with a picturesque marina, West Bay isn't anything to write home about. What is worthwhile, however, is the waterfront walkway that winds its way from here back east toward the city. The trail twists and curves through several parks, and views south through the harbor look out to the Strait of Juan de Fuca and the Olympic Mountains beyond. After about 20 minutes of walking, it may be time to take a break:

8 Spinnakers Gastro Brewpub ☕

Excellent beer brewed on the premises, combined with an above-average patio, make **Spinnakers Gastro Brewpub** a dangerously time-consuming port of call. For those looking for more substantial fare, the pub grub's very good, and the entrees are above average. The on-site bakery makes inspired beer bread, as well as a range of more delicate goods. 308 Catherine St. ✆ **250/386-BREW** (250/386-2739). See p. 258.

From the pub, continue along the shoreline until you see the totem pole standing at:

9 Songhees Point

The point is named for the First Nations tribe that once lived on the site. The Songhees had originally set up their village close to Fort Victoria, near the current site of Bastion Square, but relations with the Hudson's Bay Company were always strained. In 1844, a dispute over a pair of company oxen slaughtered by the Songhees was settled only after Commander Roderick Finlayson blew up the chief's house. A few years later, after a fire started in the native village, spread, and nearly burned down the fort, Finlayson told the Songhees to relocate across the Inner Harbour. They refused at first, pointing out quite rightly that as it was their land, they could live

The Spirit of Lakwammen totem pole at Songhees Point.

wherever they liked. They assented to the move only after Finlayson agreed to help dismantle and transport the Songhees' longhouses. The totem pole here is called the **Spirit of Lakwammen,** presented to the city to commemorate the 1994 Commonwealth Games.

Continue on the pathway around the corner. The patio of the Delta Victoria Ocean Pointe Resort (p. 239) provides a great view of the Fairmont Empress. A little farther on is the:

10 Johnson Street Bridge

The same guy who designed San Francisco's Golden Gate Bridge also designed Victoria's Johnson Street Bridge. Alas, while the soaring Golden Gate span is justly famous for its elegance, this misshapen lump of steel and concrete is something designer Joseph Strauss would likely wish forgotten.

Cross the bridge, walk past the Esquimalt and Nanaimo (E&N) Railway station and turn left onto Store St. Walk 1 block north to Swift St., turn left and walk downhill to the end of the street:

11 Canoe ☕

While having a drink at **Canoe,** it's hard to know whom to admire more: the 19th-century engineers who built everything with brick and beam, and always twice as thick as it had to be; the restorers who took this old building (once the site of the City Light Company) and turned it into a sunlit cathedral of a room; the owner, who had the vision to pay the restorers; the chef, who made the delicious plate of appetizers now quickly disappearing from your table; or the brew master, whose copper cauldrons produce such a superior brew. Try the taster option—six small glasses of different brews for about the price of a pint—and toast them all. 450 Swift St. ℂ **250/361-1940.** See p. 257.

Salutations complete, wander back up Swift St., turn right and continue south down Store St. for 2 blocks, where Store St. becomes Wharf St. Walk another 3 blocks until you reach:

12 Bastion Square

This pleasant public space stands on the site of the Hudson's Bay Company's original Fort Victoria. The fort was demolished in 1863 and the land sold off for development. When the BC government bought and renovated the Rithet Building on the southwest corner of the square, workers uncovered Fort Victoria's original water well, complete with mechanical pump. It's now in the building's lobby. The square is home to the Maritime Museum. (p. 275).

Continue south on Wharf St. another 2 blocks until you come to the pinkish Dominion Customs House. Built in 1876, the Second Empire style was meant to impart a touch of European civilization in the midst of this raw wilderness town. Take the walkway by the Customs house down to the waterline and walk out on the:

13 Floatplane Docks

Early in the morning, these docks buzz with activity as floatplanes fly in and out on their way to and from Seattle, Vancouver, and points farther north. The docks are also the place to come to arrange diving and whale-watching tours.

Back up on Wharf St., you're just a hop, skip, and a jump from the Visitor Centre tower, where the tour began.

WALKING TOUR 2: # THE OLD TOWN & CHINATOWN

START & FINISH: **The Fairmont Empress, 721 Government St.**

TIME: **2 hours, not including shopping, sightseeing, and eating stops.**

BEST TIME: **Any day before 6pm.**

WORST TIME: **Any day after 6pm, when the shops close.**

1 The Fairmont Empress

At 721 Government St., this architectural delight was designed by Francis Rattenbury (see "Francis Rattenbury: Famous Architect and Murder Victim," in chapter 2).

Walking north up Government St., you'll find a number of historic buildings. British Columbia's oldest brick structure, at 901 Government St., is the:

2 Windsor Hotel building

Built in 1858 as the Victoria Hotel, the building's actually a perfect metaphor for the city. The original structure was a robust yet stylish piece of frontier architecture, with heavy red bricks formed into graceful Romanesque arches. Then, in the 1930s, when the city began pushing the "little bit of England" shtick, the original brick was covered with stucco and fake

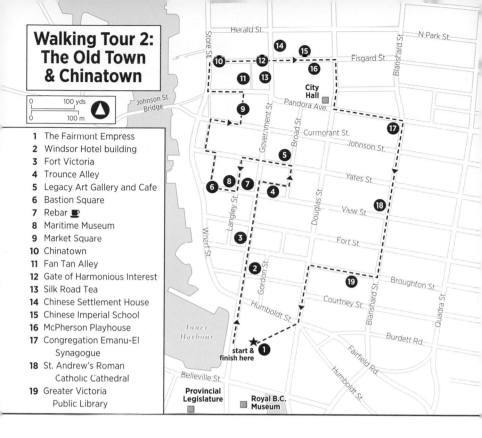

Walking Tour 2: The Old Town & Chinatown

0 — 100 yds
0 — 100 m

Tudor half-timbering. Somewhere under the phony gentility, however, the robust frontier structure survives. (It's been through worse: In 1876, the hotel underwent major unexpected remodeling after the owner searched for a gas leak with a lit candle.)

On the next block, you'll find a brass sidewalk plaque at 1022 Government St., indicating the former site of:

3 Fort Victoria

The fort was constructed in 1843 by the Hudson's Bay Company as the western headquarters of its fur-trading empire. Bound by Broughton and View streets, between Government and Wharf streets, the fort had two octagonal bastions on either side of its tall cedar picket walls. It was torn down during the 1860s gold boom to make room for more businesses. You can get an idea of its size and shape from the line of light-colored bricks—inscribed with the names of early settlers—in the sidewalk that delineates the boundaries of the original walls. The first school in British Columbia was built on this site in 1849.

Continue north 2 more blocks, just past View St., where a little byway cuts off on the right, running 1 block to Broad St. It's known as:

4 Trounce Alley

This is where miners and mariners spent their extra cash on the ladies. The alley is still lit by gas lamps, hung with heraldic crests, and ablaze with flower baskets and potted shrubs. You can stroll through shops selling jewelry, fashions, and crafts, or stop for a bite to eat. Trounce Alley ends abruptly at Broad Street.

Turn left on Broad St., walk north 1 block, turn left on Yates St. and walk west 1 block until you come to the:

5 Legacy Art Gallery and Cafe

At 630 Yates St., this ex-bank building is one of the city's finest examples of the Moderne style,

Organic juices at the funky rebar.

but what makes it worth a visit is the gallery inside, which was recently renovated (© **250/381-7670;** www.legacygallery.ca). When Victoria art collector and architectural preservationist Michael Williams died in 2000, he willed his collection of contemporary Canadian art to the University of Victoria, which shows it here, along with changing exhibitions. Williams was one of the leading figures in the fight to save Victoria's Old Town. There's a gallery shop and a deli-style cafe, as well. The gallery is open Wednesday to Sunday from 10am to 5pm.

From here, go 1 more block west on Yates St. Between Government and Store sts., on the north side of the block, is a collection of mid-19th-century brick storefronts, including the former Majestic Theatre, at 564 Yates St., dating from 1860. From Yates St., turn left on Langley St. and go 1 block south. Turn right on View St. and you're in:

6 Bastion Square

This square was a bustling area with waterfront hotels, saloons, and warehouses during the late 19th century. Earlier, it had been the site of one of Fort Victoria's octagonal gun bastions. In 1963, the area was restored as a heritage square. This is a good place to take a break:

7 rebar ☕

If you're in the mood for a big, healthy glass of organic juice or some delicious vegetarian grub, stop in at **rebar,** downtown Victoria's best and funkiest spot for wholesome food and drinks. 50 Bastion Sq. © **250/361-9223.** See p. 263.

The provincial courthouse and hangman's square were once located on Bastion Square, but now you'll find the:

8 Maritime Museum

At 28 Bastion Sq., you can get a glimpse into Victoria's naval and shipping history (p. 275). The museum is housed in Victoria's original courthouse and jail, which opened in 1889.

Turn north up Commercial Alley. Cross Yates St. and a few steps farther west, turn north again up Waddington Alley. On the other side of Johnson St. is:

9 Market Square

This restored historic site was once a two-story complex of shipping offices and supply stores. It now contains more than 40 shops that sell everything from sports equipment and crafts to books and toys. In the summer, musicians often perform and restaurants set up outdoor seating in the large open-air court. More than a century ago, Victoria's business was transacted in this area of winding alleys and walkways. Warehouses, mariner's hotels, and shipping offices have been carefully restored into shops, restaurants, and galleries. You'll occasionally find historic plaques explaining the function of a building before it was renovated.

Go north 1 block on Store St. and turn right (away from the harbor) onto Fisgard St. You're now in North America's oldest:

10 Chinatown

Established in 1858, when the first Chinese arrived as gold seekers and railroad workers, this 6-block district (roughly btw. Store and Blanshard sts., and Herald St. and Pandora Ave.) fell into decline after World War I (as did many west coast Asian communities when the U.S. and Canadian governments restricted Asian immigration). What remains is a fascinating peek into a well-hidden and exotic heritage.

On your right, halfway up the block, you'll find:

11 Fan Tan Alley

The world's narrowest street, it's no more than 1.2m (4 ft.) wide at either end, and expands to a little more than 1.8m (6 ft.) in the center. Through the maze of doorways (which still have their old Chinese signage) are entries to small courtyards leading to even more doorways. During the late 1800s, this was the main entrance to "Little Canton," where the scent of legally manufactured opium wafted from the courtyards. Opium dens, gambling parlors, and brothels sprang up between the factories and bachelor rooms where male immigrants shared cramped quarters to save money.

Today, you won't find any sin for sale here—just a few little shops dealing in crafts and souvenirs. You can enter the **Chinatown Trading Company** (551 Fisgard St.) from Fisgard Street or via a back door facing Fan Tan Alley. Hidden in its back room are a couple of mini-museums cleverly displaying artifacts from old Chinatown, including the original equipment from a 19th-century Chinese gambling house.

When you're finished exploring the alley, return to Fisgard St. and continue heading east. At the corner of Government and Fisgard sts. is the:

12 Gate of Harmonious Interest

This lavishly detailed, dragon-headed red-and-gold archway was built in 1981 to commemorate the completion—after years of deterioration—of Chinatown's revitalization by the city and the Chinese Consolidated Benevolent Association. The gate is guarded by a pair of hand-carved stone lions imported from Suzhou, China.

A half-block down, at 1624 Government St., is:

13 Silk Road Tea

A modern twist on an ancient art, this tea emporium sells more than 300 blends of exotic teas and all manner of tea paraphernalia. Enjoy a flight of teas at the tasting bar and pick up some tea spa products to use later in a relaxing bath or re-energizing foot massage.

Head back up one block to 1715 Government St., the former location of the:

14 Chinese Settlement House

Newly arrived Chinese families once lived upstairs in this balconied building and made use of social services here until they were able to secure work and living quarters. The original **Chinese Buddhist temple** has been moved from the storefront to the second floor, but it's still open to visitors. Although admission is free, hours vary. You will have to check with temple staff to see if you may enter.

A half-block up from the Gate of Harmonious Interest, at 36 Fisgard St., is the:

15 Chinese Imperial School (Zhongua Xuetang)

This red-and-gold, pagoda-style building with a baked-tile roof and recessed balconies was built by the Chinese Benevolent Society. In 1907, the Victoria School Board banned non-Canadian Chinese children from attending public school, and in response, the society started its own community elementary school the following year. The school is open to the public during the week, and it still provides children and adults with instruction in Chinese reading and writing on weekends.

Just east of the school, at 3 Centennial Sq., is the:

16 McPherson Playhouse

Formerly a vaudeville theater, this was the first of the vast Pantages Theatres chain (Alex Pantages went into showbiz after striking it rich in the Klondike gold fields). The building was restored in the 1960s and is now Victoria's main performing arts center (✆ **250/386-6121**). The center is usually open during the day, although no formal tours are given; if you ask nicely, you may be allowed to take a peek inside at the ornate interior. You could also try to get tickets to a show there. City Hall and the police department are located in the office plaza surrounding the playhouse.

When you get to the southeast corner of Centennial Square, walk east 1 more block on Pandora Ave. to Blanshard St. At 1461 Blanshard St. (at Pandora Ave.), you'll find:

17 Congregation Emanu-El Synagogue

This is the oldest surviving Jewish temple on North America's west coast. Built in 1863, it has been proclaimed a national heritage site. The temple (which is not particularly impressive on the outside) is not open to the public.

Turn south on Blanshard St. and walk 3 blocks, noting Victoria's newest landmark high-rise, the glass-spangled Atrium en route, to 740 View St., where you'll see the impressive:

18 St. Andrew's Roman Catholic Cathedral

Built during the 1890s, this is Victorian High Gothic at its best. The facade is 23m (76 ft.) across, the spire 53m (174 ft.) tall, and no frill, flounce, or architectural embellishment was left out of the design. Renovations in the 1980s incorporated the works of First Nations artists into the interior. Go inside and see the altar by Coast Salish carver Charles Elliot.

1 block south at Fort St. is the beginning of Antique Row, which stretches 3 blocks east to Cook St. Ignore that for the moment (or go explore and then come back) and continue 1 more block south on Blanshard St. Walk across the plaza to 735 Broughton St., where you'll find the:

St. Andrew's Roman Catholic Cathedral was originally built in a Victorian High Gothic style.

19 Greater Victoria Public Library

The attraction here is the huge sky-lit atrium, complete with George Norris's massive hanging artwork, *Dynamic Mobile Steel Sculpture*. Built in 1979, the library complex takes up most of the block. The library is open year-round Monday, Friday, and Saturday from 9am to 6pm; Tuesday to Thursday 9am to 9pm; October through April Sunday 1 to 5pm.

Duck out through the portal on Broughton St. and walk west to Douglas St.; turn left and walk 1½ blocks south on Douglas St. until you see the entrance to the Victoria Convention Centre. Walk in and admire the indoor fountain and aviary. The Centre connects to the Fairmont Empress, which was our starting place.

16 BIKING TOUR: **DALLAS ROAD**

START & FINISH: **Cycle BC Bike Rental, 685 Humboldt St.**

TIME: **2 hours, not including picnic stops, sightseeing, shopping, or food breaks.**

BEST TIMES: **Clear, sunny days when the Olympic Mountains are revealed in all their glory.**

WORST TIMES: **Gray, rainy days.**

Victoria cries out to be biked. The hills are modest, the traffic light and very polite, and the views incredible. When touring around by bike, you rarely have time to stop and pull out a point-by-point guide, so the descriptions offered here are shorter than for walking tours. The route is designed to take you a bit beyond what would be possible on foot, without getting into an expedition-length tour.

This tour is about 15km (9¼ miles) long and stays on bike paths through much of its length, although some of the streets in the second half of the tour are lightly trafficked. The ride from the Dallas Road shoreline to Craigdarroch Castle involves an elevation gain of about 150m (492 ft.).

Start at **Cycle BC Bike Rental** (685 Humboldt St.; ☎ **250/380-2453;** www.cyclebc.ca), on the corner of Douglas Street, then head down to **Thunderbird Park:** Have a look at the totem poles. From there, continue east along Belleville Street past the **Legislature** and the **Coho ferry terminal;** then go round the corner onto Kingston Street and left through the small park to **Fisherman's Wharf.** From here, continue south along **Dallas Road,** past the heli-jet pad and the cruise ship terminal, and stop at the entrance to the breakwater at **Ogden Point.** By this time, if the sky's clear, you should have a fabulous view of the Olympic Mountains. Park your bike and wander out along the breakwater, or stop in at the **Ogden Point Cafe** (199 Dallas Rd.) for the same view without the wind.

The opulent Craigdarroch Castle.

Continue east along the seaside bike path or on Dallas Road. Stop here and there as the mood strikes for some beachcombing. A little ways on, past Douglas Street, cross Dallas Road and cut north into **Beacon Hill Park** (p. 282). Stop at the petting zoo, look at the 38m (125-ft.) totem pole, or just enjoy Victoria's favorite park. Exit the park by the northeast corner on Cook Street and cycle a few blocks north into **Cook Street Village.** This is a good spot to stop for a coffee and dessert, or to shop for picnic supplies at the local deli or supermarket. Head back south on Cook Street to Dallas Road; turn left and continue east a kilometer or so to **Clover Point,** a short peninsula sticking out into the Strait of Juan de Fuca. It makes a fine picnic spot. From here, head east to **Ross Bay Cemetery** (p. 282), Victoria's second oldest, where many local notables are buried, including former governor James Douglas and painter Emily Carr (see "Emily Carr: Visionary from Victoria," in chapter 2). From the north side of the cemetery, ride up the hill on **Stannard Street,** skirting the eastern edge of **Government House** (p. 283), the official residence of the lieutenant governor.

When you reach **Rockland Avenue,** turn right and ride a few hundred meters past the many fine homes of this elite enclave to the main entrance to Government House. Though the residence itself is closed to the public, the formal gardens are open and well worth a wander. Round back, the hillside of Garry oaks is one of the last places to see what the area's natural fauna looked like before European settlers arrived. The rose garden in front is sumptuous. Just west of the gate on Rockland Avenue, turn right onto **Joan Crescent** and ride up the small hill to opulent **Craigdarroch Castle** (p. 273), built by coal magnate Robert Dunsmuir for his wife, Joan. The castle is open for self-guided tours. From here, continue up Joan Crescent to Fort Street; turn right and go a very short way east to Yates Street; turn left and go 1 block to Fernwood Street; turn right and go 1 block north to **Pandora Street;** then turn left again and ride west down the hill. Watch for the **Christian Science church** at 1205 Pandora St. (where the street widens to include a boulevard in its center). Another 6 blocks west, and you're at **Pandora** and **Government streets,** with **Chinatown** (see stops 10–14 of "Walking Tour 2," above) to your right, **Market Square** (see stop 9 of "Walking Tour 2," above) to your left, and the Fairmont Empress and the bike-rental spot just a few blocks south.

VICTORIA
17
SHOPPING

V
ictoria has dozens of specialty shops, and because the city is built on a pedestrian scale, you can easily wander from place to place seeking out whatever treasure you're after. Nearly all of the areas listed below are within a short walk of the Fairmont Empress; for those shops located more than 6 blocks from the hotel, bus information is provided. Stores generally open Monday through Saturday from 10am to 6pm; some are open on Sundays during the summer.

THE SHOPPING SCENE

Explorers beware: The brick-paved **Government Street promenade,** from the Inner Harbour 5 blocks north to Yates Street, is a jumble of cheap souvenir shops. There are gems in here—Irish linen, fine bone china, quality Pacific Coast Native art, and thick Cowichan sweaters—but to find these riches, you'll have to pass T-shirt stores and knickknack emporiums galore. Just off Government, near the Bay Centre, **Broad Street** and **Trounce Alley** have intriguing finds.

Farther north, the **Old Town district, Lower Johnson** (nicknamed LoJo), and **Market Square** feature a fascinating blend of heritage buildings and up-to-date shops. Victoria's **Chinatown** is tiny, and since most of the city's Chinese population has moved elsewhere, it lacks the authenticity and vitality of China-towns elsewhere. The area has been charmingly preserved, however, and there are several gallery-quality art and ceramic shops, and quirky back alleys (including Canada's thinnest commercial street, Fan Tan Alley).

A small new **Design District,** lined with home furnishing stores, begins 1 block north of Chinatown on Herald Street and stretches west to Wharf Street and south along Wharf. On the eastern edge of downtown, **Antique Row** is known for its high-quality British collectibles which, increasingly, are mixed with more modern home furnishings from the 1950s and 1960s. And if you're at all interested in the Native art of the Pacific Northwest, Victoria is a good place for pieces to add to your collection. A growing number of galleries featuring all genres of Canadian work are setting up shop behind the Empress in an up-and-coming shopping district called **Humboldt Valley.**

SHOPPING A TO Z
Antiques

Victoria has long had a deserved reputation for antiques—particularly those of British origin. Many of the best stores are on **Antique Row,** mentioned above, and is where to find two auction houses: **Lund's Auctions** (926 Fort St., © **250/386-3308;** www.lunds.com) and **Kilshaw's Auctioneers** (1115 Fort

PREVIOUS PAGE: **Faith Grant's Connoisseur Shop is the best place to shop for antiques in Victoria.**

309

St., ℂ **250/384-6441;** www.kilshaws.com), both of which can offer deals and entertainment value if you happen to be around on a bidding night.

In addition to those listed below, check out **Romanoff & Company Antiques** (837 Fort St.; ℂ **250/480-1543**) and, for furniture fans, browse **Applewood Antiques** (1028 Fort St.; ℂ **250/475-1028;** www.applewood antiques.com).

David Robinson Antiques Here, you'll find Oriental rugs, silver, oil paintings, brass, porcelain, and period furniture. Though it's not as large as Faith Grant's shop (see below), Robinson's pieces—especially his furniture—are particularly well chosen. 1023 Fort St. ℂ **250/384-6425.** Bus: 10 to Blanshard St. or Cook St.

Faith Grant's Connoisseur Shop Ltd. ♟ The farthest from downtown, this shop is also the best. The 16 rooms of this 1862 heritage building contain everything from Georgian writing desks to English flatware, not to mention fine ceramics, prints, and paintings. Furniture is especially strong here. Sadly, the property is for sale so this fabulous trove may be relocating; though by reputation alone, it should be easy to find. 1156 Fort St. ℂ **250/383-0121.** www.faithgrantantiques.com. Bus: 10 to Fort and Cook sts.

Vanity Fair Antiques & Collectibles ⚑ This large shop is fun to browse, with crystal, glassware, furniture, and lots more. If you're feeling flush, it's certainly possible to spend here, but many items can be snapped up without taking out a bank loan. 1044 Fort St. ℂ **250/380-7274.** www.vanityfairantiques.com. Bus: 10 to Blanshard St. or Cook St.

Art

Fran Willis Gallery Soaring white walls and huge arched windows make this one of Victoria's most beautiful gallery spaces. The collection is strong in contemporary oils, mixed media, and bronzes, almost all by BC and Alberta artists. 1619 Store St. ℂ **250/381-3422.** www.franwillis.com. Bus: 5 to Douglas and Fisgard sts.

Open Space When does self-confidence start edging into pretension? This artist-run gallery and self-declared flag-bearer of the avant-garde has trod on both sides of that line since 1972. Mostly, they get it right, so the gallery is usually worth a visit. Exhibits run the full gamut, from paintings and sculpture to literary and dance performances. 510 Fort St. ℂ **250/383-8833.** www.openspace.ca.

Sidestreet Studio Everything here—jewelry, pottery, wood tunings, glass, and textiles—is Canadian, handcrafted, and one-of-a-kind. Prices are more affordable than some of the large, established galleries. 729 Humboldt St. ℂ **250/590-4644.** www.sidestreetstudio.com.

Winchester Galleries This slightly daring gallery features contemporary work from sought after names like Toni Onley and Jack Shadbolt alongside such historical pieces from the Group of Seven. Unlike elsewhere in town, the gallery hangs few wildlife paintings. 796 Humboldt St. ℂ **250/382-7750.** www.winchester galleriesltd.com.

Books

Avalon Metaphysical Centre Avalon specializes in New Age books, crystals, rune stones, body oils, and videotapes of gurus who've already trodden the path to enlightenment. 62-560 Johnson St. (in Market Sq.). ℂ **250/380-1721.** www.avalon metaphysical.com.

Munro's Books is located inside a century-old heritage building.

Crown Publications   In addition to dry, but informative, government publications, this store stocks an excellent selection of books covering the history, nature, and culture of the Victoria area. Keeping up with the times, digital maps are available on CD-ROM. 563 Superior St. ⓒ **250/387-6409.** www.crownpub.bc.ca.

Munro's Books 🎁   All bookstores should look so good: a mile-high ceiling in a 1909 heritage building, complete with heavy brass lamps and murals on the walls (never mind that the building was originally a bank). The store stocks more than 35,000 titles, including an excellent selection about Victoria and books by local authors. The staff is friendly and very good at unearthing obscure titles. 1108 Government St. ⓒ **888/243-2464** or 250/382-2464. www.munrobooks.com.

Russell Books 🔖   Canada's largest used bookstore offers two floors of used, new, and remaindered books as well as out-of-print titles. 734 Fort St. ⓒ **250/361-4447.** www.russellbooks.com.

Western Canada Wilderness Committee (WCWC)   Committed to protecting Canada's endangered species and environment, the WCWC store raises funds for the cause. Choose from beautiful gift cards, posters, souvenir T-shirts, and mugs. 3 Fan Tan Alley. ⓒ **250/388-9292.** www.wildernesscommittee.org.

China & Linens

Irish Linen Stores   Everything Irish since 1910: handkerchiefs, scarves, doilies, napkins, lace, and more. 1019 Government St. ⓒ **250/383-6812.** www.irishlinen victoria.com.

Sydney Reynolds   This building opened as a saloon in 1908, became a bank in 1909, was converted into a shop in 1929, and now houses a wide array of porcelains, including tea sets and Victorian dolls. 801 Government St. ⓒ **250/383-3931.**

Tuscan Kitchen   The glorious colors of Tuscany will draw you into the store; the hand-painted Italian majolica platters, dishers, and fashionable cookware will have you stay a while; and the offer to ship world wide will likely seal the deal. 653 View St. ⓒ **250/386-8191.** www.thetuscankitchen.com.

Chinese Arts & Crafts

Chinatown Trading Company
This unobtrusive storefront on Fisgard
Street opens onto a veritable bazaar—
three connected shops stocked with
Chinese goods either useful, endear-
ingly corny, or both. Who wouldn't
want kung fu shoes or a tin pecking
chicken? Browse through bamboo
flutes, origami kits, useful and inexpensive Chinese kitchenware, and a
few small museum displays of artifacts
from Chinatown's past. Look for the
sneaky back entrance off Fan Tan
Alley. 551 Fisgard St. ℭ **250/381-5503.** Bus:
5 to Douglas and Fisgard sts.

Old Morris Tobacconist has an impressive
selection of cigars.

Cigars & Tobacco

Old Morris Tobacconist Ltd.   This small shop maintains a century-old tradition of custom-blending pipe tobacco. You'll also find an impressive selection of
cigars, including Cubans. Cuban cigars can't be brought into the United States,
but a few brands like Horvath Bances duck the blockade by importing the
tobacco into Canada and rolling the cigars here. 1116 Government St. ℭ **250/382-
4811.** www.oldmorris.com.

Department Store & Shopping Mall

The Bay Centre   The Bay Centre is named after its new anchor store, Hudson's Bay Company. Although now owned by American interests, Canada's oldest
department store still sells everything from housewares to cosmetics and the classic (and expensive) Hudson's Bay woolen point blankets. The store also has a large
china and crystal department. The rest of the complex houses a full shopping mall
disguised as a block of heritage buildings. Btw. Government & Douglas sts., off Fort &
View sts. The Bay: ℭ **250/385-1311.** Mall: ℭ **250/952-5690.** www.thebaycentre.ca.

Fashion

FOR WOMEN

Breeze   This high-energy store carries a number of trendy lines such as Mexx,
Powerline, and Mac+Jac. Shoes by Nine West and Steve Madden, plus stylish
accessories, complete the look. 1150 Government St. ℭ **250/383-8871.**

Hughes Clothing Ltd.   This local favorite features designer fashions and
trendy casual wear. 564 Yates St. ℭ **250/381-4405.** www.hughesclothing.com.

Smoking Lily   This tiny, home-based store—one of the smallest in the world—
is like a test-run showcase for new ideas in women's clothing and accessories.
Consequently, there's always something innovative on hand. 569A Johnson St.
ℭ **250/382-5459.** www.smokinglily.com.

FOR WOMEN & MEN

Still Life   Originally known for its vintage clothes, Still Life has moved to a contemporary style that includes fashions from Diesel, Workwear, and Toronto designer Damzels-in-this-Dress. 551 Johnson St. ☎ **250/386-5655.** www.stilllifeboutique. com.

W. & J. Wilson's Clothiers   Canada's oldest family-run clothing store, this shop has been owned/managed by the Wilsons since 1862. Look for sensible casuals or elegant cashmeres and leathers from British, Scottish, and other European designers. 1221 Government St. ☎ **250/383-7177.** www.wandjwilson.com.

FOR MEN

British Importers   Victoria may be laid-back, but a man still needs a power suit, and this is the place to get it. Designer labels include Calvin Klein and Hugo Boss. Ties and leather jackets are also for sale. 1125 Government St. ☎ **250/ 386-1496.**

Outlooks for Men   This is the city's most fashion-forward menswear store, geared to the younger demographic with cutting-edge labels such as Orange Label, Z Zegna, Melting Pot, and Horst. 554 Yates St. ☎ **250/384-2848.** www.outlooks formen.ca.

First Nations Arts & Crafts

Natives from the nearby Cowichan band are famous for their warm, durable sweaters knit with bold motifs from hand-spun raw wool. In addition to these beautiful knits, craftspeople create soft leather moccasins, moose-hide boots, ceremonial masks, sculptures carved from argillite or soapstone, baskets, bearskin rugs, and jewelry. The **Quw'utsun' Cultural and Conference Centre** (p. 280) also has a large gift shop where you can watch artisans at work.

Alcheringa Gallery   What began as a shop handling imports from the Antipodes has evolved into one of Victoria's truly great stores for aboriginal art connoisseurs. All the coastal tribes are represented in Alcheringa's collection, along with pieces from Papua New Guinea. The presentation is museum quality, with prices to match. 665 Fort St. ☎ **250/383-8224.** www.alcheringa-gallery.com.

Art of Man Gallery   Beautiful and expensive First Nations artwork is sold in this shop, located off the Tea Lobby in the Fairmont Empress hotel. You'll find high-quality works by some of the best-known artists in British Columbia. In the Fairmont Empress hotel, 721 Government St. ☎ **250/383-3800.** www.artofmangallery.com.

Cowichan Trading Company   A downtown fixture for almost 50 years, Cowichan Trading follows the standard layout for its displays: junky T-shirts and gewgaws in front, Cowichan sweaters, masks, and fine silver jewelry farther in. 1328 Government St. ☎ **250/383-0321.** www.cowichantrading.com.

Hill's Native Art   Hill's is the store for established artists from up and down the BC coast, which means the quality is high, and so are the prices (although you can find good-quality work for under C$300). Of course, you don't stay in business for 50 years without pleasing your drop-in customers, so Hill's has its share of dream catchers and other knickknacks. 1008 Government St. ☎ **250/385-3911.** www.hillsnativeart.com.

Food & Wine

English Sweet Shop All those old-fashioned English sweets you love but can never find in North America (such as horehound drops and lemon sherbets) are sold in this 20-year-old candy shop. They also sell English marmalade, lemon curd, jam, chutneys, tea and biscuits—you get the picture. There's a smaller version, the **British Candy Shoppe,** 2 blocks away at 638 Yates St. (✆ **250/382-2634**). 738 Yates St. ✆ **800/848-1533** or 250/382-3325. www.englishsweets.com.

The English Sweet Shop sells candies that are difficult to find on this side of the Atlantic.

Murchie's It's worth coming here just to suck up the coffee smell or sniff the many specialty teas, including the custom-made blend served at the Fairmont Empress' afternoon tea. 1110 Government St. ✆ **250/383-3112.** www.murchies.com.

Rogers' Chocolates Rogers' bills itself as "Quite possibly the best chocolates in the world," and with original Tiffany glass, old-fashioned counters, and free samples, this 100-year-old shrine could possibly live up to the claim. 913 Government St. ✆ **800/663-2220** or 250/881-8771. www.rogerschocolates.com.

Silk Road Aromatherapy and Tea Company 🐾 Before setting up shop, the two Victoria women who run this store first trained to become tea masters in China and Taiwan. Their Victoria store on the edge of Chinatown sells a wide variety of teas, including premium loose blends and tea paraphernalia such as teapots, mugs, and kettles; tea blends can be sampled at an impressive tasting

Silk Road Aromatherapy and Tea Company is run by two trained women tea masters.

bar. They also offer a full line of aromatherapy products, many of which are used in a tiny spa located in the basement. Treatments range from a 2-hour green-tea facial to a full body massage at prices that tend to be much less than the swankier spas in town. 1624 Government St. ℂ **250/704-2688.** www.silkroadtea.com. Bus: 5 to Douglas and Fisgard sts.

The Wine Barrel This shop sells more than 300 BC VQA (Vintner Quality Alliance) wines and wine accessories. It's known for carrying the largest selection of BC ice wines (a type of wine where grapes have to be picked when the temperature has been below 0°C/32°F for a certain amount of time) in Victoria. 644 Broughton St. ℂ **250/388-0606.** www.thewinebarrel.com.

Jewelry

Artina's Shop here for high-quality, handcrafted Canadian and First Nations jewelry in gold and silver. 1002 Government St. ℂ **250/386-7000.** www.artinas.com.

Jade Victoria As the name implies, jewelry is made from British Columbia jade, which is mined in northern Vancouver Island, then crafted in Victoria and China into necklaces, bracelets, and other items. 911 Government St. ℂ **250/ 384-5233.**

Le Soleil Jewellers In business since 1976, this store sells one-of-a-kind pieces created in on-site workshops using the finest of materials. 608 Courtney St. ℂ **250/388-5162.** www.lesoleiljewellers.com.

MacDonald Jewelry Ian MacDonald designs and makes all his own jewelry: diamonds cut in squares and triangles, and styles from the traditional to cutting edge. It's a great place to hunt for rings and pearls, as well as precious gems like sapphires, rubies, and emeralds. 618 View St. ℂ **250/382-4113.**

Outdoor Clothes & Equipment

Ocean River Sports This is the place to go to arrange a sea kayak tour—they'll be happy to rent (or sell) you a boat and all the gear. This is also a good spot for outdoor clothing and camping musts, such as solar-heated showers or espresso machines. 1824 Store St. ℂ **250/381-4233.** www.oceanriver.com.

Pacific Trekking An excellent source for rain and hiking gear, this store is also good for advice on local hiking trails. 1305 Government St. ℂ **250/388-7088.**

Robinson's Outdoor Store There's a plethora of outdoor gear here, including a specialty area for fly-fishing so you can get the low-down on what works on local waters. They also sell freshwater fishing licenses. For nonresidents, a 1-day license is C$20 and an 8-day license is C$50, with lower fees for BC and Canada residents. 1307 Broad St. ℂ **250/385-3429.**

Walkers Shoes This store specializes in the finest European walking shoes for men and women. 1012 Broad St. ℂ **250/381-8608.**

Public Markets

Market Square Constructed from the original warehouses and shipping offices built in the 1800s, this pleasant and innovative heritage reconstruction features small shops and restaurants surrounding a central courtyard, often the site of live performances in summer. 560 Johnson St. ℂ **250/386-2441.** www.market square.ca.

18

VICTORIA
AFTER
DARK

A quote from a visiting New Yorker, captured in the local *Monday Magazine,* sums up the historic view of the city's energy: "Victoria is God's waiting room. It's the only cemetery in the entire world with street lighting." That's harsh, but more importantly, not exactly accurate. True, with retirees and civil servants making up a sizable segment of the population, Victoria is never going to set the world on fire. But the U. Vic. students, tourists, and a small but dedicated cadre of Victoria revelers form a critical mass large enough to keep a small but steady scene alive.

Monday Magazine, a weekly tabloid published on Thursdays (go figure), is the place to start. Its listings section provides comprehensive coverage of what's happening in town and is particularly good for the club scene. If you can't find *Monday* in cafes or record shops, visit it online at **www.mondaymag.com.**

For information on theater, concerts, and arts events, contact the **Tourism Victoria Visitor Centre** (812 Wharf St.; ℭ **800/663-3883** or 250/953-2033; www.tourismvictoria.com). You can also buy tickets for Victoria's venues from the Visitor Centre, but only in person. Another useful resource is the events line run by The Community Arts Council of Greater Victoria (ℭ **250/381-ARTS** [381-2787]; www.cacgv.ca).

Whatever you decide to do with your evenings, chances are that your destination will be close at hand: One of the great virtues of Victoria's size is that nearly all of its attractions are no more than a 10-minute walk from the Fairmont Empress, and easily reached by taking bus no. 5 to the Empress Hotel/Convention Centre. For those few nightlife spots a little farther out, bus information is provided throughout the chapter.

THE PERFORMING ARTS

The **Royal Theatre** (805 Broughton St.) and the **McPherson Playhouse** (3 Centennial Sq.) share a common box office (ℭ **888/717-6121** or 250/386-6121; www.rmts.bc.ca). The **Royal**—built in the early 1900s and renovated in the 1970s—hosts concerts by the Victoria Symphony and performances by the Pacific Opera Victoria, as well as touring dance and theater companies. The **McPherson**—built in 1914 as the first Pantages Vaudeville Theatre—is home to smaller stage plays and performances by the Victoria Operatic Society.

Theater

Performing in an intimate playhouse that was once a church, the **Belfry Theatre Society ★★** (1291 Gladstone Ave.; ℭ **250/385-6815;** www.belfry.bc.ca; bus no. 22 to Fernwood St.) is an acclaimed theatrical group that stages four

PREVIOUS PAGE: **The Victoria Symphony Orchestra's Symphony Splash kicks off their season with a free performance on a barge in the Inner Harbour.**

productions (usually dramatic works by contemporary Canadian playwrights) October through April, and one show in August. Tickets are C$27 to C$38.

The **Intrepid Theatre Company** (302-1205 Broad St.; ℭ **250/383-2663;** www.intrepidtheatre.com) runs two yearly theater festivals. In spring, it's the **Uno Festival of Solo Performance** ★★, a unique event of strictly one-person performances. Come summer, Intrepid puts on the **Victoria Fringe Festival** ★★ (ℭ **250/383-2691**). Even if you're not a theater fan—*especially* if you're not—don't miss the Fringe. More

The Belfry Theatre Society performs in a former church.

than 50 performers or small companies from around the world put on amazingly inventive plays. The festival runs from late August to early September, and performances are held at six downtown venues daily noon to midnight.

Theatre Inconnu (1923 Fernwood Rd.; ℭ **250/360-0234;** www.theatreinconnu.com) is Victoria's oldest alternative theater group, celebrating 20 years of performances. The actors are local and often semiprofessional, but quality is excellent and tickets are inexpensive. They stage a two-man adaptation of Charles Dickens's *A Christmas Carol* every year as well as an annual Shakespearean Festival in July and August that takes place in St. Ann's Academy.

The **Langham Court Theatre** (805 Langham Court; ℭ **250/384-2142;** www.langhamcourttheatre.bc.ca) performs works produced by the Victoria Theatre Guild, a local amateur society dedicated to presenting a wide range of dramatic and comedic works. From downtown, take bus no. 14 or 11 to Fort and Moss streets.

Opera

The **Pacific Opera Victoria** ★★ (1815 Blanshard St.; ℭ **250/385-0222** or 250/382-1641; www.pov.bc.ca) presents three productions annually from October to April. Performances are normally at the McPherson Playhouse and Royal Theatre. The repertoire covers the classical bases, from Mozart and Rossini to Verdi and even Wagner. Tickets cost C$35 to C$140.

The **Victoria Operatic Society** (744 Fairview Rd.; ℭ **250/381-1021;** www.vos.bc.ca) presents Broadway musicals and other popular fare at the McPherson Playhouse. Tickets cost C$20 to C$45.

Orchestral & Choral Music

The well-respected **Victoria Symphony Orchestra** ★ (610-620 View St.; ℭ **250/385-9771** or 604/385-6515 for box office; www.victoriasymphony.bc.ca) kicks off its season on the first Sunday of August with Symphony Splash, a free concert performed on a barge in the Inner Harbour. Regular performances begin in September and last through May. The Orchestra performs at the Royal Theatre or the University Farquhar Auditorium. Tickets are C$15 to C$80 for most concerts.

Dance

Dance recitals and full-scale performances by local and international dance troupes, such as DanceWorks and the Scottish Dance Society, are scheduled throughout the year. Call the **Visitor Centre** at (*C*) **250/953-2033** to find out who's performing when you're in town.

Comedy & Spoken Word

Mocambo (1028 Blanshard St.; (*C*) **250/384-4468**), a coffeehouse near the public library, hosts a range of spoken-word events through the week (multimedia fusion demos, philosopher's cafes, argument for the joy of it, slam poetry), then lets loose on Saturdays with improv comedy. There is no cover.

MUSIC & DANCE CLUBS

Music Festivals

Summer in the Square Every day at noon from early July to late August, this popular festival in downtown's Centennial Square offers free music. Each day features a different band and musical style: Monday features mostly jazz; Tuesday offers a selection of Big Band golden oldies; Wednesday through Saturday is potluck (show up at noon and take your chances). The festival's showstoppers are the Concerts Under the Stars held each Sunday from 7 to 9:30pm; the series features some 15 local bands over the 6-week length of the festival. Centennial Sq. (*C*) **250/361-0388.**

Victoria Jazz Society/JazzFest International ★ The Jazz Society is a good place to call any time of year to find out what's happening; it runs a hotline listing jazz events throughout the year. Its raison d'être, however, is **JazzFest International,** held from late June to early July. The more progressive of Victoria's two summer jazz fests, this one offers a range of styles from Cuban, salsa, and world beat to fusion and acid jazz. Many free concerts are given in the Market Square courtyard; others are held in live-music venues around the city. This organization also puts on the excellent **Blues Bash** on Labour Day weekend on an outdoor stage in Victoria's Inner Harbour. (*C*) **888/671-2112** or 250/388-4423. www.jazzvictoria.ca.

Live Music

Swans Brewpub (see review under "Bars & Pubs," below) presents a live band every night.

Hermann's Jazz Club This venue cultivates a community-center feel, which is definitely and defiantly *not* chic. Still, the reasonable cover charge gets you in for some good old-time jazz and Dixieland. Open Wednesday through Saturday at 8pm, Sunday at 4:30pm. 753 View St. (*C*) **250/388-9166.** www.hermannsjazz.com. Cover C$5–C$10.

Lucky Bar This long, low, cavernous space has a pleasantly grungy feel to it, which is barely noticeable once things gear up some time after 9pm. DJs spin house and trance on the weekends, with bands often showing up earlier in the week. 517 Yates St. ℂ **250/382-5825.** www.luckybar.ca. Cover C$5–C$20.

The Upstairs Lounge One of Victoria's favorite hot spots for live music sits overtop Darcy's Wharf Street Pub (see below) on the edge of Bastion Square. The Upstairs has space, good sightlines, and a crowd of attractive Victoria locals who come for touring bands, and DJ'ed house and Top 40. It opens Friday and Saturday nights, plus weekdays for special performances. 15 Bastion Sq. ℂ **250/385-5483.** www.upstairscabaret.ca. Cover C$6–C$12.

Dance Clubs

Most places are open Monday through Saturday until 2am, and Sunday until midnight. Drinks run from C$4 to C$8.

Club 9one9 It's high-tech all the way at this DJ plus live-band local with LED ceiling, floor, and table-top displays. These guys even broadcast live over the Internet every Saturday night. 919 Douglas St. ℂ **250/383-7137.** www.club9one9.ca. Cover C$4.

Sugar Groove the night away under an old-fashioned disco ball. Open Thursday through Saturday only; lineups start at 10pm, so come early. DJs spin mostly hip-hop, house, and Top 40 tunes. 858 Yates St. ℂ **250/920-9950.** www.sugar nightclub.ca. Cover Fri–Sat C$3–C$6.

Touch Lounge With three DJs spinnin', this newly renovated club/lounge is *the* hoppin' hot spot, especially for the under-30 crowd. Each of its three rooms has a different theme so you dress to impress and/or express. 751 View St. ℂ **250/ 384-2582.**

LOUNGES, BARS & PUBS

Lounges

Bengal Lounge ★ The Bengal is one of the last outposts of the old empire—a Raffles or a Harry's Bar—except the martinis are ice-cold and jazz plays in the background (and on weekends, live in the foreground). The couches are huge and covered in leather thick enough to stop an elephant gun. The cocktail list is extensive. The combination has lately attracted the young and elegant lounge-lizard crowd. In the Fairmont Empress, 721 Government St. ℂ **250/384-8111.**

The Reef This Caribbean restaurant transforms into a funky reggae lounge when the sun has faded away. Features include great martinis and good tunes, and a DJ now and again. 533 Yates St. ℂ **250/388-5375.** www.thereefrestaurant. com.

Bengal Lounge has an extensive cocktail list.

Spinnakers Brewpub has a good selection of beers they brew on the premises.

Bars & Pubs

Big Bad John's   Victoria's first, favorite, and only hillbilly bar is a low, dark warren of a place, with thick gunk on the walls, inches of discarded peanut shells on the plank floor, and a crowd of drunk and happy rowdies. In the Strathcona Hotel, 919 Douglas St. *C* **250/383-7137.**

Canoe ★   If it's a nice night, head for this fabulous outdoor patio overlooking the Upper Harbour. The beer is brewed on the premises (try the taster option— six small glasses of different brews for more or less the price of a pint). The century-old brick-and-beam building is a joy to look at, and the food is fun and hearty. 450 Swift St. *C* **250/361-1940.** www.canoebrewpub.com.

Darcy's Wharf Street Pub   Locals would consider eating anywhere on Wharf Street second rate, but drinking? That's another story. This large, bright, harbor-front pub features a range of fine brews, pool tables, occasional live bands, and a lovely view of the sunset. The crowd is young and lively. 1127 Wharf St. *C* **250/380-1322.** www.darcyspub.ca.

Spinnakers Gastro Brewpub ★   One of the best brewpubs in town, Spin-nakers did it first and did it well. Overlooking Victoria Harbour on the west side of the Songhees Point Development, Spinnakers's view of the harbor and Legis-lature is fabulous. On sunny days, it's worth coming here for the view alone. At other times (all times, in fact), the brewed-on-the-premises ales, lagers, and stouts are uniformly excellent and the pub grub is always good. An on-site bakery sells various beer breads. The weekends often feature a band. There are also dartboards and pool tables. 308 Catherine St. *C* **250/386-2739.** www.spinnakers.com. Bus: 24 to Songhees Rd.

The Sticky Wicket   This is yet another pub in the Strathcona Hotel (see Big Bad John's, above)—but the Wicket is a standout. It's a cavernous place, but the beautiful wood interior—including dividers, glass, and a long teak bar—spent many years in Dublin before being shipped here to Victoria, making it about as original an Irish bar as you're likely to find. Elevators can whip you from deepest Dublin up three floors to the mini-Malibu on the outdoor patio balcony, complete with beach volleyball. In the Strathcona Hotel, 919 Douglas St. ⓒ 250/383-7137.

Swans Brewpub ★ Few drinking spots are more intriguing—or more enjoyable—than Swans. The intrigue comes from the founding owner's vast Pacific Northwest and First Nations art collection. The enjoyment comes from the room itself, on the ground floor of a beautifully converted 1913 feed warehouse across from the Johnson Street Bridge. The beer here is brewed on-site and delicious. There's live entertainment at the weekends. In Swans Hotel, 506 Pandora Ave. ⓒ **250/ 361-3310.**

GAY & LESBIAN BARS

Victoria's entertainment options for the gay and lesbian community are few. A good resource for local contacts can be found online at **www.gayvictoria.ca**.

Hush This straight-friendly space (crowd is about fifty-fifty) features top-end touring DJs spinning house, trance, and disco house as well as live music from visiting bands. Open Wednesday to Sunday. 1325 Government St. ⓒ **250/385-0566.** www.hushnightclub.ca. Cover on weekends C$10.

Paparazzi Lounge Drag shows, karaoke, techno, Top 40—something different every night. It's the city's only true gay and lesbian nightclub. 642 Johnson St. (entrance on Broad St.). ⓒ **250/388-0505.** www.paparazzinightclub.com.

PACIFIC RIM NATIONAL PARK RESERVE OF CANADA

19

The west coast of Vancouver Island is a magnificent area of old-growth forests, stunning fjords, rocky coastline, and long sandy beaches. The Pacific Rim National Park Reserve of Canada was established here in 1971 as Canada's first marine park.

However, it wasn't until 1991 that it really became significant in the consciousness of people outside the area. That was when thousands of environmentalists from across the province and around the world gathered to protest and blockade the clear-cutting of old-growth forests on Meares Island in Clayoquot Sound. It was the largest act of civil disobedience in Canada's history. When footage of the protests ran on the evening news, people who saw the unspoiled beauty of this coastal landscape for the first time were moved to come experience it firsthand.

Tourism in the area has never looked back, and because of its importance as a pristine marine environment, Clayoquot Sound was designated a UNESCO Marine Biosphere Reserve in 2000. This designation doesn't add any legal protection (the paper companies are again eyeing the old-growth trees), but it does boost the park's environmental visibility.

ORIENTATION

The three main areas to visit are **Ucluelet, Tofino,** and the **Long Beach section** of Pacific Rim National Park. Tofino and Ucluelet are small towns on the northern and southern edges of a peninsula about halfway up the western shore of Vancouver Island, with the Long Beach section of the park between them. From Victoria, the trip by car—along a highway considered one of the top three scenic drives in Canada—takes about 4½ hours and includes such highlights as massive old-growth trees (Cathedral Grove), an enormous mountain lake (Kennedy Lake), snow-covered peaks, and brief stretches of ocean-side highway.

The park receives about 1 million visitors a year, most of them June through August. In those high-season months, traffic between Ucluelet and Tofino becomes an all-day jam; beaches are crammed with vacationers; and every restaurant, hotel room, and B&B is full (in the summer, it's essential to book a hotel before you go). Thick fog that doesn't burn off until mid-afternoon is typical in August. As locals will tell you, September and October are actually the best times to visit, and coming out for winter storm-watching is increasingly popular. This is a coastal rainforest area, so be prepared for rain, no matter when you visit.

The town of **Ucluelet** (pronounced you-*clue*-let, meaning "safe harbor" in the local Nuu-chah-nulth dialect) sits on the southern end of the peninsula, on

PREVIOUS PAGE: **A view of Clayoquot Sound from the air.**

Long Beach stretches more than 30km (19 miles) between Tofino and Ucluelet.

the edge of Barkley Sound. It's the first town you come to if you're driving across the island from Victoria. Back when fishing was the dominant local industry, Ucluelet was the primary town on the peninsula. When tourism began to take over, Tofino became more popular (it's better developed). Ucluelet has about 2,100 permanent year-round residents; in the summer, however, its population jumps tenfold. Like Tofino, it's a small coastal town with mostly new houses and businesses, so don't expect a quaint old fishing village.

At the far northern tip of the peninsula, about a 25-minute drive from Ucluelet, **Tofino** (pop. 1,800) sits on beautiful Clayoquot Sound and is the center of the west coast's growing ecotourism business. Hikers and beachcombers come to Tofino simply for the scenery—few landscapes in the Pacific Northwest are more majestically diverse, with the Island Mountains rising to the east of island-studded Clayoquot (pronounced *clay*-oh-quot) Sound, and the thundering-surf beaches of the Pacific just to the west. The town, with its ecotour and fishing outfitters, a growing number of restaurants, and new beachfront lodges, provides all the ingredients necessary for a memorable getaway.

Long Beach stretches between Tofino and Ucluelet. The beach is more than 30km (19 miles) long, broken here and there by rocky headlands and bordered by groves of cedar and Sitka spruce. The rocky coastline is popular with countless species of birds and marine life—bald eagles routinely nest in the vicinity, and between March and May, as many as 20,000 Pacific gray whales pass by as they migrate to their summer feeding grounds in the Arctic Circle.

ESSENTIALS
Getting There
To get to Vancouver Island, see "Getting to Victoria," p. 346.

BY BOAT A 4½-hour ride aboard the Alberni Marine Transportation passenger ferry **MV *Lady Rose*** ★★ (© **250/723-8313;** www.ladyrosemarine.com) takes you from Port Alberni to Ucluelet, making brief stops along the way to deliver mail and packages to solitary cabin dwellers along the coast, and to let off or pick up kayakers bound for the Broken Islands Group. This is a wonderful way to see portions of Vancouver Island aboard a heritage vessel; the round-trip takes 11 hours. The *Lady Rose* departs at 8am Monday,

Wednesday, and Friday from June to mid-September (Tues, Thurs, and Sat the rest of the year) from Alberni Harbour Quay at 5425 Argyle St. in south Port Alberni. The round-trip fare to Ucluelet is C$74, and to Bamfield is C$70.

The MV *Frances Barkley* takes you from Port Alberni to Ucluelet, stopping along the way to deliver mail and packages.

BY BUS Greyhound Lines (© 800/ 661-8747; www.greyhound.ca) operates regular daily bus service between Victoria, Nanaimo, Port Alberni, and Tofino/Ucluelet. The 6-hour trip, departing Victoria at 7:30, 8:15am, and 1:45pm, costs from C$84 to C$155 round-trip—the lower fares for advance purchase, the higher fares for refundable tickets. During the summer months, **Tofino Bus** (© 866/986-3466 or 250/725-2871; www. tofinobus.com) provides the same route service, departing Victoria at 8:25am and arriving in Tofino at 2:30pm; the price is a fraction less than Greyhound.

BY CAR Once you are on Vancouver Island, the same scenic, easy-to-follow route takes you to Ucluelet, Long Beach, and Tofino. Considered one of the top scenic drives in Canada, the paved route, mostly two lanes, gets twisty toward the end and takes about 4 to 4½ hours from Victoria. From Victoria, take Highway 1 north along the Saanich Peninsula to Nanaimo, where you take the Island Highway (Hwy. 19) north for 52km (32 miles). Just beyond the town of Parksville, turn west on Highway 4, which leads through **Coombs,** a farming community with a good selection of crafts and picnic supplies, then past **Cathedral Grove ★★**—worth a stop to see the

Cathedral Grove is a good place to see old-growth forest.

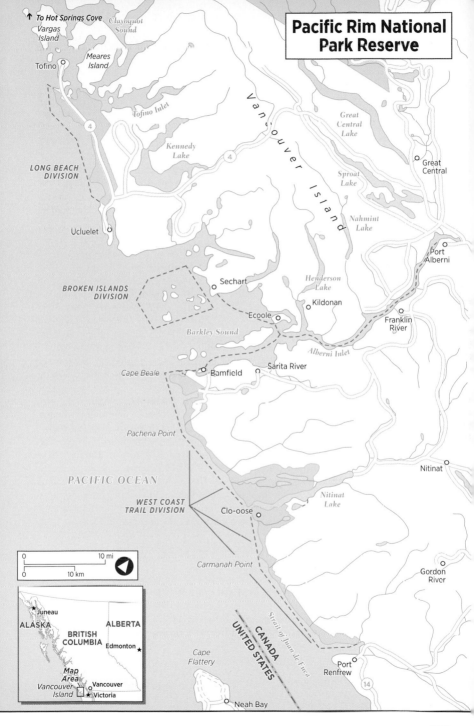

Pacific Rim National Park Reserve

To Hot Springs Cove

Vargas Island

Clayoquot Sound

Tofino

Meares Island

Tofino Inlet

Vancouver Island

Great Central Lake

Kennedy Lake

4

LONG BEACH DIVISION

Sproat Lake

Nahmint Lake

Port Alberni

Ucluelet

BROKEN ISLANDS DIVISION

Sechart

Henderson Lake

Kildonan

Franklin River

Ecoole

Barkley Sound

Alberni Inlet

Cape Beale

Bamfield

Sarita River

Pachena Point

PACIFIC OCEAN

Nitinat

WEST COAST TRAIL DIVISION

Clo-oose

Nitinat Lake

Carmanah Point

Gordon River

0   10 mi
0   10 km

Strait of Juan de Fuca

CANADA
UNITED STATES

Cape Flattery

Port Renfrew

14

Juneau

ALASKA

ALBERTA

BRITISH COLUMBIA

Edmonton

Map Area

Vancouver Island

Vancouver

Victoria

Neah Bay

old-growth inland forest—to the mid-island town of Port Alberni (about 38km/24 miles west). Highway 4 continues west, past giant Kennedy Lake, and reaches the Pacific Ocean just north of Ucluelet (103km/64 miles west of Port Alberni). Highway 4, also called Pacific Rim Highway, then turns north, passing through the Long Beach section of Pacific Rim National Park, to Tofino (34km/21 miles north of Ucluelet). If you arrive on Vancouver Island by ferry, rent a car from **Budget** (© **888/368-7368**), which offers customer pickup at all the ferry terminals in Victoria and Nanaimo. For Victoria-based cars, call **Budget** at © **800/668-9833**.

BY PLANE   Tofino's airport is tiny (only small planes can land), and the airline companies serving it change frequently. **Orca Airways** (© **888/359-6722;** www.flyorcaair.com) is currently the only Canadian company providing daily service between Vancouver/Victoria and Tofino/Ucluelet. The flight takes 55 minutes from Vancouver.

Visitor Information

The **Pacific Rim Visitor Centre** (© **250/726-4600;** www.pacificrimvisitor. ca), at the junction of Highway 4 and Ucluelet, serves as a general information gateway for Ucluelet, Tofino, Port Alberni, and Bamfield. Pick up information on area accommodations and attractions, and buy a **day-use park pass** (C$8 adults, C$7 seniors, C$4 children 6–16, C$20 families), which you'll need if you want to visit the beaches and park at any of Pacific Rim's official parking lots (passes can also be purchased with credit cards only from machines at the parking lots). The Visitor Centre is open daily April through June and September 9am to 5pm, July and August 9am to 7pm, and October through March 10am to 4pm.

The **Ucluelet Visitor Info Centre** (© **250/726-4641;** www.uclueletinfo. com), in town at 100 Main St., is open daily June through September from 9am to 5pm. The **Tofino Visitor Info Centre** (© **250/725-3414;** www.tofino-bc. com), at 380 Campbell St., outside Tofino, is open the same hours. For information on the park itself, stop in at the **Long Beach Unit of Pacific Rim National Park Reserve of Canada** (© **250/726-3500;** www.pc.gc.ca), north of Ucluelet (take the Wickaninnish Interpretive Centre exit from Hwy. 4). This park office, with a spectacular location above Wickaninnish Beach, is home to the **Wickaninnish Interpretive Centre** and a scenically stunning restaurant (p. 336). The center is open daily from mid-March through mid-October from 10am to 6pm.

Special Events

About 20,000 whales migrate past this section of Vancouver Island annually. In March, the **Pacific Rim Whale Festival** (© **250/726-7798;** www.pacificrim whalefestival.com) is held in Tofino and Ucluelet. The **Edge to Edge Marathon** in June is a distance run between Tofino and Ucluelet through Pacific Rim National Park; contact **Ucluelet Chamber of Commerce** for details (© **250/ 726-4641;** www.uclueletinfo.com).

Essentials

PACIFIC RIM NATIONAL PARK RESERVE OF CANADA

UCLUELET ★

Ucluelet is 292km (181 miles) NE of Victoria

Ucluelet enjoys a beautiful location on a sheltered harbor. You can choose from a number of fine B&Bs and cabin accommodations, but Ucluelet has yet to develop the same range of restaurants and activities as Tofino. If you want to stay in a seaside resort or lodge, head for Tofino.

Where to Stay

If you're backpacking and want budget accommodations or a place to pitch a tent, try **Ucluelet Oceanfront Hostel** (2081 Peninsula Rd., Ucluelet, BC V0R 3A0; www.cnnbackpackers.com; ✆ **888/434-6060** or 250/726-7416). The hostel, on its own private beach, provides free linens, use of a kitchen, Internet, and kayak and bike rentals. Rates are C$65 for a private room, C$25 for a single dorm bed. Campers seeking a family-friendly campground close to the park can reserve a spot at **Ucluelet Campground** (www.ucluchetcampground.com; ✆ **250/726-4355**), located at the edge of the village. The 125 campsites range from no service to full service; prices range from C$21 to C$40.

Black Rock Oceanfront Resort ★★   Ucluelet's newest and most upscale hotel sits on a rocky promontory overlooking the Pacific and surrounded by the Wild Pacific Trail. Opened in March 2009, Black Rock is carefully designed to maximize its dramatic location. Studios, and one- and two-bedroom suites feature floor-to-ceiling windows (the least expensive rooms have rainforest, not ocean, views), balconies, and a smart but unobtrusive air of contemporary luxury. Fetch, the hotel's fine-dining restaurant, sits on a surge channel with spectacular views. The center of town is a 15-minute stroll away.

596 Marine Dr., Ucluelet, BC V0R 3A0. www.blackrockresort.com. ✆ **877/762-5011** or 250/726-4800. 133 units. C$265–C$415 double; C$360–C$700 1- and 2- bedroom suite. AE, MC, V. **Amenities:** Restaurant; bar; free airport transfers; good fitness center; movie library; plunge pool; room service; spa. *In room:* TV/DVD player, hair dryer, kitchenette, minibar, MP3 docking station, Wi-Fi (free).

Pacific Rim Motel ☺   If you're looking for a clean, simple, inexpensive motel room, this is a good place to know about. The motel overlooks the harbor and offers one- and two-bedroom units, some with kitchenettes, a couple with full kitchens. The rooms are plain, the property is well maintained and well run, and you're close to the Wild Pacific Trail. They can help you arrange whale-watching or fishing tours.

1755 Peninsula Rd., Ucluelet, BC V0R 3A0. www.pacificrimmotel.com. ✆ **800/810-0031** or 250/726-7728. 55 units. C$85–C$150 double. MC, V. *In room:* TV, Wi-Fi (free).

Where to Eat

Matterson Teahouse and Garden PACIFIC NORTHWEST   Located on Ucluelet's main street, this is a good spot for lunch; sandwiches, salads, and a great seafood chowder are served in the two front rooms of a small frame house. On a nice summer day, you have the option of sitting on the shady porch or the sunny back deck. The Teahouse also serves dinner, with seafood always on the menu, along with other eclectic offerings.

1682 Peninsula Rd. ☎ **250/726-2200.** Reservations recommended for dinner in summer. Soup and sandwiches C$5–C$8; main courses C$17–C$25. MC, V. Tues–Thurs 11am–8pm; Fri–Sun 9am–8pm.

Norwoods ★ 🎒 PACIFIC NORTHWEST   Although Norwoods has all the stylings of a wine bar, its open kitchen tells you that food is the central focus of this tiny, upbeat bistro. Small plate portions encourage diners to share and experiment with an eclectic mix of styles, food fusions, and surprising combinations. All are delicious and all come with wine-pairing suggestions. Larger plates include duck, lam, and filet mignon. If dining alone or as a couple, you might enjoy a seat at counter overlooking the kitchen action.

1714 Peninsula Rd. ☎ **250/726-7001.** www.norwoods.ca. Reservations recommended. Main courses C$15–C$30. MC, V. Daily 6–11pm.

What to See & Do

Fishing remains the big outdoor activity in Ucluelet, and salmon is still the most sought-after catch. Charter companies that can take you out include **Island West Resort** (☎ **250/726-7515;** www.islandwestresort.com), **Castaway Charters** (☎ **250/726-2628** or 250/720-7920; www.castawaycharter.com), and **Long Beach Charters** (☎ **877/726-2878** or 250/726-3474; www.long beachcharters.com).

The recently completed **Wild Pacific Trail ★★★** skirts the rugged coastline with fabulous views of the Pacific and the Broken Islands; bald eagles nest along parts of the trail. For an easy and wonderfully **scenic walk,** take the 2.7km (1.7-mile) stretch from Peninsula Road in Ucluelet to the lighthouse. On this 30- to 45-minute hike along a gravel-paved trail, the path winds as close as possible to the ocean's edge, passing surge channels and huge rock formations. Check out www.wildpacifictrail.com for more information on walks and access points.

For **kayaking,** contact **Majestic Ocean Kayaking** (☎ **800/889-7644;** www.oceankayaking.com) about their half-day harbor trips (C$67), full-day paddles to Barkley Sound (C$145) or the Broken Islands (C$245), and week-long adventures in Clayoquot Sound (C$1,350).

Long Beach Nature Tours ★★ (☎ **250/726-7099;** www.longbeach-naturetours.com), run by retired Pacific Rim Park chief naturalist Bill McIntyre, does **guided beach, rainforest,** and **storm walks** that explain the ecology and wildlife of the area. Half-day hikes for 1 to 5 people cost C$225; full-day hikes for 1 to 5 people cost C$450.

Salmon fishing is the most popular outdoor activity in Ucluelet.

Housed in a converted container, the **Ucluelet Mini Aquarium** (© **604/ 987-6992;** www.uclueletaquarium.org), on Main Street at Waterfront Promenade (near Whisky Dock), is likely the world's smallest. Displays are gathered from the surrounding waters and put together with imagination, creativity, and an eye to encourage touching, stroking, ogling, and questioning of the ever-enthusiastic student marine biologists in attendance. Plans are in the works to make this a year-round deal with a permanent site, including beachside tidal gardens. Admission is C$5 adults. The aquarium is open May to October daily 10am to 6pm.

TOFINO ★★

Tofino is 316km (196 miles) NE of Victoria

The center of the environmental protest against industrial logging—and the center of the ecotourism business ever since—**Tofino** was, and to some extent remains, a schizophrenic kind of town. Until very recently, about half of the town was composed of ecotourism outfitters, nature lovers, and activists, while the other half was loggers and fishermen. Conflict was common in the early years, but gradually the two sides learned how to get along—more important than ever, now that a million visitors a year come to experience the area's natural wonders. Recently, the balance has definitely swung in favor of the eco-preservationists, who seek to manage growth and preserve the diverse habitats in a sustainable manner. But the town faces big pressures now that it's been "discovered" and has become such a popular destination.

Where to Stay

Tofino sits at the tip of Long Beach peninsula. One paved road—Highway 4—runs along the spine of the peninsula from Ucluelet up through Pacific Rim National Park to Tofino. The big resort hotels are all located on their own private roads, each of which has a name and connects to Highway 4. Big signs on Highway 4 advise drivers of the location of these private access roads, which will help you find your way to your hotel.

EXPENSIVE

Long Beach Lodge Resort ★★   This luxurious beachfront resort perched on the edge of Cox Bay, 3.2km (2 miles) south of Tofino, was built to resemble a grand West Coast–style home. The central great room (with bar and restaurant) features a massive granite fireplace and stunning ocean views. The guest rooms are luxuriously comfortable, some with fireplaces, balconies, and soaker tubs; all have marvelous beds and fine linens. Two-bedroom cottages, located in the forest and without ocean views, feature a ground-floor master bedroom and bathroom with soaker tub and separate shower, a sitting area with gas fireplace, dining area, fully equipped kitchen, private hot tub, and a second bedroom and bathroom upstairs. The dining room serves fresh regional cuisine with a hint of Asian influence.

1441 Pacific Rim Hwy., P.O. Box 897, Tofino, BC V0R 2Z0. www.longbeachlodgeresort.com. © **877/844-7873** or 250/725-2442. 61 units. C$190–C$390 double; C$320–C$630 cabin. Rates include continental breakfast. AE, MC, V. At the Pacific Rim Hwy. junction, turn right (north) and travel through Pacific Rim National Park; watch for the lodge sign on the left after you exit the park. **Amenities:** Restaurant; lounge; oceanfront health club. *In room:* TV, DVD/CD player, fridge, hair dryer, Wi-Fi (free).

The Wickaninnish Inn is the place to stay if you want the best of everything.

The Wickaninnish Inn ★★★   The Wickaninnish Inn is the most beautifully designed and built of all the Long Beach resorts, and it's the place to stay if you're looking for absolutely the best of everything. The service is exceptional, the detailing remarkable, and the setting spectacular. The inn sits on a rocky promontory, surrounded by an old-growth spruce and cedar rainforest, and the sands of Chesterman Beach. From the two buildings, no matter which room you book, you'll wake to a magnificent view of the untamed Pacific. Don't be surprised if a bald eagle soars past your window. All rooms in the original lodge feature handcrafted furniture, richly printed textiles, and local artwork, as well as a fireplace, soaker tub, and private balcony. The Wick's new wing features deluxe rooms and suites with more space, more light, and a higher price. Ancient Cedars is the hotel's on-site Aveda spa. **The Pointe Restaurant** (p. 335) is the most accomplished restaurant in the area. A stay at the Wick is a relaxing, rejuvenating, and memorable experience.

500 Osprey Lane (at Chesterman Beach), P.O. Box 250, Tofino, BC V0R 2Z0. www.wickinn.com. ✆ **800/333-4604** or 250/725-3100. Fax 250/725-3110. 75 units. C$420–C$580 double; C$540–C$620 suite; C$1,500 penthouse. AE, DC, MC, V. Drive 5km (3 miles) south of Tofino toward Chesterman Beach to Osprey Lane. **Amenities:** Restaurant; bar; babysitting; concierge; small fitness center; movie library; room service; spa. *In room:* TV/DVD player, CD player, hair dryer, minibar, MP3 docking station, Wi-Fi (free).

MODERATE

Brimar Bed and Breakfast ★   The location, right on Chesterman Beach, is what makes this place special. From your room, you can step out onto the sand and start exploring the wild Pacific. All three nonsmoking rooms have antique furnishings and lots of natural light. The upstairs Loft room features a queen-size bed, a bathroom with claw-foot tub and separate shower, and a bay window with a seat—and view of the ocean. The small Moonrise room has a queen-size sleigh bed and its own private bathroom across the hall. The larger, brighter Sunset room has a king-size bed and bathroom with shower. Breakfast and common areas look out over the ocean and are bright with natural light.

1375 Thornberg Crescent, Tofino, BC V0R 2Z0. www.brimarbb.com. ✆ **800/714-9373** or 250/725-3410. 3 units. C$160–C$300 double. All rooms C$99 in winter. Rates include breakfast. AE, MC, V. Stay on Hwy. 4 going north through Pacific Rim National Park until you pass the turnoff for the Pacific Sands Resort; take the next left on Chesterman Beach Rd. and proceed to the fork in the road. Take Thornburg Crescent (the left fork) and follow it to the end. Children 11 and under not allowed. *In room:* TV, no phone.

The Inn at Tough City   Right in town, overlooking Clayoquot Sound, this is Tofino's quirkiest small inn. Built in 1996 from salvaged and recycled material, it's filled with antiques, stained glass, and bric-a-brac. Several of the spacious rooms feature soaker tubs, fireplaces, or both. Rooms at the back enjoy views over the Sound and Tofino harbor. Three rooms on the main floor are wheelchair accessible. The excellent and reasonably priced sushi restaurant on the Inn's main floor is open for dinner only.

350 Main St., P.O. Box 8, Tofino, BC V0R 2Z0. www.toughcity.com. ✆ **877/725-2021** or 250/725-2021. Fax 250/725-2088. 8 units. C$110–C$230 double. MC, V. Drive into town and you'll see it on your right—it's impossible to miss. **Amenities:** Restaurant. *In room:* TV.

Middle Beach Lodge ★★ ☺   This appealing resort complex is on a headland overlooking the Pacific and features Middle Beach Lodge at the Beach, for adult guests only, and Middle Beach Lodge at the Headlands, a lodge and cabins suitable for families. The centerpiece of the first and smaller of the lodges is a large but rustically cozy common room with big windows that look out over crashing waves. Accommodations here are simple lodge rooms (26 of them) with private bathrooms and balconies, and no phone or TV. The 38 rooms and suites in the second lodge have more of the standard amenities, and nearby are 19 cabins designed for one to six people, with decks, kitchenettes, and wood-burning

The Inn at Tough City is Tofino's quirkiest small inn.

fireplaces, some with soaker tubs or outside Jacuzzis. This is a very comfortable, unpretentious place with a good restaurant and wonderful views of the ocean and beaches.

400 Mackenzie Beach Rd., Tofino, BC V0R 2Z0. www.middlebeach.com. ℭ **866/725-2900** or 250/725-2900. 64 units, 19 cabins. C$165–C$360 double; C$255–C$450 cabin. Rates include continental breakfast. AE, MC, V. **Amenities:** Restaurant; exercise room. *In room:* TV/DVD (in Headlands rooms), kitchenette, no phone (in Beach rooms).

INEXPENSIVE

Whalers on the Point Guesthouse ☺   Located at the foot of Main Street in "downtown" Tofino, right beside Clayoquot Sound, this 1990s building is part of the Hostelling International network of backpackers' hostels. It's clean and inexpensive, and everything in Tofino is within walking distance. As in other HI properties, you can rent a shared dorm room (four to six beds in a room), a private double room, or a larger family room. Rooms H to K, and N to Q are the best—all have views of Clayoquot Sound. There's an outdoor patio with a barbecue and a steam sauna. If hostelling isn't quite your style, there's a fully equipped deluxe condo that sleeps four, complete with flatscreen TV and free Wi-Fi.

81 West St., P.O. Box 296, Tofino, BC V0R 2Z0. www.tofinohostel.com. ℭ **250/725-3443.** Fax 250/725-3463. 17 units. C$32 dorm room; C$85–C$130 double. C$225 condo. Nonmembers pay slightly higher rates. AE, MC, V. **Amenities:** Sauna. *In room:* No phone.

CAMPGROUNDS

The 94 campsites on the bluff at **Green Point** ★★ are maintained by Pacific Rim National Park. Reservations are required in high season as the grounds are full every day in July and August, and the average wait for a site is 1 to 2 days. To

You should book ahead for a campsite at popular Green Point.

make a reservation, call ☎ **877/RESERVE** (877/737-3783) or go online at **www.pccamping.ca**. The cost is C$24 per night. You're rewarded with a magnificent ocean view, pit toilets, fire pits, and pumped well water, but no showers or hookups. The campground is closed mid-October through mid-March.

Where to Eat

Tofino is gaining a reputation for fine dining, with new restaurants opening every year, but it's also a laid-back place where you can grab a bite with the locals. For the best handmade chocolates and gelato on Vancouver Island, visit **Chocolate Tofino** (1180 Pacific Rim Hwy.; ☎ **250/725-2526;** www.chocolatetofino.com), about 3.3km (2 miles) south of town at the small, off-road complex that also houses Live to Surf and Groovy Movies.

EXPENSIVE

The Pointe Restaurant ★★★ PACIFIC NORTHWEST   Tofino's finest restaurant is perched on the water's edge in the Wickaninnish Inn (see above) with a 280-degree view of the roaring Pacific. The Relais & Château kitchen team deliciously interprets Pacific Northwest cuisine with an array of fresh and locally organic west coast ingredients, including fish, shellfish, lamb, and rabbit; there's a daily vegetarian creation, as well. To sample the best of everything, try the value-packed tasting menu. A recent one included Dungeness crab salad with English pea *panna cotta,* seared albacore tuna with fiddlehead ferns and potato-garlic puree, smoked beef tenderloin with Treviso radicchio and Puy lentils, spiced quail with sweet potato, confit fritter and saffron coconut curry, and a milk chocolate and peanut butter bar with kettle corn ice cream and salted caramel. The wine list is international in scope but also features the some of the best BC vintages. The breakfast omelet here is memorable.

In the Wickaninnish Inn (p. 332), 500 Osprey Lane (at Chesterman Beach). ☎ **250/725-3100.** Reservations required. Main courses C$34–C$52; tasting menu C$85; C$150 with wine pairings. AE, MC, V. Daily 8am–9:30pm.

The Schooner ★★ SEAFOOD/PACIFIC NORTHWEST   Established in 1949, the Schooner is the most venerable of Tofino restaurants and also one of the best for fresh seafood. The restaurant has two dining areas, one on the second floor with big windows looking out toward Clayoquot Sound. If you love fresh oysters, start with the "six pack," fresh shucked and served over ice with Tabasco and lemon. The classic signature dish here, served for more than 3 decades, is the Mates Plate, which includes fresh seafood from Clayoquot Sound (charbroiled salmon and halibut, grilled oysters, and garlic-sautéed prawns and scallops). Lamb, chicken, and pasta dishes are also available, but I'd stick with the seafood. A good wine list and wonderful desserts complement the menu.

331 Campbell St. ☎ **250/725-3444.** Reservations recommended for dinner. Main courses C$20–C$37. AE, MC, V. Mon–Sat 9–11:30am, noon–3pm and 5–9pm; Sun 9am–12:30pm, 1–3pm and 5–9pm.

MODERATE

Shelter PACIFIC NORTHWEST   Shelter is a three-in-one place: There's a casual pub area with a big-screen TV, an informal lounge area with tables and a big fireplace, and a romantic fine-dining restaurant on the second floor. The same lounge menu (halibut burger; pizza; teriyaki street bowl with fish, chicken, or tofu) is available in both areas on the main floor. If they're on the menu, try Panko-crusted Fanny Bay beach oysters—a succulent treat. Then I'd recommend the pan-seared wild salmon; it was the best sockeye salmon I've ever had. Shelter is also famous for its marinated pork chop and yellow Thai curry. This is a good place for a casual lunch, too.

601 Campbell St. ℂ **250/726-3353.** Reservations recommended in summer. Lounge meals C$11–C$18; restaurant main courses C$13–C$32. AE, MC, V. Daily 11:45am–midnight.

SOBO ★ ☺ FUSION/PACIFIC NORTHWEST   SOBO started life as a humble food truck and became so popular that it expanded into a bright, glass-walled, sit-down restaurant in "downtown" Tofino. The truck is gone now, but you can still taste the famous fish tacos made with wild salmon and halibut topped with fresh-fruit salsa; you won't find a better lunch treat in Tofino. SOBO is short for "sophisticated bohemian," which is how chef Lisa Ahier describes her cooking: She's interested in street food and tastes from all over the world. The dinner menu

SOBO is famous for its fish tacos made with wild salmon and halibut.

includes seafood tapas, soups, salads, and complete meals with offerings such as Vancouver Island seafood stew, hand-cut pasta with duck ragout, and oven-smoked-chicken pizza. There's a kids' menu, too.

311 Neill St. ℂ **250/725-2341.** www.sobo.ca. Lunch and snacks C$5–C$21; main courses C$10–C$28. MC, V. Wed–Thurs 11:30am–5:30pm; Fri–Sun 11:30am–9pm. Closed Jan and the last 2 weeks of Dec.

Wickaninnish Restaurant PACIFIC NORTHWEST   This restaurant, inside the Wickaninnish Interpretive Centre, is notable for the incredible ocean views from its wall of glass windows. It's a good lunch spot, with lots of fresh seafood on the menu, plus soups, salads, sandwiches, and fresh daily specials. Main courses include roasted chicken, baked salmon, halibut, prawns, pork tenderloin, steak, and a vegetarian offering. To reach the restaurant, you have to park in the nearby lot (the restaurant will give you a parking sticker) and follow a short boardwalk.

In the Wickaninnish Interpretive Centre (p. 328). ℂ **250/726-7706.** Reservations recommended in summer. Main courses C$19–C$44. MC, V. Daily mid-Mar to Oct 11am–9pm (until 10pm in summer). North of Ucluelet off Hwy. 4 (take Wickaninnish Centre exit).

INEXPENSIVE

Common Loaf Bakeshop COFFEE/SANDWICHES/BAKED GOODS   A cozy, comfy gathering spot, this is a good place to get a homemade breakfast sandwich or muffin, and a good cup of coffee. Service can be offhand, as in curt and/or barely there, but that doesn't seem deter the crowds. The Loaf does baked goods really well and has a modest lunch and dinner menu of soup and sandwiches.

180 1st St. ℭ **250/725-3915.** Sandwiches C$7–C$12. MC, V. Daily 8am–9pm.

Tuff Beans COFFEE/LIGHT MEALS   If you're looking for a good organic, fair-trade espresso or latte or a light meal—or want to check your e-mail—it's hard to beat Tuff Beans, located at the entrance to town. Even though the cafe is a little short on style, it serves good wraps, panini, salads, a curry bowl, and homemade soup. You can rent computers with Wi-Fi access for a nominal fee.

151 Campbell St. ℭ **250/725-2739.** Pizzas and panini C$13–C$15. MC, V. Daily 7am–9pm.

What to See & Do

For a good, overall introduction to the unique ecology of this area, stop by the 5-hectare (12-acre) **Tofino Botanical Gardens ★** (1084 Pacific Rim Hwy.; ℭ **250/725-1220;** www.tbgf.org), just south of town. The garden is laid out with paths and boardwalks that wind through the forest and along the shoreline; guided walks, special workshops, and naturalist programs are offered seasonally. The garden is open daily from 9am to dusk; admission is C$10 adults, free for children 12 and under.

Also in the gardens is the **Raincoast Education Society,** located in the Clayoquot Field Station (ℭ **250/725-2560;** www.raincoasteducation.org). Open daily in summer, this center features exhibits on local flora, fauna, and history, and often has guest speakers and nature walks; off-season hours vary, so call ahead. **Wickaninnish Interpretive Centre,** described in "Visitor Information," earlier in the chapter, has exhibits on coastal life and stunning views over Wickaninnish Beach.

The Tofino Botanical Gardens offers a good introduction to the region's ecology.

A natural, coastal hot springs about 67km (42 miles) north of Tofino, **Hot Springs Cove** is accessible only by water, makes a wonderful day trip from Tofino. Once there, you can soak in the small, steaming pools and douse yourself under a hot waterfall. A number of kayak outfitters and boat charters offer trips to the springs. I'd recommend **Jamie's Whaling Station** (606 Campbell St.; ℂ **800/667-9913** or 250/725-3919; www.jamies.com), which runs daily trips in a 12-passenger boat out of Tofino, and Ucluelet (ℂ **877/726-7444**). The 90-minute trip (each way) takes you past dozens of the quiet, green islands in Pacific Rim National Park; once you dock, there's a gorgeous and easy 30-minute hike along a boardwalk through old-growth forest to the hot springs. The cost is C$109 adults, C$99 seniors and students, and C$79 children 4 to 12. Your experience of the hot springs might be ruined if you go during the day in summer, though, when up to 70 people can jam the place. To appreciate their full magic, go on the earliest boat or floatplane, or camp overnight (Jamie's will drop you off on their last trip and pick you up in the morning). Jamie's also offers a wonderful Sea-to-Sky tour, a 5-hour trip with a boat ride, a hike through the rainforest to the hot springs, and a return to Tofino by floatplane, at the cost of C$175 adults, seniors and students, and C$165 children 4-12 years of age.

BIRDING The Tofino/Ucluelet area is directly in the path of the Pacific Flyway and attracts tens of thousands of birds and wildfowl; it's also home to bald eagles. The area celebrates its rich birdlife with the annual **Flying Geese & Shorebird Festival** every April and May. During those months, large flocks of migrating birds fill the skies and estuaries along Barkley Sound and Clayoquot Sound. Avid bird-lovers should contact **Just Birding** (ℂ **250/725-2520;** www.justbirding.com), run by keen birders who can show you the best bird spots on shore (very early in the morning) or on the open ocean. **Bird & Breakfast** (1430 Pacific Rim Hwy., Tofino, BC V0R 2Z0; ℂ **250/725-2520**) is a bed-and-breakfast run in conjunction with Just Birding. Perfect for birders, it's located adjacent to the walking trail in the Tofino Mudflat Conservation Area, right in the middle of the second-biggest shorebird pit stop this side of North America. You can also call this number to organize tours and paddles starting from C$99. April, May, and early June see literally thousands of shorebirds of all species fly by in their annual migration.

FIRST NATIONS TOURISM Clayoquot Sound is the traditional home of the Nuu-chah-nulth peoples, some of whom have recently gone into the cultural and ecotourism business. **Tla-ook Cultural Adventures ★★★** (ℂ **877/942-2663** or 250/725-2656; www.tlaook.com) runs various seasonal tours, including a 2½-hour **Inlet** (or **Sunset**) **Paddle** (C$55), in which participants paddle the local waters and learn about historical sites and local wildlife; and a 4-hour **Meares Island Tour ★★★** (C$74), which explores the ancient rainforest on Meares Island and offers insight into the trees, plants, and animals that make it their home. All tours are led by First Nations guides and often use traditional Nuu-chah-nulth canoes. These are among the most informative and memorable ecotours on Vancouver Island.

GOLF Year-round golf is available at **Long Beach Golf Course,** Grice Bay Rd., between Ucluelet and Tofino (ℂ **250/725-3332;** www.longbeachgolfcourse.com), one of the most challenging—and scenic—9-hole

Hiking through the rainforest on Meares Island is a memorable experience.

champion courses in British Columbia; guest rate is C$26. Rentals are available.

GUIDED NATURE HIKES   Owned and operated by Bill McIntyre, former chief naturalist of Pacific Rim National Park, **Long Beach Nature Tours** ★★ (✆ 250/726-7099; www.longbeachnaturetours.com) offers guided beach walks, storm-watching, land-based whale-watching, and rainforest tours customized to suit your needs. **Raincoast Education Society** (Tofino Botanical Garden; ✆ 250/725-2560; www.raincoasteducation.org) also offers seasonal guided rainforest and shore walks.

HIKING   The 11km (6.8-mile) stretch of rocky headlands, sand, and surf along the **Long Beach Headlands Trail** ★★ is the most accessible section of the Pacific Rim National Park system, incorporating Long Beach, the West Coast Trail, and the Broken Islands Group. Take the Wickaninnish Interpretive Centre exit on Highway 4.

In and around **Long Beach,** numerous marked trails .8 to 3.3km-long (.5–2.1 miles) meander through the thick, temperate rainforest edging the shore. The 3.3km (2.1-mile) **Gold Mine Trail** near Florencia Bay still has a few artifacts from the days when a gold-mining operation flourished among the trees. The partially boardwalked **South Beach Trail** (less than 1.6km/1 mile) leads through the moss-draped rainforest onto small quiet coves and rocky tidal pools of Lismer Beach and South Beach.

For a truly memorable walk, take the 3.3m (2.1-mile) **Big Cedar Trail** ★★★ through the dense rainforest on Meares Island in Clayoquot Sound. The best and most memorable way to experience Meares Island is to canoe over and enjoy a guided walk with Tla-ook Cultural Adventures (see "First Nations Tourism," above). Built in 1993 to protect the old-growth temperate rainforest, the boardwalked trail is maintained by the Tla-o-qui-aht First Nations band and has a long staircase leading up to the Hanging Garden Tree, the province's fourth-largest western red cedar.

KAYAKING Perhaps the quintessential Clayoquot experience, and certainly one of the most fun, is to slip into a kayak and paddle out into the calm waters of the sound. For beginners, half-day tours to Meares Island (usually with the chance to do a little hiking) are an especially good bet. For rentals, lessons, and tours, try **Tofino Sea Kayaking Company** (320 Main St.; ℰ **800/863-4664** or 250/725-4222; www.tofino-kayaking.com), **Pacific Kayak** (606 Campbell St., at Jamie's Whaling Station; ℰ **250/725-3232;** www.jamies.com), or **Remote Passages Marine Excursions** (71 Wharf St.; ℰ **800/666-9833** or 250/725-3330; www.remotepassages.com). Kayaking packages range from 4-hour paddles around Meares Island to weeklong paddling and camping expeditions. Instruction by experienced guides makes even your first kayaking experience a comfortable, safe, and enjoyable one. Single kayak rental averages around C$48 per day.

FROM TOP: Tofino is one of the best surfing destinations in Canada; Kayaking is perhaps the quintessential Clayoquot Sound experience.

STORM-WATCHING Watching winter storms from behind big glass windows has become very popular in Tofino. For a slight twist on this, try the outdoor storm-watching tours offered by **Long Beach Nature Tours** (ℰ **250/726-7099;** www.oceansedge.bc.ca). Owner Bill McIntyre used to be chief naturalist of Pacific Rim National Park and can explain how storms work and where to stand so you can get close without getting swept away.

SURFING The wild Pacific coast is known as one of the best surfing destinations in Canada, and most surfers work in the tourism industry around Tofino, spending all their free time in the water. To try this exciting and exhilarating sport, call **Live to Surf** (1180 Pacific Rim Hwy.; ℰ **250/725-4464;** www.livetosurf.com). Lessons start at C$55 without gear. Live to Surf also rents boards at C$25 and wet suits (don't even think

TWO trips OF A LIFETIME

These two trips are within striking distance of Vancouver or Victoria and can't be done anywhere else on Earth.

Sailing the Great Bear Rainforest ★★★

About halfway up the west coast of British Columbia, the Great Bear Rainforest is an area accessible only by boat. The lush landscape, the largest expanse of intact temperate rainforest left on the planet, encompasses fjords, rivers, streams, and waterfalls; the forest is filled with old-growth hemlock and cedar forests, and shelters the rare white spirit bear, as well as grizzlies and wolves. In 2006, a landmark agreement between First Nations tribes, environmentalists, timber companies, and the Canadian government designated the Great Bear Rainforest a protected habitat, thus preserving its unique splendor for ages to come.

With 3 decades of sailing experience in the region, Tom Ellison and his wife, Jen, run **Ocean Light II Adventures** (✆ **604/ 328-5339;** www.oceanlight2.bc.ca), the only company to offer trips to this magical part of the world on a 21m (69-ft.) sailboat. Skipper Tom Ellison is extremely knowledgeable and takes great delight in exploring the waters and coastline looking for whales, dolphins, and grizzlies. The price for a trip to the Great Bear Rainforest is C$3,600. It includes excellent home-cooked meals and comfortable, but not luxurious, accommodations aboard the *Ocean Light II.* The company also offers The Grizzlies of the Khutzeymateen, a 3-day trip (from C$1,850 per person) to Canada's only grizzly bear sanctuary. You need to book at least 6 months in advance.

Horse Trekking the Chilcotin Plateau ★★

The high plateau country of the BC interior has some of the most impressive scenery around. Soaring peaks rise above deep valleys, and mountain meadows are alive with flowers that bloom for just a few weeks in high summer. In British Columbia, one guide company is granted exclusive rights to run tours through particular sections of wilderness. The territories are typically 5,000 sq. km (1,931 sq. miles) of high-country wilderness, where you won't meet another horse team. One of the guide-outfitters closest to Vancouver is **Chilcotin Holidays Guest Ranch** (Gun Creek Rd., Gold Bridge; ✆ **250/238-2274;** www.chilcotinholidays. com), in the Chilcotin Mountains north of Whistler. Their horse-pack trips, running from 4 to 13 days and costing C$350 to C$3,450, inevitably involve encounters with wildflowers, bighorn sheep, grizzly bears, and wolves.

about going in without one) at C$20. Another option is **Pacific Surf School** (430 Campbell St.; ✆ **888/777-9961;** www.pacificsurfschool. com), or try the all-female-staff surfing school, **Surf Sister,** 625 Campbell St. (✆ **877/724-7873;** www.surfsister.com).

WHALE-WATCHING & BEAR-WATCHING   A number of outfitters conduct tours through this region, which is inhabited by gray whales, bald eagles, black bears, porpoises, orcas, seals, and sea lions. One of the oldest, **Jamie's Whaling Station** (606 Campbell St.; ✆ **800/667-9913** or 250/725-3919; www.jamies.com), uses a glass-bottomed 20m (66-ft.) power cruiser, as well as a fleet of Zodiacs for tours to watch the gray whales March through October. A combined Hot Springs Cove and whale-watching trip is offered year-round. Three-hour bear-watching trips are normally scheduled around low tides, when the bruins forage for seafood on the mudflats. Fares (for this and other companies) generally start at around C$79 per person in a Zodiac and C$99 per person in a covered craft; customized trips can run as high as C$200 per person for a full day.

Remote Passages Marine Excursions (71 Wharf St.; ☎ **800/666-9833** or 250/725-3330; www.remotepassages.com) runs 2½-hour-long whale-and bear-watching tours in Clayoquot Sound on Zodiac boats, daily March through November. Fares are C$84 adults and C$69 children 12 and under. The company also conducts a 7-hour combination whale-watching and hot springs trip at C$120 adults and C$99 children 12 and under. Reservations are recommended.

INDOOR PURSUITS   Browse the excellent selection at **Wildside Booksellers** (320 Main St.; ☎ **250/725-4222**), in the same building as the Tofino Sea Kayaking Company. Or tour some of the 20 **galleries;** the Tourist Info Centre has a pamphlet with a map and contact info for all of them. Standouts include **Sandstone Jewellery and Gifts** ★ (346 Campbell St.; ☎ **250/725-4482**) and the **Reflecting Spirit Gallery** (441 Campbell St., at 3rd St.; ☎ **250/725-2472;** www.reflectingspirit.ca). Royal Henry Vicker's **Eagle Aerie Gallery** (350 Campbell St.; ☎ **250/725-3235**) is a must-see for serious collectors of First Nations art.

PLANNING YOUR TRIP TO VANCOUVER & VICTORIA

A s with any trip, a little preparation is essential before you start your journey to Vancouver & Victoria. This chapter provides a variety of planning tools, including information on how to get there and quick, on the ground resources.

GETTING THERE

This section outlines your options for getting to Vancouver and Victoria. You'll find specific information about getting around both cities by car, on foot, and by public transportation in the chapters "Getting to Know Vancouver" (chapter 4) and "Getting to Know Victoria" (chapter 12).

Getting to Vancouver

BY PLANE   Daily direct flights between major U.S. cities and Vancouver are offered by **Air Canada** (© 888/247-2262; www.aircanada.com), **Alaska Airlines** (© 800/252-7522; www.alaskaair.com), **American Airlines** (© 800/433-7300; www.aa.com), **Continental** (© 800/231-0856; www.continental.com), **Delta Airlines** (© 800/221-1212; www.delta.com), **Frontier Airlines** (© 800/432-1359; www.frontierairlines.com), and **Northwest Airlines** (© 800/225-2525; www.nwa.com), and **United Airlines** (© 800/241-6522; www.united.com).

Domestic travelers within Canada have fewer options. **Air Canada** (© **888/247-2262**) operates flights to Vancouver and Victoria from all major Canadian cities, connecting with some of the regional airlines. Cheaper, and reaching farther all the time, is the no-frills airline **WestJet** (© **888/WEST-JET** [888/937-8358] or 800/538-5696; www.westjet.com), which operates regular flights from Vancouver and Victoria to Prince George, Kelowna, Edmonton, Calgary, Toronto, Montreal, Ottawa, Halifax, and farther afield.

Direct flights between London and Vancouver are offered by **Air Canada** (© **0871/220-1111;** www.aircanada.com). Other major carriers serving London (United, Continental, and British Airways) make stops in the U.S. before continuing on to Vancouver.

Air Canada (© **0871/220-1111;** www.aircanada.com) also flies to Vancouver from Sydney, Australia, and Auckland, New Zealand.

GETTING INTO TOWN FROM THE AIRPORT   The Vancouver International Airport is in Richmond, about a 30-minute drive south from downtown Vancouver. Ground transportation includes trains, buses, Richmond-area **hotel shuttles, rental cars, limos** and **taxis.** The latter line up in droves; expect to pay C$35 plus tip for a ride downtown. There are approximately 12 car rental agencies operating out of airport; visit www.vancouverairportcarrental.com to price compare and find your favorite agency.

PREVIOUS PAGE: **Taking a ferry boat is the best way to get from Vancouver to Victoria.**

Or, you can wait on the **AeroShuttle Service.** Operating between 8am to 8pm (to 5pm in winter), the bus leaves the international and domestic terminals on the hour and 10 minutes past the hour, respectively, and stops at most major hotels. The fare is C$15.50 one-way and C$25 round-trip. Since opening for business pre-2010 Winter Games, the **Canada Line** SkyTrain has become the fastest and most economical way to make the transfer. Services run between 5am and midnight, daily. The trip takes 25 minutes to the waterfront and costs C$8.75.

BY SHIP & FERRY Vancouver is the major embarkation point for cruises going up British Columbia's Inland Passage to Alaska. The ships carry more than 1 million passengers annually on their nearly 350 Vancouver-Alaska cruises. In the summer, up to four cruise ships a day berth at **Canada Place** cruise-ship terminal (p. 119).

The following cruises dock at Canada Place or the nearby Ballantyne Pier: **Princess Cruises** (© 800/PRINCESS [800/774-6237]; www.princess.com), **Holland America Line** (© 800/724-5425; www.hollandamerica.com), **Royal Caribbean** (© 800/398-9819; www.royalcaribbean.com), **Crystal Cruises** (© 866/446-6625; www.crystalcruises.com), **Norwegian Cruise Line** (© 866/234-7350; www.ncl.com), **Radisson Seven Seas Cruises** (© 877/505-5370; www.rssc.com), and **Carnival** (© 888/CAR-NIVAL [888/227-6482]; www.carnivalcruise.com). Public transit buses and taxis greet new arrivals, but you can also easily walk to many major hotels (the **Pan Pacific Vancouver Hotel,** perched directly atop the cruise-ship terminal, is the most convenient; p. 68).

If you're arriving from Vancouver Island or Victoria, **BC Ferries** (© **888/223-3779** or 250/386-3431; www.bcferries.com) has three daily routes. See "By Ship & Ferry," under "Getting to Victoria," below.

BY TRAIN **VIA Rail Canada** (1150 Station St., Vancouver; © **888/842-7245;** www.viarail.ca), connects with Amtrak at Winnipeg, Manitoba. From there, you can transfer to the Canadian, the western transcontinental train that travels between Vancouver and Toronto, with stops in Kamloops, Jasper, Edmonton, Saskatoon, Winnipeg, and Sudbury Junction. For travel within Canada only, the 21-day **Canrailpass** is valid for any 7 one-way trips (C$697 off-peak; C$1,114 peak) is available through www.viarail.com, with a small discount if booked 3 days in advance.

Amtrak (© **800/872-7245;** www.amtrak.com) offers daily service from Seattle, though there's currently only one train in the morning (departing Seattle 7:40am, arriving Vancouver 11:40am) and one in the evening (departing Seattle at 6:50pm and arriving in Vancouver at 10:50pm); otherwise, the Seattle-Vancouver route is covered by an Amtrak bus. Amtrak also has a route from San Diego to Vancouver. It stops at all major U.S. west coast cities and takes a little under 2 days to complete the entire journey.

BY CAR You'll probably be driving into Vancouver along one of two routes. **U.S. Interstate 5** from Seattle becomes **Highway 99** when you cross the border at the Peace Arch. The 210km (130-mile) drive from Seattle takes about 2½ hours. On the Canadian side of the border, you'll drive through or near the cities of White Rock, Delta, and Richmond, pass under the Fraser River through the George Massey Tunnel, and cross the Oak Street Bridge. The highway ends there and becomes Oak Street, a busy urban thoroughfare heading toward downtown. Turn left at the first convenient major arterial (70th, 57th, 49th, 41st, 33rd, 16th, and 12th aves. will all serve) and proceed until you hit the next major street, which will be Granville Street. Turn right on Granville Street. This street heads directly into downtown Vancouver via the Granville Street Bridge.

Trans-Canada Highway 1 is a limited-access freeway that runs to Vancouver's eastern boundary, where it crosses the Second Narrows Bridge to North Vancouver. When traveling on Highway 1 from the east, exit at Cassiar Street and turn left at the first light onto Hastings Street (Hwy. 7A), which is adjacent to Exhibition Park. Follow Hastings Street 6.4km (4 miles) into downtown. When coming to Vancouver from parts north, take exit 13 (the sign says TAYLOR WAY, BRIDGE TO VANCOUVER) and cross the Lions Gate Bridge into Vancouver's West End.

Canadian driving rules are similar to regulations in the U.S. Seat belts must be worn, children 5 and under must be in child restraints, and motorcyclists must wear helmets. It's legal to turn right on a red light after you've come to a full stop. Unlike in the U.S., daytime headlights are mandatory. Car insurance is compulsory in British Columbia.

BY BUS   **Greyhound Bus Lines** (✆ 800/231-2222 or 604/482-8747; www. greyhound.ca) offers daily bus service between Vancouver and all major Canadian cities, and between Vancouver and Seattle (at the border crossing, passengers disembark the bus and take their luggage through Customs). For information on Greyhound's cost-cutting **Canada Pass,** which allows for unlimited travel within Canada, and **Discovery Pass,** which allows for unlimited travel in the U.S. and Canada, consult their website. **Pacific Coach Lines** (✆ 800/661-1725 or 604/662-7575; www.pacific coach.com) provides service between Vancouver and Victoria (see "Getting to Victoria," below).

Getting to Victoria

BY PLANE   The **Victoria International Airport** (✆ 250/953-7500; www. victoriaairport.com) is near the Sidney ferry terminal, 22km (14 miles) north of Victoria off the Patricia Bay Highway (Hwy. 17).

Air Canada (✆ 888/247-2262 or 800/661-3936; www.aircanada. com) and **Horizon Air** (✆ 800/547-9308; www.alaskaair.com) offer direct connections from Seattle, Vancouver, Portland, Calgary, Edmonton, Saskatoon, Winnipeg, and Toronto. Canada's low-cost airline **WestJet** (✆ 888/WEST-JET [888/937-8358]; www.westjet.com) offers flights to Victoria from Kelowna, Calgary, Edmonton, and other destinations; WestJet service now extends to a few U.S. cities, as well.

Commuter airlines, including floatplanes that land in Victoria's Inner Harbour, provide service to Victoria from Vancouver and destinations within BC. They include **Jazz Air** (reached through Air Canada at ✆ 888/247-2262), **Harbour Air Sea Planes** (✆ 604/274-1277 in Vancouver or 250/384-2215 in Victoria; www.harbour-air.com), **Pacific Coastal Airlines** (✆ 800/663-2872; www.pacific-coastal.com), and **West Coast Air** (✆ 800/347-2222; www.westcoastair.com).

Kenmore Air (✆ 800/543-9595; www.kenmoreair.com) and **Helijet** (✆ 800/665-4354; www.helijet.com) offer flights between Seattle, Port Angeles, and Victoria.

PLANNING YOUR TRIP | Getting There

GETTING INTO TOWN FROM THE AIRPORT The Victoria International Airport is near the BC Ferries terminal in Sidney, 26km (16 miles) north of Victoria off Highway 17. Highway 17 heads south to Victoria, becoming Douglas Street as you enter downtown.

Airport bus service, operated by **AKAL Airport** (© 877/386-2525; www.victoriaairporter.com), takes about 45 minutes to get into town. Buses leave from the airport daily every 30 minutes, from 4:30am to midnight. The adult fare is C$18 one-way. Drop-offs and pickups are made at most Victoria area hotels. **Yellow Cabs** (© 800/808-6881) and **Blue Bird Cabs** (© 800/665-7055) make airport runs. It costs about C$50 one-way, plus tip.

Several car-rental firms have desks at the Victoria International Airport, including **Avis** (© 800/879-2847; www.avis.com), **Budget** (© 800/668-9833; www.budgetvictoria.com), **Hertz** (© 800/654-3131; www.hertz.com), and **National** (Tilden; © 800/227-7368). Car reservations are recommended from June to September and during peak travel times on holiday weekends.

BY SHIP & FERRY Car-carrying **BC Ferries** (© 888/223-3779 or 250/386-3431; www.bcferries.com) has three routes from Vancouver to Vancouver Island and Victoria. In the summer, if you're driving, it's a good idea to reserve a space beforehand, especially on long weekends.

The most direct BC Ferries route is the **Tsawwassen–Swartz Bay ferry,** which operates Monday to Saturday between 7am and 9pm (Sun 7am–10pm). Ferries run every hour, with extra sailings on holidays and in peak travel season. The crossing takes 95 minutes, but schedule an extra 2 hours for travel to and from both ferry terminals, including waiting time at the docks. Driving distance from Vancouver to Tsawwassen is about 20km (12 miles). Take Highway 99 south to Highway 17 and follow the signs to the ferry terminal.

Pacific Coach Lines (© 604/662-7575; www.pacificcoach.com) provides regular bus service from the ferry into Victoria for C$15 one-way, but you must book your seat on board the ferry and within the first 20 minutes of the ferry ride (a Pacific Coast Lines desk is on board the ferry). You can take Pacific Coach Lines all the way from Vancouver to Victoria for about C$85 round-trip, depending on the day you travel, which includes the ferry ride.

Exiting the Swartz Bay ferry terminal by **car,** you'll be on Highway 17 (there is no other option), which leads directly into downtown Victoria, where it becomes Douglas Street.

The **Vancouver-Nanaimo ferry** operates between Tsawwassen and Duke Point, just south of Nanaimo, about 100km (62 miles) north of Victoria. The 2-hour crossing runs eight times daily between 5:15am and 10:45pm.

The **Horseshoe Bay–Nanaimo ferry** has nine daily sailings, leaving Horseshoe Bay near West Vancouver (to reach Horseshoe Bay from Vancouver, take the Trans-Canada Hwy./Hwy. 99 and Hwy. 1 west across the Lions Gate Bridge) and arriving 95 minutes later in Nanaimo. From the Nanaimo ferry terminal on Vancouver Island, passengers bound for Victoria board the E&N Railiner (see "By Train," below) or drive south to Victoria via the Island Highway (Hwy. 1).

Whale-Watching on the Way to Victoria

If you're pressed for time, **Prince of Whales** (📞 888/383-4884; www.princeofwhales.com) tours offer a great way to combine whale-watching with your trip to Victoria. May to September, you can book a 5-hour whale-watching tour that leaves from Vancouver's Burrard Inlet and docks right in front of the Fairmont Empress in Victoria. The tour includes an excursion to world-famous Butchart Gardens before heading back to Vancouver. Cost is C$300 for adults, C$225 for children 13 to 17, and C$200 for children 5 to 12; check the website because the company sometimes offers special deals.

Three different **U.S. ferry** services offer daily, year-round connections between Victoria and the Washington cities of Port Angeles, Bellingham, and Seattle. All of these ferries dock at Victoria's Inner Harbour, near the Empress Hotel and Parliament Buildings, so you can walk right into town.

Black Ball Transport (📞 **250/386-2202** in Victoria or 360/457-4491 in Port Angeles; www.cohoferry.com) operates between Port Angeles and Victoria. The crossing takes 1½ hours. There are four crossings per day in the summer (mid-June to Sept) and usually two sailings a day throughout the rest of the year (with a 2-week closure in Jan).

Victoria Clipper (📞 **800/888-2535**; www.clippervacations.com) operates a high-speed catamaran between Seattle and Victoria, with some sailings stopping in the San Juan Islands. It's a passenger-only service; sailing time is approximately 3 hours, with daily runs from downtown Seattle and Victoria.

From mid-June through September, the passenger-only MV *Victoria Star,* operated by **Victoria San Juan Cruises** (📞 **800/443-4552** or 360/738-8099; www.whales.com), departs the Fairhaven Terminal in Bellingham, Washington, at 9am and arrives in Victoria at noon. It departs Victoria at 5pm, arriving in Bellingham at 8pm. This service offers special on-board salmon lunches and Victoria city-tour add-ons and overnights.

Note: If you're planning to ride the ferry between the U.S. and Canada, remember that you will need your **passport** or **passport card;** all passengers go through passport control and Customs on international ferry trips.

BY TRAIN   Travelers on the **Horseshoe Bay–Nanaimo ferry** (see "By Ship & Ferry," above) can board VIA Rail's **E&N Railiner** train at Nanaimo and wind down Vancouver Island's Cowichan River valley through Goldstream Provincial Park and to Victoria. The trip takes 2½ hours and ends at the VIA Rail Station (450 Pandora Ave.; 📞 800/561-8630 in Canada), near the Johnson Street Bridge. For more information, contact **VIA Rail Canada** (📞 **888/842-7245**; www.viarail.ca).

BY BUS   **Pacific Coach Lines** (📞 **604/662-7575**; www.pacificcoach.com) provides service between Vancouver and Victoria, with daily departures between 5:45am and 7:45pm. Pacific Coach Lines will pick up passengers from the Vancouver cruise-ship terminal and from most downtown hotels. Downtown-to-downtown fares average C$85 return, including the ferry, and depending on when you travel; ferries charge less for midweek travel. For more information, call or visit their website.

[FastFACTS] SOUTHWESTERN BRITISH COLUMBIA

Area Codes   The telephone area code for all of Vancouver Island, including Victoria and most of British Columbia, is **250.** For Vancouver and the greater Vancouver area, including Squamish and Whistler, it's **604.**

Car Rental   See "Getting Around Victoria," p. 233; and "Getting Around Vancouver," p. 55.

Cellphones   See "Mobile Phones," later in this section.

Crime   See "Safety," later in this section.

Customs   You'll pass through **Canadian Customs** (✆ **800/461-9999** in Canada or 204/983-3500) upon arrival and **U.S. Customs** (✆ **360/332-5771**), If you are traveling through the U.S., on your departure.

If you're **driving** from Seattle, you're most likely to enter British Columbia, Canada, at the Peace Arch crossing (open 24 hr.; often, there's a 30-min. or longer wait) in Blaine, Washington. You'll go through Customs when you cross the border into Canada and will need to show your passport.

Arriving by air, you'll go through Customs at the airport once you clear passport control. (Even if you don't have anything to declare, Customs officials randomly select a few passengers and search their luggage.)

Visitors arriving by **train, ferry,** or **cruise ship** from the U.S. pass through U.S. Customs before boarding, and Canadian Customs upon arrival.

What You Can Bring into Canada. Your personal items can include the following: boats, motors, snowmobiles, camping and sports equipment, appliances, TV sets, musical instruments, personal computers, cameras, and other items of a personal or household nature. If you are bringing excess luggage, be sure to carry a detailed inventory list that includes the acquisition date, serial number, and cost or replacement value of each item. It sounds tedious, but it can speed things up at the border. Customs will help you fill out the forms that allow you to temporarily bring in your effects. This list will also be used by U.S. Customs to check off what you bring out. You will be charged Customs duties for anything left in Canada.

A few other things to keep in mind:

If you're over 19, you're allowed to bring in 1.2L (40 oz.) of liquor and wine or 24 355mL (12-oz.) cans or bottles of beer and ale, and 50 cigars, 400 cigarettes, or 397g (14 oz.) of manufactured tobacco per person. Any excess is subject to duty.

Gifts not exceeding C$60 and not containing tobacco products, alcoholic beverages, or advertising material can be brought in duty-free. Meats, plants, and vegetables are subject to inspection on entry. There are restrictions, so contact the Canadian Consulate for more details or check the Canada Border Services Agency website (www.cbsa-asfc.gc.ca) if you want to bring produce into the country.

If you plan to bring your dog or cat, you must provide proof of rabies inoculation during the preceding 36-month period. Other types of animals need special clearance and health certification. (Many birds, for instance, require 8 weeks in quarantine.)

If you need more information concerning items you wish to bring in and out of the country, contact **Canada Border Services** (✆ **800/461-9999** in Canada or 204/983-3500; www.cbsa-asfc.gc.ca).

What You Can Take Home from Canada. If you're an international visitor, for information on what you're allowed to bring home, contact one of the following agencies:

U.S. Citizens: U.S. Customs & Border Protection (CBP), 1300 Pennsylvania Ave. NW, Washington, DC 20229 (📞 **877/227-5511;** www.cbp.gov).

Canadian Citizens: Canada Border Services Agency, Ottawa, Ontario, K1A 0L8 (📞 **800/461-9999** in Canada, or 204/983-3500; www.cbsa-asfc.gc.ca).

U.K. Citizens: HM Customs & Excise, Crownhill Court, Tailyour Road, Plymouth, PL6 5BZ (📞 **0845/010-9000;** www.hmce.gov.uk).

Australian Citizens: Australian Customs Service, Customs House, 5 Constitution Ave., Canberra City, ACT 2601 (📞 **1300/363-263;** from outside Australia, 612/6275-6666; www.customs.gov.au).

New Zealand Citizens: New Zealand Customs, the Customhouse, 17–21 Whitmore St., Box 2218, Wellington, 6140 (📞 **0800/428-786;** from outside New Zealand, 649/300-5399; www.customs.govt.nz).

Disabled Travelers   Vancouver's former mayor, Sam Sullivan, is keenly aware of accessibility issues, having been a quadriplegic since breaking his neck in a skiing accident at age 19. He founded several nonprofit organizations dedicated to improving the quality of life for travelers with disabilities throughout North America. However, even before Sam Sullivan, Vancouver was working to improve accessibility.

According to *We're Accessible,* a newsletter for travelers with disabilities, Vancouver is **"the most accessible city in the world."** There are more than 14,000 sidewalk wheelchair ramps, and motorized wheelchairs are a common sight in the downtown area. The stairs along Robson Square have built-in ramps, and most major attractions and venues have ramps or level walkways for easy access. Most Vancouver hotels have at least partial wheelchair accessibility; many have specially equipped rooms for travelers with disabilities. Most SkyTrain stations and the SeaBus are wheelchair accessible, and most bus routes are lift-equipped. For further information about accessible public transportation, contact **Translink** (📞 **604/953-3333;** www.translink.ca).

Many Vancouver hotels are also equipping rooms with visual smoke alarms and other facilities for hearing-impaired guests, while many crosswalks are now outfitted with beeping alerts to guide visually impaired pedestrians.

Victoria is similarly accessible. Nearly all Victoria hotels have rooms equipped to accommodate travelers with disabilities, and downtown sidewalks are equipped with ramps, though few intersections have beeping crosswalk signals for the visually impaired. The **Victoria Regional Transit System** (📞 **250/382-6161**) has a downloadable *Guide to Accessible Transit Services* on its website, **www.transitbc.com**, which includes information on which bus routes are equipped with lifts and/or low floors. The most notable spot in Victoria that isn't readily wheelchair accessible is the promenade along the water's edge in the Inner Harbour, which has only one rather challenging ramp near the Pacific Undersea Gardens.

The government of Canada hosts a comprehensive **Persons with Disabilities website** (www.accesstotravel.gc.ca) with resources for travelers with disabilities. In addition to information on public transit in cities across Canada, the site also lists accessible campsites, parks, coach lines, and a number of links to other services and associations of interest to travelers with disabilities. If you can't find what you need online, call 📞 **800/926-9105.**

Outside of Canada, organizations that offer a vast range of resources and assistance to travelers with disabilities include **MossRehab** (📞 **800/CALL-MOSS** [800/225-5667]; www.mossresourcenet.org); the **American Foundation for the Blind** (**AFB;** 📞 **800/232-5463;** www.afb.org); and **SATH** (Society for Accessible

Travel & Hospitality; (☎ **212/447-7284;** www.sath.org). **AirAmbulanceCard.com** is now partnered with SATH and allows you to preselect top-notch hospitals in case of an emergency.

Access-Able Travel Source (☎ **303/232-2979;** www.access-able.com) offers a comprehensive database on travel agents from around the world with experience in accessible travel; destination-specific access information; and links to such resources as service animals, equipment rentals, and access guides.

Many travel agencies offer customized tours and itineraries for travelers with disabilities. Among them are **Flying Wheels Travel** (☎ **507/451-5005;** www.flyingwheels travel.com) and **Accessible Journeys** (☎ **800/846-4537** or 610/521-0339; www. disabilitytravel.com).

Flying with Disability (www.flying-with-disability.org) is a comprehensive information source on airplane travel. **Avis Rent a Car** (☎ **888/879-4273**) has an "Avis Access" program that offers services for customers with special travel needs. These include specially outfitted vehicles with swivel seats, spinner knobs, and hand controls; mobility scooter rentals; and accessible bus service. Be sure to reserve well in advance.

Also check out the quarterly magazine *Emerging Horizons* (www.emerginghorizons. com), available by subscription ($17 per year in the U.S.; $22 per year outside the U.S.). The "Accessible Travel" link at **Mobility-Advisor.com** (www.mobility-advisor.com) offers a variety of travel resources to travelers with disabilities.

British travelers should contact **Holiday Care** (☎ **0845/124-9971** in the U.K.; www.tourismforall.org.uk) to access a wide range of travel information and resources for elderly people and individuals with disabilities.

Drinking Laws   The legal drinking age in British Columbia is 19. Spirits are sold only in government liquor stores, but beer and wine can be purchased from specially licensed, privately owned stores and pubs. Most LCBC (Liquor Control of British Columbia) stores are open Monday through Saturday from 10am to 6pm, but some are open until 11pm.

Driving Rules   See "Getting Around Vancouver," p. 55; and "Getting Around Victoria," p. 233.

Electricity   As in the U.S., electric current is 110 to 120 volts AC (60 cycles), compared to 220 to 240 volts AC (50 cycles) in most of Europe, Australia, and New Zealand. Downward converters that change 220 to 240 volts to 110 to 120 volts are difficult to find in North America, so bring one with you.

Embassies & Consulates   In Vancouver, the **U.S. Consulate** is at 1075 W. Pender St. (☎ **604/685-4311**). The **British Consulate** is at 800-1111 Melville St. (☎ **604/683-4421**). The **Australian Consulate** is at 2050-1075 W. Georgia St. (☎ **604/684-1177**). Check the Yellow Pages for other countries' consulates.

Emergencies   Dial ☎ **911** for fire, police, ambulance, and poison control. This is a free call.

Family Travel   Vancouver and Victoria are two of the most child-friendly cosmopolitan cities in the world. Where else would you find a market especially for kids? In addition to the standard attractions and sights, you'll find a lot of free, adventurous, outdoor activities that both you and your kids will enjoy (see "Especially for Kids," in chapters 7 and 15). Recommended family travel websites include **Family Travel Forum** (www.familytravelforum.com), a comprehensive site that offers customized trip planning; **Family Travel Network** (www.familytravelnetwork.com), an online magazine providing travel tips; and **Travelwithyourkids.com**, a comprehensive site written by parents, for parents, offering sound advice for long-distance and international travel with children. To locate accommodations, restaurants, and attractions that are particularly kid-friendly, look for the "Kids" icon throughout this guide.

Gasoline (Petrol)   Gas stations are basically the same as in the U.S., but gasoline is sold by the liter, not by the gallon. (3.8L equals 1 U.S. gal.), and by law, must be purchased in advance. Gas prices in British Columbia fluctuate, as they do everywhere else in the world; as of press time, 1 liter costs about C$1.40. Taxes are included in the printed price.

Health   Hospitals and **emergency numbers** are listed in the "Fast Facts" sections for Vancouver (p. 59) and Victoria (p. 234).

If you become ill while traveling in Canada, you may have to pay all medical costs upfront and be reimbursed later. Medicare and Medicaid do not provide coverage for medical costs outside the U.S. Before leaving home, find out what medical services your health insurance covers. To protect yourself, consider buying medical travel insurance (see "Insurance," later in this section).

If you suffer from a chronic illness, consult your doctor before your departure. Pack **prescription medications** in your carry-on luggage and carry them in their original containers, with pharmacy labels—otherwise they won't make it through airport security. Carry the generic name of prescription medicines, in case a local Canadian pharmacist is unfamiliar with the brand name.

For conditions like epilepsy, diabetes, or heart problems, wear a **MedicAlert Identification Tag** (🕾 **888/633-4298;** www.medicalert.org), which will immediately alert doctors to your condition and give them access to your records through MedicAlert's 24-hour hotline.

Holidays   For a list of holidays in Canada, see "Vancouver & Victoria Calendar of Events," in chapter 2.

Hospitals   For a list of doctors and hospitals in Vancouver, see "Fast Facts Vancouver," in chapter 4; for doctors and hospitals in Victoria, see "Fast Facts Victoria," in chapter 12.

Insurance   For international travel, most U.S. health plans (including Medicare and Medicaid) do not provide coverage, and the ones that do often require you to pay for services upfront and reimburse you only after you return home.

For information on traveler's insurance, trip cancelation insurance, and medical insurance while traveling, please visit www.frommers.com/planning.

Internet & Wi-Fi   Almost all hotels in Vancouver and Victoria provide some kind of computer access to guests traveling without their own laptops. In some cases, it's a free public computer in the lobby; in other, more high-end hotels, there may be a charge to use computers in the hotel's business center. To find cybercafes in Vancouver and Victoria, check **www.cybercaptive.com** and **www.cybercafe.com**. For those people traveling with their own computer, almost all hotels, resorts, airports, cafes, and retailers have gone to **Wi-Fi** (wireless fidelity), offering free high-speed Wi-Fi access or charging a fee for 24-hour usage. In the service information for every hotel in this guide, note whether the hotel offers free Wi-Fi or high-speed Internet access; if not, rates generally average C$15 for 24 hours. Almost invariably, it is large upscale hotels and resorts (such as Westin and the Four Seasons) that charge guests for Internet or Wi-Fi use.

To locate public Wi-Fi "hotspots," go to **www.jiwire.com**; its Hotspot Finder holds the world's largest directory of public wireless hotspots.

Gasoline (Petrol)

PLANNING YOUR TRIP

Legal Aid   While driving, if you are pulled over for a minor infraction (such as speeding), never attempt to pay the fine directly to a police officer; this could be construed as attempted bribery, a much more serious crime. Pay fines by mail, or directly into the hands of the clerk of the court. If accused of a more serious offense, say and do nothing before consulting a lawyer. In Canada, as in the U.S., the burden is on the Crown to provide a person's guilt beyond a reasonable doubt, and everyone has the right to remain silent, whether he or she is suspected of a crime or actually arrested. Once arrested, a person can make one telephone call to a party of his or her choice. The international visitor should call his or her embassy or consulate.

LGBT Travelers   Since 2003, when the Province of British Columbia announced the legalization of same-sex marriage, Vancouver and Victoria have become favored sites for **gay and lesbian weddings.** (Same-sex marriage is now legal throughout Canada.) Information about the process is listed on the invaluable **www.gayvan.com** website. Vancouver's official tourism website, **www.tourismvancouver.com**, also has information for gay and lesbian travelers.

What San Francisco is to the United States, **Vancouver** is to Canada—a hip, laid-back town with a large, thriving gay community. In fact, the largest gay population in Western Canada lives here, primarily in the **West End** and **Commercial Drive.** You'll find hotels and restaurants in Vancouver to be very gay friendly. (The straight-friendly **West End Guest House,** described on p. 79, is owned and operated by a married gay couple.)

The club, bar, and party scene is chronicled in the biweekly gay and lesbian tabloid, *Xtra! West,* available at cafes, bars, and businesses throughout the West End. For some gay nightlife options, also see the section "Gay & Lesbian Bars," in chapter 10.

The **Gay Lesbian Transgendered Bisexual Community Centre,** 2–1170 Bute St. ((✆ **604/684-5307;** www.qmunity.ca), has all kinds of information on events and the current hot spots. Also check out the **Vancouver Pride Society** website (**www. vancouverpride.ca**) for upcoming special events, including the annual Vancouver Pride Parade in June, one of the largest gay-pride events in North America. The **Vancouver Queer Film Festival** is held in mid-August; check **www.queerfilmfestival.ca** for more details. Also, check out **Gay & Lesbian Ski Week** at Whistler, located 121km (75 miles) north of Vancouver; for information, go to **www.gaywhistler.com.**

The gay and lesbian scene in **Victoria** is small but active. Explore the Pride link under "Plan Your Trip" at **www.tourismvictoria.com,** or go to the **www.gayvictoria.ca** website. At both sites, you'll find information about special places to stay and dine, plus things to do. The **Victoria Pride Parade and Festival** is held every summer in early July. For nightlife options, see chapter 18.

The International Gay and Lesbian Travel Association (IGLTA; ✆ **800/448-8550** or 954/776-2626; www.iglta.org) is the trade association for the gay and lesbian travel industry and offers an online directory of gay- and lesbian-friendly travel businesses and tour operators.

In addition to these listings, please visit Frommers.com for other specialized travel resources.

Mail   At press time, letters and postcards up to 30 grams cost C$1.03 to mail to the U.S. and C$1.75 for overseas airmail service; C59¢ within Canada. You can buy stamps and mail parcels at the main post office (for locations, see "Post Office," in "Fast Facts: Vancouver," p. 60, and "Fast Facts: Victoria," p. 235) or at any of the postal outlets inside drugstores and convenience stores. Look for a POSTAL SERVICES sign. For more information, visit www.canadapost.ca.

Mobile Phones   Canada is part of the **GSM** (Global System for Mobile Communications), a big, seamless network that makes for easy cross-border cellphone use. GSM phones function with a removable plastic SIM card, encoded with your phone number and account information. If your cellphone is on a GSM system, and you have a world-capable multiband phone such as many Sony Ericsson, Motorola, or Samsung models, you can make and receive calls across Canada. Just call your wireless operator and ask for "international roaming" to be activated on your account. (Many U.S. cellphones are already equipped with this capability and need no further modification to operate in Canada.)

You can **rent a cellphone** at a **Touristinfo Centre** at **Vancouver International Airport** (Touristinfo Centres are found in both the domestic and international terminals), or in the city at the **Vancouver Touristinfo Centre,** 200 Burrard St. (✆ **604/683-2000**), for a minimum charge (approx. C$50). For current rates and more information, contact the phone provider, **Cita Communications** (✆ **604/671-4655;** www.cita.info).

Money & Costs   Canadian monetary units are dollars and cents, with dollar notes issued in different colors. The standard denominations are C$5, C$10, C$20, C$50, and C$100. The "loonie" (so named because of the loon on one side) is the C$1 coin that replaced the C$1 bill. A C$2 coin, called the "toonie" because it's worth two loonies, has replaced the C$2 bill.

Note: If you're driving, it's a good idea to have a pocketful of toonies and loonies for parking meters. Avoid C$100 bills when exchanging money, as many stores refuse to accept these bills. Almost all stores and restaurants accept American currency, and most will exchange amounts in excess of your dinner check or purchase. However, these establishments are allowed to set their own exchange percentages and generally offer the worst rates of all.

Frommer's lists exact prices in the local currency. The currency conversions provided were correct at press time. However, rates fluctuate, so before departing consult a currency exchange website such as **www.oanda.com/currency/converter** to check up-to-the-minute rates.

THE VALUE OF THE CANADIAN DOLLAR VS. OTHER POPULAR CURRENCIES

Can$	US$	Euro (€)	UK£	NZ$	Aus$
$1	$1	€.70	£.61	NZ$1.22	A$1

The favorable exchange rate of the Canadian dollar against the U.S. dollar, the British pound, and the euro gives added value to whatever you buy. In 2011, the Canadian dollar grew considerably stronger, and at press time was virtually at par with the U.S. dollar. The Canadian dollar also gained strength against the British pound, the euro, and the Australian and New Zealand dollars. To offset this change, and because of the recession, hotels and restaurants have generally reduced their prices or kept them the same as last year. Prices in Vancouver are generally a bit higher than in Victoria.

From mid-September to April, prices for hotel rooms in both cities generally drop by at least 20%, and sometimes as much as 50%; the exception to this is Whistler, where winter is the high season and prices rise accordingly. The prices we've listed in "What Things Cost," below, are approximate.

	C$
Transfer to/from airport (transit/taxi)	4.00/45.00
Double room, moderate	200.00–300.00
Three-course dinner for one, without wine, moderate	40.00–50.00
Glass of wine	7.00–10.00
Double latte	3.75
Cup of coffee	1.75

ATMs The easiest and best way to get cash in Vancouver and Victoria is from an ATM. The **Cirrus** (✆ **800/424-7787;** www.mastercard.com) and **PLUS** (✆ **800/843-7587;** www.visa.com) networks span the globe; look at the back of your bank card to see which network you're on, then call or check online for ATM locations at your destination. Be sure you know your personal identification number (PIN) before you leave home, and be sure to find out your daily withdrawal limit before you depart. Many banks impose a fee every time a card is used at a different bank's ATM, and that fee can be higher for international transactions than for domestic ones. On top of this, the bank from which you withdraw cash may charge its own fee.

The 24-hour PLUS and Cirrus ATM systems are widely available throughout British Columbia. The systems convert Canadian withdrawals to your account's currency within 24 hours. Cirrus network cards work at ATMs at **BMO Bank of Montreal** (✆ 800/555-3000), **CIBC** (✆ 800/465-2422), **HSBC** (✆ 888/310-4722), **RBC Royal Bank** (✆ 800/769-2511), **TD Canada Trust** (✆ 866/567-8888), and at all other ATMs that display the Cirrus logo.

Credit & Debit Cards Major U.S. credit cards are widely accepted in British Columbia, especially American Express, MasterCard, and Visa. British debit cards like Barclay's Visa are also accepted. Diners Club, Carte Blanche, Discover, JCB, and EnRoute are taken by some establishments, but not as many. The amount spent in Canadian dollars will automatically be converted by your issuing company to your currency when you're billed—generally at rates that are better than you'd receive for cash at a currency exchange. However, the bank will probably add a 3% "adjustment fee" to the converted purchase price. You can also obtain a PIN for your credit card and use it in some ATMs. You usually pay interest from the date of withdrawal and often pay a higher service fee than when using a regular ATM card.

Beware of hidden credit-card fees while traveling. Check with your credit or debit card issuer to see what fees, if any, will be charged for overseas transactions. Recent reform legislation in the U.S., for example, has curbed some exploitative lending practices. But many banks have responded by increasing fees in other areas, including fees for customers who use credit and debit cards while out of the country—even if those charges were made in U.S. dollars. Fees can amount to 3% or more of the purchase price. Check with your bank before departing to avoid any surprise charges on your statement.

For help with currency conversions, tip calculations, and more, download Frommer's convenient Travel Tools app for your mobile device. Go to **www.frommers.com/go/mobile** and click on the Travel Tools icon.

20

PLANNING YOUR TRIP | Money & Costs

Newspapers & Magazines   See "Fast Facts: Vancouver," p. 60.

Packing   The proximity of mountains nudging up against the Pacific Ocean translates into mild temperatures and frequent rainfalls. Everyone here dresses West Coast casual, which means except for in some very posh restaurants, ties are unnecessary and frou frou cocktail dresses might feel over-the-top. Pack for easy layers with a fleece, umbrella, and a good pair of walking shoes stashed into your luggage. For more helpful information on packing for your trip, download our convenient Travel Tools app for your mobile device. Go to www.frommers.com/go/mobile and click on the Travel Tools icon.

Passports   Every international air traveler entering Canada is required to show a passport. *Note:* U.S. and Canadian citizens entering the U.S. at land and sea ports of entry from within the western hemisphere must now present a passport of other documents such as a passport card, compliant with the Western Hemisphere Travel Initiative (WHTI; see www.getyouhome.gov for details, the Canada Border Services Agency website is www.cbsa-asfc.gc.ca, and is also helpful).

Australia   Australian Passport Information Service (✆ **131-232,** or visit www.passports.gov.au).

Canada   Passport Office, Department of Foreign Affairs and International Trade, Ottawa, ON K1A 0G3 (✆ **800/567-6868;** www.ppt.gc.ca).

Ireland   Passport Office, Setanta Centre, Molesworth Street, Dublin 2 (✆ **01/671-1633;** www.foreignaffairs.gov.ie).

New Zealand   Passports Office, Department of Internal Affairs, 47 Boulcott St., Wellington, 6011 (✆ **0800/225-050** in New Zealand or 04/474-8100; www.passports.govt.nz).

United Kingdom   Visit your nearest passport office, major post office, or travel agency or contact the **Identity and Passport Service (IPS),** 89 Eccleston Sq., London, SW1V 1PN (✆ **0300/222-0000;** www.ips.gov.uk).

United States   To find your regional passport office, check the U.S. State Department website (travel.state.gov/passport) or call the **National Passport Information Center** (✆ **877/487-2778**) for automated information.

Police   Dial ✆ **911** for fire, police, ambulance, and poison control. This is a free call. For non-emergencies, see "Fast Facts: Vancouver," p. 60; and "Fast Facts: Victoria," p. 235.

Safety   Overall, Vancouver is a safe city, and Victoria is even safer. Violent-crime rates are quite low in both cities. However, property crimes and crimes of opportunity (such as items being stolen from unlocked cars) occur pretty frequently in Vancouver. Never leave valuable items on view in your parked car; put them in the trunk. Most hotels offer safe valet parking or parking in nearby lots.

Thanks to the mild climate and (controversially) lax laws, both Vancouver and Victoria have populations of transients living on the streets of certain neighborhoods. Vancouver's downtown East Side, between Gastown and Chinatown, is a troubled, drug-riddled neighborhood and should be avoided at night. In both Vancouver and Victoria, transients panhandle throughout downtown and tourist-heavy areas.

Senior Travel   Because BC has the mildest weather in all of Canada, Vancouver and Victoria have become havens for older and retired Canadians. Senior travelers often qualify for discounts at hotels and attractions throughout the area. Always ask; you'll be pleasantly surprised at the number of discounts available. **Discount transit**

PLANNING YOUR TRIP   Newspapers & Magazines

passes for persons 65 or older (with proof of age) may be purchased at shops in Vancouver and Victoria that display a FareDealer sign (Safeway, 7-Eleven, and most newsstands). To locate a **FareDealer vendor,** contact BC Transit (✆ **604/521-0400;** www.transitbc.com).

If you're 50 or older, consider joining **AARP** (3200 E. Carson, Lakewood, CA 90712; ✆ **800/424-3410;** www.aarp.org); their card offers additional restaurant and travel bargains throughout North America.

Smoking   Smoking is prohibited in all public areas, including restaurants, bars, and clubs. Many hotels are now entirely smoke-free. In September 2010, a ban was also instituted on smoking in public parks, including Stanley Park, and beaches.

Student Travel   The southwestern corner of BC is definitely student-oriented territory, and you'll find inexpensive youth hostels run by **Hostelling International** in Vancouver (chapter 5), Victoria (chapter 13), Whistler (chapter 11), and Tofino (chapter 19). These hostels make traveling in BC affordable and fun. For membership information, check the **Hostelling International** websites at **www.hiusa.org** and **www.hihostels.ca**. The University of British Columbia (UBC, with more than 30,000 students) in the Point Grey area, Burnaby's Simon Fraser University, and a number of smaller schools contribute to the enormous student population in **Vancouver.** Student travelers have a lot of free and inexpensive entertainment options, both day and night. Pick up a copy of *Georgia Straight* to find out what's happening. Many attractions and theaters offer discounts if you have your student ID with you. While many establishments will accept a school ID, the surest way to obtain student discounts is with an International Student Identity Card (ISIC).

In **Victoria,** the University of Victoria (referred to locally as "U. Vic.") has a sprawling campus just east of downtown. The student population accounts for most, if not all, of Victoria's nightlife. Student discounts abound. Pick up a copy of Victoria's weekly paper, *Monday Magazine* (which comes out on Thurs), for current nightclub listings.

Taxes   Hotel rooms, restaurant meals, and most consumer goods are subject to a 12% harmonized federal and provincial sales tax (HST) on most goods and services tax. Motor fuels, books, and children's clothing are taxed at 5%. For specific questions, contact the **BC Consumer Taxation Branch** (✆ **604/660-0858;** www.sbr.gov.bc.ca/rev.htm). *Note:* There is no tax rebate program for visitors.

Telephones   Phones in British Columbia are identical to phones in the U.S. The country code is the same as the U.S. code (1). Local calls normally cost C25¢. Many hotels charge C$1 or more per local call and much more for long-distance calls, although more hotels are providing free local service. You can save considerably by using a calling card or your cellphone. You can buy **prepaid phone cards** in various denominations at grocery and convenience stores.

To call Vancouver or Victoria:

1.   If you're calling from outside North America, dial the international access code: 00 from the U.K., Ireland, or New Zealand; or 0011 from Australia. (Omit this step if you're calling from the U.S.)

2.   Dial the country code 1.

3.   For **Vancouver** or **Whistler,** dial the area code **604** and then the number. For **Victoria** or **Tofino/Ucluelet,** dial the area code **250** and then the number.

20

PLANNING YOUR TRIP

Telephones

Calling within Vancouver and Whistler: If you are in Vancouver or Whistler and want to call another number in Vancouver or Whistler, you must use the area code **604,** followed by the number.

Calling within Victoria: If you are in Victoria and calling another Victoria number, you do not need to add the area code. If you are calling from Victoria to anywhere else on Vancouver Island, however, you must use the area code **250** before the number.

To make international calls: To call the U.S., dial 1, followed by the area code and phone number. To call the U.K., Ireland, Australia, or New Zealand, first dial 00 and then the country code (U.K. 44, Ireland 353, Australia 61, New Zealand 64), followed by the area code and number.

For directory assistance ("Information"): For automated toll-free directory assistance within Canada (and the U.S.), dial ✆ **800/555-1212.** You can also dial ✆ **411** if you're looking for a number inside Canada. Dial ✆ **0** (zero) for numbers to all other countries. (You will incur a charge if you use the 411 and 0 directory assistance numbers.)

For operator assistance: If you need operator assistance making a call, dial ✆ **0** (zero).

Toll-free numbers: Numbers within Canada beginning with 800, 866, 877, and 888 are toll-free from the U.S., but calling a 1-800 number in the States from Canada is not toll-free. In fact, it costs the same as an overseas call.

Time Zone   Vancouver and Victoria are in the Pacific time zone, as are Seattle, Portland, San Francisco, and Los Angeles. Pacific Standard Time is 3 hours behind Eastern Standard Time, and 8 hours behind Greenwich Mean Time.

Daylight saving time (summer time) is in effect from 1am on the second Sunday in March to 1am on the first Sunday in November. Daylight saving time moves the clock 1 hour ahead.

For help with time translations, and more, download our convenient Travel Tools app for your mobile device. Go to www.frommers.com/go/mobile and click on the Travel Tools icon.

Tipping   Tipping etiquette is the same as in the United States: In hotels, tip bellhops at least C$1 per bag (C$2–C$3 if you have a lot of luggage) and tip the chamber staff C$1 to C$2 per day (more if you've left a big mess for him or her to clean up). Tip the doorman or concierge only if he or she has provided you with some specific service (for example, calling a cab for you or obtaining difficult-to-get theater tickets). Tip the valet-parking attendant C$1 every time you get your car.

In restaurants, bars, and nightclubs, tip service staff and bartenders 15% to 20% of the check, tip checkroom attendants C$1 per garment, and tip valet-parking attendants C$1 per vehicle.

As for other service personnel, tip cab drivers 15% of the fare; tip skycaps at airports at least C$1 per bag (C$2–C$3 if you have a lot of luggage); and tip hairdressers and barbers 15% to 20%.

For help with tip calculations, currency conversions, and more, download our convenient Travel Tools app for your mobile device. Go to www.frommers.com/go/mobile and click on the Travel Tools icon.

Toilets   You won't find public toilets or "restrooms" on the streets in either Vancouver or Victoria, or at least not any you would want to use, but they can be found in hotel lobbies, bars, restaurants, department stores, railway and bus stations, and service stations. Large hotels and fast-food restaurants are often the best bet for clean facilities.

Visas   Like Canada, Australia and New Zealand are members of the British common-wealth and therefore need no special visas to travel between their respective countries, only a valid passport. U.S. citizens need only a passport to enter Canada. Visit www.cic.gc.ca/english/visit/visas.asp for a complete list of those countries which require a visa to enter or transit Canada.

Visitor Information   For tourist office locations in Vancouver, see "Visitor Information," in chapter 4; for Victoria, see chapter 12.

If you're planning to spend time outside Vancouver and Victoria, you may wish to contact the **Vancouver Coast and Mountains Tourism Region** (℗ **800/667-3306** or 604/739-9011; www.vcmbc.com). For travel information on Vancouver Island and the Gulf Islands, contact **Tourism Vancouver Island** (501-65 Front St., Nanaimo, BC V9R 5H9; ℗ **250/754-3500;** www.vancouverisland.travel).

For information about travel and accommodations elsewhere in the province, contact **Tourism British Columbia** (300-1803 Douglas St., Victoria, BC V8T 5C3; ℗ **800/ HELLO-BC** [800/435-5622] or 250/356-6363; www.hellobc.com).

Wi-Fi   See "Internet & Wi-Fi," earlier in this section.

Index

See also Accommodations and
Restaurant indexes, below.

General Index

Swiftsure International Yacht Race (Victoria), 33
Swimco (Vancouver), 183
Swimming, Vancouver, 152
Sydney Reynolds (Victoria), 311

T

Taiga (Vancouver), 188
Takaya Tours (Vancouver), 143
Tally-Ho Carriage Tours (Victoria), 285
Taman Sari Royal Heritage Spa (Whistler), 226
T&T Supermarket (Vancouver), 168, 181
Tapleys (Whistler), 228
Taxes, 357
Taxis, 52
  Vancouver, 57
  Victoria, 230, 234
  Whistler Blackcomb, 208
Telephones, 357–358
Temperatures, average high, 28
Tennis
  Vancouver, 152
  Whistler Blackcomb, 225
Ten Ren Tea & Ginseng Co. (Vancouver), 181
Thane (sailboat), 291
Theater
  Vancouver, 192
  Victoria, 317–318
Theater in the Sky (Vancouver), 132
Theatre Inconnu (Victoria), 318
Theatre Under the Stars (Vancouver), 119, 192
Thetis Lake, 287
Third Beach (Vancouver), 121, 144
Thomas Fee house (Vancouver), 162
Three Dog Bakery (Vancouver), 188
Thriller (Vancouver), 189
Thunderbird Park (Victoria), 277, 296
Tickets Tonight (Vancouver), 191
Tillicum Mall Medical Clinic (Victoria), 235
Time zone, 358
Tipping, 358
  restaurants, 108–109
Tla-ook Cultural Adventures, 338
Tofino, 324, 325, 331–342
Tofino Botanical Gardens, 337
Tofino Bus, 326
Tofino Sea Kayaking Company, 340
Tofino Visitor Info Centre, 328
Toilets, 358
Tommy Africa's (Whistler), 227
Totem poles, 22
  Vancouver, 119, 121, 128, 139, 175
  Victoria, 299, 306, 307
Touch Lounge (Victoria), 320
Tourism Vancouver Information Centre, 191

Tourism Vancouver Visitor Centre, 52–53
Tourism Victoria Visitor Centre, 230
Tourism Whistler, 208
Touristinfo Centre, 53
Tours, 37. See also Boat tours and cruises; Bus tours; Walking tours
Towing services, Vancouver, 58
Toys, Vancouver, 189
Train travel
  Vancouver, 345
  Whistler Blackcomb, 204, 208
Translink, 51
Translink (Vancouver), 55, 56
Transportation
  Vancouver, 55–59
  Victoria, 233–234
Travel with Taste (Victoria), 286
Treetops Adventure (Vancouver), 131
Treetrek, 224
Trounce Alley (Victoria), 302
True Value Vintage Clothing (Vancouver), 184
Trumpeter Swan Festival (Comox Valley), 33
Tsawwassen-Swartz Bay ferry, 347
Turnabout (Vancouver), 182
Tuscan Kitchen (Victoria), 311

U

UBC Botanical Garden & Nitobe Memorial Garden (Vancouver), 129–130
UBC Tennis Centre (Vancouver), 152
Ucluelet, 324–325, 329–331
Ucluelet Campground, 329
Ucluelet Chamber of Commerce, 328
Ucluelet Mini Aquarium, 331
Ucluelet Visitor Info Centre, 328
The Umbrella Shop (Vancouver), 188
Uniglobe Specialty Travel, 37
United Airlines, 37, 344
University Golf Club (Vancouver), 148
Uno Festival of Solo Performance (Victoria), 318
Uno Langmann Limited (Vancouver), 179
Upper, 208
The Upstairs Lounge (Victoria), 320
Urban Rush (Vancouver), 160

V

Valhalla Pure Outfitters (Vancouver), 188
Valley Trail System, 220, 222
Vancouver (magazine), 53
Vancouver Aboriginal Friendship Centre, 30

Vancouver Airport, 51–52
Vancouver Aquarium Marine Science Centre, 122–123, 139
Vancouver Aquatic Centre, 152
Vancouver Art Gallery, 123, 133, 163
Vancouver Bach Choir, 192
Vancouver Cantata Singers, 193
Vancouver Canucks, 155
Vancouver Chamber Choir, 193
Vancouver East Cultural Centre, 192
Vancouver Flea Market, 187
Vancouver Folk Music Festival, 30, 194
Vancouver Fringe Festival, 32
Vancouver General Hospital Health and Sciences Centre, 59
Vancouver Giants, 155
Vancouver International Film Festival, 32, 200
Vancouver International Jazz Festival, 30, 194
Vancouver International Marathon, 29, 155–156
Vancouver International Writers and Readers Festival, 32
Vancouver Island, 35
Vancouver Island Paragliding, 291
Vancouver Lookout, 122
Vancouver Maritime Museum, 130
Vancouver-Nanaimo ferry, 347
Vancouver Natural History Society, 153
Vancouver Olympic Centre, 144
Vancouver Olympic Village, 144
Vancouver Opera, 193
Vancouver Playhouse, 192
Vancouver Playhouse International Wine Festival, 29
Vancouver Police Museum, 124, 143, 170
Vancouver Sun Run, 29, 155
Vancouver Symphony, 193
Vancouver Taxi, 57
Vancouver TheatreSports League, 193–194
Vancouver Trolley Company, 138, 142
Vancouver Whale Watch (Richmond), 152–153
Vancouver Whitecaps, 156
Vancouver Wooden Boat Festival, 32
VanDusen Botanical Gardens (Vancouver), 135
Vanier Park (Vancouver), 174
Vanity Fair Antiques & Collectibles (Victoria), 310
Venus & Mars (Vancouver), 183
VIA Rail Canada, 345
Victoria Bobby Walking Tours, 285